Principles of
Conflict of
Laws

Cavendish
Publishing
Limited

London • Sydney

Principles of Conflict of Laws

Abla J Mayss, LLM, PhD, Licence en Droît
Lecturer in Law
University of Liverpool

Cavendish
Publishing
Limited

London • Sydney

First published in Great Britain 1994 by Cavendish Publishing Limited, The Glass House, Wharton Street, London WC1X 9PX, United Kingdom

Telephone: +44 (0) 171 278 8000   Facsimile: +44 (0) 171 278 8080

e-mail: info@cavendishpublishing.com

Visit our Home Page on http://www.cavendishpublishing.com

This title was previously published under the Lecture Notes series.

© Mayss, A   1999
First edition   1994
Second edition 1996

Mayss, Abla J
Principles of conflict of laws – 3rd ed – (Principles of law series)
1. Conflict of laws
I. Title
340.9

1 85941 460 5

Printed and bound in Great Britain

PREFACE

The law in the field of conflict of laws is constantly developing and changing. Since the second edition of this book, a number of important changes, both in terms of courts' decisions and statutory provisions, have taken place. The object of the present edition of this book is twofold: first, to take account of, and incorporate, these changes; and, secondly, to re-arrange a number of chapters in an attempt to make a notoriously difficult area of law more reader friendly. Thus, Chapters 2 and 3, both of which deal with the jurisdiction of the English court in civil and commercial matters, have been re-written to the effect that Chapter 2 now deals solely with the common law rules and Chapter 3 examines the rules under the Brussels and Lugano Conventions. Chapter 6, entitled 'Choice of Law in Tort', has been largely revised to discuss those common law rules which remain applicable to the tort of defamation, and now deals more fully with Part III of the Private International Law (Miscellaneous Provisions) Act 1995. Chapters 10 and 11 on Family Law have been greatly amended to take account of the changes brought about by the Family Law Act 1996 and to make this complicated area of law easier to read and understand. The remaining chapters have been revised and amended to take due consideration of new developments in the context of both the common law and various recent statutory provisions.

I am grateful to my colleagues in the Faculty of Law at the University of Liverpool for sparing me the time to discuss a number of issues with them, and to the students there. I am also grateful to the editorial team at Cavendish Publishing Ltd for their patience and understanding; and to the Editorial Board, for their helpful comments on the text of this book.

I have tried to state the law as it stood on 15 September 1998, although it has been possible to include some later developments.

Abla Mayss
University of Liverpool
December 1998

CONTENTS

Contents

Contents

TABLE OF APPENDICES

TABLE OF CASES

Table of Cases

TABLE OF EUROPEAN LEGISLATION

TABLE OF OTHER LEGISLATION

TABLE OF ABBREVIATIONS

STATUTES

AJA 1920	Administration of Justice Act 1920
CA 1948	Companies Act 1948
CA 1985	Companies Act 1985
CJJA 1982	Civil Jurisdiction and Judgments Act 1982
CJJA 1991	Civil Jurisdiction and Judgments Act 1991
DMPA 1973	Domicile and Matrimonial Proceedings Act 1973
FLA 1986	Family Law Act 1986
FLA 1996	Family Law Act 1996
FJA 1933	Foreign Judgments (Reciprocal Enforcement) Act 1933
MCA 1973	Matrimonial Causes Act 1973
MFPA 1984	Matrimonial and Family Proceedings Act 1984
PILA 1995	Private International Law (Miscellaneous Provisions) Act 1995
RICO	US Racketeering Influenced Corrupt Organisations Act

OTHER

EC	European Community
ECJ	European Court of Justice
EFTA	European Free Trade Association
OJ	Official Journal of the European Communities
SPBC	Special Public Bill Committee

CHAPTER 1

NATURE AND SCOPE OF CONFLICT OF LAWS

1.1 Introduction

Conflict of laws (also known as private international law) is that part of English law which comes into operation whenever the English court is faced with a case involving one or more foreign elements. This foreign element may be an event which has occurred in a foreign country, for example, an English tourist is injured in a road accident in Spain; it may be the place of business of one of the parties, for example, an English company agrees to purchase computer software from a company incorporated in New York; or it may be a foreign domicile, for example, an Englishwoman marries a man domiciled in Iran.

If the parties cannot resolve their differences amicably, then three main types of questions may arise in such cases.

1.1.1 Jurisdiction

The first question which has to be decided in a dispute involving a foreign element is whether the English court has power to hear the case. This raises the issue of whether the parties to the dispute should be free to choose the jurisdiction most favourable to their case.

1.1.2 Choice of law

Once the English court has accepted jurisdiction, the next question which has to be determined is what system of law should be applied to the dispute; that is, to determine the particular municipal system of law, by reference to which the rights and liabilities of the parties to the dispute must be ascertained. Evidently, in a conflict situation, the existence of one or more foreign elements may make it more appropriate to apply a foreign law to the dispute. The rules which direct the English court to identify the applicable law are called choice of law rules. For instance, the law which governs the question of title to immovable property is the law of the country in which the property is situated. Hence, where, for example, the English court is hearing a dispute involving the question of title to a land situated in South Africa, the choice of law rules direct the English court to apply South African law for determining that title.

1.1.3 Recognition and enforcement of foreign judgments

Under what circumstances will judgments of foreign courts be recognised or enforced in England? This type of question arises in the context where the parties litigate abroad. Suppose that a plaintiff, having obtained a judgment against an English defendant in a Turkish court for damages for negligence, decides to enforce it against the defendant's assets in England. Will the English court recognise and enforce the Turkish judgment, or will the action have to be re-tried in the English court?

1.2 Preliminary issues

1.2.1 Private and public international law

There are obvious differences between conflict of laws, or private international law, and public international law. The latter is primarily concerned with the rules that govern relations between sovereign States and consisting, in general, of customary and treaty rules which bind States in their interrelations. The former, however, is designed to regulate disputes of a private nature. Conflict of laws is that part of municipal law which only comes into play when a dispute has a connection of some kind with one or more foreign legal systems. Every modern legal system has its own rules of private international law, and they differ from one another as much as any other branch of domestic law.

In recent years, there have been strong international movements towards harmonising the various systems of conflict of laws. As this book is solely concerned with the English rules that guide an English court whenever seised of a case which involves a foreign element, it is not the intention of this author to examine the various attempts at harmonisation except in so far as they form part of English law. It suffices to say at this stage that these attempts have been framed in two different ways:

(a) the first is the unification of the internal laws of the various countries on a given topic via international conventions, so that no conflict of laws will arise. For instance, the Warsaw Convention of 1929, as amended in 1955 and supplemented by the Guadalajara Convention 1961, provides uniform rules in relation to the international carriage of persons or goods by air. This Convention was implemented in England by the Carriage by Air Act 1961;

(b) the second method attempts to unify the rules of private international law, so that a case containing a foreign element, wherever tried, will result in the same outcome. A good illustration of this method is the adoption of the Rome Convention on the Law Applicable to Contractual Obligations by the European Community in 1980. This Convention was implemented in the UK by the Contracts (Applicable Law) Act 1990.

1.2.2 Connecting factors

In many instances, the English court is faced with a range of choices as to the appropriate law which should apply to the dispute in question. Let us consider the following examples:

(a) an English company agrees to buy computer software from a New York company who manufactures them in Spain. The software, which is to be delivered to the English company's office in Rome, falls short of expectations;

(b) the carrier is an Italian company. In the course of transit through Italy, the lorry containing the software collides with a car driven by Dimitris, a Greek. Dimitris is seriously injured;

(c) an English girl of 15 marries an Iranian man in Iran. Their son is born in England.

In attempting to determine what law governs any one of the above situations, the court seeks guidance from connecting factors, that is, the factors which link an event, a transaction or a person to a country. Examples of such factors are:

(a) *lex loci contractus*: the law of the place where the contract was made;

(b) *lex loci solutionis*: the law of the place where the contract is to be performed;

(c) *lex loci celebrationis*: the law of the place where the marriage was celebrated;

(d) *lex loci delicti*: the law of the place where the tort was committed;

(e) *lex domicilii*: the law of the place where a person is domiciled;

(f) *lex patriae*: the law of the nationality;

(g) *lex situs*: the law of the place where the property is situated;

(h) *lex fori*: the law of the forum, that is, the internal law of the court in which a case is tried.

These connecting factors have no independent significance. They only provide the means to choose the appropriate law, but they cannot determine that choice. For instance, succession to immovable property is governed by the *lex situs*. The connecting factor is clearly *lex situs*, but this is part and parcel of the rule itself.

Connecting factors are nearly always determined by the law of the forum. For example, Valerie is domiciled in France according to the rules of English law of domicile. She is domiciled in England according to the rules of French law of domicile. The English court, as the forum, would decide where Valerie is domiciled according to the rules of English law of domicile. Consequently, Valerie would be domiciled in France.

It must be noted, however, that nationality as a connecting factor can only be determined by the law of the State to which a national claims to belong.

Nationality cannot be determined by the law of the forum. So, if Valerie, for example, claims French nationality in an English court, her nationality must be determined in accordance with French law rather than English law.

The process of identifying the connecting factors is the same, regardless of the nature of the dispute. However, the weight attached to a particular connecting factor varies according to the nature of the dispute. For instance, as shall be seen in due course, the law of the domicile of a person is given much more weight in a question of succession than in a question of contract.

1.2.3 The concept of personal law

Every natural and legal person is assigned a personal law defining his or her status and capacity. The connecting factor determining one's personal law varies from one legal system to another. For instance, common law systems generally adopt 'domicile' as the relevant connecting factor, civil law systems adopt 'nationality', and Islamic law assigns personal law by reference to 'religion'.

Personal law, as shall be seen in due course, is crucial in matters of family law, but increasingly less important in the context of transactions and disputes of a commercial nature. Hence, in *Bodley Head v Flegon* (1972), the court held that the capacity of the parties to a transaction is to be governed by the law applicable to the contract, rather than the personal law of the parties. On the other hand, in *Re Paine* (1940), the court applied the law of the domicile to determine whether a child is legitimate or illegitimate.

1.3 The bases of conflict of laws

What justification is there for applying a foreign law? Why not just apply the law of the forum to every case? Cheshire and North (*Private International Law*, 12th edn, p 39) put it in the following terms:

> There is no sacred principle that pervades all decisions but, when the circumstances indicate that the internal law of a foreign country will provide a solution more just, more convenient and more in accord with the expectations of the parties than the internal law of England, the English judge does not hesitate to give effect to the foreign rules.

Nevertheless, two main reasons for the application of a foreign law can be put forward.

1.3.1 Justice

An underlying reason for applying a foreign law, rather than English law, is to serve the interests of the parties to the case and achieve justice. It would be unjust to treat parties, who entered into a contract unsupported by consideration in Italy, as if they had contracted under English law, and accordingly declare their contract void for lack of consideration (see *Re Bonacina* (1912)). It is clear that English courts apply Italian law in order to do justice between the parties.

1.3.2 Comity

Although the old theory that comity is the main foundation of the conflict of laws has faded away, its impact cannot be excluded altogether. Even today, references to comity are sometimes found in English judgments (see *Travers v Holley* (1953); and *Igra v Igra* (1951)). If, for example, first cousins domiciled in Portugal marry in England: suppose that such a marriage is valid by English law, but void by Portuguese law. The English court will hold this marriage void, even if the parties wished it to be valid. (This may be inferred from the Court of Appeal decision in *Sottomayor v De Barros* (1877).) Clearly, this decision does not serve the interests of the parties, but it is based on comity, partly to protect the interests of a foreign country and partly in the expectation that the favour will be returned.

1.3.3 Public policy

Whatever the bases for the application of a foreign law are, the question is how far, if at all, should English public policy be relevant? In other words, will the English court enforce a contract for prostitution, albeit valid by its proper law? Will it enforce a contract for slavery, although valid in the *lex loci solutionis*? Scarman J observed in *In the Estate of Fuld (No 3)* (1968):

> An English court will refuse to apply a law which outrages its sense of justice or decency. But, before it exercises such power, it must consider the relevant foreign law as a whole.

Hence, it is a general principle of the conflict of laws that a rule of foreign law, which would be applicable under the *lex causae* (that is, the governing law), may be disregarded if its application would be contrary to public policy. This doctrine is clearly necessary in the context of conflict of laws, but its boundaries cannot be easily defined.

Examination of the cases in which public policy was invoked to invalidate the enforcement of rights arising under foreign laws indicate that, in general, the doctrine has been applied in cases involving foreign contracts, and those involving foreign status. These will be considered under their respective headings, and it suffices for the moment to illustrate its operation briefly. On the ground of public policy, the English court refused to enforce contracts in restraint of trade (*Rousillon v Rousillon* (1880)); contracts breaking the laws of a friendly country (*Regazzoni v Sethia* (1958)); an incapacity existing under a penal foreign law, such as the inability of persons divorced for adultery to remarry, so long as the innocent spouse remains single (*Scott v AG* (1886)); the English court also refused to recognise a marriage of a child under the age of puberty (implied in *Mohammed v Knott* (1969)).

1.4 Classification or characterisation

In a conflict case, much depends on how the issue is classified or characterised. Is it an issue of breach of contract or the commission of a tort? This may be labelled as 'classification of the cause of action'. Once this has been determined, the next stage is to ascertain the governing law which, as we have seen, depends on some connecting factors, such as the *lex situs*, the *lex loci delicti*, the *lex domicilii*, and so forth. These factors link the issue to a legal system. At this stage, a second type of classification has to be done in order to identify the legal characteristic of a particular rule. For instance, in English conflict of laws, capacity to marry is governed by the law of each party's ante-nuptial domicile, and formal validity of a marriage is governed by the law of the country where the marriage is celebrated. Is the issue of parental consent classified as a rule of capacity or formal validity? This question may arise in a different scenario; for instance, a contract between an English employer and a French employee made and to be performed in France. The applicable law to the contract is French. In an action brought in the English court for breach of this contract, the English court will apply French law to issues of formal and essential validity so long as these rules are rules of substance and not procedure. The latter is subject to English law. However, problems may arise as to whether a particular rule is to be classified as a rule of substance or procedure. This type of classification may be labelled as 'classification of a rule of law'. Each of these types will be considered separately.

1.4.1 Classification of the cause of action

Every legal system arranges its rules under different categories which must form the basis of a plaintiff's claim. These categories may be concerned with tort, contract, property, status, succession, etc. Before the English court can proceed to ascertain the *lex causae*, it has to determine the particular category into which the action falls. Does the action relate to the formal validity of a marriage, intestate succession to movables, or some other category? Given the standard categories operating in English law, the difficulty arises when some cases do not fit easily into any single one of them. An action may fall under more than one category. For example, an employee may be able to sue his employer either in contract or tort; or the action may not fall under any of them, such as the duty of a father to provide a dowry for his daughter under Greek law (*Phrantzes v Argenti* (1960)). The crucial question, therefore, is how does the English court classify the cause of action? Is the classification made according to English internal law? It is obvious that the classification process is very crucial to the outcome of cases. However, case law does not show how this process is or should be conducted. According to Cheshire and North (*Private International Law*, 12th edn, p 45):

> There can be little doubt that classification of the cause of action is in practice effected on the basis of the law of the forum ... But, since the classification is required for a case containing a foreign element, it should not necessarily be identical with that which would be appropriate in a purely domestic case.

It follows, therefore, that an English judge must not rigidly confine himself to the concepts or categories found in English internal law.

It is worthy of note, however, that in the context of both the Brussels Convention on Jurisdiction and the Enforcement of Judgments 1968, and the Rome Convention on the Law Applicable to Contractual Obligations 1980, characterisation is unlikely to be referred to the legal system of any particular Contracting State, and is rather determined in a Community sense. Indeed, as shall be discussed in Chapter 3, whether a particular relationship amounts to a contract, or whether a specific act can be characterised as a tort, have been determined in a Community sense. For instance, in the case of *Jacob Handte GmbH v Traitements Mécano-Chimiques des Surfaces* (1992) an action brought by an ultimate manufacturer of defective goods could not be classified as an action in contract for the purposes of jurisdiction under Art 5(1) of the Brussels Convention, despite the fact that it was regarded as such under French law, the law of the forum. The European Court of Justice (ECJ) expressed the view that a contractual relationship 'is not to be understood as covering a situation in which there is no obligation freely assumed by one party towards another'.

1.4.2 Classification of a rule of law

Once the legal category of a given case has been identified, the next stage is to apply the relevant choice of law rules in order to identify the *lex causae*. However, even at this stage, it may be necessary to classify a particular rule in order to determine whether it falls within one choice of law rule or another. This process can be better illustrated by examining two choice of law rules. For instance, capacity to marry is governed by the law of each party's ante-nuptial domicile (that is, the dual-domicile rule), and the formal validity of a marriage is governed by the law of the place where the marriage was celebrated. A problem of characterisation will arise if it is doubtful whether a certain rule of the domicile of one party is an issue of capacity, in which case the dual-domicile rule will apply, or whether it is an issue of formal validity, in which case it will not apply. A good illustration of this issue can be found in *Ogden v Ogden* (1908). A domiciled Englishwoman married, in England, a domiciled Frenchman aged 19. By French law, a man of that age needed his parents' consent to marry and, without such consent, the marriage was voidable. In fact, the husband had not obtained such consent. How did the court classify this issue of consent? Was it an issue of formal validity and, therefore, the rule would not be applicable, or was it an issue of capacity, in which case it would apply? The Court of Appeal classified it as a rule of formal validity and, therefore, declined to apply the dual-domicile rule, for the marriage had been celebrated in England. In this case, the issue involved a classification of a foreign rule, but what if it relates to an English rule? *Leroux v Brown* (1852) illustrates the process applied to an English rule. The case concerned an oral agreement made in France between a French employee and an English employer whereby the former was to work in France for a period longer than a year. This oral contract was governed by French law, under which the contract was formally and essentially valid. The employee brought an action in the English court to enforce the contract. The employer pleaded that the contract was unenforceable in England on the ground that the then English Statute of Frauds provided that no action shall lie upon a contract which was to last more than a year, unless the agreement was in writing.

If this provision were to be regarded as a rule of formal validity, then its application would be excluded, for the formal validity of the contract was governed by French law. However, the English court held it to be a rule of procedure and, therefore, it was applied as part of the *lex fori*. The justification given by the court was that the effect of the statute was only to prevent a party from bringing an action on a valid contract and not to make the contract void.

1.5   *Renvoi*

When an English court refers an issue to a foreign law, it nearly always refers to the domestic rules of that law. In some instances, however, the court treats this reference to the foreign law as a reference to the conflict rules of that law. This is called *renvoi*. For example, in *Re Ross* (1930), the testatrix, a British national, died domiciled in Italy. She left movable property in England and movable and immovable property in Italy. Her wills in relation to her English and Italian estates were valid by English domestic law of succession, but invalid by Italian domestic law. This was because she had not left half of the estates to her son, who contested the wills. Under English conflict of laws, the essential validity of the wills was governed by Italian law as the law of the domicile of the testatrix (in relation to the movables), and as the *lex situs* (in relation to the immovables). Under Italian conflict of laws, this issue was governed by the domestic law of the nationality of the testatrix. As a result, the English court applied English domestic law and the wills were held to be valid.

Hence, the issue of *renvoi* arises when a rule of conflict of laws refers to the whole of the law of a foreign country, but the conflict rule of the foreign country would have referred the question to the law of the first country (that is, *remission*), or the law of some other country (that is, *transmission*). There are two forms of *renvoi: single* or *partial renvoi*, and *double* or *total renvoi*.

1.5.1 Single or partial *renvoi*

Under single or partial *renvoi*, the English court accepts the reference back from the country referred to by the English choice of law rule. For instance, if an English court is referred by its own choice of law rules to the law of country X, but the choice of law rules of X refers such case back to English law, then the English court must apply its own domestic law to the case. This form has been adopted in some continental countries, but it is not part of English law.

1.5.2 Double or total *renvoi*

Under double or total *renvoi*, the English court, which is referred by its conflict rules to the foreign country, must apply the law which a court in that foreign country would apply if it were hearing the case. This means that the English court not only applies the foreign country's choice of law rule, but also its doctrine of *renvoi*. The operation of this form of *renvoi* is illustrated in *Re Annesley* (1926), where the testatrix, a British national, died domiciled in France according to English law, but domiciled in England according to French law. Her will was valid by English domestic law, but invalid by French domestic law, for she had failed to leave two thirds of her property to her children. Under the English choice of law rule, the essential validity of the will was governed by French law as the law of her domicile at the time of her death. The court applied the *total renvoi* theory and held that the will was governed by French domestic law for the following reasons: the English court took the reference to French law to mean that the case must be decided as a French court would decide it. According to French conflict rules, the succession was governed by English law as the law of the testatrix's nationality. However, a French court would apply the conflict rules of that law, that is, it would accept the *renvoi*, and apply French domestic law. Reconsider *Re Ross* (1930): the reason why English domestic law applied was because the evidence was that the Italian court would not accept the *renvoi* and would simply apply English domestic law, and that was what the English court did.

Last, but not least, *renvoi* applies to questions of intestate succession and essential validity of wills. There is some authority to the effect that it applies to 'marriage' and that it should apply to cases involving title to immovable property. *Renvoi* does not, however, find a place in the fields of contract or tort (*renvoi* will be reconsidered under the respective topics).

1.6 Proof of foreign law

Unless the foreign law is pleaded by the party relying on it, the English court will decide a case containing foreign elements as if it were a purely English domestic case. Foreign law is treated as a question of fact of which the judge has no judicial knowledge. It must be proved by 'appropriate evidence, that is, by properly qualified witnesses'. An exception, however, applies in relation to Scottish law. The latter does not have to be proved in the House of Lords, which is the common forum of both England and Scotland, for their Lordships have judicial knowledge of Scottish law.

The burden of proving the relevant foreign law lies on the party asserting it. Moreover, where the foreign law is not proved, the English court applies English law.

NATURE AND SCOPE OF CONFLICT OF LAWS

Role of conflict of laws

Conflict of laws, or private international law, comes into play whenever a dispute before the English court contains one or more foreign elements.

In such cases, three main issues have to be determined. The first issue is whether the English court is the appropriate forum to hear the case. The second issue is to ascertain which law governs the dispute in question. The third and final issue arises in relation to judgments rendered by foreign courts and is whether such judgments can be recognised and/or enforced in England.

Private and public international law

Private international law is that part of a legal system's domestic law which is primarily concerned with disputes of a private nature, whereas public international law is concerned with regulating relations between sovereign States.

Connecting factors

In order to determine the applicable law in a given dispute, an English court seeks guidance from connecting factors. Such connecting factors are, as a general rule, determined according to English law as the law of the forum.

The concept of personal law

An individual's personal law is the law which defines his status and capacity. English courts determine such a law by reference to the concept of domicile.

The bases of conflict of laws

A foreign law, rather than domestic English law, is applied to a dispute which involves foreign elements in order to serve the purpose of justice and, in some instances, to serve the interests of comity. This is so, so long as the application of such a foreign law is not contrary to public policy.

Classification or characterisation

There are two types of classification: classification of the cause of action and classification of a rule of law. In relation to the former type, English courts must determine the category to which the dispute in question belongs, whereas in relation to the latter, English courts must determine whether a particular rule is one of substance or procedure.

Renvoi

Renvoi comes into operation in circumstances where an English court refers an issue to the whole of a foreign law, including its conflict of laws rules. This process, which is rarely applied in English law, mainly operates in the areas of intestate succession and essential validity of wills.

Proof of foreign law

Unless a foreign law is pleaded and proved, the English court will determine the dispute according to English domestic law.

CHAPTER 2

JURISDICTION OF THE ENGLISH COURT IN COMMERCIAL DISPUTES: THE COMMON LAW RULES

2.1 Introduction

This chapter deals with the power of the English court to entertain actions *in personam*, that is, actions other than those concerned with matrimonial causes (which are dealt with under family law), actions for administration of estates and bankruptcy, and admiralty actions *in rem*.

The question of whether an English court has power to hear a case is a matter which must be decided according to principles of English law. However, the position is complicated by the fact that there are now two sets of rules determining the jurisdiction of English courts. In the majority of cases, jurisdiction is governed by the Brussels Convention on Jurisdiction and the Enforcement of Judgments in Civil and Commercial Matters 1968 (the Brussels Convention), as amended, and the Lugano Convention on Jurisdiction and the Enforcement of Judgments in Civil and Commercial Matters 1988 (the Lugano Convention). The rules contained therein apply to cases involving European Community (EC)/European Free Trade Association (EFTA)-based defendants, but only to the extent that the action comes under the umbrella of civil and commercial matters. In cases falling outside the scope of the Conventions, the jurisdiction of English courts is determined by the traditional common law rules. Hence, the purpose of this chapter is to examine the question of jurisdiction under the traditional common law rules only. Jurisdiction under the Brussels and Lugano Conventions are the subject matter of the next chapter.

Under the common law rules, the jurisdiction of the English court may be assumed on any one of the following grounds:

(a) where the writ is served on a defendant physically present in England;

(b) where the defendant voluntarily submits to the jurisdiction of the English court; or

(c) where the plaintiff obtains leave from the High Court to serve the writ on the defendant outside England in accordance with one or more heads under RSC Ord 11 r 1(1).

Each of these grounds will be examined separately.

2.2 Defendant present within the jurisdiction

Provided that the defendant is not domiciled within the EC/EFTA, the English court has power to hear the case when a writ is legally served on a defendant physically present in England. The application of this principle varies, depending on whether the defendant is an individual, a corporation or a partnership firm.

2.2.1 Individuals

A writ may be served on any individual who is present in England, however short his or her visit may be. For instance, in *Maharanee of Baroda v Wildenstein* (1972), the plaintiff, an Indian princess residing in France, brought an action in England against the defendant, an art expert also residing in France. The action was based on breach of a contract for the sale of a painting in France, stated to be by the artist Boucher, but which was allegedly a forgery. The writ was served on the defendant whilst he was in England on a one day visit to Ascot races. The defendant objected to the jurisdiction of the English court, but the Court of Appeal held that he had been properly served, and accordingly it had competent jurisdiction to hear the case.

2.2.2 Corporations

By virtue of ss 691, 695 and 725 of the Companies Act 1985 (CA), a corporation is deemed present in England in three situations:

(a) according to s 725, where a company is registered in England, it is deemed to be present within the jurisdiction even if it only carries on business abroad, and thus, service of the writ may be effected at its registered office in England. Where a company is registered in Scotland, and carries on business in England, the jurisdiction of the English court can be assumed by serving a writ at the company's principal place of business in England and by sending a copy to its registered office in Scotland;

(b) if the company is incorporated outside England, but has a place of business in England, then by virtue of s 691 of the CA 1985, it must file the name and address of a person in England who is authorised to accept service of the writ on its behalf. Provided that the name of such a person remains on file, service of the writ on him or her makes the company subject to the jurisdiction of the English court, regardless of the fact that the company no longer carries on business in England. This latter provision is clearly inserted to prevent foreign companies from incurring debts in England and then closing down, thus leaving creditors without a remedy. If, however, this was considered to be unfair on the defendant company, it must be noted that the latter might be able to seek successfully a stay of the English proceedings on the ground of *forum non conveniens*, that is, on the ground that there is another forum which is more appropriate than England (see below, 2.5);

(c) if no such address is filed, or if the person named dies, or for any reason the writ cannot be served in accordance with s 691 above, then by virtue of s 695 of the CA 1985, service may be effected by sending the writ to 'any place of business established by the company in Great Britain'. This provision, which replaced s 412 of the Companies Act 1948 (CA), was interpreted by the Court of Appeal in *Deverall v Grant Advertising Inc* (1955), to mean that the place must remain established at the time of service.

The above provisions give rise to the question of when a foreign company is said to have established a place of business in England. This question can only be answered by examining the activities of the defendant company in England. For instance, in *South India Shipping Corpn Ltd v Export-Import Bank of Korea* (1985) the plaintiff, a company incorporated in India, brought a claim against the defendant bank, which was incorporated in Korea where its main business was conducted. However, the bank rented an office in London for the purposes of gathering information and maintaining public relations with other banking and financial institutions in the UK and Europe. No banking transactions were concluded from the London office, nor was the office registered as a place of business under the CA 1948, then in force. The writ was served at the office in London. The defendant contended that, as they had not established a place of business in Great Britain, the writ was not duly served. The Court of Appeal held that a company was said to have established a place of business in Great Britain if it carried on part of its business activities here, and it was not necessary for those activities to be either a substantial part of, or more than incidental to, the main object of the company. Accordingly, the defendant was duly served with the writ, for it had established a place of business here. It was immaterial that the defendant neither concluded any banking transactions from the London office, nor had banking dealings with the general public. Moreover, in *Re Oriel* (1985), the Court of Appeal held that a specific location for the business was necessary in order to come within the meaning of what is now s 691 of the CA 1985. It had to be shown that there was apparently a permanent and specific location in England associated with the company, and from which it habitually or regularly carried on business, although it was not necessary for the company to own or lease such premises. Similarly, in *Cleveland Museum of Art v Capricorn Art International SA* (1990), art dealers, who had used a converted church in London both to store and display works of art, were held to have established a place of business in England. So long as the dealers were known by the art world to operate from those premises, it was immaterial that the premises did not advertise their presence therein.

2.2.3 Partnerships

In the case of partnerships, a writ can be served on any individual partner who is present in England at the time of the service. Service of the writ may now also be effected on the partnership firm by virtue of RSC Ord 81 r 1, which provides that:

> ... any two or more persons claiming to be entitled, or alleged to be liable, as partners in respect of a cause of action and carrying on business within the jurisdiction may sue, or be sued, in the name of the firm (if any) of which they were partners at the time when the cause of action accrued.

This rule means that a writ can be served at the firm's place of business in England, even if the individual partners are outside England.

2.3 Submission to the jurisdiction

At common law, the English court may have jurisdiction over the defendant if he or she submits to the court. Submission may be effected in a variety of ways. A defendant may enter an appearance to defend the case on its merits, such as disputing his or her alleged liability; or he or she may instruct a solicitor to accept service on his or her behalf in accordance with RSC Ord 11 r 1(4). Submission may also be effected where, having commenced an action in the English court as a plaintiff, he or she is faced with a counterclaim brought by the defendant and which is related to the original claim (RSC Ord 15 r 2). In all these cases, the defendant can be said to have submitted to the jurisdiction, but if he or she appears merely to contest the jurisdiction of the court, then according to *Williams and Glyn's Bank v Astro Dinamico* (1984), he or she is not deemed to have submitted thereto.

Submission may also be inferred from the terms of a contract, for example, a contract may expressly or impliedly indicate that a party has agreed to submit to the jurisdiction of the English court. Save in very exceptional circumstances, he or she will be held to that agreement.

Submission, however, applies only to actions *in personam* and does not confer jurisdiction in divorce or nullity proceedings, or in relation to an action principally dealing with an issue of title to foreign land.

2.4 Defendant outside the jurisdiction

Where the defendant has no physical presence in England, or does not submit to the jurisdiction, or if, prior to the issue of the writ, he or she goes abroad and does not return, the English court is empowered to allow service of the writ out of the jurisdiction in specific cases. This power, which is contained in RSC Ord 11 r 1(1), is discretionary. Following the Civil Jurisdiction and Judgments Act 1982 (CJJA), which implemented the Brussels Convention 1968, Ord 11 r 1(1) was substantially amended to bring it into line with Arts 5 and 6 of the Brussels Convention. The amended version came into force at the same time as the Brussels Convention, on 1 January 1987.

Service of the writ out of the jurisdiction under Ord 11 r 1(1) requires the permission of the High Court. Permission is no mere formality and it will only be granted if the case is a proper one for service out of the jurisdiction (Ord 11 r 4(2)). The onus is on the plaintiff to satisfy the court that the cause of action falls under one of the heads of Ord 11 r 1(1); that he or she has a good arguable case; that, on the merits, there is a serious issue to be tried; and that the court's discretion should be exercised to allow service out of the jurisdiction.

The fact that the plaintiff must show that he has a good arguable case means that he or she must do more than make a *prima facie* case that the dispute falls under one or more heads of r 1(1). This, however, does not mean that he or she has to satisfy the court beyond reasonable doubt. As to the merits of the case, the test was recently laid down by the House of Lords in *Seaconsar Far East v Bank Markazi Jomouri Islami Iran* (1993), where Lord Goff, giving the leading judgment, held that the correct approach was that where jurisdiction was established under Ord 11 r 1(1) and England was also established as *forum conveniens*, it was sufficient for the plaintiff to establish that there was a serious issue to be tried, rather than show a good arguable case on the merits; that is, there was a substantial question of fact or law, or both, arising on the facts disclosed by the affidavits which the plaintiff desired to have tried.

In exercising its discretion, the court will have to consider whether England is *forum conveniens*, that is, service of the writ outside the jurisdiction will only be allowed where England is clearly the appropriate forum in the interests of the parties and the ends of justice. The test is substantially similar to the test applied where an application has been made for a stay of English proceedings on the ground of *forum non conveniens*. However, in Ord 11 cases, the burden of proof is shifted onto the plaintiff. The current test was laid down by the House of Lords in *Spiliada Maritime Corpn v Cansulex Ltd* (1987). The underlying fundamental principle is 'to identify the forum in which the case can be suitably tried for the interests of all the parties and for the ends of justice'. In order to do so, 'the court must take into account the nature of the dispute, the legal and practical issues involved, such questions as local knowledge, availability of witnesses and their evidence and expense'.

It is essential to note that, for the leave to be granted, the burden is on the plaintiff to establish that England is *forum conveniens*. Since the application for leave to serve the writ outside the jurisdiction is made *ex parte*, the defendant will only become aware of the proceedings once the writ is served. At that stage, the defendant can contest jurisdiction and apply for the writ to be set aside. This process, however, must be distinguished from that of an application for a stay of proceedings in cases where the service of the writ is based on the defendant's presence within the jurisdiction. Where an application for a stay is made, the burden of proof is on the defendant to show that England is *forum non conveniens*. Conversely, where an application to have the writ set aside is made, the onus remains on the plaintiff to prove that England is *forum conveniens*.

Where the parties have agreed that any dispute arising between them shall be referred to the exclusive jurisdiction of a foreign court, leave to serve the writ outside the jurisdiction will usually be refused. For example, in *Mackender v Feldia* (1967), the Court of Appeal, reversing the decision of McNair J, set aside the leave to serve the writ outside the jurisdiction on the grounds that the contract contained an exclusive jurisdiction clause in favour of the Belgian court, and that the dispute was within the scope of that clause.

In order for the leave to be granted, the plaintiff must also show that the cause of action falls under one of the following heads of Ord 11 r 1(1). However, it must be noted that a given case may fall under more than one head.

2.4.1 General

Rule 1(1)(a): where 'relief is sought against a person domiciled within the jurisdiction'. This head is very wide and covers practically any kind of action, provided that the defendant is domiciled within the jurisdiction. 'Domicile' under this head and throughout Ord 11 is to be determined in accordance with ss 41–46 of the CJJA 1982. In general, this head can be invoked when the defendant is domiciled in England, but is abroad at the time the plaintiff intends to commence proceedings in the English court.

Rule 1(1)(b): where 'an injunction is sought ordering the defendant to do or refrain from doing anything within the jurisdiction (whether or not damages are also claimed in respect of a failure to do or the doing of that thing)'. Although the injunction does not have to be the only relief sought, it must be the substantial relief sought. Hence, leave will be refused if the injunction sought is only incidental to the cause of action. As such, this head does not cover Mareva injunctions, that is, an interlocutory injunction to freeze the defendant's assets within the jurisdiction pending the trial of an action against him or her. Additionally, according to *The Siskina* (1979), this head does not cover cases where the plaintiff only seeks a Mareva injunction and has no other cause of action in England.

Rule 1(1)(c): where 'the claim is brought against a person duly served within or out of the jurisdiction and a person out of the jurisdiction is a necessary or proper party thereto'. Leave to serve outside the jurisdiction under this head may be obtained if, for example, there are two defendants, one of whom has been duly served with the writ and the plaintiff wishes to serve the second defendant, who happened to be outside the jurisdiction. This, however, is conditional on the latter being either a necessary or a proper party to the action against the first defendant.

Furthermore, the Court of Appeal held in *Kuwait Oil Tanker Co SAK v Al Bader* (1997) that it was a prerequisite of the grant of leave under this sub-head that a defendant had already been served, either within or outside the jurisdiction, before leave to serve another defendant outside the jurisdiction could be properly granted. In this case, the plaintiffs wanted to bring an action against three defendants, the first of whom resided in England and the other two outside the jurisdiction. Before the writ was served upon either the first or the second defendant, the plaintiffs were granted leave to serve the writ on the third defendant outside the jurisdiction, under r 1(1)(c). Later the same day, the plaintiffs served the writ on the first defendant in England and, a few days later the third defendant was served outside the jurisdiction. The latter applied to have the service of the writ set aside, on the ground that the requirements of prior service under r 1(1)(c) had not been met. The Court of Appeal upheld this argument and declared the leave to be invalid. However, since this irregularity did not cause prejudice to the defendant, and as it was desirable to proceed with the action against all three defendants in the same jurisdiction, a good reason existed to justify retrospective validation of the leave in accordance with RSC Ord 2 r 1.

Essentially, the purpose of this sub-head, like Art 6 of the Brussels Convention 1968, is to alleviate the inconvenience of a dispute, involving more than one defendant, being litigated in a number of fora. It also helps to avoid the risk of irreconcilable judgments.

2.4.2 Contract

Rule 1(1)(d): a plaintiff may apply for leave to serve a writ outside the jurisdiction if the claim is brought to enforce, rescind, dissolve, annul or otherwise affect a contract, or to recover damages, or obtain other relief in respect of the breach of a contract in four different situations (see (a)–(d), below). But prior to examining these situations, it must be noted that the language of this provision appears to be sufficiently wide to embrace a claim for a declaration that no contract ever came into existence, that is, what is effectively called a negative declaration. Indeed, this view was adopted by the English High Court in *DR Insurance Co v Central National Insurance Co* (1996), concerning the existence of three reinsurance contracts entered into by Elkhorn in 1979 and 1980, one in favour of the first defendants and two in favour of the second defendants. Elkhorn was a member of a syndicate of reinsurers which wrote business through the agency of ST and Co. In 1983, Elkhorn was sold, and as part of the arrangements surrounding the sale, the business through ST and Co was transferred to the plaintiff DR. The contracts, subject of the dispute, were written in the London market. In 1986, the defendants wished to pursue claims under these reinsurance contracts, but DR declined to accept liability. In 1993, they attempted to commence arbitration against DR in Nebraska, but DR was successful in obtaining a declaration from the district court, in 1995, that the arbitration agreements were void as being contrary to the public policy of Nebraska. DR also applied to the English court for leave to serve the writ on the defendants outside the jurisdiction under Ord 11 r 1(1)(d), seeking relief by way of a declaration that the contracts in question were void and unenforcable as having been effected or carried out in contravention of the Insurance Companies Acts 1974–82. Shortly thereafter, the defendants commenced proceedings in New York seeking to enforce the contracts. They also applied to the English court to set aside the leave, contending, *inter alia*, that the claim did not fall within the scope of r 1(1)(d) on the ground that DR's claim was not one to annul or affect a relevant contract, since DR was asserting that no contracts ever came into existence. The court rejected this argument and held that the plaintiff's claim came within the ambit of r 1(1)(d). Mr Moore-Bick QC (sitting as deputy judge) explained that when seeking to ascertain the meaning of this provision, it was appropriate to have regard to the general purpose behind the rule in so far as that could be ascertained from its language. Indeed, the policy underlying r 1(1)(d) was to enable all disputes about the existence or effect of contractual rights and liabilities, falling within the scope of sub-paras (i)–(iii), to be brought before the English courts. Hence, he saw no reason why the language of this rule should be construed with such a great technicality as to exclude the present case. Accordingly, the plaintiff's claim fell within the terms of r 1(1)(d). As mentioned above, r 1(1)(d) enables a plaintiff to seek leave to serve the writ outside the jurisdiction in four contract related situations:

(a) by virtue of r 1(1)(d)(i), leave to serve the writ outside the jurisdiction may be granted if the contract was made within the jurisdiction. The place of contracting is determined according to principles of English domestic law. Thus, a contract concluded by postal correspondence is made where the acceptance is posted. The postal rule, however, does not apply to contracts concluded by the use of instantaneous communications, such as telephone, fax or telex. Indeed, in *Entores v Miles Far East Corpn* (1955), it was held that, in such cases, the contract would be made where the acceptance was received. Nevertheless, for this rule to apply, the acceptance must not be made 'subject to modifications' of the offer. For instance, in *Brinkibon Ltd v Stahag Stahl GmbH* (1983), the House of Lords held that the seller's telex, which purported to be an acceptance but had modified the terms of the offer, constituted a counter-offer. Thus, the contract was not concluded in England, where the purported acceptance was received, but was concluded in Austria, where the buyer's confirming telex was received;

(b) leave to serve the writ outside the jurisdiction is permissible under r 1(1)(d)(ii) if the contract was made by, or through, an agent trading or residing within the jurisdiction on behalf of a principal trading or residing out of the jurisdiction. Evidentially, this sub-head applies to cases where the agent, trading or residing in England, concludes the contract on behalf of a foreign principal. Additionally, according to *National Mortgage and Agency Co of New Zealand Ltd v Gosselin* (1922), this sub-head also covers cases where the contract was arranged through the mediation of the agent in England, but was actually concluded by the foreign principal. However, it must be noted that r 1(1)(d)(ii) only applies where the foreign principal is being sued as a defendant. It does not apply where he or she is suing as a plaintiff (see *Union International Insurance Co Ltd v Jubilee Insurance Co Ltd* (1991));

(c) r 1(1)(d)(iii) enables the English court to assume jurisdiction over a defendant outside the jurisdiction where the contract is, by its terms or by implication, governed by English law. Whether a contract is governed by English law must be determined by the English choice of law rules. These rules are now contained in the Contracts (Applicable Law) Act 1990, which is considered below, in Chapter 5;

(d) in accordance with r 1(1)(d)(iv), leave may be granted where a contract contains a term to the effect that the High Court shall have jurisdiction to hear and determine any action in respect of the contract. The underlying principle here is that the parties to the contract should be bound by their agreed choice of jurisdiction unless there is some strong reason to the contrary. In other words, where leave is sought under this sub-head, the English court will be more likely to exercise its discretion in favour of granting the leave than under any other heads of Ord 11. This is due to the court's policy to hold parties to their agreement. Indeed, this viewpoint was summarised by Willmer LJ, in *The Chaparral* (1968), in the following terms (p 162):

> *Prima facie* it is the policy of the court to hold parties to the bargain into which they have entered. *Prima facie* it is to be presumed, therefore, that the plaintiffs should have leave to prosecute their proceedings in this country and, in pursuance of that, serve their writ out of the jurisdiction ... I approach the matter, therefore, in this way, that the court has a discretion, but it is a discretion which, in the ordinary way and in the absence of strong reasons to the contrary, will be exercised in favour of holding parties to their bargain.

Similarly, in *Gulf Bank v Mitsubishi Heavy Industries* (1994), Hobhouse J held that, where there was a jurisdiction clause, the discretion of the court under Ord 11 r 1(1)(d)(iv) should, *prima facie*, be exercised in favour of giving effect to that clause by permitting service out of the jurisdiction. It must be noted, however, that since Art 17 of the Brussels Convention 1968 allocates exclusive mandatory jurisdiction to English courts in certain circumstances, the common law rules in this context have become less significant, to the effect that they now apply only if the parties are domiciled outside the EC or if the dispute is not within the scope of the Convention (see Chapter 3).

Furthermore, by virtue of r 1(1)(e), service of the writ out of the jurisdiction is permissible with the leave of the court where:

> ... the claim is brought in respect of a breach committed within the jurisdiction of a contract made within or out of the jurisdiction, and irrespective of the fact, if such be the case, that the breach was preceded or accompanied by a breach committed out of the jurisdiction that rendered impossible the performance of so much of the contract as ought to have been performed within the jurisdiction.

In order to fulfil this sub-head, three conditions must be satisfied: (a) the contract in question must have been entered into; (b) it must have been broken; and (c) the alleged breach must have taken place in England. The latter condition is also satisfied where the breach committed in England is only subsidiary to the substantial breach committed abroad.

2.4.3 Tort

In pursuance to r 1(1)(f), leave is permissible where the plaintiff's 'claim is founded on a tort and the damage was sustained, or resulted from an act committed, within the jurisdiction'. Whether a particular cause of action is founded on a tort is a matter which is to be ascertained in accordance with English law.

The wording of this sub-head reflects the provisions of Art 5(3) of the Brussels Convention 1968. It is intended to alleviate the problems associated with determining the place of tort where, for example, the wrongful act is committed in one jurisdiction and the resulting damage ensues in another. Thus, English courts may assume jurisdiction under this sub-head if either the wrongful act giving rise to the damage was committed in England or if the damage resulting from the tort was sustained in England.

2.4.4 Property

Leave to serve the writ on a defendant outside the jurisdiction is also permissible under the following sub-heads:

- r 1(1)(g): where 'the whole subject matter of the action is land situate within the jurisdiction (with or without rents or profits) or the perpetuation of testimony relating to land so situate';

- r 1(1)(h): where 'the claim is brought to construe, rectify, set aside or enforce an act, deed, will, contract, obligation or liability affecting land situate within the jurisdiction, such as an action to recover rent due under a lease of land, or damages for breach of covenant';

- r 1(1)(i): a leave may be granted where:

  ... the claim is made for a debt secured on immovable property or is made to assert, declare or determine proprietary or possessory rights, or rights of security, in or over movable property, or to obtain authority to dispose of movable property situate within the jurisdiction.

2.4.5 Other heads

Other heads of Ord 11 r 1 enable the court to take jurisdiction in actions brought to execute the trusts of a written instrument (r 1(1)(j)); for the administration of the estate of a person who died domiciled in England (r 1(1)(k)); in a probate action within the meaning of Order 76 (r 1(1)(l)) to enforce a foreign judgment or arbitration award (r 1(1)(m)); and actions brought under various Acts (see r 1(1)(n), (o), (p), (q), (r), (s) and (t)).

2.5 Prevention of forum shopping and the staying of actions

It appears from the foregoing discussion that English common law rules allow anyone to invoke, or become amenable to, the jurisdiction, provided that the defendant has been served with a writ. Service may be effected either by the defendant's presence, however short, in England; or if he or she was outside England, by means of RSC Ord 11 r 1(1). This approach, which has often been described as exorbitant, empowers English courts to hear cases which, in some instances, may be inappropriate for trial in England. It also leads to the plaintiff forum shopping for the best remedy available.

Lord Pearson defined forum shopping in *Boys v Chaplin* (1971) as:

[A] plaintiff bypassing his natural forum and bringing his action in some alien forum which would give him relief or benefits which would not be available to him in the natural forum.

In other words, whenever a plaintiff has a choice between a number of fora in which to litigate, he or she is bound to go for the most advantageous forum. For instance, the plaintiff may be tempted to litigate in the USA, where a contingent fee system is in operation, and where pre-trial discovery and punitive damages are available. Alternatively, he or she may choose to sue in England, where an adversarial system is in operation, whereby he or she can bring their own expert witnesses, or where the level of damages is higher than that on the continent. The plaintiff's choice of jurisdiction, albeit advantageous to him or her, is more often than not to the detriment of the defendant. Hence, questions arise as to whether plaintiffs should be allowed to forum shop for the best remedy available, and whether, and in what way, forum shopping can be controlled.

The English court has inherent jurisdiction, reinforced by statute (namely, s 49(3) of the Supreme Court Act 1981), to stay an action in England, or to restrain by injunction, a plaintiff from continuing the proceedings in a foreign court, whenever it is necessary to do so in order to preserve justice. This power is highly discretionary. It may be invoked on the ground of *forum non conveniens* in the context of stays of action, being the subject matter of this paragraph, or in the context of injunctions (examined below, 2.6) on the ground that the foreign proceedings are vexatious and oppressive.

Where the writ has been properly served, the English court will proceed with the case unless the defendant proves that England is not the natural forum and that there is another available forum which is clearly and distinctly more appropriate for the trial of the action; that is, England is *forum non conveniens*. In such cases, the defendant may base his application on one of three grounds:

- first, the defendant may simply claim that the action ought to be tried in the foreign forum rather than in England, that is, England is *forum non conveniens*;

- secondly, the defendant may apply for the English action to be stayed because proceedings had already been instituted in a foreign forum, that is, a case of *lis alibi pendens*; or

- thirdly, the defendant requests a stay of the English action on the basis that the parties had agreed that disputes of the type in question would be subject to the exclusive jurisdiction of another forum.

In all the above scenarios, the applicable test is essentially the same, that is, of *forum non conveniens*, but the outcome of the application for a stay may differ depending on the ground upon which the defendant bases his or her application.

2.5.1 *Forum non conveniens*

The doctrine of *forum non conveniens*, whilst it had been applied in Scotland and the USA for a number of years, was not accepted in England until relatively recently. In fact, it was once vehemently rejected by English judges and a stay of proceedings was confined only to cases of vexation and oppression. For instance, in *St Pierre v South American Stores Ltd* (1936) Scott LJ had stated the test in relation to stays in the following terms (p 398):

> (1) A mere balance of convenience is not a sufficient ground for depriving a plaintiff of the advantages of prosecuting his action in an English court if it is otherwise properly brought. The right of access to the King's Court must not be lightly refused.
>
> (2) In order to justify a stay, two conditions must be satisfied, one positive and the other negative:
>
> > (a) the defendant must satisfy the court that the continuance of the action would work an injustice because it would be oppressive or vexatious to him or would be an abuse of the process of the court in some other way; and
> >
> > (b) the stay must not cause an injustice to the plaintiff. On both, the burden of proof is on the defendant.

Evidentially, this test was not sufficiently effective to control forum shopping. A stay would only be granted if the plaintiff 'set out deliberately to harass the defendant' by litigating in England. It was not until the House of Lords' decision in *The Atlantic Star* (1974) that a sharp movement towards a broader test was signalled. This decision is considered as the raw material from which the doctrine of *forum non conveniens* has evolved.

The process of liberalisation continued with the subsequent decision of the House of Lords in *MacShannon v Rockware Glass Ltd* (1978), which effectively repudiated the old vocabulary and acknowledged a new test, hard to distinguish from *forum non conveniens*. Lord Diplock reformulated the second part of Scott LJ's test as follows (p 812):

> In order to justify a stay, two conditions must be satisfied, one positive and the other negative: (a) the defendant must satisfy the court that there is another forum to whose jurisdiction he is amenable in which justice can be done between the parties at substantially less inconvenience and expense; and (b) the stay must not deprive the plaintiff of a legitimate personal or juridical advantage which would be available to him if he invoked the jurisdiction of the English court.

Final express acceptance of the application of the doctrine *forum non conveniens* in cases of stays came in the House of Lords decision in *The Abidin Daver* (1984), where Lord Diplock was able to declare that 'judicial chauvinism has been replaced by judicial comity to an extent which I think the time is now right to acknowledge frankly [that the test applicable to stays] is ... indistinguishable from the Scottish legal doctrine of *forum non conveniens*' (p 411).

However, the law was exhaustively re-examined and restated by the House of Lords in *Spiliada Maritime Corpn v Cansulex Ltd* (1986), which landmarked the modern law on stays of action. Notwithstanding that this case was concerned with the exercise of the discretion to serve a writ out of the jurisdiction under RSC Ord 11 r 1(1), the House of Lords set out a number of principles, on the basis of which the discretion with regard to stays should be exercised:

(a) the basic principle is that a stay will only be granted on the ground of *forum non conveniens* where the court is satisfied that there is some other available forum, having competent jurisdiction, which is the appropriate forum for the trial of the action, that is, in which the case may be tried more suitably for the interests of all the parties and the ends of justice [p 854];

(b) in considering whether there was another forum which was more appropriate, the court would look for that forum with which the action had the most real and substantial connection, for example, in terms of convenience or expense, availability of witnesses, the law governing the relevant transaction, and the places where the parties resided or carried on business [p 844];

(c) the burden of proof rests on the defendant to persuade the court to exercise its discretion to grant a stay ... if the court is satisfied that there is another available forum which is *prima facie* the appropriate forum for the trial of the action, the burden will then shift to the plaintiff to show that there are special circumstances by reason of which justice requires that the trial should nevertheless take place in this country [pp 854–55];

(d) the fact that the granting of a stay of English proceedings ... might deprive the plaintiff of a legitimate personal or juridical advantage available to him under the English jurisdiction would not, as a general rule, deter the court from granting a stay ... if it was satisfied that substantial justice would be done to all the parties in the available appropriate forum [p 844].

Accordingly, the test in *The Spiliada* is a two stage process. At the first stage, the defendant must satisfy the court that England is not the appropriate forum and that there is another available forum which is *prima facie* the appropriate one for the trial of the action. In identifying the appropriate forum, the search is for the one which has the most real and substantial connection with the dispute. This is ascertained by weighing relevant connecting factors, such as convenience and expense, availability of witnesses, the place where the parties reside or carry on business, the law governing the cause of action, and so forth. The degree of weight accorded to each connecting factor varies depending on the circumstances of each particular dispute. Whilst a specific factor may be of great significance in one case, it may be irrelevant in another. It is only by examining the harvest of decided cases that one is able to determine the practical importance of the various connecting factors in ascertaining the appropriate forum.

It is evident that where the parties lack territorial connection with the jurisdiction, then *prima facie*, England is not the appropriate forum. Indeed, this was a decisive factor in favour of granting a stay of action in the case of *De Dampierre v De Dampierre* (1987). In this case, a husband and wife, both French nationals married in France, moved to London, where the husband carried on business on the family estate. Soon after, the wife had a child and the husband bought them a house in London. A few years later, the wife established a business in New York, where she took her child, and declared her unwillingness to return to England. The husband started divorce proceedings in France and the wife issued a divorce petition in the English court. Following the husband's application for a stay of the English proceedings, the House of Lords applied the *Spiliada* test and held that the wife's connection with England was tenuous. She was resident in the USA and had voluntarily severed all connection with England before instituting her English divorce proceedings. She was a French national, and was married in France, where she could litigate as easily as in England. Furthermore, the husband had, by then, sold his property in England and returned to reside in France. Hence, there were practically no factors connecting the case with England. Accordingly, *prima facie*, France clearly provided the appropriate forum for the resolution of the dispute, to the effect that a stay would be granted unless justice required the contrary.

English courts have attached considerable weight to the availability of witnesses, additional expense, delay and inconvenience when establishing the appropriate forum. In *Cleveland Museum of Art v Capricorn Art International SA* (1990), the Ohio court was held to be the appropriate forum on the grounds that the proceedings had been under way in that court for over two years; the defendant had already expended a considerable sum in legal costs in those proceedings; Ohio was the more convenient forum for the witnesses; the contract was for loan for an exhibition in the USA; and the proceedings in the Ohio court were only stayed for a period of time and pending the outcome of the English proceedings. Hence, since it was not certain that the Ohio proceedings would be stayed permanently, continuing the English action would cause additional expense, delay and inconvenience.

The place where the relevant events occurred and the language of the documentary evidence can also be important connecting factors. In *Re Harrods (Buenos Aires) Ltd (No 2)* (1991), the plaintiff was a minority shareholder in a company incorporated and registered in England, but its business was conducted and it was managed exclusively in Argentina. He claimed that the company's affairs were being conducted in a manner unfairly prejudicial to it and presented a petition, under the Companies Act 1985, for orders to be granted directing the defendant, the majority shareholder, to purchase its shares, or alternatively that the company be compulsorily wound up under the Insolvency Act 1986. On the facts, the Court of Appeal held that Argentina was the natural forum for the trial of the issues raised in view of the strong connection the case had with Argentina; that is, all the relevant events took place in Argentina and all the evidence would be in Spanish. Similarly, in *The Al Battani* (1993), the fact that much of the documentary evidence, as well as the surveyor's report, were in English, and which would have had to be translated into Arabic should litigation take place in Egypt, militated against trial in Egypt and in favour of England. Essentially, this accords with the view adopted in *The Magnum* (1989) where Parker LJ stated (p 51):

> Where the decision depends upon the construction of a document or documents in one language and the rival courts whose native language is that of the document and, on the other hand, courts whose native language is not that of the document, it is in my view clear that the matter may most suitably be tried in the former courts. This implies no criticism whatever of the alternative courts. It merely acknowledges reality. The true meaning of words in, for example, Spanish or French can, in my view, be better decided by Spanish or French courts as the case may be than by English courts.

With regard to libel actions, it appears that the place where the plaintiff lives and carries on business, and where he or she wishes to have their reputation vindicated, is an important connecting factor pointing to the appropriate forum. For instance, in *Schapira v Ahronson* (1998), the Court of Appeal held that, where the tort of libel was allegedly committed in England against a plaintiff, resident and carrying on business in England, by Israeli newspapers who were aware that their publication would be sent to subscribers in England, the plaintiff was entitled to bring proceedings and to limit his claim to publication in England. This was the case despite the fact that the circulation of the article alleged to be defamatory was very limited in England and there was a much larger publication in Israel. Consequently, the application for a stay of the English proceedings was dismissed on the ground that England was the most appropriate forum in which the plaintiff lived and carried on business and in which he wished his reputation to be vindicated, even though much of the evidence connected the case with Israel.

As Clarkson and Hill adumbrated (*Jaffey on the Conflict of Laws*, 1997, p 117), at the first stage of the *Spiliada* test:

> ... where the factual matrix from which the dispute arises involves a multiplicity of parties, the court will have regard to the desirability of ensuring that, as far as possible, all the disputes between the parties are resolved in one set of proceedings in a single forum.

The Kapetan Georgis (1988) is a good illustration of such a desirability. This case concerned a charterparty between Virgo, the plaintiff shipowners, and Skaarup, the first defendants, who were the charterers. Skaarup entered into a further charterparty agreement with BM, an English company, who in turn entered into a subcharterparty contract with another party (the latter's involvement in the dispute was immaterial). All three contracts contained arbitration clauses. Devco, domiciled in Canada, were the shippers of a cargo of coal on the vessel in question. An explosion occurred on the vessel, causing damage and personal injuries. Virgo brought an action against Skaarup as first defendants, and BM as second defendants, for damages and indemnity. Skaarup issued a third party notice against Devco, alleging that the cargo of coal shipped was dangerous, and claiming damages. Devco applied to the English court to have service of the third party proceedings set aside on the grounds, *inter alia*, that Canada was the more appropriate forum, and that Skaarup had failed to establish a proper basis for the court's exercise of its discretion in favour of ordering service out of the jurisdiction. On this latter issue, Hirst J rejected this argument. Applying the *Spiliada* principles, he stated that (p 360):

> One of the main purposes and indeed virtues of third party proceedings is to ensure that all the relevant parties are bound by one single decision, and I am by no means persuaded that inconsistent decisions would be out of the question if there were separate sets of proceedings in England and Canada.

Similarly, in *The Goldean Mariner* (1990), where a number of interrelated disputes involved no less than 24 defendants from a number of jurisdictions, the Court of Appeal held that it was desirable in the interests of all the parties that the litigation should be conducted in a single forum. However, the court proceeded to emphasise that it must never become the practice to bring foreign defendants here as a matter of course, simply on the ground that the only alternative required more than one suit in more than one different jurisdiction. It must be noted that the same principle has been applied to the converse situation, that is, where a single foreign court has jurisdiction to entertain all the claims in question (see *The Oinoussin Pride* (1991), where Webster J set aside the service of the writ out of the jurisdiction on the ground, *inter alia*, that it was desirable to have all the claims determined in a single forum, that of Alabama).

A further factor, which is of significance to the first stage of the *Spiliada* test and which may tilt the proceedings in favour of one forum rather than another, is that of the applicable law. Nonetheless, the weight accorded to this factor varies depending on the circumstances of the case. Evidently, it is not unusual for an English court to apply a foreign law to a particular dispute and for a foreign court to apply English law. For example, in *Amin Rasheed Shipping Corpn v Kuwait Insurance Co* (1984), a case involving service out of the jurisdiction under RSC Ord 11 r 1(1), the House of Lords held that, although the contract in question was governed by English law, there was no reason why a Kuwaiti court should find any difficulty in applying the relevant English law to the facts of the case. Basically, in this case, little weight was attached to the applicable law, since the dispute was essentially one of fact. Conversely, where the applicable law is English and the dispute raises an issue of public policy, then English courts are better placed to rule on such an issue. Indeed, this factor tilted the proceedings in favour of the English court in the case of *El Du Pont De Nemours and Co v Agnew* (1987).

The material facts were that the plaintiffs, Du Pont, were insured against product liability claims by the defendant insurers. The insurance policies were plainly expressed to follow the Lloyd's policy, which was the lead policy. The plaintiffs had been sued for product liability by a third party, who was awarded a substantial sum of money, including punitive damages. The plaintiffs then brought an action in the English court against the defendant insurers for indemnity under the insurance policies. The defendants applied, *inter alia*, for a stay of the proceedings on the ground that the Illinois court was the more appropriate forum for the trial of the action. Bingham LJ, delivering the Court of Appeal's judgment, held that, as the proper law of the policies was English, an essential question would be whether there was any rule of English public policy which would preclude the plaintiffs from recovering an indemnity. If English public policy was to be held to deny the right of indemnity in these circumstances, then the English court and no other must do so. His Lordship went further to state that this question was not 'capable of fair resolution in any foreign court, however distinguished and well instructed ... [no] foreign judge could conscientiously resolve with confidence that he was reaching a correct answer' (pp 594–95).

More recently, the same view was adopted by Sir John Wood in the case of *Zivlin v Baal Taxa* (1998). The plaintiff, an Israeli national, was resident, employed and carried on business in England. The defendant, also an Israeli national, entered with the plaintiff into a series of what are called 'gentleman's arrangements' in Israel concerning the purchase, management and financing of properties in England. A dispute arose over the terms of these arrangements. The plaintiff brought an action in the English court and the defendant brought an action in the Israeli court. The defendant then sought to have the English action stayed on the ground of *forum non conveniens*. Applying the *Spiliada* principles, Sir John Wood held that, on the facts, it was clear that the proper law was English. This was the law most akin to the arrangements, because these were in connection with the purchase, management and financing of property in England. They would also necessitate looking at the mortgage and banking arrangements, which were in England. Apart from the actual issue as to the making of the arrangements, the documentary and oral evidence and the details of the contractual arrangements were all linked in England. The currency was in sterling and no doubt the tax laws of England would be relevant. Additionally, there was an allegation that the plaintiff had been negligent in managing these properties, which would attract liability in English law; and that a particular tenant had achieved a protected tenancy under the Rent Acts of England, which would be essentially a matter of English law. Accordingly, English law as the applicable law to the dispute tilted the balance against granting a stay.

As noted above, the *Spiliada* test is a two stage process. Once it is established that England is not the appropriate forum and that there is, *prima facie*, a more appropriate forum for the trial of the action, then the second stage of the test will have to be considered; notably, the plaintiff will have to show that there are special circumstances, by reason of which justice requires that the litigation should, nevertheless, proceed in England. The burden is thus shifted onto the plaintiff to satisfy the court that, in the interests of justice, he or she should not be required to litigate abroad. According to *The Spiliada*, a legitimate personal or juridical advantage available to the plaintiff in the English court, and of which he or she would be deprived should the action be stayed, is not a sufficient reason to refuse the stay of proceedings. Lord Goff used two different examples in order to illustrate the type of advantages the court might take into consideration. He said (p 859) that the fact that a foreign forum had a more limited system of discovery or lower awards of damages would not necessarily deter the court from granting a stay. On the other hand, however, where the plaintiff's claim was time barred in the appropriate forum, but came within the English limitation period, practical justice required the court not to deprive the plaintiff of the benefit of having complied with the time bar in England, provided he or she had not acted unreasonably in failing to commence proceedings within the limitation period applicable in the appropriate forum.

The difficulty with the second stage of the test is that of identifying the factors which the English court may consider decisive. Again, like the first stage of the test, one must examine decided cases in order to establish the type of factors to which the courts attach such significance as to decline the application for a stay (or to grant leave to serve the writ out of the jurisdiction under RSC Ord 11 r 1). For instance, in *Roneleigh Ltd v MII Exports Inc* (1989), albeit New Jersey was established to be, *prima facie*, the more appropriate forum, the Court of Appeal declined to set aside the leave to serve the writ outside the jurisdiction. It was held that, where the evidence showed that the plaintiff was likely to succeed in the foreign forum, but his success would, in monetary terms, be substantially adversely affected because he would have to pay much higher costs than in England, it was reasonable and proper to conclude that substantial justice was not likely to be done in the foreign forum. Accordingly, the costs advantage from litigation in England was, in the circumstances of the case, a sufficient factor against proceedings in New Jersey.

Additionally, it appears that, where the difference between the level of damages recoverable in the English court and that recoverable in the foreign court is substantial, the court may be inclined to take the view that a stay of proceedings would cause injustice to the plaintiff. This was the view adopted by Sheen J in *The Vishva Abha* (1990). This case concerned an action brought by the plaintiffs for damages arising out of a collision between two vessels which resulted in the loss of their cargo. The defendants applied for a stay of proceedings on the ground that the Durban court, South Africa, was the more appropriate forum for the trial of the dispute. A decisive factor against granting the stay was that the limit of liability in South Africa was substantially lower than that applicable in England. In monetary terms, the limit in South Africa was in the region of £367,500 as opposed to £1.5 m in England. His Lordship considered it a grave injustice to deprive the plaintiffs of their right to litigate in England and to send them to South Africa, where their chances of recovering damages would be limited to a substantially lower sum.

In *The Al Battani* (1993), the issues of costs and delay were also considered of great significance, regardless of the fact that Egypt was, *prima facie*, the more appropriate forum for the trial of the action. Sheen J's decision was influenced by the following factors: (a) were the action to be litigated in Egypt, the contractual documents and the survey reports, which were in English, would have required translation into Arabic and that would have caused delay; (b) whereas it was likely that five years would elapse before final judgment was awarded by the Egyptian court, in the English court, finality would be reached much sooner; (c) in Egypt, a successful plaintiff would only recover court fees in terms of costs, and would, therefore, be deprived of part of the fruits of victory due to the substantial sum which they would have to pay in costs; and (d) under Egyptian law, interest is awarded to a successful plaintiff on the amount of damages at the rate of 5% per year as from the date of final judgment on appeal. This meant that the plaintiff would be deprived of interest for about seven years. Accordingly, the financial burden of litigating in Egypt was so heavy that justice required that a stay should not be granted.

Furthermore, in *Banco Atlantico SA v The British Bank of the Middle East* (1990), the Court of Appeal applied the second stage of the *Spiliada* test to deny the defendant's request for a stay of the English proceedings on the basis that the alternative court of the United Arab Emirates would apply its own law to the case. This would have resulted in the plaintiffs, an English company carrying on business in England, losing their claim.

However, in *Re Harrods (Buenos Aires) Ltd (No 2)* (1991), the fact that the plaintiff would not obtain an identical remedy to the one that would be obtained in England, was not sufficient to convince the court that the plaintiff could not obtain substantial justice in Argentina.

Moreover, in *Connelly v RTZ Corpn plc* (1996) the Court of Appeal held that the availability of legal aid to the plaintiff in England, but not in the alternative forum, was irrelevant in deciding whether or not to grant a stay of the English proceedings. In this case, the plaintiff was a British national and a former employee of the defendants, a mining company in Namibia which was also registered in England. The plaintiff was diagnosed as suffering from throat cancer, as a result of which he underwent a laryngectomy. He brought an action in the English court, claiming damages on the ground that the defendants were negligent in failing to provide a reasonably safe system of work to protect him from the effect of ore dust. The defendants applied for a stay of the proceedings on the ground that Namibia was a more appropriate forum. Sir John Wood granted the stay and held that the Namibian court was 'the forum in which the case could be tried more suitably for the interests of all the parties and for the ends of justice'. The plaintiff appealed, contending principally that since legal aid was available to him only in England, it was a practical impossibility for him to sustain his claim without legal aid and, therefore, Namibia could not represent the forum in which the case would be tried more suitably for the interests of all the parties and the ends of justice. Unfortunately, although the Court of Appeal was tempted, on purely humanitarian grounds, to refuse a stay by reason alone of the plaintiff's eligibility for legal aid, when the question was answered according to the law, the response was that a stay should be granted. The Court of Appeal based its decision mainly on the provision of s 31(1)(b) of the Legal Aid Act 1988, which expressly states that the right to legal aid 'shall not affect the rights or liabilities of the parties to the proceedings or the principles on which the discretion of any court or tribunal is normally exercised'.

Subsequently, in *Connelly v RTZ Corpn plc* (1996), Connelly re-applied to the Court of Appeal for the removal of the stay, on the ground that the action should be heard in England, but in this instance, his application was based on the fact that there existed a proposed conditional fee arrangement with his solicitor. Sir Thomas Bingham, delivering the judgment of the Court of Appeal, held that, provided that the proposal to enter into the conditional fee arrangement was *bona fide*, it was in the interests of justice, and consistent with the European Convention on Human Rights 1950, to allow the action to be heard in England. This decision was based on the fact that the only accessible forum in which the plaintiff could assert his rights was England. However, the removal of the stay was conditional on the plaintiff giving the defendants notice of any intention to apply for legal aid and informing them of any alteration to the conditional fee arrangement. Consequently, in *Connelly v RTZ Corpn plc* (1997), an appeal on the above two decisions was made to the House of Lords. With regard to the issue of legal aid, it was held that s 31(1)(b) of the Legal Aid Act 1988 was never intended to apply in the case of application for a stay of the proceedings on the ground of *forum non conveniens*. In such a case, the question was whether the court is satisfied that there was some other forum, having competent jurisdiction, in which the case would be tried more suitably for the interests of all the parties and for the ends of justice. It would be strange if the application of such a broad principle of justice should be artificially curtailed by s 31(1)(b), to the effect that the receipt of legal aid by the plaintiff would be automatically excluded from the relevant factors to be considered. Moving on to apply the *Spiliada* principles, the House of Lords held that as a general rule, the court would not refuse the grant of a stay simply because the plaintiff had shown that no financial assistance, in the form of either legal aid or, failing that, a conditional fee agreement, would be available to him in the appropriate forum, even though the availability of financial assistance in England, coupled with its non-availability in the appropriate forum, might exceptionally be a relevant factor in the context of the application of *forum non conveniens*. Nevertheless, the question remained whether the plaintiff could establish that substantial justice would not, in the particular circumstances of the case, be done if the plaintiff had to proceed in the appropriate forum where no such assistance was available. Since the complexity of this case called for highly professional representation, by both lawyers and scientific experts, for the achievement of substantial justice, and since such representation could not be achieved in Namibia, the Namibian forum was not one in which the case could be tried more suitably for the interests of all the parties and the ends of justice.

2.5.2 The relevance of *lis alibi pendens*

In some instances, proceedings between the same parties arising out of the same dispute are simultaneously pending in the English court and the courts of another country. This is referred to as a case for *lis alibi pendens*.

Under the traditional rules, the English court may be asked either by the defendant to the English proceedings to stay the action in England, or by the plaintiff to the English proceedings to grant an injunction restraining the defendant from continuing with the foreign proceedings. This paragraph is concerned only with stays; injunctions are examined below, 2.6.

In principle, the applicable test is basically that of *The Spiliada* (1986). However, an important additional element to be taken into account under the doctrine of *forum non conveniens* is that to refuse a stay of the English proceedings would result in allowing two sets of proceedings being pursued concurrently in two different jurisdictions which would, thus, involve more expense, delay and inconvenience to the parties. In essence, that was one of the factors which tipped the scales in favour of granting a stay of the English proceedings in *Cleveland Museum of Art v Capricorn Art International SA* (1990).

Also, in *DR Insurance Co v Central National Insurance Co* (1996), service out of the jurisdiction was set aside because concurrent proceedings were taking place in New York. Despite the fact that England would ordinarily have been the appropriate forum for the resolution of the dispute, continuing the English action would have resulted in an undesirable duplication of proceedings. This, combined with the fact that, it may be recalled, the claim in the English court was for a negative declaration, provided strong grounds for dismissing the English proceedings. Allowing *lis alibi pendens* can also lead to conflicting judgments and problems of enforcement. Lord Goff, in *The Spiliada*, did not indicate how the reformulated test on *forum non conveniens* applied to cases of *lis alibi pendens*. However, he stated in *De Dampierre v De Dampierre* (1988) that the 'same principle is applicable whether or not there are other relevant proceedings already pending in the alternative forum'. In fact, *The Abidin Daver* (1984), which landmarked the doctrine of *forum non conveniens* in English law, was a *lis alibi pendens* case. In this case, a collision occurred within Turkish waters between the plaintiffs' ship, a Cuban vessel, and the defendants' ship, a Turkish vessel. Soon after, the defendants commenced proceedings in the Turkish court, claiming damages against the plaintiffs. The plaintiffs then commenced an action *in rem* in the English court. Following the defendants' application for a stay of the English proceedings on the ground that the Turkish court was a more appropriate forum, the House of Lords applied the doctrine of *forum non conveniens* and held that Turkey was the more appropriate forum for the trial of the action. A crucial factor pointing towards Turkey was the fact that the Turkish court had already appointed a surveyor, who prepared a report for the court.

It should be noted that the traditional rules on *lis alibi pendens*, unlike those contained in the Brussels Convention 1968, do not operate on a first come, first served basis. Whilst, under the traditional rules, the English court retains its discretion to grant a stay (or an injunction as the case may be), under Art 21 of the Brussels Convention 1968, as shall be discussed in the next chapter, the English court must decline jurisdiction in favour of the court first seised.

2.5.3 The relevance of a foreign jurisdiction clause

Under the common law rules, where the parties have agreed in a binding contract to submit their disputes to the jurisdiction of a foreign court, the English court will not, in general, allow the parties to resile from their earlier agreed choice of jurisdiction.

Where the jurisdiction clause is in favour of a foreign court, but the plaintiff initiates proceedings in England, then according to *The Eleftheria* (1970), the court's discretion should be exercised in favour of granting a stay unless a strong case for not doing so is shown. The burden is on the plaintiff to show why a stay should not be granted. In exercising its discretion, the court should take into account all the circumstances of the particular case. For instance, the court will address such questions as which is the most convenient country for the evidence; which is the cheapest; whether the dispute is governed by a foreign law; how close are the connections of the parties to the relevant countries; whether the defendant is only seeking a procedural advantage in England; and so forth.

Hence, the applicable test is basically similar to that of *forum non conveniens*. However, here the burden is on the plaintiff to show why the jurisdiction clause should not be upheld. This is so even if a part of the agreement between the parties is void. In *Trendtex Trading Corpn v Crédit Suisse* (1981), an assignment of a cause of action took place in Switzerland. The agreement included an exclusive jurisdiction clause in favour of the Swiss courts. The House of Lords granted a stay and held that, although an assignment of a cause of action is void in England for being against public policy, this did not render the whole agreement void; accordingly, the choice of jurisdiction clause remained valid. Conversely, a stay may be refused if the plaintiff can show that either the whole agreement is void and not voidable, or that the jurisdiction clause itself is void. In *MacKender v Feldia* (1967), a *lis alibi pendens* case, a contract of insurance was made in London between the plaintiffs, Lloyd's underwriters, and the defendants, diamond merchants. The policy contained an exclusive jurisdiction clause in favour of the Belgian courts, and a choice of law clause in favour of Belgian law. Some diamonds were lost in Italy and the plaintiff insurers refused to indemnify the defendants. They brought an action in the English court, claiming that the defendants had smuggled the diamonds into Italy; that the contract was void for illegality and voidable for the defendants' non-disclosure; and accordingly, the jurisdiction clause was also void. The Court of Appeal applied English domestic law and found that the alleged illegality in this instance only made the contract unenforceable; and that the non-disclosure rendered the contract voidable and not void *ab initio*. Therefore, the jurisdiction clause was valid and the action should be tried in the Belgian court (note that, since this case involved the courts of EC Member States, it would now be decided in accordance with Art 17 of the Brussels Convention 1968, which confers exclusive jurisdiction on the chosen court. Notwithstanding that the outcome would now be the same, the court's discretion does not form a part of the equation; see Chapter 3).

Additionally, it appears that where the plaintiff has acted unreasonably in allowing the expiry of the limitation period in the agreed court, the English court would not consider it a sufficient reason to permit litigation in England. This is illustrated by the Privy Council decision in *The Pioneer Container* (1994), where the relevant contractual document contained an exclusive jurisdiction clause which provided that any dispute arising thereunder was to be determined in the courts of Taiwan. Contrary to this agreement, the plaintiffs commenced proceedings in the Hong Kong court, and the defendants applied for a stay on the basis of the jurisdiction agreement. The Privy Council held, *inter alia*, that where proceedings were brought in breach of a jurisdiction agreement to refer disputes to a foreign court, the English court should exercise its discretion to grant a stay unless a strong reason for not doing so was shown by the plaintiffs. However, in this case, since the plaintiffs had gambled on being permitted to litigate in their preferred forum of Hong Kong, rather than Taiwan, and had let time run out in the agreed forum without taking the trouble even to issue a protective writ therein, they had acted unreasonably and, therefore, a stay would be granted.

In accordance with *Hamed El-Chiaty v Thomas Cook Ltd* (1992), it seems that an oral agreement on jurisdiction is as effective as a written one. In this case, the plaintiffs, an Egyptian tourist company, contracted with the defendants, an international travel company registered and based in England, to construct a cruise ship. In return, the defendants agreed to help finance the construction of the vessel and to charter it for use on their package tours. A series of written contracts were made, whereby it was agreed that the proper law of the contract was Egyptian, but they were silent as to choice of jurisdiction. The defendants claimed, however, that during negotiations, the parties had orally agreed that any disputes would be subject to the exclusive jurisdiction of the Egyptian courts. Following the failure of the defendants to supply the agreed minimum number of tourists, the plaintiffs brought an action in the English court. Hirst J held that the oral agreement on jurisdiction was effective and granted a stay. Applying the *Spiliada* test, he stated that the burden was on the plaintiffs to show that there were special circumstances, by reason of which justice required that the trial should nevertheless take place in England. He added that the fact that the contract was subject to Egyptian law was a highly material factor, not only because the Egyptian court was best fitted to adjudicate its own law, but also because it would avoid the additional expense of bringing in expert witnesses to debate the foreign law issues.

Moreover, a jurisdiction clause, albeit non-exclusive, creates a *prima facie* case that the agreed forum is the appropriate one for litigation. For instance, in *The Rothnie* (1996), the plaintiffs and defendants entered into a contract, by which the latter agreed to carry out repair and maintenance work on the plaintiffs' vessel in Gibraltar. The contract was subject to the defendants' standard terms and conditions, which expressly provided that the contract was to be governed by the law of Gibraltar and that any disputes arising therefrom were subject to the non-exclusive jurisdiction of the courts of Gibraltar. It was held that the fact that the parties had agreed that a certain forum had jurisdiction, albeit non-exclusive, created a strong *prima facie* case in favour of that forum as being the appropriate one. This was so, unless justice required that the trial should, nevertheless, take place in England. (Note that, since Gibraltar has now become a separate Contracting State for the purposes of the Brussels Convention 1968, by virtue of the Civil Jurisdiction and Judgments Act 1982 (Gibraltar) Order 1997 (SI 1997/2602, in force on 1 February 1998), this case would now be decided in accordance with Art 17 of the Convention.)

However, it must be noted that the jurisdiction clause must be a part of the actual contract between the parties, and not a part of the document which is believed to be the contract. This may be illustrated by Sheen J's decision in the case of *The Al Battani* (1993), where a dispute arose out of a contract for the carriage of a cargo from Egypt to Hamburg. The plaintiffs had initially chartered the ship and, when the cargo was shipped, bills of lading were issued, the latter containing a jurisdiction clause in favour of the Egyptian courts. The delivery of the cargo was delayed due to deviation, which resulted in the cargo deteriorating. The plaintiffs brought an action in the English court and the defendant applied for a stay, relying on the jurisdiction clause in the bills of lading. It was held that, since the jurisdiction clause was not incorporated in the charterparty, the latter being the contract between the parties to the dispute, a stay could not be granted. Therefore, the jurisdiction clause in the bills of lading did not have any effect in this instance, for the bills of lading were merely in the nature of a receipt for the goods. These would only become the contract when they are indorsed over to a third party. In contrast, where the contract provides that one of the parties is entitled to sub-contract 'on any terms', such a phrase is sufficiently wide to cover consent to the application of an exclusive jurisdiction clause to the sub-contract. This was held to be the case in *The Pioneer Container* (1994), where the plaintiffs contracted with freight carriers for the carriage of certain goods from Taiwan to Hong Kong. The bills of lading provided that the carriers were entitled to sub-contract 'on any terms' the whole or any part of the handling, storage or carriage of the goods. The carriers sub-contracted the carriage to the defendant shipowners, who issued bills of lading incorporating a choice of law clause in favour of Chinese law and a jurisdiction clause in favour of the courts of Taiwan. The vessel sank, and the plaintiffs' goods were lost. They initiated proceedings in Hong Kong, and the defendants applied for a stay by reason of, *inter alia*, the exclusive jurisdiction clause. In connection with this latter issue, the Privy Council held that the phrase 'on any terms' was wide enough to embrace express consent to the application of an exclusive jurisdiction clause, and that such a clause was not so unusual or unreasonable as to negate the wide consent given by the plaintiffs.

The English court will, nevertheless, exercise its discretion to refuse a stay where the parties have agreed to submit their disputes to a foreign jurisdiction, if the plaintiff can show that justice cannot be obtained in the agreed forum. In *Carvalho v Hull Blyth (Angola) Ltd* (1979) the defendants, a company registered in England, carried on business in Angola through subsidiaries in which the plaintiff owned a 49% shareholding. In a contract made in Angola, which was then a Portuguese province, the plaintiff, who was then living there, agreed to sell his shareholding to the defendant, the price payable in four instalments. The contract contained an exclusive jurisdiction clause in favour of the Angolan courts. When the defendants failed to pay the fourth instalment, the plaintiff, who then moved back to Portugal, brought an action for the amount due, in the English court. The defendants, relying on the jurisdiction clause, applied for a stay. The Court of Appeal held that the jurisdiction clause in favour of Angola could not be relied upon, because under the revolutionary government, the Angolan court was no longer a Portuguese court applying Portuguese municipal law. Moreover, due to the political and legal changes in Angola, the plaintiff satisfied the court that it was 'just and proper' to refuse the stay.

Similarly, an exclusive jurisdiction clause would not be upheld if its application would lead to separate additional proceedings on the same facts having to be pursued in the English court. For example, in *Citi-March v Neptune Orient Lines* (1996), the plaintiffs contracted with the first defendant, a company incorporated and carrying on business in Singapore, for the carriage of consignments of clothing to London. The bills of lading incorporated an exclusive jurisdiction clause in favour of the courts of Singapore. Following delivery in London, it was found that a quantity of the goods was missing. Consequently, the plaintiffs commenced proceedings in the English court against the first defendant and three other companies, based in England, which had stored the goods on their premises prior to delivery to the plaintiffs. The first defendant applied to have service of the English proceedings set aside on the basis of the exclusive jurisdiction clause. Colman J held that, if the jurisdiction was to be upheld, therefore requiring the plaintiffs to pursue their claim in Singapore, it was probable that separate proceedings against the three companies would have to be pursued in England. This would lead to a clear risk of inconsistent decisions on the facts. The plaintiffs would also lose the benefit of a composite trial and would be precluded from having the benefit of obtaining the evidence of all four defendants. Therefore, strong reason had been shown in favour of ignoring the jurisdiction clause and maintaining the action in the English court.

A stay of the English proceedings will also be refused where the action is time barred under the law of the foreign court designated by the clause, and where there is no substantial difference between the law of England and the law of that foreign country. Such was the case in *The Vishva Prabha* (1979), where the English court declined to grant a stay in favour of the Indian court.

Conversely, where the parties have agreed to refer their disputes to the jurisdiction of the English courts, it is highly unlikely that a stay would be granted on the ground that proceedings had started in a foreign court. This was held to be the case in *British Aerospace v Dee Howard* (1993), where, contrary to their agreed choice of jurisdiction in favour of the English court, the defendants initiated proceedings in Texas. When the plaintiffs brought an action in the English court, the defendants applied for a stay of action on the ground that proceedings were already pending in Texas. They also argued that the jurisdiction clause, which stated that '... the courts of England shall have jurisdiction to entertain any action ... and that in the event of such proceedings being commenced, each party shall forthwith notify to the other an address in

England for the service of documents', was not exclusive. The English court refused to grant the stay and held that the jurisdiction agreement was exclusive, for there was no real purpose in submitting disputes to the jurisdiction of the English court unless the intention was to make England exclusive (see, also, *Gulf Bank v Mitsubishi Heavy Industries Ltd* (1994) where a jurisdiction clause in favour of the English court, albeit non-exclusive, was upheld).

2.6 Prevention of forum shopping and anti-suit injunctions

In the above discussion, the plaintiff has come 'shopping' in the English courts. What if, when the natural forum would be England, he or she went shopping in a foreign court; or being the defendant in the English proceedings, he or she started cross-proceedings elsewhere? For example, a plaintiff suffers injuries in an air crash in the UK. The airline is incorporated in England, the aeroplane was manufactured in England by an English company, but the company is part of a group with the parent company incorporated in California. Clearly, the plaintiff has powerful incentives to sue in California for the following reasons:

(a) pre-trial discovery;

(b) jury trial;

(c) punitive damages; and

(d) contingent fee system.

In such cases, the defendant may apply to the English court for an injunction to restrain the foreign proceedings. The injunction operates *in personam*. It is granted against the plaintiff, not the foreign court itself. If it is not complied with, then the person against whom it is granted will be held in contempt of court. Lord Denning MR stated, in *Castanho v Brown and Root (UK) Ltd* (1981), that injunctions restraining foreign proceedings should only rarely be granted 'so as to avoid even the appearance of undue interference with another court'. In this case, which is considered to be the leading one in the context of injunctions, the plaintiff, a Portuguese subject resident in Portugal, was employed by the second defendants, a Panamanian company, on a US ship. The first defendants were an English company which provided shore services for the ship. Both defendants were part of a large group of companies based in Texas. The ship was in England when the plaintiff had an accident, as a result of which he suffered severe personal injury. While in hospital in England, his English solicitors issued a writ, claiming damages for his injuries. Some time later, he was contacted by a firm of Texan attorneys and, on their advice, he discontinued the English proceedings and started the action in Texas, where he would have the prospect of higher damages. The defendants applied for an injunction. The House of Lords discharged the injunction granted in the court of first instance, and held that, in order to justify the grant of an injunction, it had to be shown that the English court was a forum to which the defendants were amenable and in which justice could be done at less inconvenience and expense; and that an injunction would not deprive the plaintiff of a personal or juridical advantage available to him in the Texan jurisdiction. On the facts, since the defendants were Texas-based, with an office and substantial assets in Texas, and the plaintiff would enjoy the prospect of higher damages, the critical equation between advantage to the plaintiff and disadvantage to the defendants was solved in the plaintiff's favour.

It is worth noting that the test which the House of Lords applied in this case was similar to that then applied in cases where a stay of English proceedings was sought. This was widely criticised, because it would enable injunctions to be granted more readily, and the Privy Council, in *Société Nationale Industrielle Aérospatiale v Lee Kui Jack* (1987), decided to re-adopt the criteria used in the *St Pierre* case (1936). In the *SNIA* case, a plaintiff was killed in a helicopter crash in Brunei. The helicopter was manufactured in France by a French company, SNIA, which had a subsidiary in Texas to whom the French company sold helicopters. At the time of the crash, the helicopter was owned by an English company, and was operated and serviced by its Malaysian subsidiary under a contract to a Brunei subsidiary of an international oil company. Proceedings against the French and Malaysian companies were brought both in Brunei and Texas. The reasons for bringing the action in Texas were that Texan law was more favourable to the plaintiffs and that US courts awarded a higher level of damages. The defendants applied for an injunction restraining the plaintiffs from continuing the Texan proceedings on the ground, *inter alia*, that it was highly unlikely that the Malaysian company could be brought before the Texan courts and, therefore, SNIA would have to claim contribution from the former company in some other forum. The Court of Appeal of Brunei applied the test applicable to stays of action and refused to grant the injunction. On appeal, the Privy Council restated the test on injunctions as follows: as a general rule, a decision to grant an injunction restraining foreign proceedings would only be made if such pursuit would be vexatious and oppressive and the injunction would not unjustly deprive the plaintiff of advantages available to him in the foreign forum. This presupposed that the English court would provide the natural forum for the trial of the action and that, as a matter of justice, the injustice to the defendant, if the plaintiff was allowed to pursue the foreign proceedings, would outweigh the injustice to the plaintiff if he was not allowed to so. As the accident occurred in Brunei, the deceased and the plaintiffs were resident there, and the law governing the claim was the law of Brunei, then Brunei remained the natural forum for the action. Furthermore, it would be oppressive for the plaintiffs to proceed in Texas, because the defendants might be unable to pursue their own contribution claim against the Malaysian company. Accordingly, the injunction was granted.

Despite the fact that the *SNIA* test was a Privy Council decision and, therefore, is only of a persuasive nature, English courts have followed it consistently. For instance, in *EI Du Pont De Nemours and Co v Agnew (No 2)* (1988) the plaintiffs applied for an injunction to restrain the defendants from continuing with the proceedings in the Illinois court. The Court of Appeal elected to apply the test in the *SNIA* case, rather than the test of *forum non conveniens*, and held that an injunction would not be granted. Dillon LJ rejected the view that the principle to be applied to injunctions was the same as that to be applied to stays. This was justified on the ground that the test on stays was based on *forum non conveniens*, which meant that, once the English court was found to be a natural and appropriate forum for the action and there was no other available forum which was more appropriate, a stay would be granted. Were the same test to apply to injunctions, it would follow that an injunction would almost be automatically granted once England was found to be the more appropriate forum. This could not be right, since it would lead:

> ... to the conclusion that, in a case where there [was] simply a difference of view between the English court and the foreign court as to which [was] the natural forum, the English court [could] arrogate to itself, by the grant of an injunction, the power to resolve that dispute.

The same test was applied by the Court of Appeal in the subsequent case of *Re Maxwell Communications Corpn (No 2)* (1992), where the applicable principles were summarised by Gildwell LJ in the following terms:

(a) if the only issue is whether an English or a foreign court is the more appropriate forum for the trial of the action, that question should normally be decided by the foreign court on the principle of *forum non conveniens*, and the English court should not seek to interfere with that decision;

(b) however, if, exceptionally, the English court concludes that the pursuit of the action in the foreign court would be vexatious and oppressive and that the English court is the natural forum, that is, the more appropriate forum for the trial of the action, it can properly grant an injunction preventing the plaintiff from pursuing his action in the foreign court;

(c) in deciding whether the action in the foreign court is vexatious and oppressive, account must be taken of the possible injustice to the defendant if the injunction is not granted, and the possible injustice to the plaintiff if it is. In other words, the English court must seek to strike a balance.

The above test indicates that an injunction would not be granted unless England is the natural and more appropriate forum for the trial of the action. A question arises, however, as to whether the English courts can also grant an injunction even when the dispute is not connected with England, but rather with another country. This matter was examined in detail by the House of Lords in the recent case of *Airbus Industrie GIE v Patel* (1998). The case concerned an aircraft, owned by Indian Airlines, which crashed in 1990 as it was about to land at Bangalore Airport. The defendants to the English proceedings were English passengers who were injured or killed in the air crash. The aircraft was manufactured by Airbus Industrie in France. Indian Airlines was a domestic airline, which did not fly internationally. After the crash, a public inquiry, carried out in India, concluded that the crash was caused by the pilot's fault. The defendants sued the airline and airport company in India. They also brought an action in Texas against a large number of parties who might have had some connection with certain aspects of the aircraft or its operation, including Airbus Industrie. The latter challenged the jurisdiction of the Texas court on the ground, *inter alia*, that the US Foreign Sovereign Immunity Act entitled corporations which were more than 50% government owned to claim sovereign immunity. The district court upheld this objection and the defendants appealed. Meanwhile, Airbus obtained a declaration in the Bangalore City civil court that the defendants were not entitled to proceed in any court other than Bangalore. Airbus then applied to the English court for an injunction restraining the defendants from pursuing their appeal in Texas, on the ground that those proceedings were vexatious and oppressive.

Hence, the prime and crucial question before the court was whether the English court would grant an injunction in circumstances where there was no relevant connection between the English jurisdiction and the proceedings in question other than that the defendants, who were resident in England, were subject to the jurisdiction and, thus, could effectively be restrained by such an injunction. In the court of first instance, Colman J concluded that the existence of the substantive proceedings in England was not an essential precondition for the exercise of jurisdiction to grant an injunction. Where, however, the court is being asked to adjudicate between two foreign jurisdictions, such jurisdiction must be exercised with great caution and should only be granted where the very clearest case of oppression was made out. This, in his view, was not proven in this case. On appeal, the court stated that, unless the English courts were to grant an injunction against the defendants, the English claimants, there was no other court in this case which had the jurisdiction over them to do so. Although the Indian court had granted an injunction, in international terms that court had no jurisdiction over the defendants and no means of enforcing its orders against them. Additionally, this was an exceptional case, in that the litigation in Texas was in a forum where the principle of *forum non conveniens* was not recognised, and where the courts had no jurisdiction to consider or adjudicate upon such a question. Hence, if an order was to be made, it must be made by the English court. On appeal, the House of Lords set aside the injunction granted and held that, as a general rule, before an injunction could be granted, comity required that the English forum should have a sufficient interest in, or connection with, the matter in question to justify the indirect interference with the foreign court which such an injunction entailed. Although this rule should not be interpreted too rigidly, in the instant case the plaintiffs had not appealed from the judge's decision not to enforce the judgment of the Indian court, but were relying simply on the English court's power to grant an injunction. Thus, the court could not grant the injunction sought, for it would be inconsistent with the principle of comity.

An injunction will also be granted even where the English forum affords alternative, but not the same, causes of action compared to those afforded in the foreign court. For instance, in *Simon Engineering plc v Butte Mining plc (No 2)* (1996), where the defendants, a company incorporated in England, initiated proceedings in Montana, alleging securities fraud contrary to the US Securities Exchange Act 1934 and claiming multiple damages under the Racketeering Influenced Corrupt Organisations Act (RICO). They also claimed damages for a number of common law causes of action, notably fraud, breach of contract, negligence, breach of duty, negligent misrepresentation, constructive trust and secret profit. The plaintiffs applied to the English court for an injunction, on the grounds that England was the appropriate forum and that the Montana action was vexatious and oppressive. The defendants contended that an injunction would be prejudicial to them, since, *inter alia*, this was a single, not a choice of, forum case in that the federal causes of action, especially RICO, were only available in Montana. This argument was rejected, on the grounds that RICO provided a remedy, rather than a cause of action; and that English law afforded alternative causes of action under its own statutes with regard to securities fraud as well as the same common law causes of action which were alleged in Montana.

An injunction, however, will not be granted in cases where the plaintiff has only a single forum in which he or she can sue, as in the case of *British Airways Board v Laker Airways Ltd* (1985). Here, Laker Airways brought an action in the USA against British Airways and another British airline, claiming multiple damages for breach of US anti-trust laws by conspiring to eliminate Laker Airways as a competitor. This cause of action could only be tried in the USA, and Laker did not have a remedy in England. The House of Lords unanimously allowed the appeal against the grant of an injunction and held that, since Laker could not bring an action in conspiracy in England, and since the US anti-trust laws were purely territorial in application, the only available forum was that of the USA.

In conclusion, the test of 'vexatious and oppressive' is the one applicable to injunctions. Nevertheless, it is clear from the *British Airways Board* case that an injunction will not be granted where only the foreign court provides a remedy to the plaintiff in the foreign proceedings. As this case was decided prior to the *SNIA* case, which introduced a new test, one may wonder whether *British Airways Board* remains good law. The answer to this question can be found in the more recent case of *Channel Tunnel Group Ltd v Balfour Beatty Construction Ltd* (1993), where the plaintiffs applied for an interlocutory injunction to restrain the defendants from suspending their work. This type of injunction is not the same as the type of injunctions we are dealing with, but the relevance of this case lies in the fact that both types of injunction are provided for in s 37(1) of the Supreme Court Act 1981, which confers on the High Court a discretionary power to grant an injunction in a proper case. Mustill LJ, who delivered the House of Lords' judgment, consolidated the *ratio* in the *British Airways Board* case and re-emphasised the view that the court's discretion to grant an injunction must be exercised with caution, because it involved direct interference with the process of the foreign court concerned (p 361).

It appears that, where the bringing of an action in a foreign court involves the breach of a jurisdiction or arbitration clause in favour of England, English courts will almost certainly grant an injunction. In *Sohio Supply Co v Gatoil (USA) Inc* (1989), an injunction was granted to restrain the defendants from continuing with the proceedings in Texas on the basis that the parties had agreed to refer disputes to the English courts. Similarly, in *The Angelic Grace* (1995), the Court of Appeal granted an injunction to prevent proceedings abroad brought in breach of an arbitration agreement in favour of England. The court stated that, in such cases, an injunction would be granted unless there were special circumstances, by reason of which the court's discretion should operate against the plaintiff. Subsequently, in *Ultisol Transport Contractors Ltd v Bouygues Offshore SA* (1996), an injunction was granted to prevent the continuation of proceedings in South Africa where the parties had agreed to refer disputes to the English courts. It mattered not in this case that the proceedings in South Africa involved a third party not amenable to England. More recently, in *Svendborg v Wansa* (1997), the Court of Appeal granted an injunction restraining the defendant from continuing with the proceedings in the Sierra Leone courts on the basis that the contract in the first action, being the Melbourne case, contained a jurisdiction clause in favour of England (note that this case involved three actions, but, for the purposes of this paragraph, only the first of them is relevant). Notwithstanding that the plaintiffs had submitted to the jurisdiction of the Sierra Leone court which would have prevented them from obtaining the injunction, there were circumstances and evidence in this case which, together with other evidence that the defendant had regularly boasted that he could, in effect, manipulate the legal system in Sierra Leone, amounted to sufficient evidence of vexation and oppression to lead to the conclusion that an injunction should be granted.

JURISDICTION OF THE ENGLISH COURT IN COMMERCIAL DISPUTES: THE COMMON LAW RULES

Jurisdiction under the traditional rules

Where the defendant is not domiciled within the EC/EFTA but present in England, then jurisdiction *in personam* is assumed when the writ is served on his or her person in the case of an individual, on its principal place of business in the case of a corporation, and either on the individual partner present in England or on the partnership firm in the case of a partnership.

Where the defendant is not present in England, the English court has power to hear the case if he or she voluntarily submits to the jurisdiction, or if the plaintiff obtains leave to serve the writ outside the jurisdiction under RSC Ord 11 r 1(1). Order 11 r 1(1) provides a multiplicity of instances under which leave of the court may be obtained. The burden is on the plaintiff to show that the dispute comes under any one of the heads provided.

Prevention of forum shopping and staying of actions

The impact of the English law rules on jurisdiction, in the context of the traditional rules, clearly allows plaintiffs to forum shop. To circumvent this problem, English courts have been lent a discretionary power to stay an action brought in the English court whenever it is appropriate to do so. This power may be invoked on the grounds of *forum non conveniens, lis alibi pendens* or exclusive jurisdiction agreements.

A stay of the English proceedings is applied for by the defendant where the appropriate forum is abroad and the plaintiff comes shopping in England.

In the case where the defendant bases his application on the ground that the English court is *forum non conveniens*, the court exercises its discretion by applying the *Spiliada* test, which states that a stay will only be granted on the ground of *forum non conveniens* where the defendant can prove that there is a more appropriate forum where the action may be tried more suitably for the interests of all the parties and the ends of justice. Such factors as convenience, availability of witnesses, the law governing the relevant transaction, and the places where the parties reside or carry on business, are to be taken into consideration.

Depriving the plaintiff of a legitimate or juridical advantage would not, as a general rule, deter the English court from granting a stay if it was satisfied that substantial justice as between the parties would be obtained in the natural forum.

Where the defendant to the English proceedings applies for a stay on the ground of *lis alibi pendens*, the English court, in addition to the *forum non conveniens* test, must take into account that declining to grant a stay will involve more expense and inconvenience to the parties and may also lead to two conflicting judgments.

Where the defendant requests a stay on the grounds that the parties had agreed to submit their disputes to a foreign jurisdiction, the English court will normally stay the proceedings unless the jurisdiction agreement is void, or unless it is satisfied that justice cannot be obtained in the agreed jurisdiction.

Prevention of forum shopping and anti-suit injunctions

Where the appropriate forum is England and the plaintiff goes shopping abroad, the defendant can apply for an injunction to restrain the foreign proceedings, and if the plaintiff declines to comply with it, he or she will be held in contempt of court.

As a general rule, the applicable test is that an injunction would be granted if the proceedings in the foreign court are vexatious and oppressive to the defendant and the injunction would not unjustly deprive the plaintiff of advantages available to him or her in the foreign forum. This is the case, unless the plaintiff's only remedy is available in the foreign jurisdiction, in which case an injunction will not be granted.

Where the plaintiff applies for an injunction on the basis that the parties had agreed to refer disputes to the jurisdiction of the English court, then the court will almost certainly grant an injunction.

JURISDICTION OF THE ENGLISH COURT IN COMMERCIAL DISPUTES: THE BRUSSELS AND LUGANO CONVENTIONS

3.1   Introduction and background

As stated in the previous chapter, there are, at present, two sets of rules which ascribe jurisdiction to English courts in civil and commercial matters: notably the traditional common law rules and those prescribed under the Brussels and Lugano Conventions. Whilst the latter ascribe jurisdiction, generally, where a civil or commercial dispute involves defendants domiciled within the European Community (EC) or the European Free Trade Association (EFTA), the former rules determine jurisdiction in cases where the defendant is domiciled outside these boundaries. (Note that, since 1 February 1998, Gibraltar is to be treated as if it were a separate Contracting State. This is following the Civil Jurisdiction and Judgments Act 1982 (Gibraltar) Order 1997 (SI 1997/2602), the effect of which is to make provisions corresponding to those of the Brussels Convention, for the purpose of regulating the jurisdiction of courts and the recognition and enforcement of judgments as between the UK and Gibraltar.) This chapter focuses only on the question of jurisdiction of English courts in the context of the Brussels and Lugano Conventions.

English courts have been prevented, since 1 January 1987, from hearing cases where to do so would be in breach of the Brussels Convention on Jurisdiction and the Enforcement of Judgments 1968. This Convention was implemented into UK law by the Civil Jurisdiction and Judgments Act 1982 (CJJA). The purpose of this Convention is twofold: (a) to provide uniform rules of jurisdiction in civil and commercial matters within the EC; and (b) to facilitate the recognition and enforcement of judgments in such matters obtained in the courts of Member States. This Convention was complemented by the Luxembourg Protocol 1971, which confers on the European Court of Justice (ECJ) the power to interpret the provisions of the Convention.

The Brussels Convention 1968 was initially adopted by the six original Member States only. In order to take cognisance of the fact that new Member States would be acceding to the EC thereafter, Art 63 of the Convention was incorporated, with the effect that any such new Member State would also be required to accept the Brussels Convention as a basis for negotiations; and that any adjustments found necessary thereto would form the basis of a special accession convention. To date, there have been four accession Conventions:

(a) the Luxembourg Convention 1978 on the accession of Denmark, Ireland and the UK to the Brussels Convention and the Luxembourg Protocol on its interpretation. This Convention necessitated a number of amendments to the original text in order to embrace some common law concepts, such as the concept of trust, which are recognised and applied in the UK. The Brussels Convention, in its amended version, appears as Sched 1, and the Luxembourg Protocol as Sched 2 to the CJJA 1982;

(b) the Luxembourg Convention 1982 on the accession of Greece. The amendments made in this Convention were of a technical nature only;

(c) the San Sebastian Convention 1989 on the accession of Portugal and Spain. This Convention brought about a significant number of substantive amendments, the object of which was mainly to take into consideration the amendments brought about by the Lugano Convention 1988. It was incorporated into UK law by the CJJA 1982 (Amendment) Order 1990 (SI 1990/2591), which came into force on 1 December 1991;

(d) the Brussels Convention 1996 on the accession of Austria, Finland and Sweden (formerly, EFTA Member States). No amendments of substance were made therein.

It must be noted that the UK also adopted the Modified Convention which appears as Sched 4 to the CJJA 1982. This Convention allocates jurisdiction between the different parts of the UK (that is, England and Wales, Scotland, and Northern Ireland). It is based on broadly similar provisions as those set out in the Brussels Convention. However, in contradistinction to the Brussels Convention, the Modified Convention is not subject to interpretation by the ECJ.

In addition, the Lugano Convention 1988, also called the 'Parallel' Convention, was signed at Lugano between EC and EFTA Member States. This Convention is closely based upon the text of the Brussels Convention. It was implemented in the UK by the CJJA 1991, which came into force in the UK on 1 May 1992 (SI 1992/745).

Hence, there are currently three texts which operate on broadly similar terms, albeit that they bear some differences in detailed rules. In this chapter, reference is made only to the Brussels text as amended, and any variations between its provisions and those of the Lugano Convention will be indicated as and when necessary. The Modified Convention is examined briefly below, 3.12. Furthermore, this chapter deals with the provisions of the Conventions only in so far as they regulate jurisdiction. The provisions on the recognition and enforcement of judgments are examined in Chapter 4.

3.2   Interpretation of the Convention

By virtue of the Luxembourg Protocol 1971, the ECJ has jurisdiction to interpret the Brussels Convention. This is normally done following a reference from the national court seised of a case involving the application of the Convention. This power is exercisable by way of a preliminary ruling at the request of an appellate court of a Member State, or by way of a declaratory ruling at the request of a competent authority of a Member State (Arts 1, 2 and 3 of the Luxembourg Protocol 1971). Preliminary ruling means that the ECJ interprets the way in which a particular provision of the Convention is intended to apply, but without going into the merits of the dispute in question. A judgment rendered by the ECJ on the interpretation of the Convention is binding on all national courts. This applies to both the court which made the reference and the courts of all other Contracting States before which the application and interpretation of the same provision subsequently arises (s 3 of the CJJA 1982).

In the case of the Lugano Convention, however, no similar provision is made for the interpretation of its provisions by the ECJ or by any other supranational judicial body. Instead, its interpretation is left to the national courts of the Contracting States. This is due to the fact that the Lugano Convention is not a source of Community law. However, Protocol 2 of this Convention requires courts in Contracting States to have regard to the principles laid down in the decisions of the courts of other Contracting States, rulings of the ECJ and decisions under the Brussels Convention. Awareness of such decisions is achieved by the establishment of a procedure for the exchange of information concerning relevant judgments.

In the context of both Conventions, national courts may also refer to the explanatory reports accompanying each of them as an aid to interpreting their provisions.

3.3   Scope of the Convention

In accordance with Art 1, the Brussels Convention is limited in scope to civil and commercial matters, irrespective of the nature of the court or tribunal before which the action is brought. However, the Convention does not cover revenue, customs or administrative matters. Nor does it cover any of the following:

(a) the status or legal capacity of natural persons, rights in property arising out of a matrimonial relationship, wills and succession;

(b) bankruptcy and liquidation;

(c) social security; and

(d) arbitration.

The phrase 'civil and commercial matters' is left undefined in the Convention. Some guidance can be deduced from the ECJ decision in *LTU v Eurocontrol* (1976), where it was held that an independent Community meaning had to be given to this phrase. In this case Eurocontrol, which was a public company in the business of supplying services for the purposes of air traffic control in Western Europe, claimed charges owed to them by LTU. The ECJ held that the question that had to be asked was whether the claim in question arose from Eurocontrol's exercise of its powers, that is, traffic control services. If so, then the claim would not be within the ambit of the phrase. But if the claim arose out of activities not specific for this purpose, such as the purchase of food for consumption by the company's staff or the acquisition of furniture for staff offices, then it would be covered by the Convention. Similarly, in *Netherlands v Rüffer* (1980), the ECJ ruled that the concept 'civil and commercial matters' did not extend to a claim made by the Netherlands State for the recovery of costs incurred in the course of removing a vessel's wrecks from a public waterway. This ruling was again based on the ground that the Netherlands State was acting in its capacity as the public authority in charge of administering public waterways in accordance with the provisions of an international convention.

Conversely, according to the ECJ in *Sonntag v Waidmann* (1993), where the standard or duty of care required of a public authority is that applicable to all individuals, then a claim for the breach of such a duty is within the ambit of 'civil and commercial matters'. In this case, Sonntag, a school teacher employed by the German Government, took a group of school children on a trip to the Italian Alps. One of the children fell and died. Sonntag was prosecuted and convicted on a charge of homicide before the Italian courts. The next of kin of the victim joined in the criminal proceedings as *parties civiles*, claiming damages which the Italian courts ordered Sonntag to pay. An order for the enforcement of this judgment was granted by the German court of first instance and was confirmed by the Court of Appeal. On appeal to the *Bundesgerichtshof*, Sonntag and the State Government contended, *inter alia*, that the judgment of the Italian court ordering the payment of compensation was not a 'civil matter' and therefore did not fall within the meaning of Art 1 of the Convention. This was based on the ground that Sonntag was acting in his capacity as a public servant and his liability, therefore, concerned an administrative matter. With regard to this particular issue, the ECJ ruled that, as the standard of care required of Sonntag was that applicable to all individuals, whether be it school teachers, State employees or ordinary individuals, his liability should be treated as ordinary civil liability, thus falling within the scope of Art 1 of the Convention.

It is important to re-emphasise that the ECJ has given the concept of 'civil and commercial matters' an autonomous meaning independent from the meaning given to it in the national laws of the different Member States. As illustrated in the *Sonntag* case, the concept also covers civil claims made in the course of criminal proceedings despite the fact that the notion of *parties civiles* in criminal proceedings is not known in the national law of all Member States.

As adumbrated above, where the defendant is being sued on a matter covered by the Convention and is domiciled in a Contracting State, the action must usually be brought in the courts of that State. Hence, service of the writ under the 'traditional' rules cannot found jurisdiction where the defendant is domiciled in a Contracting State. Whether or not a person is domiciled in a particular State is to be determined by the law of that State (Art 52). Thus, provided that the claim is within the scope of the Convention, English courts must accept jurisdiction where the defendant is domiciled in England. This is so irrespective of the fact that the dispute could be determined more appropriately by a court outside England.

3.4   The concept of domicile

In essence, the defendant's domicile is the point at which the Convention's jurisdictional rules hinge.

The concept of domicile, albeit central to the operation of the Convention, is undefined. All the Convention does is indicate which system of national law should apply to determine the defendant's domicile.

3.4.1   Domicile of individuals

In the case of individuals, Art 52(1) states that:

> In order to determine whether a party is domiciled in the Contracting State whose courts are seised of a matter, the court shall apply its internal law.

> If a party is not domiciled in the State whose courts are seised of the matter, then, in order to determine whether the party is domiciled in another Contracting State, the court shall apply the law of that State.

Hence, if an English court has to determine whether or not a party is domiciled in England, it must apply English law. Where it is established that the person in question is not domiciled in England, but is allegedly domiciled in France, for example, then the English court must apply the French definition of domicile in order to ascertain whether he or she is so domiciled. A question arises at this stage as to how the court seised would solve the problem of a defendant having two domiciles in two different Contracting States. For instance, a defendant may be domiciled both in the UK, where he or she has been resident for the last three months, and in Belgium, where his or her name is entered in the register of population. It is important to note that Art 52 directs the court seised to its internal law without any reference to its conflict of laws rules. Accordingly, if the Belgian court, as the court seised, establishes that the defendant is domiciled in Belgium, then it is not necessary to consider whether or not he or she is domiciled in the UK.

It is noteworthy that the traditional English concept of domicile (which remains applicable to family law and succession matters) puts emphasis on a person's permanent home. Since, as will be seen in due course, this has often proved difficult to ascertain, a new definition of domicile, closer to that used on the continent, had to be adopted by the UK. The new definition, found in ss 41–46 of the CJJA 1982, applies in relation to civil and commercial disputes.

Section 41 deals with domicile of individuals, and provides that an individual is domiciled in the UK if, and only if, he or she is *resident* in the UK, and the nature and circumstances of his or her residence indicate that the individual has *substantial connection* with the UK (s 41(2)) (note that s 41(3) makes provision in respect of identifying whether an individual is domiciled in a part of the UK). Neither residence nor substantial connection are defined, but s 41(6) provides that if an individual has been resident in the UK for the past three months or more, then the requirement of substantial connection is presumed to have been met unless the contrary is proven. The question of determining a defendant's domicile is one of fact. The Court of Appeal in *Canada Trust Co v Stolzenberg (No 2)* (1988), held that the burden of proof was on the plaintiff to show a good arguable case that a defendant was domiciled in the jurisdiction. Applying this principle in *Petrotrade Inc v Smith* (1998), Thomas J held that where the defendant would have returned to Switzerland after a few days of his arrest had it not been for the condition imposed as a term of his bail that he must remain in the UK, there was no good arguable case that he was domiciled in the UK for the purposes of the Convention. Furthermore, his enforced presence in the UK did not indicate the 'substantial connection' with the country as required by s 41 of the CJJA 1982.

The same criteria apply to determine whether an individual is domiciled in a part of the UK (s 41(4)). However, the presumption of three months' residence contained in s 41(6) cannot be used for the purposes of s 41(4).

If an individual is alleged to be domiciled in a State other than a Contracting State, then the English court, by virtue of s 41(7), applies English law to determine his or her domicile. This provides for the application of the same criteria as above, but here the three months' presumption does not apply.

3.4.2 Domicile of corporations and associations

With regard to a corporation or association's domicile, Art 53(1) of the Convention provides that this refers to the seat of the relevant body as determined by the conflict of laws rules of the court seised. The material text of Art 53(1) provides that:

> For the purposes of this Convention, the seat of a company or other legal person or association of natural or legal persons shall be treated as its domicile. However, in order to determine that seat, the court shall apply its rules of private international law.

It follows that the court seised is required to apply its own definition of 'seat', even when ascertaining whether a corporation has its seat in another Contracting State. With regard to the UK, s 42(3) of the CJJA 1982 indicates that a corporation or association has its seat therein if:

(a) it was incorporated in the UK and has its registered office, or some other official address in the UK; or

(b) its central management and control is exercised in the UK.

According to s 42(4), the same criteria apply to determine whether a corporation has its seat in a part of the UK. However, this provision adds a further alternative. That is, a corporation or association has its seat in a part of the UK where it also has a place of business in that part. In other words, if a company has a place of business in England and Wales, its registered office in Scotland and its central management and control in Northern Ireland, this company is regarded as having a domicile in each of the three parts of the UK, and therefore can be sued in any of these parts. Evidently, it is possible under this provision that a corporation may have a seat in more than one Contracting State. This may lead to the problem of multiplicity of proceedings in more than one Contracting State. Nonetheless, it appears that the provisions of Arts 21 and 22 on *lis alibi pendens*, which are considered below, 3.11, are capable of solving this problem by ascribing competent jurisdiction to the court first seised.

Section 42(6) determines whether a corporation or association has its seat in a Contracting State other than the UK by using the same test as that applicable for the UK. This approach, however, may lead to contradictory results. For instance, the UK may regard a corporation as having its seat in France, whereas France, applying its different concept of a seat, may regard the corporation as having its seat in the UK. Therefore, in order to avoid such a danger, s 42(7) provides that a corporation is not to be regarded as having its seat in a Contracting State if the court of the latter State would not regard it as having its seat there.

Furthermore, s 43 lays down a different definition of a seat intended to apply in the context of Art 16(2) of the Brussels Convention, which provides for exclusive jurisdiction over certain disputes connected with matters related to company law. Section 44 defines the domicile of a branch, agency or other establishment for the purposes of the Convention's special provisions on insurance and consumer contracts. Finally, s 45 deals with the domicile of a trust, and s 46 provides a criterion for the determination of the domicile of the Crown.

3.5 The primary basis of jurisdiction

The primary basis of jurisdiction in the Convention is set out in Art 2 which provides that the action must usually be brought in the courts of the State in which the defendant is domiciled. This provision is mandatory, with the effect that the competent court must accept jurisdiction, provided that the dispute comes within the scope of the Convention, and irrespective of the fact that the dispute could be litigated more appropriately in the courts of another Contracting State. Consequently, the English doctrine of *forum non conveniens* under the traditional rules has no application in cases where a defendant is sued before an English court in accordance with the rules ascribed by the Convention. This view conforms with two relatively recent first instance decisions, notably, *S and W Berisford plc v New Hampshire Insurance Co* (1990); and *Arkwright Mutual Insurance v Bryanston Insurance* (1990). In both cases, the court held that Art 2 of the Convention was mandatory, in spite of the fact that the competing forum was a non-Contracting State forum. Nevertheless, in the subsequent case of *Re Harrods (Buenos Aires) Ltd* (1991), the Court of Appeal overruled the two decisions above, and held that, pursuant to s 49 of the CJJA 1982, *forum non conveniens* remained applicable to cases where to do so is not inconsistent with the Convention. In *Re Harrods*, an action was brought for, *inter alia*, the winding up of an English incorporated company. The company's registered office was in England, but its business was carried on, and it was managed and controlled exclusively, in Argentina. The Brussels Convention applied by virtue of the company's domicile in England. However, the defendant argued that the English proceedings should be stayed, because Argentina was the most appropriate forum for the trial of the action. He also claimed that Art 2 of the Convention did not have a wide mandatory effect where the only conflict was between the courts of a Convention country and the courts of a non-Convention country. Unexpectedly, the Court of Appeal upheld this argument and granted a stay of the English proceedings. A fundamental distinction was drawn between cases where the alternative forum was in a non-Contracting State and cases where it was in a Contracting State, and as such the Convention was intended and designed to regulate relations only as between Convention countries. Accordingly, the court retained its discretion under s 49 of the 1982 Act to stay or dismiss the action on the grounds of *forum non conveniens* where the more appropriate forum was in a non-Contracting State.

This decision has been widely criticised for having misinterpreted the Convention and for creating uncertainty in the law (see Cheshire and North, *Private International Law*, 12th edn). Nevertheless, it has been followed by a subsequent decision, *The Po* (1991), where the doctrine of *forum non conveniens* was applied in the context of the Collision Convention 1952. Although the House of Lords had referred the question of stays in *Re Harrods* to the ECJ (OJ C219/4, 1992), the case was settled. Hence, it seems that this will be the law until an ECJ ruling indicates otherwise.

As stated earlier, where the defendant is domiciled in a non-Contracting State, the question of jurisdiction is remitted to the internal law of the Contracting State whose courts are seised of the dispute (Art 4). Essentially, this means that whether a court has competent jurisdiction is determined by the traditional pre-existing rules of the Member States. Art 4, however, expressly states that it is subject to the provisions of Art 16 on exclusive jurisdiction (see below, 3.8). Furthermore, as will be discussed in due course, it appears that Article 4 is also subject to the provisions of Arts 8 and 14, which apply to insurance and consumer contracts respectively; Art 17 on jurisdiction agreement; Art 18, which deals with a defendant's submission by appearance; and possibly Art 21 on *lis alibi pendens*.

In addition to the primary jurisdictional basis under Art 2, Art 3 provides that a defendant may also be sued in the courts of another Contracting State, but only in accordance with the bases specified in Arts 5–18 of the Convention. Each of these bases will be examined separately.

3.6   Special jurisdiction

Articles 5 to 6A of the Convention supplement the primary rule of the defendant's domicile and confer 'special' jurisdiction to the courts of another Contracting State in a number of situations. Whilst the bases of jurisdiction under Art 5 rely on the existence of a factual connection between the subject matter of the dispute and the court specified, the bases under Arts 6 and 6A address cases of multiplicity of defendants and liability actions in certain circumstances. Before dealing with the various heads available, it is important to note that the court's discretion to refuse jurisdiction is not permitted. In fact, the 'special jurisdiction' grounds enable a plaintiff to forum shop, save where Art 16 is invoked. It will, therefore, be crucial for plaintiffs to consider which is a more advantageous forum before commencing an action. It is also worthy of note that Arts 5–6A bear an apparent close resemblance to the provisions of the revised RSC Ord 11, regulating service of a writ overseas.

3.6.1   Contract

Article 5(1) provides for the first alternative basis of jurisdiction. It states that, in matters relating to a contract, a defendant may also be sued 'in the courts for the place of performance of the obligation in question'. Thus, if that place is in Belgium, for instance, then the Belgian courts can also have jurisdiction, although the defendant may be domiciled in England. In *Industrie Tessili v Dunlop* (1977), the ECJ gave some guidance as to how the place of performance is to be ascertained. In this case, the ECJ ruled that the place of performance of the obligation in question was to be determined by the law which governed that obligation. That law would be ascertained by the national court before which the matter was brought, in accordance with its own private international law rules. Where, however, the place of performance has been indicated by the parties in a clause which is valid by the law applicable to that contract, then pursuant to *Zelger v Salinitri* (1980), such a clause would generally be upheld.

In relation to the phrase *'obligation in question'*, the Convention gives no guidance as to what it means. In *De Bloos v Bouyer* (1977), the ECJ held that the phrase referred to the contractual obligation which formed the basis of the plaintiff's action, and not to any other obligation under the contract. Therefore, where, for example, a claim is brought by a seller of goods for non-payment by the buyer, then, clearly, the obligation in question is that of the buyer to pay the agreed price. Conversely, where the buyer brings an action against the seller for non-delivery of goods, then the obligation in question is that of the seller to deliver.

The recent case of *Fisher v Unione Italiana De Riassicurazione SPA* (1998) provides a good illustration of this point. AG, an Italian insurance company, reinsured the risk in question with the defendant. The latter retroceded part of the risk to London underwriters, including the plaintiff on terms that the proposed reinsured, that is, the defendant, was to retain an amount of the risk. The plaintiff argued that the defendant did not retain any part of the risk and sought a declaration from the English court for non-liability by reason of the defendant's breach of warranty. The plaintiff obtained leave to serve the defendant in Rome, on the basis of Art 5(1) of the Convention, that the place of performance of the plaintiff's obligation to pay was England. The defendant, on the other hand, argued that the courts of Rome had jurisdiction, since the case centred on an alleged breach of the retention warranty which was to be performed in Italy. Colman J set aside the writ and held that where a party claimed a negative declaration that he was not bound to perform some obligation in the contract, it would be to the courts of the country where the obligation was to be performed that jurisdiction would lie. But, where the claim for relief was based on the non-performance of an obligation by the other party, it would be that term that was the relevant obligation. Hence, it was the defendant's obligation to retain an interest that was in dispute, and accordingly the claim should be brought before the Italian courts.

Where, however, the subject of the dispute entails more than one obligation, then according to the ECJ in *Shenavai v Kreischer* (1987), the phrase referred to the principal obligation as determined by the national court seised of the dispute. This principle was subsequently applied in *Union Transport v Continental Lines* (1992). The plaintiff brought an action in England against the defendant, a Belgian company, for failure both to nominate and provide a vessel to carry a cargo of telegraph poles from Florida to Bangladesh under a charterparty agreement. Thus, the plaintiff alleged breach of two obligations: the first was to nominate a vessel, and the second was to provide that vessel to load the cargo. The House of Lords held that the principal obligation in this case was the obligation to nominate the vessel. Since this obligation was to be performed in England, where the plaintiff were to receive the nomination, the English court had competent jurisdiction under Art 5(1). It was irrelevant that Florida was the place where the vessel should have been made available for the purposes of loading the cargo. Another recent example can be found in *Source Ltd v TUV Rheinland Holding* (1997), where the plaintiffs, an English company, had contracted to buy promotional goods direct from suppliers in Hong Kong and Taiwan for importation to, and direct resale in, England. Payment for the goods was to be by way of a letter of credit upon presentation by the suppliers of certificates of quality issued by the plaintiffs. The latter engaged the defendants, two German companies, to conduct quality control inspections of the goods in the Far East and to report to the plaintiffs in England. In reliance on the reports, the plaintiffs instructed the defendants to issue the suppliers with certificates of quality, thereby enabling the latter to obtain payment. The plaintiffs subsequently received complaints about the quality of the goods and brought an action in England alleging, *inter alia*, that they were in breach of contractual duty to exercise reasonable care and skill. The defendants applied to set aside service of the writ on the ground that they should be sued in Germany pursuant to Art 2 of the Convention; and that the English court had no special jurisdiction under Art 5(1), for the place of performance of the obligation in question was in the Far East. Staughton LJ, delivering the judgment of the Court of Appeal, held, *inter alia*, that there were a number of obligations under this contract: an obligation to inspect; an obligation to refer defects to the factories; an obligation to write a report and send it to the plaintiffs in England; and possibly an obligation to transmit a certificate to the sellers. The principal obligation, however, was the inspection of the goods, rather than the delivery of the reports in England. Thus, the place of the performance of the obligation in question was in the Far East, and accordingly Art 5(1) did not apply to confer jurisdiction on the English court.

Due to some divergent differences between the national legal systems, the phrase 'matters relating to a contract' has been given an independent Community meaning. Thus, this concept is said to cover any relationship which is contractual whereby the defendant has voluntarily undertaken to fulfil an obligation towards the plaintiff, but subject to the privity rule. In *Peters GmbH v Zuid Nederlande AV* (1983), the ECJ extended the meaning of this concept to cover an obligation to pay money arising from a relationship between an association and its members. Furthermore, where the dispute between the parties is as to the existence of the contract itself, then by virtue of *Effer v Kantner* (1982), such a dispute is also within the meaning of this concept. The English Court of Appeal has applied this principle even to a case where the plaintiff denied the existence of the contract. In *Boss Group Ltd v Boss France SA* (1996), the facts simply stated, the plaintiff, an English company, terminated a contract of exclusive distributorship of its products with the defendant, a company domiciled in France. The latter considered the act to be a breach of the said contract and commenced proceedings against the plaintiff in France, claiming damages. The plaintiff then commenced proceedings in England under Art 5(1), seeking a declaration that no contract had existed between the parties. The Court of Appeal held, *inter alia*, that the word 'contract' in Art 5(1) could not be read as only including cases where the existence of the contract was unchallengeable or unchallenged. Indeed, the Art 5(1) provision was not confined to actions to enforce, or to obtain recompense for the breach of, a contract. On the contrary, it referred generally to matters relating to contract;

and since the defendant had sought to enforce the contract in France, this was sufficient to establish that the plaintiff's claim was a matter relating to contract under Art 5(1) of the Convention.

Despite the wide meaning this phrase has been given by the ECJ, it would seem to be restricted to cases where there is a direct undertaking between the parties to the dispute. In *Jacob Handte GmbH v Traitements Mécano-Chimiques des Surfaces* (1992), the ECJ held that an action by a buyer against the manufacturer, rather than the vendor of a defective product, did not come under the provision of Art 5(1). Basically, this type of action is allowed under French law where it is classified as a contractual remedy and is called *action directe*. In general terms, under this type of remedy, a purchaser of a product which is found to be defective can sue the manufacturer directly, irrespective of the lack of privity between them. Moreover, the Court of Appeal held in *Barclays Bank v Glasgow City Council* (1994), that the phrase 'matters relating to a contract' required either an actual relationship or a consensual relationship closely akin to a contract. Nevertheless, in *Agnew v Lansfösäkringsbølagens* (1996) (a case decided under Art 5(1) of the Lugano Convention), Mance J held that Art 5(1) was sufficiently wide to cover an action for the breach of a duty to make a fair presentation of the risk by not giving full disclosure and for misrepresentation during the negotiation of a contract of reinsurance. This was because, in his view, Art 5(1) drew no express distinction between obligations arising in the context of negotiation of a contract and obligations arising under or after the contract.

It is worthy of note that a revised version of Art 5(1) includes separate provision dealing with matters relating to individual contracts of employment, the purpose of which is to provide jurisdictional protection for employees. This provision is examined below, 3.7.

3.6.2 Tort

By way of derogation from the primary basis of jurisdiction under Art 2, Art 5(3) provides for special jurisdiction in matters relating to tort, delict or quasi-delict, to the effect that a person domiciled in a Contracting State may also be sued 'in the courts for the place where the harmful event occurred'. The meaning of 'tort, delict or quasi-delict' has been considered by the ECJ in *Kalfelis v Schröder, Münchmeyer, Hengst and Co* (1988), where it was held that the phrase must be given an independent Community meaning, and covered all proceedings which were brought against a defendant for any liability that did not involve contractual matters. Thus, whether the proceedings concern 'matters relating to tort' or 'matters relating to contract', they cannot be determined by reference to the internal law of Contracting States. For instance, where the proceedings concern 'matters relating to tort', a plaintiff cannot invoke the jurisdiction of the French courts under Art 5(1), on the basis that the action can be framed in contract under French internal law. Similarly, where the action relates to a contractual matter, an English court cannot be jurisdictionally competent under Art 5(3), simply because English internal law classifies it as a matter relating to tort. Furthermore, pursuant to the *Kalfelis* case, where the proceedings against the defendant are partly related to tort and partly related to contract, a court which has competent jurisdiction in tort under Art 5(3) can only deal with that part which is based on tort. Such a court is not competent to deal also with that part of the proceedings which is contractual. Conversely, where a claim may be based alternatively in contract and in tort, the claim will be regarded for the purposes of the Convention as being contractual in nature. Therefore, where the action in *Source Ltd v TUV Rheinland Holding* (1997) was brought on the basis of both the defendants' contractual obligation to use reasonable skill and care in carrying out the inspections, and their breach of duty in the form of a negligent misstatement, the Court of Appeal held that the plaintiff's alternative claim in tort was excluded from the special jurisdiction in Art 5(3).

The key element under Art 5(3) is 'the place where the harmful event occurred'. This phrase was interpreted by the ECJ in *Bier BV v Mines de Potasse d'Alsace SA* (1976). Here, the plaintiff, a Dutch market gardener, alleged that the defendants, a company domiciled in France, had polluted the waters of the Rhine in France. The pollution of these waters, which he used for the purpose of irrigation, resulted in damage to his plants. He brought an action in the Dutch court as the court for the place where the harmful event occurred. The jurisdiction of the Dutch court was contested and the matter was referred to the ECJ, which ruled that Art 5(3) was intended to cover both the place where the damage occurred, and the place where the event giving rise to the damage occurred. Hence, according to this decision, a plaintiff suing in tort may have as many as three options. He or she may choose to bring the action in any one of the following courts:

(a) in the courts for the place where the defendant is domiciled (Art 2);

(b) in the courts for the place where the damage occurred (Art 5(3)); or

(c) in the courts for the place where the event giving rise to the damage took place (Art 5(3)).

The question of identifying the place where the harmful event occurred was again referred to the ECJ in the recent and complicated case of *Shevill v Presse Alliance* (1995), which related to the tort of defamation. In a simplified account of the facts, the plaintiffs, Shevill, domiciled in the UK, along with three other companies established in different Member States, brought an action against the defendant, Presse Alliance, alleging libel as a result of an article published in the newspaper *France-Soir*, which suggested that the plaintiffs were involved in a drug trafficking network. The action in the English court was for damages, on the ground that the plaintiffs had suffered harm in France and in the other States, as well as in England. The plaintiffs subsequently limited their claim to damages for the harm suffered in England. The newspaper was mainly distributed in France (237,000 copies), but with a small circulation in England (230 copies). The defendants contested the jurisdiction of the English court on the ground that the harmful event within the meaning of Art 5(3) had occurred in France and not in England. The House of Lords referred a number of questions to the ECJ.

With regard to the question relating to where the harmful event occurred, the ECJ ruled that this was either the place where the publisher was established, that is, France, since in that place the harmful event originated; or the place where the damage occurred. As this case was one of international libel through the press, the damage occurred in the places where the publication was distributed and where the victims were known. Therefore, the courts of each Member State in which the defamatory publication was distributed, and in which the victims suffered injury to their reputation, had jurisdiction, but only to the extent of harm suffered within that jurisdiction.

The end result of this case is that, in international libel cases, Art 5(3) confers jurisdiction on the courts of the place where the publisher is established or on the courts for the places where the harm was suffered. However, with regard to the latter, the courts of each place have jurisdiction only to the extent of damage suffered within that place. The place of the harmful event in connection with the tort of negligent misstatement was recently considered by the English court in *Domicrest Ltd v Swiss Bank Corpn* (1998), where Rex J held that this place was where the misstatement originated. In his view, the place from which the misstatement was put into circulation was as good a place in which to found jurisdiction as the place where the misstatement was acted upon, even if receipt and reliance were essential parts of the tort. Indeed, it was the representor's negligent speech, rather than the hearer's receipt of it, which best identified the harmful event which set the tort in motion, and no distinction was to be drawn between a written document, an oral, or other instantaneous communications. Furthermore, in *Mecklermedia v DC Congress* (1998), the place of the harmful event in respect of the tort of passing off was held to be in England; that is, the place where the harm was done to the plaintiff's goodwill and its effect on their reputation therein.

With regard to the plaintiff's option to bring proceedings in the courts for 'the place where the damage occurred', the question arises as to whether the phrase embraces cases involving economic loss, direct or indirect, as opposed to personal injury and damage to property. Suppose that a parent company, domiciled in France, suffers loss as a consequence of its German subsidiary becoming insolvent when acting on the defendant's negligent advice. Evidently, the German subsidiary has suffered economic loss in Germany as a direct result of the negligent advice; and presumably it should be able to bring proceedings in Germany. However, would the French courts have jurisdiction under Art 5(3) on the basis of the indirect loss suffered by the French parent company? This question was addressed by the ECJ in *Dumez France SA v*

Hessische Landesbank (1990), wherein similar facts were the subject matter of the proceedings. The ECJ expressed the view that the damage which located jurisdiction under Art 5(3):

> ... can be understood only as indicating the place where the event giving rise to the damage, and entailing tortious, delictual or quasi-delictual liability directly producing its harmful effects upon the person who is the immediate victim of that harmful event [p 71].

Hence, the underlying principle in this judgment is that Art 5(3) applies to allocate jurisdiction to the courts for the place where the direct damage occurred, and does not cover cases of indirect damage.

A similar line or reasoning was adopted by the ECJ in *Marinari v Lloyds Bank plc* (1996), wherein the plaintiff, domiciled in Italy, had received a set of promissory notes issued in the Philippines in favour of a company trading in the Lebanon. The notes, which had an exchange value of $752 m, were deposited with Lloyds Bank in England. The bank, suspecting that the notes were of dubious origin, informed the police, who arrested the plaintiff and confiscated the notes. Following criminal proceedings in England, the plaintiff was acquitted, but the notes were not returned. Subsequently, he brought an action in the Italian courts, claiming damages to the value of the notes. The Italian action was brought in reliance on Art 5(3), on the ground that he suffered financial loss in Italy as a result of the conduct of the bank staff, which had taken place in England. He argued that the Italian courts had jurisdiction, since it was in Italy that the harmful consequences had occurred. However, the ECJ rejected this argument and ruled that the Italian courts did not have jurisdiction. As in the *Dumez* case, the ECJ drew a distinction between the place where the damage had arisen, that is, England, where the bank's employees had acted and where the promissory notes were confiscated; and the place where the damage was suffered, that is, Italy, where the alleged consequential loss was felt. The place where the damage occurred under Art 5(3) must be taken to cover only the place of direct damage and did not include the place where the consequential financial loss was suffered.

3.6.3 Restitutionary claims

Much controversy has surrounded the question of whether restitutionary claims, such as claims for unjust enrichment, breach of fiduciary duty, *quantum meruit* payment, breach of constructive trust, etc, are covered by the Convention. It is evident that the primary basis jurisdiction under Art 2 encompasses restitutionary claims. It is less clear, however, whether the special bases of jurisdiction under Art 5(1) and (3) embrace such claims.

It must be noted that the ECJ has not addressed this question to date. But two controversial English judgments highlight the difficulties with classifying such claims. *Kleinwort Benson Ltd v Glasgow City Council* (1997), which concerned a rather new type of financial transaction known as interest rate swap agreements, arose under the Modified Convention. In plain terms, such a transaction consists of an agreement between two parties, whereby one party pays the other sums of money over a period of months or years. The sums in question are calculated by reference to the difference between a fixed rate of interest and the current rate of interest from time to time. The main feature of the agreement is that it is a futures contract, whose financial outcome depends on future movements in interest rates. A number of local authorities, including Glasgow City Council, used these contracts in 1982 in an attempt to improve financial income. The facts of this case are as follows: Glasgow City Council entered into seven transactions with Kleinwort. In 1991, the House of Lords held, in *Hazell v Hammersmith and Fulham London Borough Council* (1991), that all such transactions were void for lack of capacity, on the part of the local authorities, to enter into them. Consequently, Kleinwort brought an action against Glasgow City Council in the English court, claiming restitution of the sum of £807,230, being the balance standing to the credit of the city council under the transactions, on the basis of unjust enrichment. The defendant challenged the jurisdiction of the English court on the ground that it was domiciled in Scotland and, therefore, the action should be brought in the Scottish courts pursuant to Art 2 of the Modified Convention. Conversely, the plaintiff contended, *inter alia*, that the English court had jurisdiction under Art 5(1), or alternatively under Art 5(3), since the claim was for restitution in respect of money paid to the defendant under a contract which was a nullity, because one of the parties did not have capacity to enter into it; and that England was 'the place of performance of the obligation in question' or 'the place where the harmful event occurred'. The Court of Appeal held (Leggatt LJ dissenting) that the correct approach in determining whether a claim was to be regarded within the ambit of Art 5(1) was to ask whether the defendant should broadly be regarded as being sued in a matter relating to a contract. It was incorrect to ask whether the claim would be classified as contractual under domestic law. Hence, a contract was a consensual arrangement intended both to create legal relations and be legally enforceable, and that included a void contract. As for the phrase 'place of performance of the obligation in question', this meant the intended place of performance of the supposed obligation. Accordingly, the English court had jurisdiction under Art 5(1) to adjudicate the claim of the plaintiff for restitution in respect of money paid under the terms of the interest rate swap contracts. The Court of Appeal then found it unnecessary to decide whether a claim of this type also fell under Art 5(3).

On appeal to the House of Lords, however, the decision of the Court of Appeal was reversed, and it was held that the claim fell under neither Art 5(1) nor Art 5(3). The House of Lords took the view that a claim could only fall within Art 5(1) if it was based on a particular contractual obligation, the place of performance of which was within the jurisdiction of the court. On the facts, however, the plaintiff's claim was for the recovery of money paid under a supposed contract which had never existed in law. Thus, the claim was not based on a contractual obligation, but rather on the principle of unjust enrichment. Since no express provision was made in respect of such claims in Art 5(1), the defendants must be sued in the courts of their domicile. With regard to Art 5(3), again, the House of Lords held that the claim did not fall within its ambit, for such a claim did not, apart from exceptional circumstances, presuppose either a harmful event or a threatened wrong. Accordingly, the English court did not have jurisdiction to entertain the action.

The question of classifying restitutionary claims also arose in *Atlas Shipping v Suisse Atlantique Société d'Armement Maritime SA* (1995), which concerned a constructive trust created by memoranda. The plaintiffs, brokers on behalf of the sellers, sought to recover from the buyers the commission they were due as a result of the sale of two vessels. The plaintiffs had no contractual relationship with the buyers, but the latter had the right to deduct 2% commission from the purchase price under the terms of the contracts. The plaintiffs contended that, by necessary implication, where the deduction was taken, the buyers had contracted with the sellers to pay the identified commission to the brokers. Consequently, the buyers and sellers had created a trust, of which the buyers were trustees and the plaintiffs were the beneficiaries. The buyers were domiciled in Switzerland, but the plaintiffs brought the action in England, in reliance on Art 5(1) as an exception to Art 2 of the Lugano Convention. The buyers contested the jurisdiction of the English court on the ground that they were not sued in matters relating to contract, but rather by reason of a constructive trust created by memoranda. Nevertheless, Rix J held that the obligation, which was being enforced in this case, was the obligation owed by the buyers to the sellers to pay the brokers. It made no difference that the contractual promise had been given with the intention of creating an irrevocable trust in favour of a third party; the obligation in question was contractual. Indeed, the buyers were being sued 'in matters relating to a contract'; the obligation in question was the alleged promise given by them that they would pay over the deduction in the form of commission to the brokers; and the place of performance of that obligation was England. Thus, the plaintiffs' claim was within both the spirit and letter of Art 5(1).

Essentially, the English courts reached a differing conclusion as to whether the restitutionary claims in question came within the scope of Art 5(1). Indeed, the *status quo* is far from clear since not all restitutionary claims can be based on a contract. It appears that unless and until the ECJ considers such a question, this area of law remains uncertain.

3.6.4 Maintenance

By virtue of Art 5(2), a person domiciled in a Contracting State may be sued in another State:

... in matters relating to maintenance, in the courts for the place where the maintenance creditor is domiciled or habitually resident or, if the matter is ancillary to proceedings concerning the status of a person, in the court which, according to its own law, has jurisdiction to entertain those proceedings, unless that jurisdiction is based solely on the nationality of one of the parties.

Notwithstanding that the Convention does not apply to marriages or matrimonial property, it applies to maintenance (note that a new EC Convention on Jurisdiction and the Recognition and Enforcement of Judgments in Matrimonial Matters was signed in Brussels on 28 May 1998. It is designed to regulate jurisdiction and recognition and enforcement of judgments in respect of divorce, legal separation, marriage annulment, parental responsibility and child abduction). Under this provision, thus, a maintenance creditor can sue the defendant in the courts of the creditor's domicile or habitual residence. Evidently, this is in lieu of bringing proceedings in the courts of the defendant's domicile, being the primary basis of jurisdiction under Art 2.

As claims for maintenance are most likely, in practice, to be combined with the main proceedings for divorce, Art 5(2) further provides that in such cases, the court which has competent jurisdiction over the main proceedings, according to its own law, also has jurisdiction in respect of maintenance claims. This is the case, provided that jurisdiction over the main proceedings is not assumed on the basis of one of the parties' nationality. (This provision is re-examined in Chapter 11.)

It must be noted that the notion 'maintenance proceedings ancillary to proceedings of status' under Art 5(2) has given rise to problems of interpretation, especially when considered in the light of matters relating to 'rights in property arising out of a matrimonial relationship' which are excluded from the ambit of the Convention (Art 1). The Convention provides no guidance on this issue, but a number of ECJ judgments have elucidated what this notion might entail. In *De Cavel v De Cavel (No 1)* (1979), it was ruled that a judicial decision, which had authorised protective measures concerning the property of the spouses and pending the outcome of divorce proceedings, was not covered by Art 5(2) of the Convention. Equally, in *CHW v GJH* (1982), it was held that, where the main proceedings related to the husband's management of the wife's property, the application for provisional measures to secure the delivery of a certain document, so as to prevent it from being used as evidence in the main proceedings, did not fall within the scope of the Convention. Nonetheless, according to *De Cavel v De Cavel (No 2)* (1980), an application for the enforcement of an interim order, made in the course of divorce proceedings, was covered by the Convention; the reason being that such an order was in the nature of maintenance, providing financial support to the spouse.

More recently, in *Van den Boogard v Laumen* (1997), the ECJ explained how to draw the distinction between decisions regulating matrimonial property under Art 1, and those relating to maintenance under Art 5(2). In this case, a former spouse applied to the Dutch courts to enforce an order made by the English court following divorce proceedings. The order was for payment in respect of her claim for ancillary relief; and the payment thereunder was to be made by a combination of a lump sum and the transfer of ownership of certain property. The husband contended that the order concerned rights in property arising out of a matrimonial relationship and, therefore, could not be enforced under the Convention. The ECJ drew a distinction between those aspects of a decision which regulated matters of maintenance, and those which regulated the matrimonial relationship of the parties, stating that:

> ... if this shows that a provision awarded is designed to enable one spouse to provide for himself or herself or if the needs and resources of each of the spouses are taken into consideration in the determination of its amount, the decision will be concerned with maintenance [p 306].

Where, on the other hand, the decision is solely concerned with dividing property between the spouses, it will then be related to matrimonial relationship and cannot be enforced under the Convention.

Furthermore, the term 'maintenance creditor' was interpreted by the ECJ in *Farrell v Long* (1997) to cover not only persons applying for maintenance, but also persons bringing a maintenance action for the first time.

3.6.5 Civil claims in criminal proceedings

In relation to a civil claim for damages or restitution which is based on an act giving rise to criminal proceedings, the plaintiff may also sue in the court seised of the criminal proceedings, provided that such a court can entertain the civil claim under its own law (Art 5(4)). This provision is not likely to be operative in England, for English law does not generally confer jurisdiction upon criminal courts to deal with civil claims. Article 5(4) is intended to cover such cases as *Sonntag v Waidmann* (1993), where the deceased's next of kin were allowed to join in the criminal proceedings in the Italian court for the purpose of claiming civil compensation.

3.6.6 Branch, agency or other establishment

Pursuant to Art 5(5), where the dispute arises out of the operations of a branch, agency or other establishment, a defendant may also be sued 'in the courts for the place in which the branch, agency or other establishment is situated'. At first glance, this provision appears to embrace a wide extension of jurisdiction likely to cover any dispute arising out of the operation of any secondary establishment. Initially, the ECJ had given the phrase 'branch, agency or other establishment' a narrow Community meaning. For instance, in *De Bloos v Bouyer* (1976) an exclusive distribution agreement was granted by *Bouyer*, a French company, to *De Bloos*, a Belgian company, for the marketing by the latter of the former's products in a number of Contracting States. *De Bloos* brought an action in the Belgian courts, claiming breach of contract and seeking dissolution of the distribution agreement. The jurisdiction of the Belgian court was invoked on the ground that *De Bloos* should be regarded as a branch, agency or other establishment within the meaning of Art 5(5). The ECJ, however, rejected this view and held that one of the essential characteristics of this concept was that the branch or agency had to be subject to the direction and control of the parent body. Similarly, in *Blankaert and Willems v Trost* (1981), the ECJ held that an independent commercial agent, who could also represent other rival firms and who merely conveyed orders to the parent body without being involved in the performance of the contracts, could not be classed as a branch, agency or other establishment. Furthermore, in *Somafer SA v Saar-Ferngas AG* (1978), an action was brought against the defendant, a French company, in the German courts. The defendant company had its registered office and principal place of business in France, but its notepaper also had a business address in Germany. This business, however, was not registered as a branch in Germany and was carried on only by one of the defendant's employees. The ECJ ruled that, for an action to come within the meaning of Art 5(5), it had to be shown that the branch, agency or other establishment had a fixed permanent place of business, was subject to the direction and control of the parent body, and acted as an extension of the parent body.

Nevertheless, in the subsequent case of *Sar Schotte GmbH v Parfums Rothschild SARL* (1987), the ECJ appears to have moved towards adopting a wider meaning to this concept. The plaintiff, a German company, supplied goods to a French subsidiary of another German company. Following a dispute over the quality of the goods supplied, the plaintiff brought an action in the German courts on the basis of Art 5(5), that is, the German parent company was considered as a branch, agency or other establishment of the French subsidiary, for it had conducted business with the plaintiff on behalf of the subsidiary. The ECJ confirmed this view, and ruled that the vital question was to look at the way in which the two companies were behaving and how they presented themselves to third parties. Indeed, the ECJ stated that:

> ... third parties doing business with the establishment acting as an extension of another company must be able to rely on the appearance thus created and regard that establishment as an establishment of the other company, even if the two companies are independent of each other [p 4920].

Moreover, in order to invoke jurisdiction under Art 5(5), it needs to be established that the claim arises out of the 'operation' of the branch, agency or other establishment itself. The word, 'operation', was given an independent Community meaning by the ECJ in *Somafer SA v Saar-Ferngas AG* (1978). This includes actions relating to the management of the branch, agency or other establishment. Such actions are those:

... concerning the situation of the building ... the local engagement of staff, torts committed in the course of the branch's activities, and undertakings entered into in the name of the parent and which are to be performed in the place where the branch, agency or other establishment is situated.

Additionally, in *Lloyd's Register of Shipping v Société Campenon Bernard* (1995), the ECJ went further, to decide that it was not necessary for the operation giving rise to the dispute to take place in the Contracting State where the secondary establishment was situated. The case concerned a contract between the plaintiff, a French company, and the defendant, an English company with various branches in a number of Contracting States, including France and Spain. The contract, which was concluded in France through the defendant's subsidiary therein, was to be performed in Spain, wherein the defendant was to examine certain steel through their branch there. Following a dispute, the plaintiff brought an action in the French courts on the basis of Art 5(5). The defendant contested the jurisdiction, contending that since the steel was to be examined in Spain, that is, the place where the undertaking was to be performed, the requirements of this provision were not satisfied. Nonetheless, the ECJ took the view that such an undertaking would form part of the operations of a secondary establishment within the meaning of the provision, even though it was to be performed outside the Contracting State where such an establishment was situated.

3.6.7 Trusts

Article 5(6) provides for special jurisdiction in relation to trusts, to the effect that the courts of the Contracting State in which the trust is domiciled will also have jurisdiction. In order for this provision to be invoked, the trust must have been created by the operation of a statute, or by a written instrument, or created orally and evidenced in writing.

3.6.8 Salvage

Article 5(7) provides for special jurisdictional rules in relation to remuneration for the salvage of a cargo. These are outside the scope of this book.

3.6.9 Further alternative bases of jurisdiction

Articles 6 and 6A of the Convention provide for further alternative bases of jurisdiction which are designed both to reduce the expense and inconvenience of litigating in different Member States, and to avoid the risk of irreconcilable judgments resulting from separate proceedings in different States.

Article 6(1) applies in the case of co-defendants and provides that a person domiciled in a Contracting State may be sued, where he or she is one of a number of defendants, in the courts of the State where any one of them is domiciled. Pursuant to *Canada Trust Co v Stolzenberg (No 2)* (1998) and *Petrotrade Inc v Smith* (1998), the time for determining the domicile of the person whose domicile determined the jurisdiction under Art 6 is the date of the issue of the writ, and not the date when the writ was served.

Moreover, by virtue of Art 6(2), he or she may be sued, as a third party in an action on a warranty or guarantee, in the court seised of the original proceedings. This is so unless such proceedings were instituted in order to avoid the jurisdiction of the court which would be competent in this case.

In relation to a counterclaim arising from the same contract or facts on which the original claim was based, Art 6(3) provides for jurisdiction in favour of the court in which the original claim is pending.

Both the San Sebastian and Lugano Conventions introduced a new Art 6(4). This provision may be invoked in matters relating to a contract, but only if the action may be combined with an action against the same defendant and is related to a right *in rem* in immovable property. Where these requirements are met, the defendant many also be sued in the court where the property is situated.

Finally, when, by virtue of the Convention, a court of a Contracting State has jurisdiction in actions relating to liability arising from the use of a ship, then according to Art 6(A) any claims for limitations of such liability are subject to the jurisdiction of that court.

3.7   Protective measures

Title II of the Convention sets out a number of provisions dealing with jurisdiction in relation to three specific types of contract; notably, individual contracts of employment (Art 5(1)), insurance contracts (Articles 7–12A), and certain consumer contracts (Arts 13–15). These provisions supplement Arts 5 and 6 and are designed to protect certain categories of persons who are considered to be the weaker party to the contractual relationship.

3.7.1   Individual contracts of employment

The original text of the Brussels Convention did not address the question of jurisdiction over individual contracts of employment, but both the Lugano and San Sebastian Conventions, in a revised version of Art 5(1), added a separate provision to deal with such matters. The purpose of this provision is to incorporate the earlier decisions of the ECJ in *Ivenel v Schwab* (1983), *Shenavai v Kreischer* (1987), and the first part of the judgment in *Six Constructions v Humbert* (1989). The new provision in both Conventions ascribes special jurisdiction in matters relating to individual contracts of employment, to the place 'where the employee habitually carries out his work'. However, where the employee does not habitually carry out his work in any one country, then, according to the provision in the San Sebastian Convention, which differs slightly from that in the Lugano Convention, 'the employer may also be sued in the courts for the place where the business which engaged the employee was or is now situated'. As for the Lugano text, it provides that the place of performance refers to the 'place of business through which he was engaged'.

In effect, this new provision means that, in individual contracts of employment, either party can sue the other in the courts of the Member State where the employee works. Hence, if the employee works in France, then either party can sue the other in the courts of France as the place of performance of the obligation. Where, however, the employee carries out his work in more than one country, even if one or more of these countries are outside the EC, then the San Sebastian Convention allows the employee (but not the employer) to sue in the place where the business through which he was engaged was then situated or in the place where this business is now situated. For instance, if the employee was engaged through a business then situated in England to carry out his work in France, Germany and Liberia, and that business moved subsequently to Spain, he can sue the employer either in England or in Spain. According to the Lugano Convention, on the other hand, the employee can only sue in the courts where the business through which he was engaged was situated. In other words, the Lugano provision not only restricts the employee's choice, by failing to take account of a change of the place of business after the employee is engaged, but also, unlike the San Sebastian Convention, allows for both employer and employee to be sued in that place of business. This means that whilst, under the Lugano Convention, an employee as well as an employer may be sued in that place, under the San Sebastian Convention, only the employee has this additional option.

The meaning of the concept 'place of habitual work' has been addressed by the ECJ in two instances. Whilst the first was based on the pre-1989 version of Art 5(1), the second was based on the new amended text. Nonetheless, in both instances, the ECJ applied the same criteria. In *Mulox IBC v Geels* (1993), the plaintiff, domiciled in the Netherlands and living in France, was employed by the defendant, an English company. He was to carry out his work in Belgium, Germany, the Netherlands, Scandinavia and subsequently in France. During his employment, he used his place of residence in France as his base for his work. The defendant terminated the contract of employment and he brought an action for wrongful dismissal in the French courts on the basis of Art 5(1). The ECJ held that, where an employee carried out his work in more than one Contracting State, then Art 5(1) accorded jurisdiction to the courts of the Contracting State in which the work was principally carried out. Hence, since France was the place where the employee had principally carried out his work, the French courts had competent jurisdiction. Similarly, in *Rutten v Cross Medical Ltd* (1997), where the employee carried out his work in the Netherlands, the UK, Belgium, Germany and the USA, the ECJ ruled that Art 5(1) of the Convention:

... must be understood to refer to the place where the employee has established the effective centre of his working activities, and where, or from which, he in fact performs the essential part of his duties vis à vis his employer [p 214].

By virtue of Art 17(5), where there is a jurisdiction agreement between the employer and employee to refer their dispute to the courts of a particular Contracting State, such an agreement is subject to the restrictions provided therein. The latter provision was inserted by both the San Sebastian and Lugano Conventions, but alas, again in slightly different terms. In general terms, such a jurisdiction agreement is valid only if entered into after the dispute has arisen, or alternatively if the employee invokes it to bring the action in the courts other than those of the defendant's domicile or those specified in Art 5(1), the latter alternative is allowed under the San Sebastian Convention only.

3.7.2 Jurisdiction in matters relating to insurance

Articles 7 to 12A apply to matters relating to insurance. These provisions have to be read in conjunction with s 44 of the 1982 Act, which defines the domicile of a branch, agency or other establishment for the purposes of Arts 7–12A on insurance contracts, and Arts 13–15 on consumer contracts. The provisions in Arts 7–12A are exclusive, but without prejudice to the provisions of Arts 4 and 5(5). In general, the rules are in favour of the policyholder rather than the insurer. By virtue of Art 8, the policyholder can sue the insurer either in the courts of the State where the latter is domiciled, or in the courts of the State where the policyholder is domiciled. If the defendant is a co-insurer, then the policyholder can sue him or her in the courts of the State where the leading insurer is being sued. In addition, in the case of liability insurance, or insurance of immovable property, he or she can also sue in the courts of the State where the harmful event occurred (Art 9). However, this special jurisdiction is not reciprocated in the sense that the policyholder may be sued only in the courts of the State where he or she is domiciled. This is in accordance with Art 11, which provides:

> ... an insurer may bring proceedings only in the courts of the Contracting State in which the defendant is domiciled, irrespective of whether he is the policyholder, the insured or the beneficiary. The provisions of this Section shall not affect the right to bring a counterclaim in the court which, in accordance with this Section, the original claim is pending.

The meaning of this provision was elaborated by the Court of Appeal in *Jordan Grand Prix v Baltic Insurance Group* (1998). The plaintiff in the original action was an English company which ran a Formula One racing team. It agreed to make bonus payments to its employees if it finished in the top six of a world championship, and it insured that contingent liability with the defendant insurer, a Lithuanian company. The latter had a managing agent in Belgium,

CIU. The plaintiff's primary case was that the requisite insurance cover was effected with the defendant through CIU and with the participation of another Belgian intermediary, SRI. The plaintiff also had a secondary claim against SRI. Q Ltd, an Irish company, of which D and G, both domiciled in Ireland, were directors, agreed with the plaintiff to sponsor the team and to pay a certain sum if the team finished in the top six. In the event, the team finished fifth, but the insurer refused to pay, alleging that the bonus scheme and sponsorship agreement were not genuine, and that the plaintiff and Q Ltd were parties to a conspiracy to defraud the insurer. The plaintiff brought proceedings in the English court against the insurer, claiming the sum due under the policy. The defendant served a defence and a counterclaim alleging conspiracy and fraud. As well as being against the plaintiff, the counterclaim was made against various individuals associated with the plaintiff, and against Q Ltd and SRI. Before the counterclaim had been served on Q Ltd, the latter served proceedings in the Belgian court against the defendant, SRI and CIU, and then applied to the English court for a declaration that the court did not have jurisdiction to entertain the counterclaim against them, relying on Art 11 of the Convention. The defendant insurer contended that Art 11 only applied to an insurer domiciled in a Contracting State; that the word 'counterclaim' in Art 11 meant any claim counter to the original claim and was not restricted to one against the original plaintiff; and that the reference in Art 11 to the defendant being 'the policyholder, the insured or a beneficiary' was intended to be an exhaustive list. The Court of Appeal held, however, that Art 11 was not limited to an insurer domiciled in a Contracting State, for, having regard to the absence of any reference to the domicile of a plaintiff insurer therein, such domicile was irrelevant. In respect of the insurer's second contention, it was held that the word 'counterclaim' in Art 11 was limited to a counterclaim against the original plaintiff. This was because the basic principle underlying the last part of Art 11 was that, by becoming a litigant within the jurisdiction, a plaintiff submitted himself or herself to the incidents of such litigation, including liability to a counterclaim. Additionally, the words 'the policyholder, the insured or a beneficiary' in Art 11 were not intended to be an exhaustive list of those capable of taking advantage of this provision, but rather elaborated the meaning of 'defendant'. Accordingly, the declaration sought by Q Ltd was granted.

It must be noted that the above provisions can be departed from by an agreement on jurisdiction in accordance with Art 12, the latter requiring such an agreement to satisfy one of five requirements. These are as follows:

(a) the agreement is entered into after the dispute has arisen;

(b) it allows the policyholder, the insured or a beneficiary to bring proceedings in courts other than those indicated in Arts 7–12A;

(c) it is concluded between a policyholder and an insurer, both of whom having their domicile or habitual residence in the same Contracting State. Such an agreement must also have the effect of conferring jurisdiction on the courts of that State, even if the harmful event were to occur abroad. This is so, provided that such an agreement is not contrary to the law of that State;

(d) the agreement is concluded with a policyholder who is not domiciled in a Contracting State unless the insurance is compulsory or is related to immovable property in a Contracting State; or

(e) the agreement relates to a contract of insurance which covers one or more of the risks set out in Art 12A, that is, risks connected with carriage by air and by sea.

3.7.3 Jurisdiction over consumer contracts

In order to protect consumers, Arts 13–15 of the Convention contain special provisions for jurisdiction over certain consumer contracts. These provisions are exclusive but without prejudice to Arts 4 and 5(5). Article 13 defines the 'consumer' as a person who concludes the contract 'for a purpose which can be regarded as being outside his trade or profession'. It also defines a 'consumer contract' to include a contract for the sale of goods on instalment credit terms; a contract for a loan repayable by instalments, or for any other form of credit, made to finance the sale of goods; or any other contract for the supply of goods or a contract for the supply of services. Such contracts must also be preceded by a specific invitation addressed to the consumer or by advertising in the State of the Consumer's domicile, and the consumer took in that State the necessary steps for the conclusion of the contract.

By virtue of Art 14, the consumer may bring proceedings against the other party to the contract (that is, seller or lender) either in the courts of the State where the defendant is domiciled, or in the courts of the State in which the consumer is domiciled. However, if a consumer is to be sued, then proceedings against him or her can only be brought in the courts of the State in which the consumer is domiciled. Last, but not least, Art 15 severely restricts the power of the other party to the contract to depart from these provisions by means of a jurisdiction agreement in the contract to the following situations:

(a) the jurisdiction agreement is entered into after the dispute has arisen; or

(b) the jurisdiction agreement allows the consumer to bring proceedings in courts other than those indicated in Article 14; or

(c) both parties to the jurisdiction agreement are domiciled or habitually resident in the same Contracting State to whose courts jurisdiction is conferred, so long as such an agreement is not contrary to the law of that state.

It must be noted that only a person who is the original consumer can rely on the provisions of Arts 13–15. This may be illustrated by the ECJ ruling in *Shearson Lehmann Hutton Inc v TVB GmbH* (1993). In this case, a German consumer had entered into contracts with Hutton Inc, American brokers, for financial services and advice. His investment was nearly a total loss. The consumer was thought to have a claim against Hutton Inc, based, *inter alia*, on their failure to indicate the risks involved in such transactions. Rather than suing them himself, he elected to assign his right to sue to a German company, TVB. The latter brought an action in the German court on the basis of Art 14. The defendant contested the jurisdiction of the German court which, in turn referred the issue to the ECJ. It was held, *inter alia*, that Arts 13–15 did not apply in this instance, because these provisions were intended to apply only to cases where both the parties to the contract were consumer and supplier, and the parties to the litigation were consumer and supplier. As the plaintiff in this case was not a private consumer, though the assignee of a consumer's claim, it was not entitled to avail itself of Arts 13–15 of the Convention. Similarly, in *Benincasa v Dentalkit* (1997), where the defendant, an Italian company specialising in the sale of dental hygiene equipment, entered into a franchising contract with the plaintiff, an Italian national, with a view that the plaintiff would set up and operate a shop in Germany, trading in goods supplied by the defendant. The plaintiff set up a shop, paid the defendant an initial agreed sum, and made several purchases of products for which he never paid. He then ceased trading. He brought proceedings in the German court seeking to have the franchising contract and all subsequent contracts declared void, and argued that, as he had not commenced trading, he should be regarded as a consumer under Arts 13 and 14 of the Convention, and therefore he should be permitted to bring the action in Germany, where he was domiciled. Nevertheless, the ECJ ruled that the concept of a 'consumer' within the meaning of the Convention had to be construed strictly to mean a private, final consumer. It did not extend to a person who concluded a contract with the intention of pursuing a trade or profession, either at the present time or in the future. Hence, the plaintiff could not be classed as a consumer.

3.8   Exclusive jurisdiction

Article 16 provides for the exclusive jurisdiction of the courts of a particular Contracting State irrespective of the domicile of the defendant. In other words, if an action is within the provisions of Art 16, then the designated courts will have exclusive jurisdiction and the courts of the defendant's domicile must decline jurisdiction unless these are the designated courts under these provisions. Moreover, it is irrelevant whether or not the defendant is domiciled in a Contracting State, so long as the subject matter of the dispute is within the scope of Art 16. Hence, Art 16 is overriding in character and applies regardless of domicile, submission by appearance and jurisdiction agreements.

Exclusive jurisdiction is given to courts of Contracting States in the following situations:

- *Art 16(1): immovable property.* Where proceedings have as their object rights *in rem* in, or tenancies of, immovable property, then 'the courts of the Contracting State in which the property is situated' shall have exclusive jurisdiction. Article 16(1) was amended by both the San Sebastian and Lugano Conventions, but in slightly different terms. The effect and intent of both amendments was to reverse the ECJ judgment, in *Rösler v Rottwinkel* (1985), relating to short term tenancies. This provision is more fully examined in the context of immovable property in Chapter 8. At this stage, it suffices to mention that Art 16(1) became Art 16(1)(a), and a new Art 16(1)(b) was added;

- *Art 16(2): companies and associations.* Where proceedings have as their object the validity of the constitution, the nullity or the dissolution of companies or other legal associations, or the decisions of their organs, then the courts of the Contracting State in which the company or association has its seat shall have exclusive jurisdiction;

- *Art 16(3): public registers.* Where the proceedings have as their object the validity of entries in public registers, the courts of the Contracting State where the register is kept shall have exclusive jurisdiction;

- *Art 16(4): intellectual property.* Where the subject matter of the proceedings is concerned with the registration or validity of patents, trade marks, designs, or other similar rights required to be deposited or registered and the deposit or registration has been applied for, has taken place, or deemed to have taken place under the terms of an international convention in a Contracting State, then the courts of that State shall have exclusive jurisdiction;

- *Art 16(5): enforcement of judgments.* Where the proceedings are concerned with the enforcement of judgments, then the courts of the Contracting State in which the judgment is sought to be enforced shall have exclusive jurisdiction.

3.9 Jurisdiction agreements

In addition to Art 16, Art 17 of the Convention confers exclusive jurisdiction in cases where there is a jurisdiction agreement to submit disputes to the courts of a Contracting State. Article 17(1) was significantly amended by both the Lugano and San Sebastian Conventions in identical terms. As adumbrated earlier, both Conventions also added a new Art 17(5) which applies to jurisdiction agreements in individual contracts of employment.

The amended version of Art 17(1) states that 'if the parties, one or more of whom is domiciled in a Contracting State, have agreed that a court or the courts of a Contracting State are to have jurisdiction to settle any disputes which have arisen or which may arise in connection with a particular legal relationship, that court or those courts shall have exclusive jurisdiction', provided that the jurisdiction clause is either:

(a) in writing or evidenced in writing; or

(b) in a form which accords with practices which the parties have established between themselves; or

(c) in international trade or commerce, in a form which accords with a usage of which the parties are or ought to have been aware and which in such trade or commerce is widely known to, and regularly observed by, parties to the contracts of the type involved in the particular trade or commerce concerned.

Article 17(1) further provides that in such a situation, 'the courts of other Contracting States shall have no jurisdiction over their disputes unless the court or courts chosen have declined jurisdiction'.

Hence, for a jurisdiction agreement to be valid, the first of the above alternative requirements is that it must be in 'writing or evidenced in writing'. The meaning of this requirement was elucidated by the ECJ in *Tilly Russ v Nova* (1984), where it was held that the jurisdiction clause must be contained in a document signed by both parties. Where, however, the written contract incorporating the jurisdiction clause stipulates that it can be renewed only in writing, but the parties continued to rely on its terms after it had expired, this does not imply that the jurisdiction clause is no longer valid. This was held in *Iveco Fiat v Van Hool* (1986), where the ECJ adopted the view that if the law applicable to the contract allowed the parties to renew the original contract other than in writing, then the jurisdiction clause would be effective, provided that the other party, to whom a confirmation must be given, did not object. Moreover, the ECJ held, in *Powell Duffryn v Petereit* (1992), that a jurisdiction clause covering disputes between a company and its shareholders and contained in the constitutional documents of the company, such as its articles of association, satisfied the formal requirements of 'writing or evidenced in writing' within the meaning of Art 17(1). Equally, where the jurisdiction clause was agreed orally and the written confirmation thereof was received by the party without raising any objection, then according to *Berghoefer v ASA* (1985), the agreement would satisfy the requirement of 'evidenced in writing'. Nevertheless, following the ECJ ruling in *Galeries Segoura v Bonakdarian* (1976), a contract concluded orally, subject to the general conditions of sale which incorporate a jurisdiction clause, would not satisfy this requirement unless the seller's written confirmation was accompanied by a notification of the general conditions and these were accepted by the purchaser in writing.

If the agreement on jurisdiction does not satisfy the requirement of 'writing or evidenced in writing', it may still be valid if it 'accords with practices which the parties have established themselves'. Thus, in *Tilly Russ v Nova* (1984), where the shipper and carrier concluded a contract for the carriage of goods orally and, subsequently, the carrier issued a bill of lading incorporating a jurisdiction clause, it was held that the clause was effective provided that the parties had a continuing trading relationship governed by the carrier's general conditions; the latter containing the jurisdiction clause. In the absence of such a trading relationship, the jurisdiction clause may remain valid if it is made 'in a form which accords with a usage of which the parties are or ought to have been aware and which in such trade or commerce is widely known to, and regularly observed by, parties to contracts of the type involved in the particular trade or commerce concerned'. The meaning and application of this provision was clarified by the ECJ in *Mainschiffahrts-Genossenchaft v Les Gravières Rhénanes* (1997). The case concerned a charterparty concluded between the plaintiff, domiciled in Germany, and the defendant, domiciled in France. Following completion of negotiations, the plaintiff forwarded a letter of confirmation, incorporating a jurisdiction clause in favour of the Würzburg courts, to the defendant. A reference to that clause was also made on invoices which the plaintiff paid without challenging them in any way. It was held that consensus on the part of the Contracting Parties as to the jurisdiction clause would be presumed where the commercial practices in the relevant branch of international trade or commerce existed, and of which the parties were or ought to have been aware. In this case, the fact that the defendant did not react to the letter of confirmation or to the invoices would be deemed to constitute consent to the jurisdiction clause. The ECJ went further, to give guidance to national courts as to how they should determine whether a contract came under a head of international trade or commerce, whether there was a practice in the branch of international trade or commerce in which the parties were operating, and whether they were or ought to have been aware of that practice. First, it should be considered whether a contract, concluded between two companies domiciled in different Contracting States, came under the head of international trade. Secondly, the question of whether a practice existed must not be determined by reference to the law of one Contracting State. Nor should it be determined in relation to international trade in general, but to the branch of trade in which the parties in question were operating. Finally, actual or presumptive awareness of such a practice would be established where, in particular, the parties had had trade relations between themselves or with other parties operating in the same sector; or where, in that sector, a particular course of conduct was generally and regularly followed when a contract of the type in question was concluded.

The requirement of consensus was addressed by the English court in *IP Metal v Ruote* (1993), where the plaintiffs and defendants entered into seven contracts for the sale by the plaintiffs to the defendants of quantities of aluminium. The telexes confirming the sales contained a clause nominating English law as the applicable law and England as the competent forum. In reliance on that clause, the plaintiffs brought an action against the defendants in relation to six contracts. An action in relation to the seventh contract had already been commenced by the defendants in the Italian court. The defendants then applied to the English court for a stay of the proceedings on the ground, *inter alia*, that Art 17(1) did not apply in this case, for there was no agreement, nor sufficient consensus in relation to jurisdiction. Waller J rejected this argument and held that, in the context of metal trade, as was the case here, it was common form that the terms would be negotiated over the telephone, because some of the terms would go without saying, and that there would then be a confirmation of those terms by telex immediately thereafter. Unless the defendants made it clear that they were not prepared to accept a particular term, they must be taken to have agreed to it. Therefore, the jurisdiction clause was valid and accorded to the provisions of Art 17(1).

Where an agreement conferring exclusive jurisdiction, within the provision of Art 17, is contained in the contract, this agreement has been held by the ECJ to confer exclusive jurisdiction on the designated court also where the action seeks, in particular, a declaration that the contract containing that clause is void (see *Benincasa v Dentalkit* (1997)).

The opening sentence of Art 17(1) stipulates that 'one or more of the parties' must be domiciled in a Contracting State. This suggests that it need not be the defendant, especially since at the time of the agreement on jurisdiction it is uncertain as to which of the parties will be the defendant and which of them will be the plaintiff in future disputes. Hence, if one or more of the parties is domiciled in a Contracting State, then provided that their agreement complies with one or more of the above requirements, the courts designated in the agreement shall have exclusive jurisdiction over the actions. However, if none of the parties is domiciled in a Contracting State, then Art 17(1) proceeds to state that the courts of other Contracting States shall have no jurisdiction, unless the court chosen has declined jurisdiction. Therefore, depending on where the parties to the agreement are domiciled, the agreement will either give the court chosen exclusive jurisdiction, or merely preclude the courts of other Contracting States from having jurisdiction.

Article 17(2) makes provision for jurisdiction clauses in relation to trust instruments.

Article 17(3) imposes two limitations on the effectiveness of a jurisdiction agreement. The first limitation applies in relation to Art 16 of the Convention, to the effect that a jurisdiction agreement shall have no legal force if it purports to exclude the courts of the Contracting State which have exclusive jurisdiction by virtue of Art 16. In other words, Art 16 is of an overriding nature. The second limitation applies where the jurisdiction agreement is contrary to the provisions of Art 12 which applies to contracts of insurance and Art 15 which applies in the context of certain consumer contracts. In such cases, the agreement shall have no legal force.

Two further qualifications on the effectiveness of jurisdiction clauses are contained in Art 17(4) and (5). If the jurisdiction agreement was concluded for the benefit of only one of the parties, then by virtue of Art 17(4), that party shall retain the right to bring proceedings in any other court which has jurisdiction under the Convention. So, because the agreement is only for the benefit of one party, that party is given the right to waive that benefit. The question of whether or not a clause is for the benefit of one party must be answered by examining the terms of the clause, that is, it must be either express or implied. Such an implication is to be deduced from evidence or the surrounding circumstances. However, in line with the ECJ judgment in *Anterist v Crédit Lyonnais* (1986), the fact that the chosen court is that of the country where that party is domiciled must not be taken to presume that the choice is for his or her benefit.

Article 17(5) is confined to jurisdiction agreement in matters relating to individual contracts of employment. As adumbrated earlier in this chapter, this is a new qualification introduced by the San Sebastian and Lugano Conventions in order to complement the provisions added by Art 5(1). The agreement on jurisdiction will only have legal force if it is entered into after the dispute has arisen, or if it is invoked by the employee as plaintiff in order to seise courts other than the court of the defendant's domicile or those courts specified in Art 5(1). The latter alternative is only available under the San Sebastian Convention.

A question arises at this stage as to whether a jurisdiction clause conferring jurisdiction on the courts of more than one Contracting State can be taken to confer exclusive jurisdiction on the courts of these States to the exclusion of all others. If one examines the wording of Art 17, an agreement conferring jurisdiction gives the court exclusive jurisdiction; there is nothing in the wording which indicates that the agreement must be exclusive. Indeed, this effect may be deduced from Hoffman J in the case of *Kurz v Stella Musical GmbH* (1992).

It should be noted that a similar version of Art 17 contained in Sched 4 of the Civil Jurisdiction and Judgments Act 1982, which deals with cases where the defendant is domiciled within the UK, omits the requirement that the jurisdiction agreement must be in writing.

3.10 Submission

By virtue of Art 18 of the Convention, the courts of a Contracting State, before whom a defendant enters an appearance, shall have jurisdiction. This is so, except where his appearance was solely to contest the jurisdiction, or where another court has exclusive jurisdiction under Art 16. However, by only mentioning Art 16, Art 18 seems to prevail over an agreement conferring jurisdiction under Art 17. This line of reasoning was confirmed by the ECJ in *Elefanten Schuh v Jacqmain* (1981), where Art 18 was held to override an earlier agreement conferring jurisdiction on the courts of another Contracting State.

3.11   *Lis alibi pendens* and related actions

In some instances, proceedings between the same parties arising out of the same dispute are simultaneously pending in the English court and the courts of another country. This is referred to as a case for *lis alibi pendens*.

In cases where the concurrent proceedings are in the courts of the UK on one hand, and the courts of another EC or EFTA State on the other, the Conventions give no discretion to a court to stay proceedings on the ground of *forum non conveniens* or similar grounds. Article 21, which was significantly amended by both the Lugano and San Sebastian Conventions, reads as follows:

> Where proceedings involving the same cause of action and between the same parties are brought in the courts of different Contracting States, any court other than the court first seised shall of its own motion stay its proceedings until such time as the jurisdiction of the court first seised is established.

> Where the jurisdiction of the court first seised is established, any court other than the court first seised shall decline jurisdiction in favour of that court.

This provision has the effect of requiring the court, other than the one first seised, to stay its proceedings of its own motion. The stay will be for a limited period of time and until the court first seised establishes whether or not it has competent jurisdiction over the parties and the cause of action. If so, then any court other than the court first seised has an obligation to decline jurisdiction. The object of Art 21 is to prevent parallel proceedings from taking place in two different Contracting States for the purpose of avoiding the risk of irreconcilable judgments and in the interests of the administration of justice.

Whilst Art 21 applies to concurrent proceedings in Contracting States only, there appears to be no requirement that either party should be domiciled in a Contracting State. Indeed, this was ruled by the ECJ in *Overseas Union Insurance Ltd v New Hampshire Insurance Co* (1992). Here, the defendant, a company incorporated in the USA, carried on business in England and in France. The plaintiffs were three companies, two of which were incorporated in England and the third in Singapore. Following the defendant's initiation of proceedings in France, the plaintiffs sought declarations, relating to their rights against the defendant, from the English court. The Court of Appeal, which was satisfied that the proceedings involved the same parties and the same cause of action within the meaning of Art 21 of the Convention, referred to the ECJ, *inter alia*, the question of whether Article 21 applied where one of the parties is not domiciled within the EC. The ECJ answered this question in the affirmative and ruled that Art 21 applied to any proceedings before a court of a Contracting State, regardless of the parties' domicile.

What is meant by the notion 'the same cause of action'? The ECJ, in *Gubisch Maschinenfabrik v Giulio Palumbo* (1987), whilst ruling that this notion had to be given an independent Community meaning, appears to have attributed a wide interpretation to it. The case concerned a dispute over a contract for the sale of a machine by a German seller to an Italian buyer. The seller brought an action for payment of the price in the German court. The buyer brought an action in the Italian court, seeking the annulment of the contract, and/or rescission of the contract on the basis of delay in the delivery of the machine. The ECJ held that Art 21 extended to a case where one party brought an action in the courts of one Contracting State claiming annulment or rescission of a contract when another action for the enforcement of the contract was simultaneously pending in the courts of another Contracting State. Moreover, in *The Maciej Rataj* (1994), an action seeking to establish the defendant's liability in contract for causing loss to a cargo was held to have the same object as earlier proceedings brought by the defendant and seeking a declaration that he was not liable for that loss.

However, in *Sarrio v KIA* (1997), the Court of Appeal held that a claim for damages based on negligent misrepresentation did not constitute the same cause of action as a claim for sums for non-performance of the contract, despite the fact that both sets of proceedings involved the same parties. (Note that there followed, in this case, an appeal to the House of Lords on the basis of Art 22, which is examined below.) Equally, in *Boss Group v Boss France* (1996), the Court of Appeal held that proceedings of a provisional nature and proceedings adjudicating the merits of the case were not classed as the same cause of action. Additionally, in *Mecklermedia Corpn v DC Congress* (1998), it was held that a claim based on the infringement of a trade mark registration was not the same as a passing off action.

Article 21 also requires that the concurrent proceedings must be between the same parties. This notion was confirmed by the ECJ in *The Maciej Rataj* (1994). Thus, where two sets of proceedings do not involve the same parties, Art 21 cannot come into operation. Indeed, a mere licensee who happens to be working for a company could not be regarded as 'the same party' as that company itself. This was also held in *Mecklermedia Corpn v DC Congress* (1998). However, the ECJ held in *Drouot Assurances v Consolidated Metallurgical Industries* (1998) that, where an insurer, by virtue of its right of subrogation, brings or defends an action in the name of its insured without the latter being in a position to influence the proceedings, the insurer and insured must then be considered to be one and the same party. But the application of Art 21 cannot have the effect of precluding the insurer and the insured, where their interests diverge, from asserting their respective interests before the courts as against the other parties concerned by the proceedings. Whether the interests of the insurer can be considered as identical to and indissociable from those of its insured is for the national courts to ascertain. It is worthy of note that, according to *Dubai Bank Ltd v Abbas* (1998), once the cause of action promoted in the foreign proceedings, even though entirely contingent, is the same as the cause of action promoted in the English proceedings, the court should stay the English proceedings. The same case, however, is also authority for the principle that

Arts 21 and 22 of the Convention do not apply to proceedings in Contracting States concerning the recognition and enforcement of judgments given in civil and commercial matters in non-Contracting States.

Article 21 ascribes priority to the court first 'seised' of proceedings. In *Zelger v Salinitri (No 2)* (1984), the ECJ interpreted the term to require the action to be 'definitively pending'. However, the question of whether a court is 'definitively seised' at the time when the writ is issued or at the time it is served must be determined in accordance with the law of the State to which the court in question belongs. From the information placed before the ECJ in this case, it appeared that in all six original Member States (that is, Belgium, France, Germany, Italy, Luxembourg and the Netherlands), a court would only be definitively seised when the writ was served. In relation to England, the Court of Appeal, in *Neste Chemicals SA v DK Line (The Sargasso)* (1994), ruled that an English court became 'seised' of proceedings on service of the writ and not on granting provisional measures such as the Mareva injunction.

The Convention is silent as to the problem of concurrent proceedings pending before the courts of a Contracting State and the courts of a non-Contracting State. There has been no ECJ ruling on this point, but it is suggested that national courts might be inclined to apply the pre-existing rules of jurisdiction to such a situation.

Article 22 of the Convention allows a court to stay its proceedings where the cause of action, not the same but related, is pending in another State first seised of the matter. By virtue of Art 22(3), 'related proceedings' are proceedings which are closely connected so that it is expedient to hear them together to avoid the risk of irreconcilable judgments resulting from separate proceedings. It must be noted in this context that, because Art 21 has been given a wide interpretation, the importance of Art 22 has been greatly reduced. The meaning of the concept 'related actions' has been considered in a number of cases. For instance, in *Sarrio v KIA* (1998), the House of Lords held that there should be a broad common sense approach to the question of whether actions are related, bearing in mind the objective of Art 22, applying the simple wide test set out in that Article, and refraining from an over-sophisticated analysis of the matter. Thus, a claim based on negligent misrepresentation and one for sums for non-performance of the contract were 'related actions' within the meaning of Art 22, since the same allegations about the role of the defendant in the negotiations for the sale of the plaintiff's business underpinned the litigation in both jurisdictions and raised a risk of irreconcilable judgments. Furthermore, in *Blue Nile Shipping Co Ltd v Iguana Shipping and Finance Inc* (1992), two vessels, *The Darfur* and *The Happy Fellow*, travelling in opposite directions, collided in the River Seine. The owners of *The Happy Fellow* arrested *The Darfur* in Rouen and then commenced proceedings in France, claiming damages. The charterers of *The Darfur* brought an action against its owners in the English court, claiming damages for breach of the charterparty and other relief in respect of the collision. The owners of *The Darfur* instituted limitation proceedings in the same court. Subsequently, a claimant in the collision proceedings in France applied to the English court for a stay of its proceedings on the grounds that the limitation proceedings were related to those brought in France within the meaning of Art 22 of the Convention. The Court of Appeal held that the two actions were related so that, if the English action were not stayed, there was a real risk of irreconcilable judgments. However, in *Mecklermedia Corpn v DC Congress* (1998), the action in the English court was for passing off, and the action in the German court was for the infringement of the German trade mark registration; these were held to be not related, in that there was no risk of irreconcilable judgments.

Article 23 of the Convention applies where two Contracting States have exclusive jurisdiction over the same dispute. The court first seised has jurisdiction.

A question arises at this stage as to the relationship between Art 17 and Art 21 of the Convention. Suppose that the parties had agreed in their contract to refer their dispute to the jurisdiction of the English court. Contrary to this agreement, one of the parties commenced proceedings in the Greek court. The other party then brought an action in the English court in accordance with the jurisdiction agreement. If Art 21 were to prevail, then the English proceedings would have to be stayed. Conversely, if Art 17 were to prevail, then the Greek proceedings would have to be stayed. There is no ECJ ruling on this point yet, but the English court of Appeal took the view, in *Continental Bank v Aeokos Cia Naviera SA* (1994), that Art 17 prevailed over Arts 21 and 22. It was held that the court had power, by virtue of an exclusive jurisdiction clause in favour of the English courts, to grant an injunction restraining a group of borrowers and guarantors from bringing legal proceeding in another Contracting State, namely Greece. Even though the court first seised of the proceedings was the Greek court, the Court of Appeal stated that Art 17 of the Brussels Convention applied in this case, to take precedence over the provisions of Arts 21 and 22. Furthermore, there was nothing in the Convention which was inconsistent with a power vesting in the English court to grant an injunction, the objective of which was to secure enforcement of an exclusive jurisdiction agreement.

3.12 Jurisdiction within the UK: the Modified Convention

Section 16 of the CJJA 1982 allocates jurisdiction within the UK. This is set out in Sched 4 to the Act and it applies a modified form of the provisions on jurisdiction in the Brussels Convention. According to s 16, the modified rules apply if the following three conditions are satisfied:

(a) the issue must concern allocation of jurisdiction within the UK;

(b) the subject matter of the proceedings must be within the scope of the 1968 Convention; and

(c) the defendant must be domiciled in the UK, or the dispute must come within the scope of Art 16 of the Convention.

The most important modifications of substance are as follows:

(a) Art 5(3) provides an additional ground of 'special' jurisdiction in relation to 'threatened wrongs', which gives jurisdiction to the courts of the part of the UK where the threatened wrong is likely to occur;

(b) a new Art 5(8) allocates jurisdiction in relation to, inter alia, proceedings to enforce debts secured on immovable property. The courts of the part of the UK in which the property is situated shall have jurisdiction;

(c) a new Art 5A deals with certain company law matters and confers jurisdiction on the courts of that part of the UK in which the company has its seat;

(d) there is no specific provision for insurance contracts;

(e) Art 13, which applies to consumer contracts, excludes the references to advertising;

(f) Art 17 is modified so as to exclude the requirement of 'writing' in relation to jurisdiction agreements; and finally

(g) the provisions relating to *lis alibi pendens* and related actions are omitted.

JURISDICTION OF THE ENGLISH COURT IN COMMERCIAL DISPUTES: THE BRUSSELS AND LUGANO CONVENTIONS

Where the defendant is domiciled within the EC/EFTA, the English court must ignore the traditional common law rules and assume jurisdiction in accordance with the provisions of either the Brussels Convention or the Lugano Convention.

As a general basis of jurisdiction, the essential criterion is the domicile of the defendant. The courts of the Contracting State in which the defendant is domiciled will have jurisdiction to entertain a dispute within the scope of the Conventions.

Alternative bases of jurisdiction are provided by virtue of the provisions on special jurisdiction, that is, in relation to contract, tort, maintenance, etc. In such cases, the plaintiff is given a choice, to bring his action either in the courts of the Member State where the defendant is domiciled, or in the courts of the Member State designated by those provisions.

Specific provisions on jurisdiction are adopted in the Conventions for the purposes of protecting the weaker party to the contract in certain specific matters. These relate to individual contracts of employment (Arts 5(1) and 17(5)); insurance contracts (Arts 7–12A); and certain consumer contracts (Arts 13–15).

This is so unless the provisions on exclusive jurisdiction under Art 16 come into operation. The effect of such basis of jurisdiction is that the designated courts of the Contracting State shall have exclusive jurisdiction and the courts of the defendant domicile will have to decline jurisdiction. Such exclusive jurisdiction applies in relation to issues of immovable property, companies and associations, intellectual property, enforcement of judgments, etc.

Additionally, and subject to Art 16, further provisions for exclusive jurisdiction apply in relation to jurisdiction agreements and a defendant's submission to the jurisdiction of a Member State other than that of his domicile. Art 17 states that the designated court shall have exclusive jurisdiction, provided that the jurisdiction agreement satisfies certain requirements, and so long as it is not inconsistent with Art 16.

The Convention makes provision for *lis alibi pendens* and related actions under Arts 21 and 22 thereof. In effect, the courts first seised of the action have priority over the question of jurisdiction.

An exclusive jurisdiction clause in favour of the English court between the parties under Art 17 has been held to allow that court to grant an injunction against a plaintiff who, in contravention of this agreement, had brought proceedings in the court of another Contracting State.

In relation to jurisdiction within the UK, s 16 of the CJJA 1982 applies similar, but slightly modified, provisions of the Brussels Convention.

CHAPTER 4

RECOGNITION AND ENFORCEMENT OF FOREIGN JUDGMENTS

4.1   Introduction

Suppose that a plaintiff brings an action against a defendant in the court of New York, claiming breach of contract. He obtains a judgment for damages, but only tzo discover that the judgment cannot be satisfied in New York because the defendant has removed all his assets to England. The question arises as to whether the plaintiff can enforce the New York judgment in England, or whether he has to bring fresh proceedings against the defendant there. The basic rule is that, due to the doctrine of territorial sovereignty, a judgment delivered in one country cannot be directly recognised or enforced in another unless there exists an international agreement between the two countries in question. Nevertheless, English law has long allowed the recognition or enforcement of a foreign judgment in England, provided that the judgment meets certain requirements.

Due to the UK's accession to both the Brussels and Lugano Conventions, there are currently two sets of rules in relation to recognition and enforcement of foreign judgments, depending on where the judgment in question was rendered. If it was rendered within EC/EFTA States and related to a civil or commercial matter, then the issue would be exclusively governed by the Civil Jurisdiction and Judgments Acts 1982 and 1991 (CJJA). However, if the judgment was rendered outside those States, then the traditional rules would apply. Matters are complicated further by the fact that the traditional law rules comprise three sets of rules. There are those rules which govern judgments of courts of Commonwealth countries to which the Administration of Justice Act 1920 applies, and those which govern judgments of courts of other countries to which the Foreign Judgments (Reciprocal Enforcement) Act 1933 (FJA) applies, and those of the common law which apply to judgments of courts of other countries.

Before moving on to examine both the traditional rules, which include the 1920 and 1933 Acts respectively, and the Brussels and Lugano Conventions rules, it is worth illustrating the distinction between recognition and enforcement. Whilst a foreign judgment must be recognised before it can be enforced, not every recognised judgment need be enforced. Recognition simply means that the English courts take note of the result of the judgment. Hence, if English law recognises a foreign divorce decree, this simply means that it will consider the couple as unmarried. However, there may be an order ancillary to such a decree which may be capable of enforcement, such as an order that the husband should pay maintenance to the wife.

It should be noted that there are special rules on the recognition of foreign matrimonial judgments which are not within the scope of this chapter. These rules will be examined in the context of family law below, in Chapter 11.

4.2 Recognition and enforcement at common law

At common law, foreign judgments have been recognised and enforced by English courts since the 17th century. This was initially based on the ground of comity. However, this theory has been superseded by the 'doctrine of obligation', which was stated in *Schibsby v Westenholz* (1870) in the following terms:

> ... the true principle on which the judgments of foreign tribunals are enforced in England is ... that the judgment of a court of competent jurisdiction over the defendant imposes a duty or obligation on the defendant to pay the sum for which judgment is given, which the courts in this country are bound to enforce; and consequently that anything which negatives that duty, or forms a legal excuse for not performing it, is a defence to the action.

In other words, once a court of competent jurisdiction has rendered a judgment for a sum to be paid by the defendant, this sum becomes a legal obligation which may be enforced in England by an action for the debt. Consequently, the burden lies on the defendant to prove to the English court why he or she should be excused from performing this obligation.

Prior to the coming into force of the CJJA 1982, a plaintiff, who obtained a foreign judgment for a debt and the judgment could not be satisfied where it was rendered, had the option of either bringing an action in England for the debt, or bringing fresh proceedings against the defendant on the original cause of action. This latter option, however, has been abolished by s 34 of the CJJA 1982, which provides that:

> No proceedings may be brought by a person in England and Wales ... on a cause of action in respect of which a judgment has been given in his favour in proceedings between the same parties or their privies, in a court in another part of the United Kingdom or in a court of an overseas country, unless that judgment is not enforceable or entitled to recognition in England and Wales.

Hence, if a foreign judgment is entitled to recognition or is enforceable in the English courts, then according to s 34, the plaintiff has to sue on the foreign judgment rather than bring fresh proceedings on the original cause of action. This is so, irrespective of whether the foreign judgment is entitled to recognition or enforcement at common law, by statute, or under the Brussels or Lugano Conventions. The application of s 34 can be seen in the recent case of *Republic of India v India Steamship Co Ltd* (1998), wherein the plaintiff brought an action in India, claiming short delivery of a cargo of munitions which was shipped from Sweden to India. During transit, a fire occurred in the hold and caused a number of shells and charges to jettison. The plaintiff was successful at first instance in India, but an appeal was still pending at the time of the English proceedings. During the Indian proceedings at first instance, the plaintiff commenced an action *in rem* in the English courts. The defendants argued that the latter claim was excluded by virtue of s 34 of the CJJA 1982, which acted as an absolute bar to English proceedings brought on a cause of action on which judgment had been given by an overseas court. The House of Lords held that, where proceedings in England were commenced before judgment had been given in the court of an overseas country, but are continued after judgment, those proceedings could naturally be described as brought on a cause if action in respect of which a judgment had been given within the meaning of s 34.

4.2.1 Requirements for recognition and enforcement

At common law, a successful litigant seeking to enforce a foreign judgment in England has to institute fresh legal proceedings, that is, he or she must sue on the obligation created by the judgment. Alternatively, he or she may plead the judgment *res judicata* in any proceedings which raise the same issue. If a fresh action is brought in England, he or she can apply for summary judgment under RSC Ord 14, so long as the defendant has no defence to the claim as was held by *Grant v Easton* (1883). This is so, provided that the action in England satisfies the English rules as to jurisdiction and service of writs.

The above provisions are reinforced by statutory rules which operate a slightly more direct process of registration of foreign judgments. The two most important statutes are the Administration of Justice Act 1920 (AJA) and the FJA 1933. Section 13 of the AJA 1920 provides for the enforcement, by registration within the UK, of judgments obtained in a superior court of any part of the Commonwealth party to the Act. Basically, according to s 9(1), a person who has obtained a judgment in any part of the Commonwealth may apply, within 12 months, to the High Court to have the judgment registered. Registration, however, is discretionary and not as of right, since the registering court can refuse the application unless 'in all the circumstances of the case ... [it] thinks it just and convenient that the judgment should be enforced in the United Kingdom'.

This policy of facilitating the direct enforcement of foreign judgments received further progress by the FJA 1933, which applies the principle of registration to countries of the Commonwealth as well as to politically foreign countries. This Act, although drafted in much more detail, applies provisions similar to those of the AJA 1920. However, by the virtue of s 2 of the FJA 1933, a successful litigant may apply to the High Court for the registration of a foreign judgment at any time within six years, and no discretion is given to the High Court, which *shall* order the judgment to be registered, provided it complies with the other provisions of this Act. Both the AJA 1920 and FJA 1933, however, rely very much on reciprocity and, consequently, a foreign judgment is not registrable within the UK unless the provisions of the Acts extend by Order in Council to the country in which the judgment has been obtained.

As both the AJA 1920 and FJA 1933 are restricted in scope and limited to geographical boundaries, the common law rules are still extensively relevant. Moreover, whilst the provisions of both Acts tend to reproduce the common law closely, there remain diverging differences in a few detailed rules, which will be examined as and when necessary.

In general, recognition or enforcement of foreign judgments may not be allowed if the foreign court acted without competent jurisdiction, or if the defendant can avail himself or herself of any of the limited number of defences available.

4.2.2 Jurisdiction of the foreign court

The most essential requirement for recognising or enforcing foreign judgments in England, whether at common law or under both the AJA 1920 and FJA 1933, is that the foreign court which rendered the judgment in question had jurisdiction in the international sense to entertain the action. In other words, the English court would not effect a foreign judgment unless the foreign court was jurisdictionally competent according to the English conflict of laws rules. Buckley LJ, in an often cited *obiter* in *Emanuel v Symon* (1908), stated (p 309):

> In actions *in personam*, there are five cases in which the courts of this country will enforce a foreign judgment: (1) where the defendant is a subject of the foreign country in which the judgment has been obtained; (2) where he was resident in the foreign country when the action began; (3) where the defendant in the character of plaintiff has selected the forum in which he is afterwards sued; (4) where he has voluntarily appeared; and (5) where he has contracted to submit himself to the forum in which the judgment was obtained.

In relation to the first case mentioned in the above statement, the nationality of the defendant can no longer be relied upon to justify the jurisdiction of the foreign court. Indeed, nationality as a basis of jurisdiction has been doubted by Diplock J in *Blohn v Desser* (1962), by McNair J in *Rossano v Manufacturers Life Insurance Ltd* (1963), and by Ashworth J in *Vogel v R and A Kohnstamm Ltd* (1973) respectively.

The second case stated by Buckley LJ relates to residence, which is the most common basis for jurisdiction in this context. Finally, the last three cases come under the umbrella of submission, which is another basis for jurisdiction. Nevertheless, whatever the basis of jurisdiction is, according to *Adams v Cape Industries plc* (1990) the onus of proof lies on the plaintiff seeking to enforce the judgment of a foreign court.

4.2.3 Residence

It is a well settled principle that the residence of the defendant in the foreign country when the action began is a sufficient ground for jurisdiction. Although the term residence has been used in numerous case law and it appears in s 4(2)(a)(iv) of the FJA 1933, it is not precisely defined. Clearly, residence includes physical presence, but whether presence alone will suffice is doubtful. However, there has been some support for this principle in *Carrick v Hancock* (1895), and more recently in *Adams v Cape Industries plc* (1990), where the Court of Appeal took the view that 'the voluntary presence of an individual in a foreign country, whether permanent or temporary and whether or not accompanied by residence, is sufficient to give the courts of that country territorial jurisdiction over him under our rules of private international law'. However, to base jurisdiction on the casual presence within the foreign jurisdiction may not be very desirable, since though it remains a basis for English jurisdiction, the English rules on jurisdiction operate in conjunction with the doctrine of *forum non conveniens*. Nevertheless, one may safely state that there has been no single decision reported in which the English court declined to enforce a foreign judgment by reason only that the defendant was merely present, but not resident, within the jurisdiction of the foreign court.

In relation to a corporate defendant, there seems to be no doubt that there must be a fixed place of business within the jurisdiction of the foreign country, and from which the corporation operates. The test was set out by the Court of Appeal in *Adams v Cape Industries plc* (1990) (p 530). It has to be shown that:

(a) [the corporation] has established and maintained at its own expense (whether as owner or lessee) a fixed place of business of its own in the other country, and for more than a minimal period of time has carried on its own business at, or from, such premises by its servants or agents (a 'branch office' case); or

(b) a representative of the overseas corporation has, for more than a minimal period of time, been carrying on *the overseas corporation's* business in the other country at, or from, some fixed place of business.

In relation to the second requirement, if business is carried on by a representative, then the question whether he or she has been carrying on the overseas corporation's business, or has been doing no more than carry on his or her own business, will necessitate an examination of his or her functions and all aspects of his or her relationship with the overseas corporation. This is likely to involve such questions as the acquisition of business premises, reimbursement of costs and expenses, contributions by the overseas corporation, method of payment (whether by commission or regular wages), degree of control by the overseas corporation and display of the overseas corporation's name, and whether the representative has power to bind the corporation contractually. The fact that he or she never makes contracts, whether with or without prior approval, in the name of the overseas corporation so as to bind it, is a powerful factor pointing against presence.

In the *Adams* case, the Court of Appeal applied the above principles to the situation where the overseas corporation carried on business through its subsidiary in the USA. It was held that a subsidiary normally acted for itself and not for the overseas parent corporation, especially since, in this case, the subsidiary had no power to (and never did) bind the parent corporation contractually. Parent and subsidiary are to be treated as separate legal entities.

The AJA 1920 appears to apply the same criteria as that applied under the common law. For instance, in *Sfeir v National Insurance Co of New Zealand Ltd* (1964), the defendants, a New Zealand company, who were allegedly carrying on business in Ghana through an appointed agent, contended that the English court should decline to enforce a judgment obtained against them in the courts of Ghana on the ground, *inter alia*, that they were not resident in Ghana when the action began, in accordance with s 9(2) of the AJA 1920. Mocatta J held that, although the defendants had business carried on by their agent in Ghana, such business was the agent's own business and not that of the defendants, since the former only carried on minor tasks on the defendants' behalf as well as business for other companies.

As far as the FJA 1933 is concerned, s 4(2)(a)(iv) requires that the corporation must have its 'principal' place of business in the foreign country.

4.2.4 Submission

Submission to a foreign court's jurisdiction may be effected in various ways. The first and most obvious way is when a person voluntarily invokes the jurisdiction of the foreign court. This may take the form of either bringing the action as a plaintiff, or making a counterclaim or cross-action as a defendant. In this situation, he or she renders himself or herself liable to a judgment of the foreign court, and he or she cannot afterwards, if sued upon the judgment in England, contend that the foreign court did not have jurisdiction. This was held in *Schibsby v Westenholz* (1870) and is stipulated in s 4(2)(a)(ii) of the FJA 1933. Similarly, where the defendant voluntarily appears in the foreign court, he or she is taken to have submitted to the jurisdiction if he or she pleaded to the merits of the case, regardless of the fact that the defendant also contested the jurisdiction (see also s 4(2)(a)(i) of the FJA 1933). However, if the defendant appeared before the foreign court merely to protest against the jurisdiction of that court, it is now a settled principle, by virtue of s 33 of the CJJA 1982, that he or she will not be regarded as having submitted to the jurisdiction. Section 33 provides that:

> (1) For the purpose of determining whether a judgment given by a court of an overseas country should be recognised or enforced ... the person against whom the judgment was given shall not be regarded as having submitted

to the jurisdiction of the court by reason only of the fact that he appeared (conditionally or otherwise) in the proceedings for all or any one or more of the following purposes, namely:

    (a) to contest the jurisdiction of the court;

    (b) to ask the court to dismiss or stay the proceedings on the ground that the dispute in question should be submitted to arbitration or to the determination of the courts of another country;

    (c) to protect, or obtain the release of, property seized or threatened with seizure in the proceedings.

(2) Nothing in this section shall affect the recognition or enforcement ... of a judgment which is required to be recognised or enforced ... under the 1968 Convention or the Lugano Convention.

(Section 33(2) was amended by the CJJA 1991 so as to include the phrase 'Lugano Convention'.)

Section 33 only applies to a judgment rendered by the courts of an overseas country. It does not make a distinction between enforcement and recognition at common law or by statute. In relation to enforcement under the FJA 1933, s 33 of the CJJA 1982 replaced the similarly worded provision of s 4(2)(a)(i) of the FJA 1933. One restriction, however, is that s 33 remains subject to both the Brussels and Lugano Conventions.

The provision of s 33 has the impact of reversing the Court of Appeal decision in *Henry v Geoprosco International Ltd* (1976). Here, the plaintiff brought an action in England to enforce, at common law, a judgment obtained from the court of Alberta. That judgment was for breach of contract which was governed by English law and which contained an arbitration clause. The defendant was neither resident in Alberta, nor carried on business there. When served with the writ, the defendant appeared in the Alberta court and argued that the service of the writ should be set aside on the ground that Alberta was not *forum conveniens*, and that a stay of the proceedings should be granted due to the arbitration clause in the contract. Both arguments failed and the defendant took no further part in the proceedings. However, the Court of Appeal held that the judgment given by the Alberta court was enforceable in England; and that where the defendant had asked the court to exercise its discretion to decline jurisdiction by staying the action or to decline to assume a jurisdiction which it had under local law, the defendant would be taken to have submitted thereto.

The meaning and application of s 33 was examined in the recent case of *Chief Harry Akande v Balfour Beatty Construction Ltd* (1998), wherein the plaintiff had obtained a judgment in Nigeria, for which registration under s 20 of the AJA was secured in England. The defendant sought to have the registration set aside on the grounds that it did not submit to the Nigerian jurisdiction within the meaning of s 33 of the CJJA 1982. It was held that the law applicable in the foreign court on the significance of a conditional appearance was irrelevant, since the test to be applied in English courts in relation to submission was to be found in s 33. However, s 33 was not an exhaustive test of what did not amount to submission to the jurisdiction of the foreign court. The appropriate test was whether the party alleged to have waived his or her other objection had taken some step which was only necessary or only useful if the objection had been actually waived, or if the objection had never been entertained.

Another way of submission is where there is an agreement which provides that all disputes between the parties shall be referred to the exclusive jurisdiction of the foreign court in question. This may also take the form of an agreement to accept service of process at a designated address.

In general, an agreement to submit disputes to the jurisdiction of a foreign court must be express rather than implied. Moreover, it was held in *Dunbee Ltd v Gilman and Co (Australia) Pty Ltd* (1968) that, if the parties agreed that disputes under their contract shall be governed by the law of a particular foreign country, it could be inferred that their dispute was also subject to the jurisdiction of the courts of that country.

4.3 Further requirements for enforcement

A foreign judgment *in personam*, albeit rendered by a court having competent jurisdiction according to the English conflict of laws rules, will not be enforced in England unless it meets certain requirements. These requirements vary, depending on whether the application for enforcement is based on the common law rules, the AJA 1920 or the FJA 1933.

4.3.1 At common law

In order for a foreign judgment to be enforced at common law, it must be: (a) for a fixed sum of money; (b) final and conclusive; (c) on the merits; and (d) not a judgment in relation to foreign revenue, penal or other public laws.

(a) An action brought by a plaintiff to enforce a foreign judgment in England, which is considered as an action based on a debt, must be for a fixed sum. Otherwise, the English court will refuse to enforce it. For instance, in *Sadler v Robins* (1808), where a court in Jamaica had held that the defendant was to pay the sum of £3,670 1s 9d to the plaintiff, but subject to the full costs expended by the defendant as taxed by a master of the court to be deducted therefrom, the English court held that the judgment could not be enforced since, until taxation, the sum due remained indefinite. The same principle was held to apply in relation to a foreign maintenance order by instalments, where the foreign court can vary the instalments payable. However, if the foreign court has no power to vary the amount for past instalments, then the arrears can be recovered in England. Similarly, following *Beatty v Beatty* (1924), this requirement is satisfied where the debt can be ascertained by a simple arithmetical process. It follows that a plaintiff cannot enforce a foreign judgment for specific performance, injunctions or any judgment which orders the defendant to do more than pay a certain amount of money.

(b) The foreign judgment must be final and conclusive. If the case can be re-opened in the same court, or if there remain some issues to be dealt with, then the English court will not enforce the judgment. This can be illustrated by the House of Lords decision in *Nouvion v Freeman* (1889). Here, the plaintiff in the original action had sold certain land to the defendant. He brought summary proceedings in Spain against the defendant and obtained a *remate* judgment for a sum of money. Under this type of proceedings, as opposed to ordinary *plenary* proceedings, a Spanish court, on proof of a *prima facie* case, made an order for the attachment of the defendant's property without giving notice to the defendant before the order was made. Notice of this order was given to the defendant, and he was at liberty to appear and defend the action on a limited number of grounds, but he could not set up any defence to deny the validity of the transaction which he was sued upon. By Spanish law, if any of the party failed in this action, that party could institute plenary/ordinary proceedings before the same judge and then could use every available defence. The House of Lords held that this *remate* action could not be enforced in England, since it was liable to be abrogated by the adjudicating court. However, if the foreign judgment is subject to an appeal, this will not render the judgment unenforceable, although a stay of the English proceedings would be ordered pending the outcome of the appeal. This was said to be the case in *Colt Industries Inc v Sarlie (No 2)* (1966)).

(c) The foreign judgment must be on its merits. In *The Sennar (No 2)* (1985), Brandon LJ elaborated on the meaning of this notion. He stated that (p 499):

[A] decision on the merits is a decision which establishes certain facts proved or not in dispute, states what are the relevant principles of law applicable to such facts, and expresses a conclusion with regard to the effect of applying those principles to the factual situation concerned.

A foreign judgment on the merits can be used as a defence against proceedings in England. This is known as estoppel, which can take two forms: cause of action estoppel and issue estoppel. Cause of action estoppel is used as a defence where the plaintiff attempts to sue on the same cause of action in England as that which has been determined by the foreign court. Issue estoppel, on the other hand, is where the plaintiff to the English proceedings, albeit the cause of action is different, is prevented from raising a particular issue which had been decided by a foreign court.

(d) For a foreign judgment to be enforced in England, it must not be for foreign revenue, penal or other public laws. Hence, the English court will not enforce a foreign judgment ordering the payment of taxes or penalties (see *Huntington v Attrill* (1893) and *Rossano v Manufacturers Life Insurance Co Ltd* (1963)). However, the English court will enforce a foreign compensation order made by a criminal court for the benefit of a victim; for instance, in *Raulin v Fischer* (1911), where the defendant, an American lady, while recklessly riding her horse in France, seriously injured the plaintiff. She was prosecuted for her criminal negligence by the French authorities. The plaintiff intervened in the proceedings and made a claim for damages, as allowed under French law. On an action by the plaintiff to enforce the compensation order, the English court held that the French judgment was severable. The compensation order, although combined with a penal judgment, was actionable in England as creating a separate cause of action, and was, therefore, enforceable.

Moreover, in *SA Consortium General Textiles v Sun and Sand Agencies Ltd* (1978), a case under the FJA 1933, in which the defendant raised an objection against the enforcement of part of a French judgment for the sum of FFr10,000, which was awarded on the basis of the defendant's unjustifiable opposition to the plaintiff's claim. The objection was based on the ground that this sum was for punitive or exemplary damages and, therefore, a penalty. The Court of Appeal rejected this argument and Lord Denning MR stated that the 'word penalty ... means a sum payable to the State by way of punishment and not a sum payable to a private individual, even though it is payable by way of exemplary damages'.

If the judgment of the foreign court is one which that court had jurisdiction to give, the English court will not otherwise inquire into the grounds of the decision. For instance, in *Godard v Gray* (1870), the plaintiffs, who were Frenchmen, sued the defendants, who were Englishmen, on a charterparty in the French court. The proper law of the charterparty was designated to be English law. The charterparty contained a clause which stated: 'Penalty for non-performance of this agreement estimated amount of freight.' Under English law, such a clause did not have the effect of specifying the exact amount of damages, but instead, such damages would be assessed according to the actual loss suffered. However, the French court gave the language of this clause a literal interpretation and assessed the damages at the exact amount of freight. The English court rejected the defendants' plea, that the French court was mistaken in its assessment of damages, on the ground that it would not inquire into the merits of the foreign judgment.

The same principle has been applied in relation to the recognition of foreign arbitral awards. For example, in *Dallal v Bank Mellat* (1986), the English court held that an arbitration award made in The Netherlands in favour of the defendant was entitled to be recognised as binding, and consequently the English court refused to go into the merits of the award.

4.3.2 Administration of Justice Act 1920

A person who has obtained a judgment in a *superior* court of any part of the Commonwealth (s 13), may, within 12 months, apply to the High Court in England or Northern Ireland, or the Court of Session in Scotland, for its registration, provided that it is for a fixed sum of money (s 12). Registration of a judgment is not as of right, but discretionary (s 9(1) and (2)). A judgment registered under the AJA 1920 has the same force and effect as if it had been rendered by the registering court (s 9(3)).

However, a judgment may not be registered if an appeal is pending, or if the defendant is entitled and intends to appeal (s 9(2)(e)). By virtue of s 9(5), a plaintiff remains free to bring his or her action on the foreign judgment under the common law rules. However, if he or she chooses to do so, then he or she will not usually be able to recover the costs.

The AJA 1920 is based on reciprocity, which means that a foreign judgment is not rendered registrable within the UK unless the provisions of the Act have been extended by Order in Council to the country in which the judgment has been obtained. The Order in Council will not be made unless Her Majesty is satisfied that provisions have been made by the country in question for the enforcement there of UK judgments (s 14 as amended by s 35(3) of the CJJA 1982).

4.3.3 Foreign Judgments (Reciprocal Enforcement) Act 1933

The FJA 1933 was intended to replace gradually the AJA 1920. With this object in mind, s 7 of the FJA 1933 provides the Crown with the power to make an Order in Council to extend the application of the Act to any Commonwealth country, preventing in this way the further extension of the AJA 1920. However, the FJA 1933 does not substitute the AJA 1920. In other words, it does not automatically apply to any Commonwealth country party to the AJA 1920; for that to be done a further specific Order in Council is required. The FJA 1933 applies the principle of registration, not only to the Commonwealth, but also to foreign countries.

The FJA 1933 also operates on reciprocity. A creditor of a judgment, rendered in a foreign country to which the Act has been extended, may apply to the High Court in England or Northern Ireland, or to the Court of Session in Scotland at any time within *six years* of the date of the judgment, to have it registered in that court. Unlike the AJA 1920, the court has no discretion and must order the judgment to be registered, provided that it satisfies the requirements of the Act (s 2). The Act applies to any judgment of a court and, unlike the AJA 1920, the judgment does not have to be delivered by a superior court, provided that it is for a sum of money, final and conclusive, and not rendered in respect of taxes or penalties (s 1(2A) added by s 35(1) and Sched 10, para 1 of the CJJA 1982). A judgment is considered final and conclusive although an appeal against it is pending (s 1(3)). However, by virtue of s 5, the court has a discretionary power to set aside the registration or to adjourn the application, if it is satisfied that an appeal is pending or that the defendant is entitled and intends to appeal. Moreover, according to s 4(1)(b), a registration may be set aside if the registering court is satisfied that there is a previous final and conclusive judgment on the same cause of action which was rendered prior to the foreign judgment in question by a court having competent jurisdiction. Unlike the AJA 1920, s 6 of the FJA 1933 prevents the party seeking enforcement from bringing an action in England on the foreign judgment.

4.3.4 Restrictions

All the above instances are subject to s 5 of the Protection of Trading Interests Act 1980, which provides that a court in the UK cannot enforce a judgment for multiple damages. That is, a judgment 'for an amount arrived at by doubling, trebling or otherwise multiplying a sum assessed as compensation for the loss or damage sustained by the person in whose favour the judgment is given'. Neither can a court in the UK enforce any judgment specified by the Secretary of State as being concerned with the prohibition of restrictive trade practices. Clearly, the reference to multiple damages seems to target US anti-trust laws. This prohibition applies whether a judgment creditor is seeking to enforce a foreign judgment at common law, under the AJA 1920, or under the FJA 1933. Section 5 does not, however, apply in the context of the Brussels Convention or the Lugano Convention.

4.4 Defences

There are a number of defences which the defendant can raise in order to escape liability for the foreign judgment. When considering these defences below and unless otherwise stated, it is to be assumed that they may be raised at common law, in the context of the AJA 1920, or in relation to the FJA 1933. The defences which a defendant may plead are as follows.

4.4.1 Fraud

It is a well established rule that a foreign judgment, like any other judgment, may be refused recognition or enforcement upon proof that it was obtained by fraud. Such fraud may take various forms. It may be that the foreign court itself has acted in a fraudulent manner, as in *Price v Dewhurst* (1837), or it may be that the successful party had produced forged evidence or had kept from the foreign court vital evidence, or it may be that he or she bribed the foreign court.

If fraud is alleged by the defendant, the question arises as to whether the English court will go into the merits of the action which led to the foreign judgment in the absence of fresh evidence. The Court of Appeal, in no less than four instances, upheld the view that no fresh evidence is required. In *Abouloff v Oppenheimer* (1882), Lord Esher said (p 306):

> I will assume that in the suit in the Russian courts the plaintiff's fraud was alleged by the defendants and that they gave evidence in support of the charge ... that the defendants gave the very same evidence which they propose to adduce in this action; nevertheless, the defendants will not be debarred at the trial of this action from making the same charge of fraud and from adducing the same evidence in support of it.

Similarly, in *Vadala v Lawes* (1890), the Court of Appeal unanimously held that, even if an allegation of fraud was fully considered by the foreign court prior to rendering its judgment, this would not stop the English court from investigating the same allegation again. Also, in *Syal v Heyward* (1948), the same principle was applied, although the plaintiff deliberately refrained from raising the issue of fraud in the original action.

The above decisions were approved and followed in two more recent cases, *Jet Holdings Inc v Patel* (1990) and *Owens Banks Ltd v Bracco* (1992). In the latter case, which concerned registration of a foreign judgment under the AJA 1920, the House of Lords treated all the above cases as binding and held that, in relation to fraud, the enforcement of a foreign judgment, unlike the enforcement of an English one, did not require fresh evidence before the case could be re-opened. However, the Court of Appeal decision in *House of Spring Gardens Ltd v Waite* (1991), which required the defendant to produce fresh evidence, was distinguished on the ground that the issue of fraud had been tried in Ireland in a separate and second action from the original one. Accordingly, in this case, the judgment of the second action created an estoppel, and unless fresh evidence of fraud was obtained, the original action could not be re-opened.

Finally, although the *Owens* case was brought under the provisions of the AJA 1920, Lord Bridge, with whom the other Lords concurred, indicated that both s 9(2)(d) of the 1920 Act and s 4(1)(a)(iv) of the FJA 1933 incorporated the concept of fraud from the common law and, therefore, they bore the same interpretation. He felt, however, that the concept of fraud needed to be updated so as to take into consideration the changed circumstances of the 1990s, but that to alter the common law rule without altering the statutory rules would result in anomalies, and this was out of the question.

4.4.2   Contrary to natural justice

At common law, a foreign judgment may be refused recognition or enforcement if the proceedings were opposed to natural justice. Although the limits of this defence are not clear, when applied in the context of foreign judgments, it concerns alleged irregularities in the procedure by which the foreign court reached its judgment and does not extend to the merits of the case. For many years, it has been held that the defence may be invoked if the defendant was not given due notice of the proceedings or was denied a proper opportunity to be heard (see *Jacobson v Frachon* (1927)). However, subsequently, in the case of *Adams v Cape Industries plc* (1990), the Court of Appeal held that the concept of natural justice extended to any situation which would amount to a breach of the English court's views of 'substantial justice', such as an absence of a judicial determination of damages. More recently, the Supreme Court of Bermuda held that it was contrary to natural justice to require a defendant in the original proceedings to put up, as a condition of defending, a security he or she could not meet (*Muhl v Adra Insurance Co Ltd* (1997)).

In relation to both the AJA 1920 and the FJA 1933, neither of them provides for such a defence. Section 9(2)(c) of the AJA 1920 provides that an application to register a foreign judgment may be declined if the defendant was not duly served or did not appear in the original proceedings, and s 4(1)(a)(iii) of the FJA 1933 provides that the registration of a foreign judgment must be set aside if the defendant in the original proceedings did not receive notice of the proceedings in sufficient time to enable him or her to defend the case and did not appear therein.

4.4.3 Contrary to public policy

A foreign judgment will neither be recognised nor enforced in England if it is contrary to the English principles of public policy. In *Re Macartney* (1921), a maintenance order was made in the Maltese court against a man domiciled in England. The order was to provide maintenance for his illegitimate daughter, who was born in Malta. The English court refused to enforce this order on the grounds, *inter alia*, of public policy, in the sense that English law did not at the time allow for such a maintenance order in favour of an illegitimate child to be enforced against its father or his estate. According to *Israel Discount Bank of New York v Hadjipateras* (1984), the concept of public policy is wide enough to embrace undue influence, duress and coercion. Public policy provisions are also made under s 9(2)(f) of the AJA 1920 and s 4(1)(a)(v) of the FJA 1933.

4.4.4 Section 32 of the Civil Jurisdiction and Judgments Act 1982

An additional and important defence which may be invoked, irrespective of whether recognition or enforcement is sought at common law or under statute, was introduced by s 32 of the CJJA 1982. However, this section does not affect judgments required to be recognised and enforced under either the Brussels or Lugano Conventions (s 32(4) of the CJJA 1982, as amended by CJJA 1991). Section 32 provides:

(1) ... a judgment given by a court of an overseas country in any proceedings shall not be recognised or enforced in the United Kingdom if:

    (a) the bringing of those proceedings in that court was contrary to an agreement under which the dispute in question was to be settled otherwise than by proceedings in the courts of that country; and

    (b) those proceedings were not brought in that court by or with the agreement of the person against whom the judgment was given; and

    (c) that person did not counterclaim in the proceedings or otherwise submit to the jurisdiction of that court.

Section 32 applies to judgments given only by the courts of an *overseas country*, which means that it applies to any territory outside the UK, but it does not apply to judgments rendered by the courts of Scotland or Northern Ireland.

For s 32 to apply, three requirements must be met. First, the bringing of the proceedings must be in breach of an agreement between two parties to settle the dispute in question otherwise than by proceedings in the courts of the country where the proceedings were brought. This situation would arise if, for instance, proceedings were brought in Belgium when an agreement provided that disputes arising were to be settled by arbitration in Belgium; or proceedings were brought in California when an agreement provided that disputes arising were to be settled in English courts. The second requirement which must be met is that the person, against whom the judgment was obtained, neither brought nor agreed to the bringing of the proceedings in that court. Thirdly, it must be shown that the person against whom the judgment was given did not counterclaim in the proceedings or did not submit to the jurisdiction of that court. To decide whether that person submitted to the jurisdiction of that court, guidance is sought from s 33 of the 1982 Act. If all the above requirements are satisfied, then the judgment in question shall be neither recognised nor enforced in the UK. This defence, however, would not apply if, according to s 32(2), the agreement was 'illegal, void or unenforceable or was incapable of being performed for reasons not attributable to the fault of the party bringing the proceedings in which the judgment was given'.

The operation of s 32 was considered by the Court of Appeal in the case of *Tracomin SA v Sudan Oil Seeds Co Ltd (No 1)* (1983) where the sellers, a Sudanese company, made two contracts for the sale of ground nuts to the buyers. The contracts provided that they were governed by English law and that any dispute arising out of the contracts, including any question of law, should be referred to arbitration in London. A dispute arose and the buyers brought an action in the Swiss court, contrary to the arbitration agreement. The sellers applied for a stay of the proceedings in the Swiss court on the basis that the dispute should be determined by arbitration. The Swiss court, however, refused to stay the action on the ground that the arbitration clause was of no effect under Swiss law because it had not been properly incorporated in the contracts. Under English law, the arbitration clause was valid. The buyers then applied to the English court for an injunction to restrain the sellers from arbitrating. This was based on the fact that the Swiss decision, invalidating the arbitration clause, had produced an estoppel, which meant that the sellers could no longer claim that there was an effective arbitration in England.

The Court of Appeal held that the requirements of s 32 had been satisfied in this case, and accordingly refused to recognise the Swiss judgment. The reasons for this view were explained by Staughton J at first instance: (a) the contracts contained an agreement to refer disputes to arbitration, so s 32(1)(a) was satisfied; (b) the Swiss proceedings were not brought with the agreement of the sellers, so s 32(1)(b) was satisfied; and (c) the sellers did not submit to the jurisdiction of the Swiss court since they merely appeared to contest that jurisdiction, so s 32(1)(c) was satisfied. (Note that Swiss judgments are now covered by the Lugano Convention.)

4.4.5 Limitation of actions

Section 3 of the Foreign Limitation Periods Act 1984 provides that:

> Where a court in any country outside England and Wales has determined any matter wholly or partly by reference to the law of that or any other country (including England and Wales) relating to limitation, then, for the purposes of the law relating to the effect to be given in England and Wales to that determination, that court shall, to the extent that it has so determined the matter, be deemed to have determined it on its own merit.

This provision means that the dismissal of the action in the foreign court on the ground that it was time barred under a statute is deemed to be a judgment on the merits, that is, this judgment is treated as conclusive.

4.4.6 *Res judicata*

English courts will not recognise a foreign judgment if it is inconsistent with a previous judgment pronounced by a competent English court. For instance, a Belgium nullity decree was refused recognition in *Vervaeke v Smith* (1983) on the ground, *inter alia*, that it was inconsistent with an earlier English judgment which had determined such a matter. Hence, the earlier English judgment was *res judicata*. Moreover, according to *Showlag v Mansour* (1994), the same principle appears to apply in the context of two inconsistent foreign judgments. Indeed, the Privy Council held that where there were two conflicting judgments (in this case an English judgment and a Jersey judgment), each of which was pronounced by a court of competent jurisdiction and each of which was final and not open to impeachment on any ground, then, as a general rule, the earlier of them in time would be recognised and given effect to the exclusion of the latter.

4.5   EC/EFTA judgments

It may be recalled that the provisions on jurisdiction of both the Brussels and Lugano Conventions were examined in Chapter 3. In this paragraph, their provisions in respect of recognition and enforcement of judgments will be dealt with. It may also be recalled that, in Chapter 3, it was indicated that the provisions of the Lugano Convention are closely based on the Brussels Convention, but not identical to it. Therefore, for the benefit of avoiding repetition, the Brussels Convention will be examined and any marked differences under the Lugano Convention will be dealt with as and when necessary.

The provisions on recognition and enforcement only apply to judgments rendered in a Contracting State within the EC and EFTA, provided that the judgment is within the scope of the Conventions as defined in Art 1. However, by virtue of Art 25, 'judgment' means 'any judgment given by a court or tribunal of a Contracting State'. Therefore, the Conventions, unlike the common law, apply not only to money judgments, but also to injunctions, orders for specific performance, decisions or writs of execution as well as the determination of costs and expenses, provided they are not made *ex parte*, that is, made in the absence of the defendant and intended to be enforced without due notice. For instance, in *Denilauler v SNC Couchet Frères* (1981), a French company, Couchet Frères, was in the business of transporting goods for the defendant, Denilauler. When the defendant failed to make payment, the plaintiff brought an action in the French court. A French order, known as a *saisie conservatoire*, similar to the English Mareva injunction, was issued to freeze the defendant's bank account in Germany. This order was made *ex parte* and without notice to the defendant. The ECJ ruled that such a protective measure could not be enforced in this instance, as it was made without the party, against whom it was directed, having been summoned to appear and without prior notice to that party. However, arbitration awards do not come within the ambit of Art 25, which is not surprising, because Art 1 excludes arbitration from the scope of the Conventions.

In relation to *recognition*, Art 26 provides that: 'A judgment given in a Contracting State shall be recognised in the other Contracting States without any special procedure being required.' But, in relation to *enforcement*, Art 31 provides that: 'A judgment given in a Contracting State and enforceable in that State shall be enforced in another Contracting State when, on the application of any interested party, it has been declared enforceable there.' Hence, it can be seen that recognition is automatic and without any conditions having to be satisfied (subject to Art 27), whereas enforcement requires that some procedure be followed. Before dealing with the mechanism for enforcement, it is important to note that the Conventions' provisions on recognition and enforcement apply to all judgments of Contracting States, provided that they are within the scope of Conventions, that is, civil and commercial matters within the meaning of Art 1. These judgments may be recognised and enforced, regardless of whether or not the defendant is domiciled in a Contracting State, that is, regardless of which rules on jurisdiction have been applied. Thus, a judgment rendered in a Contracting State after jurisdiction was assumed under the traditional national rules rather than the Conventions' rules, against a defendant domiciled in a non-Contracting State, will be recognised and enforced in other Contracting States in accordance with the provisions of the Conventions.

4.5.1 Mechanisms for enforcement

The procedure for the enforcement of judgments in the UK is a two stage process. First, it involves an *ex parte* application under s 4 of the CJJA 1982 and an order for enforcement. The second stage relates to subsequent appeals. When the application is made, the defendant does not have the right to be heard, or even informed of the application. Clearly, this provision is intended to prevent the defendant from removing his or her assets from the jurisdiction where the judgment is sought to be enforced. Once the enforcement of the judgment is authorised and registered, it has, by virtue of s 4(3) of the 1982 Act, the same force and effect as if it has been rendered by the registering court in England. In addition, the costs of registration are recoverable as part of the judgment. Although the Conventions do not deal with the issue of interest for the period after the judgment is given, s 7 of the 1982 Act provides that interest can be recovered on registered judgments provided that it is recoverable under the judgment in accordance with the law of the Contracting State in which the judgment was given.

Special provisions are provided for the enforcement of maintenance orders under s 5 of the CJJA 1982.

Once enforcement is authorised, notice of the registration is served on the defendant who, according to Art 36, has a month from the date of the authorisation, or two months where the defendant is not domiciled within the jurisdiction, in which to appeal. In England, the appeal must be made to the High Court and the judgment rendered on appeal is subject to one further appeal, but only on a point of law (s 6).

On the other hand, if the application for enforcement is refused, then the applicant may re-apply to the High Court (Art 40). The outcome of this appeal will be subject to one further right of appeal by either of the parties, but only on a point of law (Art 41).

4.5.2 Defences

Articles 27 and 28 of the Brussels Convention provide for a number of defences; if any of them is established, then the judgment will not be recognised. As recognition is a prerequisite for enforcement, Art 34 expressly states that these defences apply equally to enforcement. They are as follows:

(a) if recognition is contrary to public policy in the State in which recognition is sought (Art 27(1));

(b) where the judgment was given in default of appearance, if the defendant was not duly served with the document which instituted the proceedings in sufficient time so as to enable him to arrange for his defence (Art 27(2));

(c) if the judgment is irreconcilable with a judgment given in a dispute between the same parties in the State in which recognition is sought (Art 27(3));

(d) if the original court:

> ... has decided a preliminary question concerning the status ... of natural persons, rights in property arising out of a matrimonial relationship, wills or succession, in a way that conflicts with a rule of the private international law of the State in which recognition is sought ... unless the same result would have been reached by the application of the rules of private international law of that State ...

(Art 27(4)); or

(e) if the judgment:

> ... is irreconcilable with an earlier judgment given in a non-Contracting State involving the same cause of action and between the same parties, provided that this latter judgment fulfils the conditions necessary for its recognition in the State addressed [Art 27(5)];

(f) if the judgment conflicts with the jurisdictional provisions in Arts 7–12A (insurance matters), Arts 13–15 (consumer contracts), or Art 16 (exclusive jurisdiction) (Art 28). Although Art 28(3) provides that the jurisdiction of the court of the State of origin may not be reviewed, an exception to this is made if jurisdiction was taken contrary to the provisions of the above articles. However, according to Art 28(2), in examining jurisdiction, the recognising court is bound by the findings of fact on which the original court based its jurisdiction;

(g) if the case is provided for under Art 59 (Art 28(1)). That is, if jurisdiction was taken contrary to the provisions of another convention protected under Art 59 with regard to arrangements with non-Contracting States.

It must be borne in mind, however, that the court, in which recognition or enforcement is sought, is, under no circumstances, entitled to review a foreign judgment as to its substance (Arts 29 and 34(3)).

In addition to the above defences, the Lugano Convention introduced four new defences to recognition and enforcement. The first is contained in Art

54B(3) which gives the recognising court a discretionary power to refuse recognition or enforcement of a judgment 'if the grounds of jurisdiction on which the judgment has been made differs from that resulting from this Convention'. This defence will only apply where the party, against whom recognition or enforcement is sought, is domiciled in an EFTA State. The second defence is found in Art 57(4), which deals with the situation where jurisdiction was assumed by virtue of some other international convention, such as the Warsaw Convention on International Carriage by Air 1929. The third defence, contained in Protocol 1, applies in relation to Art 16(1)(b). Finally, the fourth defence, also contained in Protocol 1, which is of limited application both in time and in geographical scope, gives Switzerland the right to decline recognition or enforcement if the jurisdiction of the Contracting State in question was based only on Art 5(1).

4.6   Recognition and enforcement within the UK

A judgment rendered in one part of the UK may be enforced in another part if it meets the requirements of s 18 of the CJJA 1982. Enforcement can only be made by way of registration under Sched 6 of the Act (for money judgments) or Sched 7 (for non-money judgments). Section 18 initially defines 'judgment' in a wide manner and then gives a detailed list of the judgments it does not cover. For example, it does not cover judgments given in a magistrate's court, judgments in bankruptcy or winding up of companies, maintenance orders, orders concerning the status of an individual, and orders for provisional measures other than interim payment (see s 18(3), (5), (6) and (7)).

Registration *must* be set aside if it is contrary to the provisions of Scheds 6 and 7. It *may* be set aside if the registering court is satisfied that the subject matter of the dispute had been previously decided by another court with competent jurisdiction. None of the common law defences, however, may be invoked.

Finally, s 19 applies in relation to recognition of judgments within the UK.

RECOGNITION AND ENFORCEMENT OF FOREIGN JUDGMENTS

Recognition and enforcement at common law

Since 1982, a plaintiff who has obtained a foreign judgment for a debt can only bring an action in England for the debt and can no longer bring fresh proceedings on the original cause of action.

A plaintiff seeking to enforce a foreign judgment in England may either sue on the obligation created by the judgment, or plead the judgment *res judicata* in proceedings which raise the same issue.

Under the Administration of Justice Act 1920, a person who obtained a judgment in any part of the Commonwealth may apply to the High Court to have the judgment registered. Registration is, however, discretionary.

Under the Foreign Judgments (Reciprocal Enforcements) Act 1933, registration of a foreign judgment in England is as of right and not discretionary, and the successful litigant can make his application at any time within six years.

Requirements under the traditional common law rules

The foreign court must have been jurisdictionally competent to try the action. Competence is tested in the context of residence of the defendant in, and/or his submission to, the foreign court.

Where the plaintiff seeks enforcement at common law, under the AJA 1920, or under the FJA 1933, rather than mere recognition, the judgment must be for a fixed sum of money, final and conclusive, and not rendered in matters of foreign revenue, penal or other public laws, provided that it is not inconsistent with the provisions of the Protection of Trading Interests Act 1980. One main distinguishing feature, however, under the AJA 1920 is that the judgment must have been rendered by a superior court.

Defences

The defences which may be raised by the defendant against the enforcement of a foreign judgment are fraud, public policy, natural justice, breach of s 32 of the CJJA 1982, and *res judicata*.

EC/EFTA judgments

The provisions of the Conventions apply to any judgment given by a court or tribunal of a Contracting State, regardless of whether or not the defendant is domiciled in a Contracting State, including injunctions, specific performance, writs of executions, etc, and provided that the judgment was not made *ex parte*.

A judgment given in a Contracting State must be recognised in all other Contracting States without any special procedures required.

In relation to enforcement, however, such a judgment must be enforced in another Contracting State when, on the application of any interested party, it has been declared enforceable there.

Mechanisms for enforcement

This involves a two stage process. First, the plaintiff makes an *ex parte* application for an order for enforcement. At this stage, the defendant does not have the right to be heard. Secondly, once the judgment is authorised, notice of the registration is served on the defendant, who has the right to appeal.

Defences

A defendant may raise one or more of seven defences, such as public policy, non-reconciliation, lack of jurisdiction, etc. A further four defences may be invoked where the judgment is sought to be enforced within EFTA States.

Recognition and enforcement within the UK

Enforcement can only be effected by way of registration, which must be set aside where the subject matter of the dispute had been previously decided by another court with competent jurisdiction.

CHAPTER 5

CHOICE OF LAW IN CONTRACT

5.1 Introduction

In a conflicts situation, once an English court has ascertained its competence as to jurisdiction, it proceeds to determine the law governing the dispute.

Where a contract containing one or more foreign elements is the subject matter of proceedings in an English court, the difficult and complicated question of ascertaining the applicable law arises. Such difficulty stems from the multiplicity and diversity of connecting factors which can be raised by the facts of the case. For instance, each of the following factors may have arisen in a different jurisdiction: the place where the contract was made; the place of performance; the place of business of the parties; the place of payment; the currency of payment; the domicile or nationality of the parties; and so on. Which of these connecting factors will be considered as the decisive one is the subject matter of this chapter. The weight attached to each of them will depend greatly on the type of contract in question, for example, contract of sale, carriage of goods by sea or insurance, etc, and on the nature of the dispute, for example, validity, illegality, non-performance, or capacity, etc.

The law in this area has undergone fundamental changes. Until relatively recently, the flexible common law doctrine of *the proper law of the contract* governed most issues. This, however, has been replaced to a great extent by the Contracts (Applicable Law) Act 1990, which came into force on 1 April 1991. This Act implements the EC Convention on the Law Applicable to Contractual Obligations 1980, known as the Rome Convention. The Act affects contracts entered into only after the date of its coming into force. This means that the common law rules continue to apply to contracts concluded before 1 April 1991. In addition, the common law rules remain relevant in relation to certain contracts which are excluded from the ambit of the Convention, such as certain contracts of insurance, arbitration agreements, and bills of exchange. Hence, the Rome Convention, as implemented by the Contracts (Applicable Law) Act 1990, will form the main basis of discussion in this chapter, and the common law rules will be examined partly to compare the traditional English approach to that of the Convention, and partly to highlight the continuing relevance of some of these rules in relation to some contractual issues which fall outside the scope of the Convention.

5.2 The Contracts (Applicable Law) Act 1990; the Rome Convention 1980

The Contracts (Applicable Law) Act 1990 implements the Rome Convention 1980 on the Law Applicable to Contractual Obligations. The text of the Convention is appended to the 1990 Act by Sched 1.

The Rome Convention marks a further move towards the harmonisation of the laws of EC Member States, so that, to a large extent, the same choice of law will be applied irrespective of the Member State in which the proceedings are brought. This uniformity would have the effect of minimising the unfairness which can result from forum shopping, for the Convention is intended to operate in such a way as to identify the same applicable law, regardless of where and in which Member State the action is brought.

The Act came into force on 1 April 1991 and applies to any contract within the scope of the Convention, provided that it is made after that date (Art 17 of the Rome Convention). Thus, the Convention replaces, with very few exceptions, the English common law rules on choice of law in contract.

As is the case with the Brussels Convention, and many other EC Conventions, an explanatory report on the Rome Convention was published in the Official Journal 1980 (the Giuliano-Lagarde Report, OJ C282/1, 1980). Section 3(3)(a) of the Act enables this Report to be consulted when ascertaining the meaning or effect of any provision of the Convention. Moreover, the Brussels Protocol, conferring the power to give preliminary rulings on the interpretation of the Convention to the ECJ, was concluded in Brussels on 19 December 1988. This Protocol is also appended to the Act by virtue of Sched 3. These measures will enable any question on the interpretation of the Convention to be referred to the ECJ, especially where clarity is necessary to decide a particular case. This requirement is consolidated in s 3(1) of the 1990 Act, which adds that any question of interpretation, if not referred to the ECJ, shall 'be determined in accordance with the principles laid down by, and any relevant decision of, the European Court'. The above provisions on interpretation are buttressed by Art 18 of the Convention, which provides that, in the interpretation and application of the rules laid down in the Convention, 'regard shall be had to their international character and the desirability of achieving uniformity in their interpretation and application'.

5.2.1 Scope of the Convention

Article 1(1) provides that the choice of law rules set out in the Convention apply to *contractual obligations* in any situation involving a choice between the laws of different countries. Therefore, for the Convention to apply, there must be a contractual obligation which must involve a choice between the laws of different countries, that is, a contract which involves one or more foreign elements. It is also important to note that, unlike the Brussels Convention, the countries concerned under the Rome Convention are not limited to Member States. Indeed, Art 2 expressly provides that any law specified by the Convention shall be applied whether or not it is the law of a Contracting State. Furthermore, notwithstanding the provisions of Art 19(2), which states that the Convention does not have to apply when the conflict is solely between the laws of different territorial units within the same State, s 2(3) of the 1990 Act, which accords with the provision of Art 19(1) of the Convention, provides that the Convention shall apply in the case of conflicts between the laws of different parts of the UK.

It must be noted that the phrase 'contractual obligations' is not defined in the Convention. In addition, as one may expect, the domestic laws of various Member States are likely to differ as to what types of obligations are characterised as contractual. A simple example may be that, whilst Italian domestic law classifies an agreement unsupported by consideration as a contract, English domestic law requires consideration to exist before an agreement can be recognised as a contract. What if such an Italian contract were to be the subject of dispute in an English court? Would the English court declare the Italian contract void for lack of consideration? Under the traditional common law rules, this question was considered by the Court of Appeal in *Re Bonacina* (1912), where the proper law of the contract was applied. It was held that, as the contract was valid by Italian law, it would be recognised and enforced in England. However, as the differences between the laws of Member States can be much more complex than that in the above example, it is expected that the ECJ will interpret this phrase so as to confer on it an autonomous Community meaning in line with Art 5(1) of the Brussels Convention 1968.

5.2.2 Matters excluded from the ambit of the Convention

The Convention does not apply to all contractual matters. Article 1, paras (2) and (3) set out a list of issues which are excluded from its scope. These are as follows:

(a) questions involving the status or legal capacity of natural persons, but subject to Art 11;

(b) contractual obligations relating to wills and succession;

(c) contractual obligations relating to rights in property arising out of matrimonial relationships;

(d) family law matters;

(e) obligations arising under bills of exchange, cheques and promissory notes and other negotiable instruments to the extent that the obligations arise out of their negotiable character;

(f) arbitration and jurisdiction agreements;

(g) questions governed by the law of companies and other bodies corporate or unincorporate such as the creation, legal capacity, internal organisation or winding up, and the personal liability of officers and members as such for the obligations of the company or body;

(h) the question whether an agent is able to bind a principal, or an organ to bind a company or body corporate or unincorporate, to a third party;

(i) the constitution of trusts and the relationship between settlors, trustees and beneficiaries;

(j) evidence and procedure, but subject to Art 14; and

(k) contracts of insurance which cover risks situated in the territories of the Member States of the EC.

In relation to the latter exclusion, whether a risk is situated within the territories of a Member State is a matter for the court of that State to determine by applying its internal law. The Convention, however, applies to contracts of re-insurance (Art 1(4)). As far as English law is concerned, all the above exclusions will continue to be governed either by the common law rules relating to contract, if and when they are classified as contractual, or by the choice of law rules applicable to whatever classifications they may belong.

As for arbitration and jurisdiction agreements, their exclusion from the scope of the Convention was justified on the ground that the validity of jurisdiction clauses is covered, to a large extent, by the provisions of Art 17 of the Brussels Convention 1968, and the validity of arbitration clauses is governed by the New York Convention on the Recognition and Enforcement of Foreign Arbitral Awards 1958, to which almost all EC Member States have acceded. It does not follow, however, that the substantive contract incorporating a jurisdiction or an arbitration clause is not covered by the Rome Convention. In fact, according to the Giuliano-Lagarde Report, such clauses may be taken into account when ascertaining the applicable law under Arts 3 and 4 of the Convention.

5.2.3 The applicable law: express and/or inferred choice of law

Like the English common law rules, the Convention makes a basic distinction between the situation where the applicable law is chosen by the parties and the situation where, in the absence of choice, the applicable law is to be ascertained objectively. Similarly, any reference to an applicable law under the Convention is a reference to the domestic law of the country in question, and accordingly the doctrine of *renvoi* is specifically excluded (Art 15).

By virtue of Art 3(1) of the Convention, a contract is to be governed by the law chosen by the parties, provided that the choice is express or demonstrated with reasonable certainty by the terms of the contract or the circumstances of the case. Thus, parties are given the freedom to pick and choose the applicable law. This bears close resemblance to the view upheld under the English common law rules, where Lord Wright held, in *Vita Food Products Inc v Unus Shipping Co Ltd* (1939), that 'provided the intention expressed is *bona fide* and legal and there is no reason for avoiding the choice on the grounds of public policy', the parties' express choice would be upheld.

Moreover, according to the last sentence of Art 3(1), which reads that 'the parties can select the applicable law to the whole or part of the contract', the parties can choose different laws to govern different parts of the contract. This clearly allows for '*dépeçage*', that is, the act of severing the contract between different legal systems. Hence, the parties may choose different legal systems to govern different issues in their contract. For instance, they can choose a law to govern the interpretation of the contract and a different law to govern its discharge. In the context of the common law rules, although such a *dépeçage* did not apply, it had some support. For instance, MacDermott LJ, dissenting, in *Kahler v Midland Bank* (1950), took the view that *dépeçage* could be relied upon where unusual and compelling circumstances existed. Also, in *Sayers v International Drilling Co* (1971), the Court of Appeal held that an exemption clause was governed by the proper law of the contract, whilst the remaining issues were governed by tort rules.

In the absence of an express choice, Art 3(1) stipulates that a choice of law can be inferred, provided that it is 'demonstrated with reasonable certainty by the terms of the contract or the circumstances of the case'. No guidance as to how such an inference may be determined is given in the Convention. However, the Giuliano-Lagarde Report provides examples of certain factors which may be of assistance to the court's attempt to infer a choice of law. Such factors may be: a choice of jurisdiction or arbitration clause; a reference to a particular system of law in the contract; the use of a standard form; and so forth. These factors, however, are not conclusive. They are merely factors to be taken into account. Guidance as to how an implied choice of law may be inferred under Art 3(1) can be found in the recent case of *Egon Oldendorff v Liberia Corpn* (1996). In this case, a contract was made between a Japanese company and a German company without any express choice of law provision. The contract, however, provided for arbitration in London and was in a well known English charterparty which contained standard clauses with well known meanings in English law. Clarke J held that the contract was subject to Art 3(1) of the Convention. Although the parties had not expressly agreed whether English or Japanese law applied, the plaintiff had demonstrated with reasonable certainty that the parties had intended English law to apply. He stated that (p 390):

> In short, having agreed English arbitration for the determination in London of disputes arising out of a well known English language form of charterparty

which contains standard clauses with well known meanings in English law, it is in my judgment to be inferred that the parties intended that law to apply.

By way of analogy, the English common law rules had operated in the past to infer a choice of law on the basis of broadly similar factors. Indeed, Clarke J in the *Egon* case expressed the view that Art 3(1) was similar to the position at common law and accordingly a similar test could be applied. At common law, in *Miller (James) and Partners Ltd v Whitworth Street Estates (Manchester) Ltd* (1970), the use of a standard form was held to be a strong indication pointing to the law of the country to which such a form owed its origin. Nevertheless, the indication would not be sufficiently strong to infer a choice of law where such a standard form was adopted throughout the world. In this case, the English court would look for other factors which would enable such an indication to be deduced. This was the case in *Amin Rasheed Shipping Corpn v Kuwait Insurance Co* (1984), where the majority of the House of Lords inferred from the terms of the contract that English law was the applicable law. The plaintiffs, a Liberian company carrying on a business in Dubai, insured a vessel with the defendants, a Kuwaiti insurance company. The insurance policy was a standard Lloyd's policy, as set out in the Marine Insurance Act 1906. The House of Lords held that the parties intended their contract to be governed by English law. This inference was not, however, based on the ground that the policy was in English form, as such policies had been adopted widely throughout the world, but on the ground that it was not possible to interpret the policy without recourse to the British Act and to the judicial interpretation of that Act.

Furthermore, English courts adopted the view that, where the parties did not choose a law, but chose a forum, either for litigation or arbitration, then that choice would form a strong indication that the parties intended the law of that forum to govern their contract. However, the importance of this factor would pale into insignificance where other factors pointed to the application of another law. This view may be illustrated by the judgment of the House of Lords in *Compagnie d'Armement Maritime SA v Compagnie Tunisienne de Navigation SA* (1971), where a shipping contract was made in Paris on an English language printed form containing a clause providing for the settlement of disputes by arbitration in London. Under this contract, the defendants, French shipowners, agreed to carry for the plaintiffs, a Tunisian company, a large quantity of oil over a period of some months from one Tunisian port to another. The freight was payable in French francs in Paris, and French commercial law prevailed in Tunisia. The House of Lords held that French law was the proper law of the contract. Lord Wilberforce stated (p 600) that:

> ... an arbitration clause must be treated as an indication, to be considered together with the rest of the contract and relevant surrounding facts. Always, it will be a strong indication ... But, in some cases, it must give way where other indications are clear.

In this case, the contract was made in France, the freight was payable in French francs, the contract was to be performed in Tunisia, a country which applied French law, and the only connection with England was in terms of the arbitration clause. Accordingly, there was a clear balance in favour of French law.

Article 3(2) of the Convention goes on to add that the parties' choice of law can be made at any time, even after the conclusion of the contract. They can also vary any choice of law that was done previously, provided that the variation of the choice does not prejudice the formal validity of the contract under the rules set out in Art 9, or adversely affect the rights of third parties. This provision enables the parties to have maximum freedom as to when a choice of law can be made. Thus, a choice of law can be made either at the time of contracting, or before or after the conclusion of the contract.

Although the parties are free to choose any law, whether or not connected with the contract, this choice is qualified by the rule laid down in Art 3(3) of the Convention which provides:

> The fact that the parties have chosen a foreign law ... shall not, where all the other elements relevant to the situation at the time of the choice are connected with one country only, prejudice the application of rules of the law of that country which cannot be derogated from by contract, hereinafter called 'mandatory rules'.

The effect of Art 3(3) may be illustrated in the following example: suppose that the parties to an entirely English contract containing exemption clauses, choose, for example, Swiss law to govern. Then, by virtue of Art 3(3), the court of any Contracting State which tries the action is required to apply any controls on exemption clauses which are part of English law, such as those contained in the Unfair Contract Terms Act 1977, or in the Employment Rights Act 1996.

If a dispute arises as to whether one of the parties has consented to the choice of the applicable law, then according to Art 3(4), the existence and validity of the consent are to be determined in accordance with the provisions of Art 8 in relation to material validity, Art 9 in relation to formal validity and Art 11 in connection with issues of incapacity.

5.2.4 Applicable law in the absence of choice

If the parties have failed to choose a law either expressly or impliedly, then the applicable law will be determined in accordance with Art 4. Paragraph (1) of this Article provides that:

> To the extent that the law applicable to the contract has not been chosen in accordance with Art 3, the contract shall be governed by the law of the country with which it is most closely connected.

This is an objective test under which the applicable law is ascertained by looking objectively at the connecting factors. Here, again, as under Art 3(1), there is room for *dépeçage*, notably provided by the last sentence of Art 4(1) which states that:

> Nevertheless, a severable part of the contract which has a closer connection with another country may by way of exception be governed by the law of that country.

This provision, however, only applies in exceptional cases, which means that *dépeçage* is only intended to operate in very limited circumstances.

By way of comparison, under the traditional English rules and in the absence of a choice of law, either express or implied, English courts adopted a test in favour of the 'law most closely connected' with the contract. Note, however, that there is a slight difference between this test and that employed in the Convention. The latter refers to the 'country', rather than the 'law', most closely connected with the contract. Whether this will result in the application of a different test under the Convention remains to be seen (for details on the importance of this difference, see Stone, *The Conflict of Laws*, 1995, pp 239–40).

Both the Convention and the common law adopt an objective test to ascertain the applicable law. However, the similarities stop here. Whilst Art 4 proceeds to give three rebuttable presumptions for determining the country with which the contract is most closely connected, English common law considered such presumptions to be of little value. In fact, any attempt to use rebuttable presumptions was aborted long ago, towards the end of the 19th century.

Article 4(2) provides that:

> ... it shall be presumed that the contract is most closely connected with the country where the party, who is to effect the performance which is characteristic of the contract, has, at the time of conclusion of the contract, his habitual residence, or, in the case of a body corporate or unincorporate, its central administration. However, if the contract is entered into in the course of that party's trade or profession, that country shall be the country in which the principal place of business is situated or, where under the terms of the contract the performance is to be effected through a place of business other than the principal place of business, the country in which that other place of business is situated.

The meaning of Art 4(2) can be explained as follows: it is to be presumed that the contract is most closely connected with the country where the party who is to effect the characteristic performance of the contract has his habitual residence at the time of conclusion of the contract. It must be emphasised that it is the country of the characteristic performer that matters when identifying the applicable law under this provision, rather than the place where the characteristic performance was effected. Characteristic performance, albeit undefined under the Convention, is explained in the Giuliano-Lagarde Report as being, usually, the performance for which the payment is due, such as the delivery of goods, the provision of a service, the granting of the right to make use of an item of property, and which is usually the centre of gravity and the socio-economic function of the contractual obligation.

By way of illustration, suppose that S, habitually resident in Germany, makes a contract with B, habitually resident in Italy. The contract provides that S is to supply goods to B in three different countries: Germany, Belgium and Kuwait, for an agreed price. When a dispute arises, the applicable law will be presumed to be that of Germany, the reason being that the party, who is to effect the characteristic performance, that is, S, is habitually resident in Germany at the time of the conclusion of the contract. German law remains the applicable law even if, at the time of performance or at the time the dispute arises, S is habitually resident in another country. If, however, S is a corporate or unincorporate body, such as a company or a partnership, registered in Germany but with its central administration in England, then the applicable law will be presumed to be that of England.

Thus, although Art 4(2) places emphasis on 'characteristic performance', the applicable law is the law of the country where the party who is to effect it has his 'habitual residence', or, in the case of a corporate or unincorporate body, its 'central administration', as at the time of the conclusion of the contract. As 'habitual residence' and 'central administration' are not defined, then presumably the forum will have to apply its national definitions.

If the relevant party was acting in the course of his trade or business, then it is to be presumed that the contract is most closely connected with the country in which that party has his principal place of business. If, however, under the terms of the contract, the performance is to be effected in a place of business other than the principal one, then it is to be presumed that the country is that in which that other place of business is situated. So, if B is acting in the course of his trade or business, for example, a producer supplying goods he has produced, and his principal place of business is in England, then it is to be presumed that English law is the applicable law. If, however, B has his principal place of business in England, but he supplied the goods from his secondary place of business in Germany, then German law is presumed to be the applicable law.

In many instances, identifying the characteristic performance will present no difficulty. Indeed, the case of *Machinale Glasfabriek De Maas BV v Emaillerie Alsacienne SA* (1984) is a good illustration on this point. (This case was decided by the Dutch courts on the basis of Art 4(2), albeit prior to the coming into force of the Rome Convention, the provisions of which had been at the time incorporated as part of the Dutch national rules of conflict of laws.) The case concerned a contract for the sale of goods by a Dutch seller to a French buyer. The characteristic performance was held to be the seller's obligation to deliver the goods. Consequently, since the seller's place of establishment was in The Netherlands at the time of the conclusion of the contract, the applicable law was the law of that country. It must be noted, however, that the characteristic performance in some commercial contracts, such as contracts connected with letters of credit, can prove more difficult to ascertain. This may be illustrated by the recent English decision in *Bank of Baroda v Vysya Bank* (1994). In a simplified account of the facts, Vysya was an Indian bank with no branch in England. It was instructed by an Indian seller to issue a letter of credit in favour of Granada, an Irish company which had an office in London. The letter of credit was in respect of the shipment of a cargo of pig iron. Baroda was another Indian bank with an office in London. Baroda was instructed to confirm the credit in London and to pay the Irish company on tender of the shipping documents. Subsequently, Vysya alleged that there had been fraud in the contract of sale, and that the documents did not conform with the credit, and accordingly Vysya withdrew the authorisation to reimburse Baroda in respect of the payment made to the Irish company. One of the questions which had to be determined by the English court was which law governed the contractual relationship between Vysya and Baroda. Evidently, the applicable law depended on the place of residence of the party who was to effect the characteristic performance. What was the characteristic performance in this case? Was it Baroda's confirmation of the credit and the honouring of the liability accepted thereby? Or was it Vysya's obligation to reimburse Baroda upon their presentation of confirming documents? Mance J held that the relationship between Vysya and Baroda was one of agency, the characteristic performance of which was Baroda's confirmation and honouring of liability to the Irish company. The liability of Vysya, the issuing bank, to reimburse Baroda, the confirming bank, did not characterise the contract. Accordingly, since the place of business of Baroda was London, the presumption in Art 4(2) pointed to English law as the applicable law.

Article 4(3) of the Convention provides that, where the subject matter of the contract is a right in immovable property or a right to use immovable property, then the presumption in Art 4(2) does not operate. Instead, it is to be presumed that the contract is most closely connected with the country where the immovable property is situated.

A further special presumption is provided in relation to contracts for the carriage of goods under Art 4(4), whereby the presumption refers to the law of the country in which the carrier has his principal place of business provided that this country is also either the place of loading, the place of discharge, or the principal place of business of the consignor at the time of the conclusion of the contract.

By virtue of Art 4(5), however, the basic presumption in Art 4(2) shall not apply if the *characteristic performance* cannot be determined, and all the above presumptions (including Art 4(2)) are to be disregarded if it appears from the circumstances as a whole that the contract is more closely connected with another country. The object of this provision is to give national courts a degree of discretion to disregard the applicable law identified by Art 4(2) when the circumstances of the case so require. The application of this provision was addressed by Mance J in *Bank of Baroda v Vysya Bank* (1994) where, it may be recalled, Vysya requested Baroda to confirm and honour a letter of credit in favour of Granada, an Irish company. On the question of which law governed the contract between Vysya and Granada, the application of the presumption under Art 4(2) pointed to Indian law as the place of central administration of Vysya. This was the party effecting the characteristic performance of the contract between Vysya and Granada. This meant, however, that two contracts, one between Vysya and Granada, and another between Vysya and Baroda, were governed by two different laws, even though both contracts related to the same provision of credit. In essence, Mance J concluded that this was a classic example of the need of Art 4(5). Accordingly, by virtue of Art 4(5), the contract between Vysya and Granada was held to be governed by English law.

5.3   Special rules for specific contracts

The Convention contains special rules in relation to two types of contracts, that is, certain consumer contracts and individual employment contracts. These contracts have been singled out because it was felt that special provisions are necessary to protect consumers and employees who are considered to be the weaker parties to the contract. Each of these will be examined separately.

5.3.1   Certain consumer contracts

Article 5(1) defines a consumer contract as one:

> ... the object of which is the supply of goods or services to a person ('the consumer') for a purpose which can be regarded as being outside his trade or profession, or a contract for the provision of credit for that object.

In such a case, any choice of law made by the parties shall not have the effect of depriving the consumer of the protection afforded to him by the mandatory rules of the law of the country in which he or she has his or her habitual residence, that is, rules of law which cannot be derogated from by contract. It must be noted, however, that Art 5 does not apply to all consumer contracts, but only to a number of transactions, and only where one or more of the situations envisaged in Art 5(2) apply.

Hence, where a choice of law is expressly made in the contract, such a law shall not have the result of depriving the consumer of the protection afforded to him by the mandatory rules of the law of the country in which the consumer has his or her habitual residence, provided that:

(a) in that country, the conclusion of the contract was preceded by a specific invitation addressed to him or by advertising, and he had taken in that country all the steps necessary on his part for the conclusion of the contract; or

(b) the other party or his agent received the consumer's order in that country; or

(c) the contract is for the sale of goods and the consumer travelled from that country to another country and gave his order there, provided that the consumer's journey was arranged by the seller for the purpose of inducing the consumer to buy.

If any of the above circumstances apply and a choice of law is made, then that choice will apply, but subject to the relevant mandatory rules of the law of the country of the consumer's habitual residence.

However, in the absence of choice of law and where one or more of the above circumstances exist, Art 5(3), excluding the operation of Art 4, provides that the contract shall be governed by the law of the country in which the consumer has his or her habitual residence. As can be seen, this provision is worded to identify the only applicable law and, therefore, does not operate as a presumption.

Article 5 excludes from its scope contracts of carriage and contracts for the supply of services where the services are to be supplied exclusively in a country other than the country of the consumer's habitual residence (Art 5(4)). Nevertheless, its provisions apply to contracts which, for an inclusive price, provide for a combination of travel and accommodation (Art 5(5)).

5.3.2 Individual employment contracts

Individual contracts of employment are the subject of the provisions in Art 6. No actual definition of what may be considered as an 'individual contract of employment' is specified in the Convention. It is expected, however, that the ECJ would accord to it such an independent Community meaning as to correspond to that accorded to the provisions of Art 5(1) of the Brussels Convention 1968 (see Chapter 3).

Where a choice of law is made in the contract, it should be upheld, but only insofar as it does not deprive the employee of the protection afforded to him by the mandatory rules of the law which would be applicable under Art 6(2) in the absence of such choice (Art 6(1)). In the absence of choice, Art 6(2) provides that the contract shall be governed by the law of the country in which the employee habitually carries out his work in performance of the contract, even if he is temporarily employed in another country. If, however, the employee does not habitually carry out his work in any one country, then the applicable law shall be the law of the country in which the place of business, through which he was engaged, is situated.

Suppose that A, an Italian employer, employs B, a Greek employee, to work in Italy. The contract provides that it is to be governed by Greek law. By virtue of Art 6(1), Greek law will apply, but only in so far as it does not deprive B of the protection afforded to him by the would be applicable law to the contract as determined by Art 6(2). In accordance with the latter provision, the would be applicable law is that of Italy, where the employee habitually carries out his work. The end result is that Greek law applies as the law chosen by the parties, but without prejudice to the protection afforded to the employee by the Italian employment protection legislation. If no choice of law is made, then Italian law will apply to the above scenario, even if B is temporarily employed in another country.

In parallel with the provision in Art 5(1) of the Brussels Convention, which ascribes jurisdiction in respect of individual contracts of employment, and following the ECJ ruling in *Rutten v Cross Medical Ltd* (1997), the base from which the employee carries out his work will be of great importance in determining the place where the employee habitually carries out his work for the purposes of Art 6(2) of the Rome Convention. It may be recalled that in this case (see Chapter 3), the employee carried out his work in The Netherlands, UK, Belgium, Germany and the USA, though he used an office in The Netherlands as a base from which he organised his working activities. The ECJ ruled that the habitual place of work referred to the place where the employee had established the effective centre of his activities and from which he, in fact, performed the essential part of his duties.

Where, however, B habitually carries out his work in more than one country, for example, Greece, Germany and Kuwait, then the applicable law will be that of the country in which the employer's place of business, through which B is employed, is situated. So, if B is employed through A's place of business in Greece, Greek law applies; or through that in Germany, German law applies; or through that in Kuwait, Kuwaiti law applies.

Article 6 has the effect of preventing an employer from evading the mandatory rules relating to employment protection. Mandatory rules are defined in Art 3(3) as those rules which cannot be derogated from by contract. For example, under English law, s 204 of the Employment Rights Act 1996 stipulates that 'for the purpose of this Act it is immaterial whether the law which (apart from this Act) governs any person's employment is the law of the United Kingdom, or of a part of the United Kingdom, or not'. Hence, this Act, which regulates maternity leave, redundancy, written terms of employment, minimum periods of notice, and unfair dismissal, will apply to a contract of employment which would be governed by English law in accordance with Art 6(2), regardless of the fact that the contract was expressly governed by the law of another country.

Article 6(2), unlike Art 5(2), but like Art 4, operates as a presumption which may be rebutted where the contract is more closely connected with another country, in which case the contract shall be governed by the law of that country.

5.4 Specific issues

The Rome Convention, having set out the rules on the applicable law, goes on to deal with the specific issues of material validity, formal validity, incapacity, and a number of other issues. These will now be examined.

5.4.1 Material validity

Article 8 of the Convention deals with the issue of material validity of the contract, a term which seems to embrace what English law would consider as matters relating to the formation of the contract, such as offer, acceptance, and consideration, as well as issues in relation to the validity of the contract and issues in relation to the terms of the contract. Article 8(1) provides that the validity of such issues is to be governed by the law which would govern the contract under the Convention. In other words, Art 8(1) provides for the application of what is called 'the putative proper law' in order to determine the existence and validity of a contract or any of its terms.

This largely reflects the English common law rules in this area. For instance, in *Albeko Schuhmaschinen v Kamborian Shoe Machine Co Ltd* (1961), the English court applied the putative proper law in order to decide whether an agreement was made. In this case, an offer was posted to Switzerland from England. An acceptance was alleged to have been posted in Switzerland, but was never received by the offeror. The question arose as to whether a contract came into existence. By English law, there would have been a contract immediately the acceptance was posted. By Swiss law, however, a contract could not come into existence unless the acceptance was posted and received. Salmon J applied Swiss law, as the would be applicable law had the contract been formed, and held that there was no contract.

Similarly, with regard to consideration, the Court of Appeal in *Re Bonacina* (1912) applied the putative proper law to the question of whether a contract unsupported by consideration, though not valid by English law, could be enforced as it was valid by Italian law. Accordingly, the contract was held to be valid.

Moreover, Art 8(1) appears to extend to issues of 'illegality'. This means that the question of 'illegality' is governed by the applicable law rather than the law of the place of contracting or that of the place of performance. Equally, under the common law rules, the English court would not enforce a contract if it was illegal by its proper law. For instance, in *Kahler v Midland Bank* (1950), in which certain bonds were held by Midland Bank in London, the plaintiff was, in theory, entitled under the contract, whose proper law was Czech, to withdraw these bonds. However, Midland Bank refused to release them on the ground that, under the Czech currency control regulations, it was prohibited from doing so, despite the fact that the plaintiff had left Czechoslovakia and became a US citizen. The House of Lords held that Czech law was the proper law of the contract, and accordingly the bonds could not be released (illegality under the common law rules is also considered below, 5.6.2).

There is a special safeguard in relation to consent contained in Art 8(2), which provides that:

> ... a party may rely upon the law of the country in which he has his habitual residence to establish that he did not consent, if it appears from the circumstances that it would not be reasonable to determine the effect of his conduct in accordance with the law specified in the preceding paragraph.

This provision is designed to protect a party who, for example, did not reply to an offer. Whilst silence may amount to acceptance in some countries, it may not be so under the law of the country where the offeree has his or her habitual residence. Hence, to avoid any unfairness, Art 8(2) allows that party to plead the law of his or her habitual residence to deny the existence of the contract.

5.4.2 Formal validity

Article 9 of the Convention deals with the question of formal validity of the contract. It contains general provisions as to formal validity and specific provisions in relation to consumer contracts and contracts relating to immovable property. Before dealing with the provisions of Art 9, the meaning of 'formal validity' requires consideration.

Because English law has only a few requirements for the formal validity of contracts, English lawyers are likely to have particular difficulty classifying whether an issue is one of form or one of substance. However, the Giuliano-Lagarde Report gives guidance as to what may be classified as a matter of form. Form includes 'every external manifestation required on the part of a person expressing the will to be legally bound and, in the absence of which, such expression of will would not be regarded as fully effective'. Such matters include, for example, the requirement that the contract must be made in duplicate, that the contract must be in writing, that there must be two signatures to the contract, that a non-competition clause in a contract of employment must be in writing, and so forth.

The concept of formal validity, however, does not cover the issue of what may be required for an act to be valid against third parties, that is, the requirement that a retention of title clause, for example, must be registered before it can be valid against a third party, will not be treated as an issue of formal validity under the Convention.

By virtue of Art 9(1), where a contract is concluded between persons who are in the same country, then it is formally valid if it satisfies either the formal requirements of the governing law, or the formal requirements of the law of the country where the contract is concluded. However, if the contract is concluded between persons who are not in the same country, then according to Art 9(2), it is formally valid if it meets the formal requirements of either the governing law or the law of any of the countries in question. Moreover, for the purposes of the above two paragraphs of Art 9, para (3) provides that, where a contract is concluded by an agent, then the country in which the agent acts is the relevant country. For instance, if S and B concluded a contract in Italy where they both were, and the contract is governed by German law, then the contract is formally valid if it satisfies the requirements of form of either Italy or Germany. If, however, S was in Greece and B was in Italy, and the contract is governed by German law, then the contract is formally valid if it meets the requirements of either Germany, Greece or Italy.

With regard to the traditional English rules, a contract would be formally valid if it complied with the requirements of either the proper law (see *Van Grutten v Digby* (1862)) or the *lex loci contractus* (see *Guépratte v Young* (1851)). However, an exception to this rule seems to apply in relation to what is classified as 'a rule of procedure', such as the requirement incorporated in s 4 of the Statute of Frauds 1677 which formerly provided that no action could be brought on certain contracts unless evidenced in writing. The classification of this rule was illustrated in *Leroux v Brown* (1852), where an oral agreement was made in France whereby the defendant, resident in England, agreed to employ the plaintiff, resident in France, for a period longer than one year. This contract was valid and enforceable by French law, which was the proper law. However, by English domestic law, though valid, it would be unenforceable by virtue of s 4 of the Statute of Frauds, which required such a contract to be in writing. Despite the fact that the proper law of the contract was French, the English court classified the requirement of s 4 as a rule of procedure and held that the contract was unenforceable.

According to Art 9(4), an act which is intended to have legal effect relating to an existing contract, such as notice of termination, or repudiation, is formally valid if it satisfies the formal requirements of the governing law or the law of the country where the act was done.

Special rules relating to the formal validity of consumer contracts, which are concluded in accordance with the provisions of Art 5(2) of the Convention, are contained in Art 9(5). The formal validity of such contracts is to be governed by the law of the country in which the consumer has his or her habitual residence.

Special rules also apply to contracts for rights in immovable property or rights to use immovable property. By virtue of Art 9(6), the formal validity of such contracts shall be subject to the mandatory requirements of the *lex situs*, regardless of the governing law or the law of the country where the contract was concluded.

5.4.3   Capacity

The issue of capacity comes into play where one of the parties to the contract lacks power to make or be bound by a contract. As discussed earlier in this chapter (see 5.2.2), Art 1(2) of the Convention excludes the question of capacity of corporations altogether from the ambit of the Convention. In relation to the status or legal capacity of natural persons, the exclusion is qualified, for it is made subject to Art 11 which provides that:

> In a contract concluded between persons who are in the same country, a natural person who would have capacity under the law of that country may invoke his incapacity resulting from another law only if the other party to the contract was aware of this incapacity at the time of the conclusion of the contract or was not aware thereof as a result of negligence.

Article 11 only applies to contracts concluded between persons who are in the same country, and has the effect of allowing a natural person, who would have capacity under the law of that country, to invoke his or her incapacity resulting from another law. This is subject to the requirement that, at the time of the conclusion of the contract, the other party was either aware or, as a result of negligence, unaware of this incapacity.

With regard to the English common law rules, which remain relevant post the Convention, but subject to Art 11, the question of what law governs capacity in the context of commercial transactions is open to speculation. This is partly due to the lack of case law on this point, and partly because the age of majority has been reduced from 18 to 16. The only modern authority on this point can be found in the case of *Bodley Head Ltd v Flegon* (1972), where a Russian author signed a power of attorney in Moscow which authorised a Swiss lawyer to deal with the author's works outside the Soviet Union. The author had no capacity under Russian law, but had capacity under Swiss law, which was the proper law of the contract. Brightman J appeared to suggest that the question of the author's capacity was governed by Swiss law, the proper law of the contract.

With regard to immovable property, English law appears to apply the *lex situs* to both capacity to dispose of land and capacity to contract to do so (see further details in Chapter 8).

5.5   Scope of the applicable law under the Convention

The applicable law identified by virtue of the Convention provisions does not necessarily govern all issues of a given contract. For instance, as already noted, it does not govern some issues of formal validity, nor does it govern issues of capacity. Material validity is, however, governed by the applicable law. Article 10 lists some examples to which the applicable law extends. These are embodied in Art 10(1) as follows:

(a) *interpretation* of the contract: this reflects the position under the traditional English rules (see *Bonython v Commonwealth of Australia* (1951) where it was held that the interpretation of a contract was governed by the applicable law);

(b) *performance*: according to the Giuliano-Lagarde Report, performance is likely to involve such issues as conditions as to the time and place of performance, alternative obligations, pecuniary obligations, the diligence with which the obligation must be performed, and so forth;

(c) within the limits of the powers conferred on the court by its procedural law, the consequences of the breach, including the assessment of damages in so far as it is governed by rules of law. 'The consequences of the breach,' according to the Giuliano-Lagarde Report, entail such issues as the liability of the party who is responsible for the breach, claims for termination of the contract for breach, and any requirement of service of notice on the party to assume his liability. The consequences of breach include the 'assessment of damages', but in so far as it is governed by rules of law. The Giuliano-Lagarde Report gives examples of cases where the question of assessment is one of law, such as where the contract prescribes the level of damages in relation to non-performance, or where there is an international convention which imposes a limit on the right of compensation;

(d) the various ways of extinguishing obligations, and prescription and limitation of actions. Similarly, the English common law rules invoke the applicable law to decide whether a particular obligation has been discharged either as a result of a breach or by frustration. For instance, in *Jacobs v Crédit Lyonnais* (1884), the defendants agreed to sell to the plaintiffs in London some goods to be shipped from Algeria on board ships provided by the latter. On failing to deliver part of the goods, the defendants contended that, due to the military operations in Algeria, the performance of the contract was rendered impossible and that by French law, which prevailed in Algeria, *'force majeure'* was an excuse for non-performance. The Court of Appeal, however, rejected this argument and held that the proper law of the contract was English and, because such a defence was not admissible under English law, the defendants were liable in damages.

Equally, by virtue of s 1(1) of the Foreign Limitation Periods Act 1984, all limitation periods, whether it be English or foreign, are governed by the applicable law;

(e) the consequences of nullity of contract: this provision is not part of UK law. Indeed, the UK entered a reservation on this provision on the basis that the consequences of nullity of contract form part of the law of restitution. As discussed in Chapter 3, there exists in English law a problem as to the classification of claims for unjust enrichment. English conflict of laws is still in its infancy as to whether such claims are to be classed as contractual, tortious, or quasi-contractual. It is suggested, however, that a claim arising out of a null contract may be regarded as one of unjust enrichment rather than one of contract (see the House of Lords' decision in *Kleinwort Benson Ltd v Glasgow City Council* (1997), in respect of unjust enrichment and the Brussels Convention). Clarkson and Hill have submitted that it is for this reason that Art 10(1)(e) was not implemented into UK legislation (*Jaffey on the Conflict of Laws*, 1997, pp 273–78).

A further reference to performance is made in Art 10(2), which provides that:

> In relation to the manner of performance and the steps to be taken in the event of defective performance, regard shall be had to the law of the country in which performance takes place.

In other words, despite the fact that the applicable law governs performance, the law of the country of the place of performance should be considered when the issue is related to the manner of performance and the steps to be taken in the event of defective performance. As to the issues which are likely to fall within the notion of 'manner of performance', the Giuliano-Lagarde Report provides some examples, such as the manner in which goods are to be examined, and the consequences and the steps to be taken in case of refusal to accept delivery. Presumably, it will be for the law of the forum to decide whether or not a particular issue is one relating to the 'manner of performance'. The provisions of Art 10(2) are rendered more vague by the fact that, in such cases, the court is merely required to have regard to that law, but the extent to which such law should affect the outcome of a case is not specified. Perhaps this is a provision which must await elucidation and clarification by case law.

5.6 Limitations on the applicable law

There are two limitations on the applicable law, that is, 'mandatory rules' under Art 7 and '*ordre public*' (public policy) under Art 16 of the Convention.

5.6.1 Mandatory rules

The concept of mandatory rules is one of the key issues in the Rome Convention, where it is used under at least six different provisions, namely Arts 3(3), 5(2), 6(1), 9(6), 7(1) and 7(2). Whilst the first four provisions apply in very limited circumstances, the last two are of a much wider scope.

Article 7(1) is related to the mandatory rules of a foreign country, and Art 7(2) is related to the mandatory rules of the forum. Only the latter provision is given effect in English law, and, therefore, it will form the starting point. Article 7(2) provides that:

> Nothing in this Convention shall restrict the application of the rules of the law of the forum in a situation where they are mandatory irrespective of the law otherwise applicable to the contract.

Mandatory rules are defined in Art 3(3) as rules 'which cannot be derogated from by contract'. Rules of this type are contained in what is called 'overriding statutes' in English law. The operation of such rules may be illustrated by the case of *The Hollandia* (1983). In this case, the plaintiffs shipped a machine on board a Dutch vessel belonging to the defendant carriers for carriage from Scotland to the Dutch West Indies. The bill of lading contained a choice of law clause in favour of Dutch law, and an exclusive jurisdiction clause in favour of the court of Amsterdam. While the machine was being unloaded, it was dropped and severely damaged. The damage was estimated at about £22,000, and the plaintiffs brought an action *in rem* against the ship's sister *The Hollandia* in the English court. The carriers, relying on both the jurisdiction and the choice of law clauses, applied for a stay of the English proceedings. Dutch law at the time still applied the Hague Rules, whereby the carrier was able to limit his liability to about £250. English law, however, applied and still applies the amended Hague/Visby Rules implemented by the Carriage of Goods by Sea Act 1971, whereby the limitation of liability was in the region of £11,000. Moreover, the Hague/Visby Rules provide that the Rules *shall* apply to, *inter alia*, every bill of lading if the carriage of goods is from a port in a Contracting State. They also provide that any agreement lessening the carrier's liability for loss or damage to the goods otherwise than as provided in the Rules *shall* be null and void and of no effect. On the issue of the choice of law clause, the House of Lords held that the Hague/Visby Rules were of an overriding nature and that the English court would not give effect to a choice of law clause that would result in limiting the carrier's liability to a sum lower than that dictated by these Rules. Accordingly, the choice of law clause was null and void.

Similarly, in *Boissevain v Weil* (1950), the English court refused to enforce a contract entered into in Monaco under Monégasque law, on the ground that it contravened the now repealed UK Exchange Control Act 1947, which was of an overriding nature.

The Giuliano-Lagarde Report cites some examples of the type of rules which Contracting States were keen to preserve as mandatory overriding rules. These include rules on competition and restrictive practices, consumer protection, employment protection legislation and certain rules on carriage.

An important example of modern mandatory rules in English law may be found in the Unfair Contract Terms Act 1977, which imposes restrictions on the validity of exclusion or exemption clauses in various types of contracts. More important is the provision of s 27(2) of this Act, which states:

> This Act has effect notwithstanding any contract term which applies or purports to apply the law of any country outside the United Kingdom, where (either or both):
>
> (a) the term appears to the court, or arbitrator or arbiter to have been imposed wholly or mainly for the purpose of enabling the party imposing it to evade the operation of this Act; or
>
> (b) in the making of the contract, one of the parties dealt as consumer, and he was then habitually resident in the United Kingdom, and the essential steps necessary for the making of the contract were taken there, whether by him or by others on his behalf.

It is essential to note that the above sub-section provides for the operation of the restrictions on the use of exclusion clauses in the international context. It is not, however, of a universal character. It is only intended to prevent the parties to a contract most closely connected with the UK from contracting out of the restrictions laid down by the 1977 Act, by choosing the law of a country outside the UK. If the requirements of s 27(2) are met, the courts of the UK will not strike the parties' choice of a foreign law, but will apply it to the contract subject to the restrictions of the 1977 Act. Article 7(2) of the Convention will, therefore, apply to cases coming within s 27(2) of the 1977 Act.

In relation to the mandatory rules of other countries, Art 7(1) provides that:

> ... when applying under this Convention the law of a country, effect may be given to the mandatory rules of the law of another country with which the situation has a close connection, if and in so far as, under the law of the latter country, those rules must be applied whatever the law applicable to the contract. In considering whether to give effect to these mandatory rules, regard shall be had to their nature and purpose and to the consequences of their application or non-application.

The application of Art 7(1) in the UK is specifically excluded by s 2(2) of the Contracts (Applicable Law) Act 1990, in accordance with Art 22 of the Convention. Therefore, it is sufficient to note that it is both wide and vague. As it stands and without further elucidation by guidance from case law, it is likely to be difficult to determine its parameters for two reasons. First, it refers to the mandatory rules of a country which 'has close connection', which is very vague to determine. Secondly, it gives a discretion to the forum as to whether or not to apply these mandatory rules by providing 'effect may be given ...'.

5.6.2 Public policy

Article 16 provides that:

> ... the application of a rule of the law of any country specified by this Convention may be refused only if such application is manifestly incompatible with the public policy ('*ordre public*') of the forum.

Hence, even if there is no 'overriding statute', the English courts may still refuse the application of a law identified as applicable by the Convention, provided that it is manifestly contrary to public policy.

At common law, English courts refused to enforce a contract where to do so would contravene the principles of English public policy. For instance, English courts would not enforce a contract which, though valid by its proper law, contravened the law of a friendly country. In *Regazzoni v KC Sethia Ltd* (1958), a contract for the sale of jute bags from Indian defendants to Swiss purchasers provided for English law as the applicable law. The defendants knew that the purchasers intended to transport the jute to South Africa, and both knew that such a transport was illegal by Indian law. The defendants failed to supply the goods and relied on the illegality by Indian law. The House of Lords held that, although the contract was legal by its proper law, the English court, as a matter of public policy, would not enforce a contract where the parties have set up to break the law of a foreign and friendly State.

The principles of public policy could equally be invoked where a contract, though valid by its proper law, involved the *commission* of an act which was unlawful by the *lex loci solutionis*, that is, the law of the place of performance. For instance, in *Ralli Brothers v Compania Naviera Y Aznar* (1920), which concerned a contract to carry jute from India to Spain, the contract was subject to English law and provided that payment of freight would be made on delivery in Spain. During transit, a Spanish decree came into force and made it illegal for payment of freight to exceed a certain amount. Such statutory amount was much lower than that agreed in the contract. The Court of Appeal applied English law as the proper law of the contract and held, however, that the Spanish decree had the effect of frustrating the obligation to pay any excess over and above the statutory limit.

5.7 Exclusion of *renvoi*

The Rome Convention excludes the application of *renvoi* in express terms. Article 15 provides that any reference to the applicable law of a country, specified by the provisions of the Convention, is taken to mean the application of the domestic law of that country excluding its rules of private international law. Similarly, under the English common law rules, *renvoi* was expressly excluded by the judiciary. For instance, in *Re United Railways of Havana and*

Regla Warehouses Ltd (1960), Lord Jenkins stated that the principle of *renvoi* found no place in the field of contract; and in *Amin Rasheed Shipping Corpn v Kuwait Insurance Co* (1984), Lord Diplock elaborated on this issue and stated that the proper law of a contract 'is the substantive law of the country which the parties have chosen as that by which their mutual legally enforceable rights are to be ascertained, but excluding any *renvoi*, whether of remission or transmission, that the courts of that country might themselves apply if the matter were litigated before them'. He proceeded to give an example and said that if 'a contract made in England were expressed to be governed by French law, the English court would apply French substantive law to it notwithstanding that a French court applying its own conflict rules might accept a *renvoi* to English law as the *lex loci contractus* if the matter were litigated before it'.

CHOICE OF LAW IN CONTRACT

The Contracts (Applicable Law) Act 1990

This Act implements the Rome Convention 1980. It came into force on 1 April 1991.

Where the parties have made a choice of law in their contract, this will be upheld unless, where all the other relevant elements are connected with one country only, that choice prejudices the application of that country's mandatory rules.

Where no such choice of law is made, the contract will be governed by the law of the country with which it is most closely connected.

It is to be presumed that the contract is most closely connected with the country where the party who is to effect the characteristic performance of the contract has his habitual residence at the time of the conclusion of the contract.

Where, however, the subject matter of the contract is a right in immovable property, then the contract is presumed to be most closely connected with the *lex situs*.

Contracts for the carriage of goods are presumed to be most closely connected with the country in which the carrier has his principal place of business, provided that this country is also the place of loading, discharge, or the principal place of business of the consignor.

These presumptions may be rebutted if it appears that the contract is more closely connected with another country.

Special rules on choice of law are also made in relation to consumer contracts and individual employment contracts.

In general, the application of the law identified by the Convention must not restrict the application of the mandatory rules of the forum which cannot be derogated from by contract.

Equally, the application of the proper law may be refused if it is manifestly incompatible with the public policy of the forum.

Renvoi is expressly excluded from the scope of the Convention.

Material validity

Issues of material validity are to be governed by the law which would govern the contract had the latter been validly created.

Formal validity

Issues of formal validity are determined as follows:

(a) where the parties are resident in the same country, the contract is formally valid if it meets the requirements of either the law of that country or the law identified by the Convention;

(b) where the parties are not in the same country, formal validity is tested by the law of either country or by the proper law of the contract;

(c) formal validity of consumer contracts is subject to the requirements of the law of the country where the consumer is resident;

(d) formal validity of contracts for rights in immovable property must be subject to the formal requirements of the *lex situs*.

Scope of the applicable law under the Convention

The applicable law under the Convention governs such issues as interpretation of the contract, performance, the consequences of breach, discharge, and the manner of performance and the steps to be taken in the event of defective performance.

CHAPTER 6

CHOICE OF LAW IN TORT

6.1 Introduction

The question of choice of law in tort is a difficult and complicated one. Its difficulty stems from the many types of torts which exist, such as negligence, assault, defamation, etc; and the various kinds of scenarios in which a claim in relation to a particular tort may arise. Moreover, unlike contracts, where disputes can be anticipated and a choice of law clause to this effect may be inserted by the parties, tort injuries are most unexpected and parties are hardly likely to give advance thought to any choice of law. Until injuries occur and the injured party decides to pursue a claim for compensation, the issue of choice of law in tort will not arise.

This question has become even more complicated since the latter half of the 19th century, largely due to technological advances, modern means of transport, and the fact that the marketing of products is no longer restricted to national boundaries. Suppose that a drug is manufactured in country A and marketed in country B, where X consumes it and suffers personal injuries as a result. Y, a French tourist, is injured in a car accident driven by Z, an English domiciliary, in Belgium. Defamatory letters are written by N against M in Germany, and published in London. An aircraft negligently manufactured in Japan crashes over England, injuring and causing the deaths of passengers from 15 different countries. An English employee suffers injuries as a result of an industrial accident in Libya. If an action is brought in England on any of these torts, which law will an English court apply?

To apply the law of the forum may lead to injustice and inconvenience, for a defendant may be held liable for an act which may constitute a tort in England, but not in the place where it was committed. Besides, if the law of the forum were to apply as a general rule, then that would give the plaintiff an incentive to forum shop for a place where the law is more favourable to him or her than that of the place where the tort was committed. On the other hand, to apply the law of the place of tort, though probably giving effect to the natural expectations of the parties, may provoke doubts as to whether that law is the most appropriate one to apply, especially in the case where the parties have little or no connection with that place. One solution would be to apply the proper law of tort, that is, 'the law which has the most significant connection with the chain of acts and circumstances in the particular case in question'. This latter approach, though appearing sound and fair, sacrifices the advantages of certainty and predictability.

6.2   The English approach

Until recently, the question of choice of law in tort had been governed by the common law rules. However, due to their unsatisfactory impact, these rules have been repealed, to a large extent, by virtue of Pt III of the Private International Law (Miscellaneous Provisions) Act 1995 (PILA). Part III came into force on 1 May 1996 and only affects the choice of law rules applicable to torts which occur after that date. Hence, the common law rules will remain relevant for some time to come, partly because they still apply to claims where the tort occurred prior to that date, and partly because the new provisions under Pt III of the Act exclude the tort of defamation from their scope.

Since the tort of defamation is excluded from the scope of Pt III, and, therefore, remains governed by the common law rules, the analysis of these rules will form the starting point. This will also help the reader to appreciate more fully the impact of the new provisions. Additionally, the common law rules may be of indirect relevance to English courts when determining the relationship between the general rule, under s 11 of the PILA 1995, and the exception, in s 12, for the common law rules operated within a similar basic framework, that is, a general rule and an exception.

6.3   The common law rules

The common law rules on choice of law in tort could generally be seen as a compromise between the law of the forum and the law of the place where the tort was committed. These rules, however, have been often described as 'raising one of the most vexed questions in the conflict of laws'. The choice of law rules in this field differ, depending on whether the tort was committed in England or abroad. It must be noted that determining the place of tort may no longer be required in cases where Pt III of the PILA 1995 is applicable. Nevertheless, where the tort is one of defamation, this distinction remains important to ascertain the choice of law.

6.3.1   Torts committed in England

Where a tort is found to have been committed in England, the English courts always apply English law. This is the case irrespective of how limited the parties' connection is with England. This rule could be illustrated by the case of *Szalatnay-Stacho v Fink* (1947), where the defendant, an official of the Czech Government in exile in England, sent some documents to the President of the Czech Republic who was also in England. These documents, which were published in England, alleged misconduct by the plaintiff, who was the Czech Acting Minister in Egypt. The plaintiff brought an action for defamation. Under Czech law, the publication of these documents fell within the defence of absolute privilege, which meant that no action for defamation could be brought under that law. Under English law, however, the defence of qualified privilege applied. This meant that the defendant would not be liable where, having had information placed upon him, he was under a duty to disclose them. The Court of Appeal held that, as the documents had been published here, the tort was committed in England, and therefore, English law was the governing law.

This principle was confirmed by the Court of Appeal in *Metall und Rohstoff AG v Donaldson Lufkin and Jenrette Inc* (1990), where it was stated that, if the tort was committed in England, then English law would apply to the dispute.

6.3.2 Torts committed abroad

Where the tort is alleged to have been committed abroad, then the rule in *Phillips v Eyre* (1870), also known as the double-actionability rule, applies. In this case, the plaintiff brought an action for assault and false imprisonment by the defendant, the Governor of Jamaica, during a rebellion on the island. The defendant argued, however, that the grievances complained of were necessary measures implemented to suppress the rebellion and were, therefore, reasonable and in good faith for the purpose of putting an end to it. In his judgment, Willes J laid down his famous *dictum* (p 28) as follows:

> As a general rule, in order to found a suit in England for a wrong alleged to have been committed abroad, two conditions must be fulfilled. First, the wrong must be of such a character that it would have been actionable if committed in England ... Secondly, the act must not have been justifiable by the law of the place where it was done.

Hence, in an action on a foreign tort, the applicable law would be determined according to the above formula, that is, the alleged wrong must be actionable in England, and it must not be justifiable by the law of the place where it was committed. The phrase 'not justifiable' was subsequently replaced by the word 'actionable', as a result of the House of Lords decision in *Boys v Chaplin* (1971). What this formula means, and how it has been applied, will be dealt with in due course. It suffices to note at this stage that the opening words of Willes J indicated that this formula is to be applied as a general rule. However, as the rule only applies to foreign torts, it is necessary to deal first with the question of how the place of tort is ascertained.

6.4   Place of tort

There have been very few cases where the question of ascertaining the place of tort has arisen in the choice of law context. Indeed, until 1987, this question had arisen in the context of jurisdiction where it had been necessary for the English courts to determine the place of tort for the purpose of granting leave to serve the writ outside the jurisdiction under what used to be RSC Ord 11 r 1(1)(h). That rule allowed the English court to exercise its discretion to grant such leave where the action was founded upon a tort committed within the jurisdiction. Alas, the test which was devised by the English courts for the purpose of that rule has been also applied in the small number of cases where the question of ascertaining the place of tort has arisen in the choice of law context.

This policy is questionable, on the grounds that a decision to grant leave for service out of the jurisdiction was and remains discretionary, and that a court, whilst it 'may be prepared to hold that a tort is committed in several places for the purposes of a jurisdictional rule, it should insist on one single place of the tort in the choice of law context' (Cheshire and North, *Private International Law*, 12th edn, pp 552–54). In addition, the new rule, which replaced r 1(1)(h), now contained in r 1(1)(f), no longer requires the allocation of the place of tort, for it allows the English court to exercise its discretion either where the tort is committed, or where the damage occurred, in England (see Chapter 2). Nevertheless, the fact remains that the same test has been employed to ascertain the place of tort in the context of choice of law. For instance, in the recent case of *Metall und Rohstoff AG v Donaldson Lufkin and Jenrette Inc* (1990), the Court of Appeal ascertained the place of tort by reference to cases decided under the old tort head of Ord 11, and applied the test of 'where in substance did the cause of action arise'.

Notwithstanding that the same test has been applied, the place of tort varies in accordance with the subject matter of the dispute in question. Therefore, it is necessary to look at how this test operated in the context of particular torts. As adumbrated earlier, however, save for the tort of defamation, which remains governed by the common law rules, the determination of the place of tort may no longer be required under Pt III of the PILA 1995. Thus, this paragraph will focus on the tort of defamation, but as the common law rules are still relevant in respect of torts committed before 1 May 1996, the other types of tort will be discussed briefly.

6.4.1 Defamation

In *Bata v Bata* (1948) the Court of Appeal held that where defamatory letters had been written in Switzerland, but published in England, the tort was committed in England. This was because publication was the essential element of the tort of libel. Hence, the place of publication would be treated as the place where the tort was committed. Indeed, this could also be inferred in the choice of law case of *Church of Scientology v Metropolitan Police Commissioner* (1976). Here, the plaintiffs, the Church of Scientology of California resident in England, brought an action for libel against the defendant, the Commissioner of the Metropolitan Police in England. It was alleged that four police officers, acting under the defendant's control, had published to the then Federal Police Authority of West Germany, a report relating to the plaintiffs' activities which was defamatory to them. Notwithstanding that this case dealt with the choice of law question, the Court of Appeal proceeded on the assumption that the tort was committed in Germany where the report was published.

6.4.2 Negligence

In *George Monro Ltd v American Cyanamid and Chemical Corpn* (1944), the Court of Appeal laid down the test as being: 'Where was the wrongful act, from which the damage flows, in fact done?' The question was not where the damage was suffered, even though damage might have been the gist of the action. In this case, it was held that the wrongful act was done in New York, where the goods were negligently manufactured, and not in England, where they caused injury and damage to a farmer who used them on his land. However, in *Distillers Co (Bio-Chemicals) Ltd v Thompson* (1971), the Privy Council modified the test by addressing the question of: 'where in substance did the cause of action arise?' The case concerned a drug, Distaval, which was manufactured in England and marketed in New South Wales, Australia. The exporting company neither warned the importing company nor put a warning on the drug disclosing the risks involved when taken by pregnant women in the early weeks of pregnancy. The plaintiff's mother purchased the drug in Australia, where she consumed it whilst pregnant. This resulted in the baby being born with physical deformities. An action was brought in the Australian court. On appeal to the Privy Council, the substance test was applied and it was held that the tort was committed in Australia. Unlike the above case, where the tort consisted of negligent manufacture in New York, here the tort consisted of negligent failure to give adequate warnings as to the drug's harmful side effects in Australia, where it was marketed. (See, also, *Castree v Squibb Ltd* (1980), where it was held that, in ascertaining the place of tort, the court had to look back over the series of events which were said to constitute the tort and decide where in substance the cause of action arose. The plaintiff's cause of action arose in England, since it was not the mere manufacture of the defective machine which constituted the tort, but the act of placing it onto the English market with no warning as to its defects. Accordingly, the tort was committed in England.)

6.4.3 Fraudulent misrepresentation

Where the alleged tort is one of fraudulent misrepresentation made by instantaneous communications, then according to *Diamond v Bank of London and Montreal Ltd* (1979), the tort is committed when the message was received and acted upon. Equally, in *Armagas Ltd v Mundogas SA* (1986), the Court of Appeal held that the tort of fraudulent misrepresentation was committed where the misrepresentation was communicated orally and acted upon in Denmark.

6.4.4 Economic torts

Economic torts entail such issues as intimidation, interference with contractual rights and inducing a breach of contract. In *Metall und Rohstoff AG v Donaldson Lufkin and Jenrette Inc* (1990), a Swiss company brought an action in the English court against two US companies for, *inter alia*, inducing a breach of contract. The acts which led to the alleged inducement occurred in a series of meetings in the USA, as a result of which the plaintiff's brokers committed breaches of contract in England. The Court of Appeal held that the tort was committed in England, where the breaches of contract and the resulting damage occurred, even though the acts of inducement took place in the USA (it must be noted that the above case was overruled in the subsequent case of *Lonrho plc v Fayed* (1991), but on a different point).

6.5 The double-actionability rule for defamation

As previously stated, where a tort is committed in England, English law applies; but where it is committed abroad, the double-actionability rule in *Phillips v Eyre* (1870) applies. As a general rule, to found a suit in England for a tort alleged to have been committed abroad, two conditions must be satisfied:

(a) the act must be *actionable* as a tort in England; and

(b) it must be *actionable* by the law of the place where it was committed.

The first limb of the rule, requiring actionability as a tort in England, has been subject to much criticism. It owes its origin to the Privy Council decision in *The Halley* (1868), where an action for the employer's vicarious liability was dismissed on the ground that such a tort was then unknown to English law.

The second limb of the rule, when initially formulated by Willes J in *Phillips v Eyre* (1870), had imposed a requirement of 'non-justifiability' by the law of the place where the wrongful act was committed. This, however, was taken to mean that the second limb of the rule would be satisfied even if the defendant's act did not amount to civil liability by the law of that place. For instance, in *Machado v Fontes* (1897), the defendant had published a defamatory statement against the plaintiff in Brazil. Under the law of Brazil, the defendant's conduct attracted criminal liability, but no civil claim for damages was allowed. The Court of Appeal held that, whilst the first limb of the rule would only be satisfied if the defendant's conduct was actionable as a tort in England, to satisfy the second limb it was sufficient that the conduct was wrongful by the *lex loci delicti*. Hence, the fact that the defendant was only criminally liable was held to satisfy the requirement of 'non-justifiability' by the law of the place where the act was committed. This case was, however, overruled by the House of Lords in *Boys v Chaplin* (1971), where the second limb of the rule in *Phillips v Eyre* was modified and the phrase 'non-justifiable' was replaced by *actionable*.

6.5.1 An exception to the rule

Boys v Chaplin (1971) was of further importance, as it paved the way towards establishing an exception to the general rule. Here, the plaintiff and defendant were both resident in England, but temporarily stationed in Malta in the British armed forces. While both were off duty, the plaintiff was seriously injured in a road accident as a result of the defendant's negligent driving. Under the law of Malta, the plaintiff could only recover special damages for his expenses and proved loss of earnings. Under English law, however, he could also recover general damages for pain and suffering. The House of Lords unanimously held that the plaintiff should recover damages assessed according to English law. This was a most unsatisfactory decision, for their Lordships' conclusion was based on divergent reasoning:

(a) Lord Hodson stated that 'the question of right to damages for pain and suffering is a substantive right'. English law, however, was applied on the basis that the rule in *Phillips v Eyre* should be flexibly interpreted;

(b) Lord Guest rejected the proper law approach and was of the view that the right to claim damages for pain and suffering was a procedural matter and English law should be applied as the law of the forum;

(c) Lord Donovan was of the view that while the double actionability rule should be preserved, the English court should apply its own law to the issue of damages, as this was a procedural issue;

(d) Lord Wilberforce stated that the issue of damages was substantive and should be governed by the applicable law, which was Maltese law. However, English law should apply on the basis that the general rule must apply with flexibility and should be departed from in the presence of clear and satisfying grounds to do so;

(e) Lord Pearson, by way of second preference, concurred with both Lord Hodson and Lord Wilberforce that the issue before the court was substantive. Although the rule in *Phillips v Eyre* stood as good law, it should be applied with flexibility. However, he applied English law as the substantive law, on the basis that, as the law of forum, it should play a predominant role in determining the cause of action.

Despite the variety of reasons expressed by their Lordships, it is submitted that this decision is authority for the proposition that the general rule should apply with flexibility and should be departed from when necessary to do so.

There has been a wide acceptance of the view that the proposition above, which originated in Lord Wilberforce's judgment, constituted an exception to the general rule in *Phillips v Eyre*. Even though great uncertainty has surrounded its nature and extent, it has been taken in numerous cases to mean that it is an exception in favour of the proper law of the tort. One such instance could be found in *Johnson v Coventry Churchill International Ltd* (1992). In this case, the defendants were an English employment agency which recruited personnel to work abroad. The plaintiff, following an advertisement in a newspaper, was hired to work in Germany under a contract which provided that he was at all times to work as and where directed by the defendants and their clients. Whilst working in Germany, the plaintiff was injured on a building site. West German law did not impose liability on an employer for personal injuries suffered by his employees as a result of the former's negligence. The plaintiff brought an action in the English court, claiming damages on the ground that the defendants had failed to provide a safe system of work. The defendants contended, *inter alia*, that the action should fail on the ground that the double actionability rule was not satisfied. It was held, however, that the defendants' negligence was an issue which fell within the scope of the exception to the general rule of double-actionability. Under this exception, a wrong allegedly committed in a foreign country was actionable as a tort according to English law in circumstances where justice to the plaintiff dictated that English law should be applied as the law of the country having the most significant relationship with the occurrence of the act and the parties. The facts that the parties were both English, the contract was expressly made subject to English law, and the defendants, by taking out insurance to protect their position as employers of English workers abroad, were unlikely to be taken unawares by the consequences of applying English law, tipped the scales in favour of English law.

The exception to the general rule has been widely recognised, but successfully applied in a couple of cases post-*Boys v Chaplin* and merely to govern a particular issue in a given case. However, its application had resulted only in ousting the law of the place of tort in favour of the law of the forum. Accordingly, many questions remained unanswered: for instance, whether the exception could apply to the whole case rather than a single issue, whether it would apply where the parties to the action were domiciled in different countries, and whether it could operate to oust the law of the forum in favour of the law of the place where the tort was committed. It was not until the case of *Red Sea Insurance Co Ltd v Bouygues SA* (1994) that some of these questions were resolved and the extent of the exception was somewhat elaborated.

6.5.2 The exception in the *Red Sea* case

In July 1994, Lord Slynn delivered the Privy Council judgment in *Red Sea Insurance Co Ltd v Bouygues SA*. The facts of this case could be summarised as follows.

The 23 plaintiffs, participants in a construction project in Saudi Arabia, brought an action in the Hong Kong court against an insurance company, Red Sea, incorporated in Hong Kong. The plaintiffs claimed indemnity under the insurance policy for loss and expenses incurred as a result of correcting certain structural damage. Red Sea argued that such a loss was not insured under the policy. However, it counterclaimed that, if it was liable, then the fourth to 13th plaintiffs, PCG, who were suppliers of precast building units, were in breach of their duty of care towards the other plaintiffs and that, as insurer of the project, Red Sea was subrogated to the plaintiffs' rights. PCG applied to strike out the counterclaim. At that stage, Red Sea further claimed that it was entitled, by virtue of Saudi Arabian law, to sue PCG directly for the damage caused to the other plaintiffs.

The court of Hong Kong applied the double-actionability rule and ordered the counterclaim to be struck out. This was based on the grounds that, under Hong Kong law, no right of subrogation could arise until payment had been made by the insurer; that such proceedings had to be brought in the name of the insured; and that Saudi Arabian law alone could not be relied upon to determine liability in tort in the courts of Hong Kong. On appeal, the Court of Appeal of Hong Kong set aside the order, striking out the counterclaim, and held that Red Sea had the right to try to establish that it had indirect claim by way of subrogation under the law of Saudi Arabia. Nevertheless, Red Sea could not sue PCG directly for negligence by relying solely on the *lex loci delicti*.

However, on appeal to the Privy Council, Lord Slynn, who delivered the court's judgment, held that the general rule with regard to foreign torts required double-actionability both in the *lex fori* and the *lex loci delicti*. However, exceptionally and in an appropriate case, a plaintiff could rely on the *lex loci delicti* exclusively, even if under the *lex fori* his or her claim would not be actionable. The fact that the court would be required to apply a foreign law when its own law would not give a remedy should nevertheless be taken into account in deciding whether the exception should be invoked. He further held that the exception could be applied to the whole claim as well as to merely a specific isolated issue. Accordingly, since all the significant factors connected the case with Saudi Arabia, the exception to the general rule should be applied. Furthermore, the Court of Appeal decision – that the defendant's direct cause of action against PCG, relying solely on Saudi Arabian law , was unsustainable – was wrong.

Hence, the decision in this case has widened the extent of the exception. It expressly indicated that the exception could apply either to the whole case or to specific issues arising in a particular case. The exception could also operate to oust the *lex fori* in favour of applying the *lex loci delicti* and vice versa.

6.6   Scope of the double-actionability rule

Suppose that a news reporter, in the course of his or her employment, published in a foreign country a statement defamatory to a certain individual. By the law of that country, the reporter was liable in tort, but the employer was not, that is, there was no provision for vicarious liability under the foreign law.

However, under English law, such liability existed. Thus, the tort would be actionable under both English law and the foreign law, but not against the same defendant. The question arises as to whether that would be sufficient to invoke the double-actionability rule. The same question would equally arise in relation to the issue of plaintiffs and the issue of contractual defences. Each of these will be examined separately.

6.6.1 The same defendant

For the double-actionability rule to be applied, it is not sufficient for the plaintiff to show merely that the wrongful act would give rise to liability in the foreign country; he or she also has to show that the tort would be actionable against the same defendant. This could be illustrated by the decision in *The Mary Moxham* (1876), where an action was brought in England against the owner of a British ship for causing damage to the plaintiff's pier in Spain. The plaintiff's action failed because the doctrine of vicarious liability, though part of English law, did not apply under Spanish law. The latter would regard only the master and crew, but not the shipowner, as the defendants.

6.6.2 The same plaintiff

In addition to the defendant having to be the same in both the *lex fori* and the *lex loci delicti*, the plaintiff also has to be the same. There is very little authority in relation to this issue in English law, but regard could be had to some Australian authorities. For instance, in *Corcoran v Corcoran* (1974), where both the plaintiff and defendant were domiciled in Victoria, where their car was also registered. The wife was injured when she was travelling as a passenger in a car negligently driven by her husband in New South Wales. By the law of New South Wales, the wife could not sue her husband, because he was immune by statute from being sued by his wife in tort. By the law of Victoria, however, she could. So, the wife brought her action in the court of Victoria. The Supreme Court of Victoria held that, were the general rule in *Phillips v Eyre* to apply strictly, the wife's action should fail. Nevertheless, according to the House of Lords in *Boys v Chaplin*, this rule should apply flexibly when clear and satisfying grounds required so. Therefore, as, in this case, the plaintiff, defendant and car were all connected with Victoria, and the only connection with New South Wales was the occurrence of the accident, the exception to the rule would apply. Accordingly, the plaintiff's action succeeded.

This line of reasoning was also applied in *Red Sea Insurance v Bouygues* (1994) where, it may be recalled, Red Sea contended, *inter alia*, that by virtue of Saudi Arabian law, but not Hong Kong law, it was entitled to sue PCG directly for the damage caused to the other plaintiffs. By way of an exception to the double-actionability rule, the Privy Council held that Red Sea was entitled to do so.

6.6.3   Contractual defences to claims in tort

The issue of raising contractual defences in a tort claim was far from being resolved under the common law. This is still so, even after the adoption of the PILA 1995, for Pt III thereof is silent on this point.

Hence, the pre-existing common law rules remain relevant.

In some instances, a contract may contain a clause limiting or excluding liability for, *inter alia*, personal injury or damage to property. If an injured party was to bring an action in tort against the defendant, could the clause contained in the contract operate so as to deny the plaintiff his or her claim for compensation in tort? In other words, would the defendant be able to raise such a clause in the contract as a defence to prevent the plaintiff from recovering in tort? The validity of this question was examined by the Court of Appeal in *Sayers v International Drilling* (1971). The plaintiff, an Englishman, entered into a contract of employment with the defendants, a Dutch company, to work on their oil rig in Nigerian waters. The contract contained a clause stating that the plaintiff should accept the benefits provided by the company's Disability Compensation Programme as his exclusive remedy in the event of accidental injury or disability in lieu of any claims, rights or action under English law or the law of any other nation. The clause was valid by Dutch law, but was invalid by English law. Soon after arriving in Nigeria, he was injured in a serious accident, allegedly caused by the negligence of his fellow employees. He brought an action in tort against his employer in England. The defendant raised the exclusion clause as a defence to the action. The Court of Appeal unanimously held that the plaintiff's claim should fail, but on two different grounds. The majority of their Lordships came to the conclusion that the proper law of the contract was Dutch law and accordingly any claim in tort was defeated by the exemption clause. Lord Denning MR, however, was of the view that the claim was one in tort, the proper law of which was Dutch law. Although he said that the proper law of the contract was English law, he concluded that as the court 'cannot apply two systems of law, one for the claim in tort, and the other for the defence in contract', the issue of liability should be determined by Dutch law.

The outcome of this case was that the majority of the Court of Appeal treated the validity of such a clause as a purely contractual issue. However, their Lordships failed to consider the relevance of Nigerian law as the *lex loci delicti*, despite the fact that the plaintiff had brought his action in tort.

This issue was further explored in the subsequent case of *Coupland v Arabian Gulf Oil Co* (1983). Here, the plaintiff, while working as a technician in Libya for the defendant oil company, had an accident as a result of which his leg was amputated from below the knee. He received payments for his injuries under Libyan social security and labour laws and under an insurance policy taken out by the employer. In an action for negligence against the defendants, the Court of Appeal held that the plaintiff was entitled to his claim. It was further held that Libyan law was the proper law of the contract of employment, but since the plaintiff's claim was based on a tort committed abroad, then the rule in *Phillips v Eyre* would apply. Accordingly, English law would apply in so far as the claim in tort was not excluded or restricted under the terms of the contract. The Court of Appeal, however, did not explain the further implications in such cases. As such, it is not sufficiently clear what the general rule in relation to a contractual defence raised in a tort claim would be.

6.7 Problems associated with the double-actionability rule and the tort of defamation

It is clear and beyond doubt that the double-actionability rule is in need of certainty and clarity. The nature and extent of the exception requires further elaboration. The distinction between English and foreign torts adds unnecessary complications. More importantly, the general rule of double-actionability could lead to very unjust results. This latter deficiency was described by the Lord Chancellor, Lord MacKay of Clashfern, in the course of the proceedings of the Special Public Bill Committee (SPBC, HL, Paper 36, Session 1994–95, March 1995, p 3) in the following terms:

> The law is to the advantage of the defendant, because, as a general rule, the plaintiff cannot succeed in any claim unless both the law of the forum and the law of the place where the wrong occurred make provision for it, whereas the defendant can escape liability by taking advantage of any defence available under either law. This appears unfair to plaintiffs, because it ensures that they cannot succeed to a greater extent than is provided by the less generous of the two systems of law concerned.

Indeed, such injustice could be illustrated by the often cited Scottish case of *M'Elroy v M'Allister* (1949) where the plaintiff's husband was killed in an accident at Shap in England, 40 miles south of the border, when a lorry was being driven by another fellow employee in the course of business for their Scottish employer. All parties were Scots. The plaintiff sued in Scotland in her capacity as the husband's *executrix-dative*, claiming: (a) solatium under Scots law *(lex fori)*; (b) and (c) by English law *(lex loci delicti)* under the Law Reform Act 1934 on behalf of his estate and under the Fatal Accidents Act 1846; and (d) by both laws, the funeral expenses. The court applied the rule in *Phillips v Eyre* and held that (a) was not actionable under English law; (b) and (c) were not actionable under Scots law; and (d) was the only head of damages recoverable under both laws. Accordingly, all the wife was able to obtain was the funeral expenses.

It is evident that a double-actionability test can lead to absurd and anomalous results. Notwithstanding that the *Red Sea* case enables English courts to exercise a greater degree of flexibility, the fact remains that such flexibility is an exception to a harsh general rule. This can be illustrated by the following example. Suppose that A, domiciled in England, publishes a defamatory statement in Spain about B, a very successful businessman. B is unknown in England, albeit domiciled there, but is well known in Spain, where all his business dealings are conducted. Suppose also that in England, the defence of qualified privilege applies to exonerate the tortfeasor from liability, but in Spain no such defence exists. By applying the double-actionability rule, B will fail in his claim unless the English court considers the case as one in which it is appropriate to invoke the flexible exception, as expanded by the *Red Sea* case.

Although the common law rules have now been abolished by Pt III of the PILA 1995, they remain in force in respect of defamation by virtue of s 13(1), which stipulates that:

> Nothing in this Part applies to affect the determination of issues arising in any defamation claim.

Defamation is defined in s 13(2) as being 'any claim under the law of any part of the UK for libel or slander or for slander of title, slander of goods or other malicious falsehood and any claim under the law of Scotland for verbal injury' and any claim under the law of any other country corresponding to, or in the nature of, this description.

It is worthy of note that when the Law Commission (Report No 193, 1990, leading to the adoption of Pt III of the PILA 1995) considered the question of whether or not special provisions should be made in relation to particular torts, they concluded that, with regard to defamation, there should not be any *prima facie* applicable law, since it was believed that it would be best dealt with by way of English general rules. However, due to the fact that there is no uniform concept of defamation in the different systems of private international law, and the fact that the relevant law might impose liability when UK law did not, it was recommended that whenever the tort in substance occurs in the UK, the law of the relevant part of the UK applies. As this would not solve the case of the statement originating in this country and subsequently published abroad, it was further recommended that, where the UK was the country of origin of the statement in question, UK law should apply irrespective of where the alleged wrong was subsequently published. Moreover, in order to prevent parties from obtaining the automatic application of English or Scots law simply by repeating the defamatory statement in the UK, it was also recommended that only when a statement was published abroad, and simultaneously or previously published in the UK, would the applicable law be that part of the UK where the proceedings were brought.

Part III of the Act, however, excludes the tort of defamation from its scope altogether. This exclusion, which was a result of immense pressure by the press following the publication of the Bill, was justified on the ground that the Law Commission's recommendations, if implemented, would have an adverse impact on the freedom the expression. Hence, by virtue of s 13, the double actionability rule remains applicable to claims for defamation.

6.8 Part III of the Private International Law (Miscellaneous Provisions) Act 1995

The PILA 1995 (Pts I–III) received Royal Assent on 8 November 1995. Part III (ss 9–15), which makes provisions for choice of law in tort or delict, came into force on 1 May 1996. (Part I makes provisions in relation to interest on judgment debts and arbitral awards, and Pt II makes provisions in relation to the validity of marriages under a law which permits polygamy.)

Part III extends in application to England and Wales, Scotland, and Northern Ireland. It largely implements the Law Commissions' draft Bill. Basically, Pt III adopts a general rule which identifies the applicable law. It also provides for an exception which applies in appropriate circumstances. Moreover, contrary to the Law Commission's recommendations, the provisions in Pt III apply equally to both UK and foreign torts. Two issues are, however, left outside its scope. These relate to the tort of defamation, which has been examined above, and to the complex question of the possibility of raising contractual defences in a tort action. In respect of the latter issue, s 9(1) provides that the provisions of the Act apply to ascertain the law applicable to 'issues relating to tort'. Can contractual defences raised in a tort action be classed as issues relating to tort? The answer to this question may be found in s 9(2), which states that 'the characterisation for the purposes of private international law of issues arising in a claim as issues relating to tort or delict is a matter for the courts of the forum'. Hence, it is very probable that the common law rules remain applicable to determine whether such defences can be invoked in a tort action.

In accordance with s 9(6), the new statutory regime appears to apply both to English torts as well as foreign torts. The material text of this provision states that 'this Part applies in relation to events occurring in the forum as it applies in relation to events occurring in any other country'. At first sight, it appears that s 9(6) has the effect of abolishing the common law rule that where the tort is committed in England, English law applies. Nonetheless, s 9(6) is expressly made subject to s 14; the latter stipulating that nothing in this Act 'affects any rules of law (including rules of private international law) except those abolished by s 10 above', that is, the double-actionability rule and the exception thereof. On the one hand, this may be taken to mean that the choice of law rule on English torts under the common law is still in force. On the other hand, if this rule is considered to be a necessary consequence of the double-actionability rule, the abolition of the latter has the implication of abolishing the former. What view the English courts will adopt on this issue remains to be seen.

6.8.1 The new general rule

Section 10 of the Act abolishes the double-actionability rule and its exception as they applied to any claim in tort or delict, except for the tort of defamation. Section 11(1) introduces a new general rule which identifies the applicable law as that of the country in which the tort is committed. Where, however, the elements of the tort occur in different countries, s 11(2) provides for a number of presumptions to help identify the applicable law. Section 11(2) states:

> Where elements of those events occur in different countries, the applicable law under the general rule is to be taken as being:
>
> (a)　for a cause of action in respect of personal injury caused to an individual or death resulting from personal injury, the law of the country where the individual was when he sustained the injury;
>
> (b)　for a cause of action in respect of damage to property, the law of the country where the property was when it was damaged; and
>
> (c)　in any other case, the law of the country in which the most significant element or elements of those events occurred.

Accordingly, where the elements of the tort occur in a single country, the applicable law will be the law of that country. Conversely, where they occur in different countries, the applicable law is identified by having recourse to specific presumptions. Where the cause of action is in respect of personal injury or death, it is to be presumed that the applicable law is that of the country where the injury was sustained. Where the cause of action is in respect of damage to property, the applicable law is that of the country where the damage was sustained. Thus, if A, a Greek tourist in Northern Ireland, is negligent in causing an accident there, resulting in injury to B, an American tourist, the applicable law under s 11(1) is that of Northern Ireland. In contrast, if C, an English drug manufacturer, negligently produces a defective product which causes personal injury to D in Spain, E in Germany and F in Belgium, then by virtue of s 11(2), D's claim will be determined by Spanish law, E's claim will be determined by German law and F's claim by Belgian law, provided of course that the exception in s 12 does not apply.

Where the cause of action is not one for personal injury or death, or property damage, then pursuant to s 11(2)(c), the applicable law is that of the country in which 'the most significant element or elements' of the tort occurred. This provision will operate in respect of economic torts, such as economic loss resulting from fraudulent misrepresentation or inducement of breach of contract. The applicable law in these cases is that of the country where the most significant elements occurred. This is a flexible rule, which enables English courts to exercise considerable discretion when locating the most significant elements of the tort. It is submitted, however, that since a similar test is applied to locate the place of tort under the common law rules, English courts will have recourse to such cases as *Metall und Rohstoff AG v Donaldson Lufkin and Jenrette Inc* (1990); *Diamond v Bank of London and Montreal Ltd* (1979); and *Armagas Ltd v Mundogas SA* (1986), when ascertaining the applicable law under s 11(2)(c).

6.8.2　Exception to the general rule

Section 12(1) allows for an exception to the general rule and provides:

> If it appears, in all the circumstances, from a comparison of:
>
> (a)　the significance of the factors which connect a tort or delict with the country whose law would be applicable under the general rule; and
>
> (b)　the significance of any factors connecting the tort or delict with another country, that it is substantially more appropriate for the applicable law for determining the issues arising in the case, or any of those issues, to be the law of the other country, the general rule is displaced and the applicable law for determining those issues or that issue (as the case may be) is the law of that other country.

Hence, this proper law exception may be invoked where the comparison between the significance of the factors connecting the tort with the country identified under the general rule and that of the factors connecting the tort with another country, indicates that it is *substantially* more appropriate to apply the law of that other country to determine any or all of the issues arising in the case.

It is worthy of note that s 12(1) clearly indicates that either the whole case or a single issue in the case can be governed by the exception. The word 'substantially' must be emphasised here. It appears to provide a clear indication that the exception should not be readily invoked. Furthermore, by virtue of s 12(2), the factors which may be taken into account when attempting to invoke the exception include those relating to the parties, to any of the events which constitute the tort or delict in question, or to any of the circumstances or consequences of those events.

It is suggested that this exception would be invoked in such cases as *Boys v Chaplin* (1971); and *Red Sea Insurance v Bouygues* (1994), where the circumstances thereof made it more appropriate to displace the law identified by the double-actionability rule. It is also suggested that the exception in s 12 will operate to displace either the *lex loci delicti* in favour of the *lex fori*, or vice versa. Whether it will operate to apply the law of a third country is doubtful, since the *substantial connection* forms the point at which the application of the exception hinges.

6.8.3 Miscellaneous

The Act contains further miscellaneous provisions. For instance, s 14(1) ensures that the reforms contained in Pt III of the Act do not have retrospective effect. They only apply to torts committed after 1 May 1996. Section 14(2)(b) preserves the application of various procedural rules which remain governed by the law of the forum. Section 14(2)(a) preserves both the power of the English court to decline the application of a particular law on the grounds of public policy, and its power not to give effect to foreign penal, revenue or other public laws. Last, but not least, s 9(5) expressly excludes the application of *renvoi* in this area of choice of law.

CHOICE OF LAW IN TORT

The common law

Under the common law rules, where a tort was found to have been committed in England, English law applied. Where it was found to have been committed abroad, the rule in *Phillips v Eyre* applies.

Place of tort

English courts, when determining the place of tort in the choice of law context, applied the same basic test used in relation to the old Ord 11 r 1(1)(h) on jurisdiction, which is the question of where in substance the cause of action arose.

In relation to negligence, the test was applied in various ways to the effect that a tort was held to have been committed in the place where the goods were manufactured, or where they were marketed without adequate warnings.

In relation to defamation, the tort was held to be committed in the country where the statement was published.

As for fraudulent misrepresentation made by instantaneous communications, the tort was held to be committed in the place where the message was received and acted upon.

In the context of inducing a breach of contract, the tort was said to have been committed in the place where the breach of contract and the resulting damage occurred.

The rule in *Phillips v Eyre*

Where a tort was committed abroad, the double-actionability rule applied, that is the tort must be actionable in England, and it must be actionable by the law of the place where it was committed.

An exception to the general rule appeared to have been adopted in favour of the application of the proper law of tort, though great uncertainty surrounded its nature and extent.

Scope of the double-actionability rule

For the rule to apply, the tort must be actionable against the same defendant in both jurisdictions.

Equally, the plaintiff must be the same in both jurisdictions.

In relation to contractual defences against claims in tort, the law was and remains far from clear and settled. Such defences may sometimes be used so as to negate liability in tort.

Certainty, clarity and justice were the main reasons for calls for reform.

Reform

In 1984, the Law Commission published its Consultation Paper No 87, whereby recommendations as to reform were proposed. The main proposal was that the first of the rules should be abolished, and from that stemmed two possible models for reform.

These recommendations were re-examined by the Law Commission in its Report No 193, where a modified version of Model 1 was proposed.

Part III of the PILA 1995

Under the new law and as a general rule, the applicable law is that of the *lex loci delicti*. Where, however, the elements of the tort occur in different countries, a number of presumptions are adopted in order to help identify the applicable law. In case of personal injury or damage to property, the applicable law is the law of the place where the person or property was when the injury or damage occurred. In case of death, it is the law of the place where the deceased was when the fatal injury was inflicted. In all other cases, the applicable law is the law of the territory in which the most significant elements in the sequence of events occurred.

As an exception to the general rule, the applicable law is the law of the place with which the tort has the most substantial connection.

The tort of defamation is excluded from the scope of Pt III and, therefore, remains governed by the common law rules.

CHAPTER 7

JUDGMENTS IN FOREIGN CURRENCY

7.1 Introduction

Suppose, for example, that a plaintiff brings an action in the English court for damages for loss of earnings, the amount of which is expressed in a foreign currency rather than sterling. Alternatively, suppose that a plaintiff brings an action in the English court to recover, for instance, payment due to him or her under a transnational contract, and that amount is expressed in a foreign currency. Can the English court give its judgment for damages in that foreign currency rather than sterling? Until 1975, the rule that had formerly applied to the enforcement by court proceedings of an obligation expressed in a foreign currency was that the claim, the judgment and any process of execution of such judgment in England, had to be in sterling. Furthermore, the rate of conversion was the exchange rate applicable at the date when the amount was due, that is, the date of payment in the case where the sum was agreed in the contract, as in *Tomkinson v First Pennsylvania Banking and Trust Co* (1961); the date of the breach in the case of a claim for damages, pursuant to *Di Ferdinando v Simon, Smits and Co Ltd* (1920); and the date when the loss was suffered as a result of the commitment of a tort according to *Celia v Volturno* (1921). This rule was clearly stated by Lord Denning in the case of *Re United Railways of Havana and Regla Warehouses* (1961) in the following terms (pp 1068–69):

> If there is one thing clear in our law, it is that the claim must be made in sterling and the judgment given in sterling. We do not give judgments in dollars any more than the United States courts give judgments in sterling.

7.2 The new approach

However, when sterling fluctuates significantly in relation to other currencies, as occurred in the 1970s, the substantive rule above may result in great injustice. This led the House of Lords to reverse its own previous decision in the *United Railways* case and to adopt a new approach in the case of *Miliangos v George Frank (Textiles) Ltd* (1976). Here, a contract was made in 1971 between a Swiss national and an English textile company for the sale of yarn to the company. The proper law of the contract was Swiss law and the currency in which the contract price was expressed was Swiss. The price was SFr415,000, which equated to £42,000 at the date of the contract. The buyer failed to pay on the due date fixed in the contract. However, owing to the depreciation of sterling at the time of the hearing, the sterling equivalent of SFr415,000 became £60,000. The House of Lords held the defendant had to pay the Swiss seller

SFr415,000 or the sterling equivalent at the date of the actual payment (that is, the defendant had to pay the greater sterling sum).

The approach adopted in *Miliangos* not only remedied the injustice caused by any devaluation in sterling, but created a completely new principle, whereby the courts accepted the need to give judgments in foreign currency. It must be noted, however, that although the House of Lords made the foreign currency the standard by which to determine the amount to be paid by the judgment debtor, the debtor still had the option of paying in sterling.

The decision in the *Miliangos* case was restricted to two issues. First, it was limited in application to claims for liquidated damages. Secondly, it was restricted to contracts which were governed by a foreign law and where the currency of account and payment was that of the foreign country. Indeed, the House of Lords declined to re-examine the whole law in this field and restricted their judgment to the case before them. Nevertheless, a number of subsequent judgments extended the application of this principle to a variety of issues.

7.2.1 Breach of contract

The *Miliangos* rule has been held to apply to a claim for damages for breach of contract, that is, unliquidated damages. Such was the decision of the House of Lords in *Services Europe Atlantique Sud (Seas) v Stockholms Rederiaktiebolag Svea (The Folias)* (1979), which concerned a charterparty, made between the Swedish shipowners and a French company, for carriage of goods by sea from the Mediterranean to the east coast of South America. The contract contained a clause providing for arbitration in London, and the freight was expressed to be payable in US dollars. The French company shipped a cargo of onions in Spain for carriage to Brazil. The cargo arrived in a damaged condition due to the failure of the ship's refrigerating facilities. Consequently, the company had to compensate the receivers of the cargo, so they bought Brazilian cruzieros with French francs. The latter was the currency in which the company had kept its accounts. Subsequently, the cruziero declined in value by 50%.

The question before the House of Lords was: in which currency should the company be able to recover damages? It was held that, where the contract failed to provide a decisive interpretation, the damages would be calculated in the currency which most fully expressed the plaintiff's loss. The plaintiff, which was a French company with its place of business in Paris, had to use French francs to purchase other currencies in order to settle cargo claims. Accordingly, the currency best suited to achieve an appropriate and just result was French francs.

7.2.2 Damages in tort

Equally, the rule has been applied to actions for damages for tort. This was held in *The Despina R* (1979) where two Greek ships, *The Eleftherotria* and *The Despina R*, collided off Shanghai, as a result of which the former ship sustained damage. The collision was due to the negligence of the master and crew of *The Despina R*. Consequently, *The Eleftherotria* underwent some temporary repairs both in Shanghai and Yokohama and then proceeded to Los Angeles for permanent repairs. As such, the loss and expenses were incurred in three different currencies, that is, Chinese yuan, Japanese yen and US dollars. The question arose as to in which currency the plaintiffs should be compensated, bearing in mind that the ship was managed by agents whose principal place of business was in New York and the bank accounts used for all payments in respect of the operation of the ship was in US dollars.

The House of Lords, applying the normal principles which govern the assessment of damages in cases of tort, held that the judgment must be in US dollars, for this was the currency in which the loss was felt. That is, the loss sustained was measured, not by the immediate currencies in which the loss first emerged, but by the amount of the plaintiff's currency which was, in the normal course of operation, used to obtain those currencies.

In addition, the English court, in the case of *Hoffman v Sofaer* (1982) went further, to give a judgment for damages for tort partly in sterling and partly in US dollars. Here, the plaintiff was a US citizen who came to England on holiday. Whilst in this country, he suffered trouble in his right arm for which he was negligently treated. As a result, his arm became useless to the extent of 84%. The amount of damages for his pain, suffering and loss of amenity was assessed at £19,000. Moreover, the plaintiff was at the time the president of an American company. However, due to his injury he had to resign his position and take on a less important position with another company, which he subsequently lost due to the reorganisation of that company. His misfortune resulted in an additional loss of US$266,049, assessed in terms of special and general damages. The main question before the English court was, in which currency should the judgment be given. Talbot J considered the rule in *Miliangos* and held that the plaintiff's loss was most closely linked with the US currency. Accordingly, apart from the damages for pain, suffering and loss of amenities which were calculated at £19,000, the judgment would be in US dollars. This was because the losses which arose as a result of the plaintiff's injury had to be met by him in US dollars.

7.2.3 Restitution

Similarly, the English court can now award a judgment in foreign currency for claims for restitution under s 1(3) of the Law Reform (Frustrated Contracts) Act 1943. Indeed, this view was held in *BP Exploration Co (Libya) Ltd v Hunt (No 2)* (1982). The plaintiffs alleged that they had entered into a contract, governed by

English law, with the defendants for the sharing of an oil concession which had been originally granted to the defendant, and that the contract had been frustrated due to the expropriation by the Libyan government of the plaintiffs' half share in the concession. As a result, the plaintiffs claimed an award of a just sum under s 1(3) of the Law Reform (Frustrated Contracts) Act 1943. At first instance, Robert Goff J held that the plaintiffs were entitled to an award in US dollars, that is, the currency of the defendant's benefit rather than that of the plaintiffs' loss, in respect of the oil concession contract and oil received by the defendants. He also made an award in sterling in respect of services rendered by the plaintiffs. In addition, the learned judge ordered that interest, by virtue of s 3(1) of the above Act, be paid from the date when the plaintiffs had clearly indicated that they intended to claim restitution. On appeal by the defendant, both the Court of Appeal and the House of Lords upheld this judgment.

7.3 Issues arising

A number of issues can be deduced from *Miliangos* and subsequent case law. These can be summarised as follows:

(a) in order to determine the money of account, that is, the currency in which the contractual obligation is to be assessed, the English court applies the proper law of the contract. However, if the contract provides for a different money of account and money of payment (that is, the currency in which payment is to made), then it is likely that they will measure the loss and give judgment in the currency of account where the proper law of the contract is English. Otherwise, the English court will put the question to the foreign proper law;

(b) in order to determine the currency in which to give damages for breach of contract, the English court applies the principles laid down by Lord Wilberforce in *The Folias* (1979):

- whether an award should be given in a particular foreign currency depends on the general law of contract and on the rules of conflict of laws. The former involves the principle of *restitutio in integrum* with due regard to the reasonable contemplation of the parties. The latter, however, requires the ascertainment and application of the proper law of the contract;

- if the proper law is English, the first step is to see whether the contract itself expressly or impliedly answers that question, that is, whether the parties have chosen a 'damages' currency;

- if not, damages should be calculated in 'the currency in which the loss was felt by the plaintiff'. The court should search for 'the currency, payment in which will as nearly as possible compensate the plaintiff in accordance with the principle of restitution, and whether the parties must be taken reasonably to have had this in contemplation';

- the currency in which damages for breach of contract should be awarded is always a matter for determination by the proper law of the contract;

(c) damages in tort would be given in the currency in which the loss was effectively felt or borne by the plaintiff. The burden of proof is on the plaintiff, who has to show that either:

  - it is the currency which he would normally use to meet his expenditure; or

  - his loss could only appropriately be measured in that currency;

(d) a plaintiff does not have a choice to claim judgment either in sterling alone or in a foreign currency alone. Indeed, Donaldson J stated in *Ozalid Group (Export) Ltd v African Continental Bank Ltd* (1979) that, according to *The Folias* and *The Despina R*, the plaintiff did not have such a choice. He had to select the currency in which to make his claim and prove that a judgment in that currency would most truly express his loss;

(e) if a debtor fails to pay a debt and subsequently the currency of the debt is severely devalued, the question to consider is whether the debtor should still be held to the currency of the debt or its sterling equivalent at the date of payment, that is, at the date of the judgment or the date of its enforcement. For instance, the debt is to be paid in US dollars in 1992 but, at the date of the judgment in 1996, the US dollar has fallen in value against sterling. Can the judgment creditor choose to be paid in sterling?

In the *Ozalid* case, Donaldson J awarded the creditors damages, in order to compensate them for the devaluation in the currency of account. In this case, the plaintiff, an English company carrying on business in England, agreed to sell certain machinery and equipment to a Nigerian company in March 1977. The price was expressed in US dollars and the payment was to be made by irrevocable letter of credit valid for six months. The buyers arranged for the latter to be issued by the defendants, a Nigerian bank with a branch in London. The plaintiffs were subject to the UK exchange control regulations, under which the plaintiffs were allowed to hold a US dollars account but were obliged to sell any excess dollars to an authorised bank in exchange for sterling. Payment by the defendants ought to have been made not later than 5 October 1977. However, such payment was not made until 12 December 1977. The plaintiffs suffered loss as a result of this delay and brought an action claiming:

- £2,987.17 in respect of their loss consequent upon the change in the exchange rate between 5 October and 12 December 1977;

- interest on the sterling equivalent of US$125,939.22 which was due on 5 October for the period until 12 December; and

- £40 paid to the plaintiffs' solicitors for their services prior to the issue of the writ.

Donaldson J allowed all three claims and held, *inter alia*, that although the price of the goods was agreed to be paid in US dollars, it was clear that the plaintiffs' loss was incurred in sterling and this was foreseeable by the defendants. He further held that, once it was proved that the plaintiffs' true loss was to be measured in sterling, any payment made in a different currency fell to be credited against that sterling loss at the rate of exchange ruling at the time of payment.

Furthermore, in a purely English case, *Wadsworth v Lydell* (1981), which was approved by the House of Lords in *President of India v La Pintada Compania Navigacion SA* (1984), the Court of Appeal held that a party to a contract was entitled to special damages in respect of loss suffered by him as a result of the failure by the other party to pay money, providing that the loss was foreseeable by the debtor. In this case, the creditor had to borrow money at a high rate of interest because the debtor had not paid him. However, in *President of India v Lips Maritime Corpn (The Lips)* (1987), Lord Brandon, delivering the House of Lords' judgment, stated that *La Pintada* did not apply to claims to recover currency exchange losses;

(f) the rule in *Miliangos* appears to be a rule of procedure and not a rule of substance. That is, English law is applied as the law of the forum.

7.4 The Law Commission

The law in this field was examined by the Law Commission in 1981 (Working Paper No 80) where it was concluded that the *Miliangos* rule was satisfactory and should be retained. Hence, it was felt that legislative intervention was not required. In 1983, the Law Commission re-examined this area of law in their Report No 124. Again, they recommended the retention of the *Miliangos* rule, but made a number of proposals for changes to relevant procedural rules. The recommendations were as follows:

(a) the *Miliangos* principle is a good one and should be retained;

(b) the present rule that conversion of a foreign currency judgment into sterling is to be effected at the date of actual payment or the date on which the court authorises enforcement of the judgment, whichever is the earlier, is practical and should be retained;

(c) it should be possible to obtain and/or enter a judgment in sterling alone or a foreign currency alone. This, however, should be left to the discretion of the court. Much emphasis should be put in a contract case on the intention of the parties as to the form of payment;

(d) a plaintiff should not be able to obtain judgment in sterling in the case of the enforcement of a claim which ought properly to be expressed in a foreign currency. Nevertheless, no legislative intervention is necessary, for the judiciary can appropriately deal with this matter;

(e) the present rules governing questions of currency conversion in relation to the enforcement of foreign judgments in this country are satisfactory and need not be amended;

(f) parties should continue to be free to agree that payment in England and Wales should be made in a particular foreign currency and that the debtor has no option to pay in sterling. Similarly, they are free to agree the date at which the conversion of any currency is to be made and/or the rate of exchange to be applied;

(g) with regard to interest, the present law is that the right to claim interest on the basis of a contractual term is a matter of substance and is governed by the *lex causae*. This is probably also the case where interest on a debt is claimed on a sum payable as damages for breach of contract or tort (see para 2.30 of the report). This rule is satisfactory and should be retained;

(h) the rate of interest on damages should be determined by the application of English law as the law of the forum.

In relation to interest on judgment debts and arbitral awards in foreign currency, the Law Commission recommended legislative intervention and a draft clause to that effect was appended to their report. This clause has been adopted, with minor amendments, by Parliament and is now implemented in Pt I of the PILA 1995, which received royal assent on 8 November 1995. With the exception of s 3 thereof (now repealed), this Part came into force on 1 November 1996 (SI 1996/2515).

7.5 Part I of the Private International Law (Miscellaneous Provisions) Act 1995

Part I, which now embodies three separate provisions (ss 1, 2 and 4), applies to England and Wales, but not to Scotland. It changes the law regarding the rate of interest payable on judgment debts expressed in foreign currency (note that s 3, which made provisions in respect of interest on arbitral awards has been repealed). It has the purpose of giving English courts, in the case of foreign currency judgments, the flexibility to order a rate of interest at their discretion.

Prior to the PILA 1995, interest on High Court and county court judgments was prescribed at a fixed rate, then 8%. This statutory rate, which could be altered from time to time, reflected generally the level of interest rates normally prevailing in the UK. It did not, however, reflect the rate appropriate to any particular foreign currency. As such, it was thought that the statutory rate would often be entirely inappropriate to the foreign currency in question.

The amendments brought about by Pt I of the PILA 1995 are of a procedural nature and have the effect of treating sterling and foreign currency judgment debts on an equal basis. Section 1, which deals with interest on judgment debts expressed in currencies other than sterling, amends s 44 (interest on judgment debts) of the Administration of Justice Act 1970 by inserting a new s 44A. This additional provision reads as follows:

(1)   Where a judgment is given for a sum expressed in a currency other than sterling and the judgment debt is one to which s 17 of the Judgments Act 1838 applies, the court may order that the interest rate applicable to the debt shall be such as the court thinks fit.

(2)   Where the court makes such an order, s 17 of the Judgments Act 1838 shall have effect in relation to the judgment debt as if the rate specified in the order were substituted for the rate specified in that section.

Section 2 of the 1995 Act makes similar amendments in relation to county court judgment debts by adding a new sub-s 5A to sub-s 5 of s 74 of the County Courts Act 1984. The new provision states that:

The power conferred by sub-s (1) includes power to make provision enabling a county court to order that the rate of interest applicable to a sum expressed in a currency other than sterling shall be such rate as the court thinks fit (instead of the rate otherwise applicable).

Section 3 had made similar provisions in relation to interest on arbitral awards. However, s 3 has now been repealed by virtue of the Arbitration Act 1996, which deals with all aspects of arbitration awards, including interest, as stipulated in s 49 thereof. Arbitration is outside the scope of this book, but it is worth mentioning that ss 1–84 of this Act came into force on 31 January 1997 (SI 1996/3146).

It must be noted that the amendment in s 1 of the Act does not have a retrospective effect. That is, it does not apply in relation to judgments made before the commencement of Pt I.

JUDGMENTS IN FOREIGN CURRENCY

Judgments in foreign currency

Prior to 1975, the English court applied the rule that, in a claim for the enforcement by court proceedings of an obligation expressed in foreign currency, the judgment and any process of execution in England had to be in sterling.

The rule in *Miliangos*

As this substantive rule might lead to great injustice in the case where sterling fluctuates, the House of Lords departed from it and adopted a new approach known as the *Miliangos* rule. By virtue of this principle, English courts are now able to give judgments in foreign currency or its sterling equivalent at the date of payment.

Extension of the rule in *Miliangos*

The rule in *Miliangos* has been extended to cover claims for unliquidated damages for breach of contract and tort. In this context, the test which applies is that the damage would be calculated in the currency which most fully expressed the plaintiff's loss. The rule has also been held to apply to claims for restitution under s 1(3) of the Law Reform (Frustrated Contracts) Act 1943. Lord Goff held that, in such a case, the damage should be assessed in the currency of the defendant's benefit, rather than that of the plaintiff's loss.

Issues arising

English courts apply the proper law of the contract in order to assess the currency of the contractual obligation.

The currency in which English courts award damages for breach of contract is determined by the proper law of the contract.

As for damages in tort, the currency is that in which the loss was effectively felt or borne by the plaintiff. The burden of proof is on him to show that the currency in question is either that which he would normally use to meet his expenditure, or that in which his loss could be appropriately measured.

Statutory intervention

The Law Commission reviewed this rule and published its Report No 124 in 1983, whereby it recommended that the substantive law in this field was satisfactory and did not require legislative intervention. However, a rule of procedure giving the English court the power to award interest on judgment debts was felt necessary. Consequently, a new clause to that effect was appended to the report. Save for minor amendments, that clause was implemented in Pt I of the PILA 1995. The new provisions change the law regarding the rate of interest payable on judgment debts expressed in foreign currency and have the effect of treating them as equal to those expressed in sterling.

CHAPTER 8

LAW OF PROPERTY

8.1 The distinction between movables and immovables

English domestic law classifies the subject matter of ownership of, and other interests in, property into reality and personality. However, for the purposes of the conflict of laws, the classification is between movables and immovables. This is basically because the former distinction is not known to civil law systems or any other system not based on the English common law. Moreover, as shall be seen, the application of the governing law which determines rights over property differs depending on whether the right in question is one over immovable or movable property.

Where there is a conflict between the law of the forum and the law of the *situs* as to whether a particular right may be characterised as one relating to movable or immovable property, it is well settled that, in such a situation, the law of the *situs* determines the characterisation. For instance, in *Re Berchtold* (1923), Russell J held that where an interest in the proceeds of sale of English freeholds was subject to a trust, which was for sale, but not yet sold, this was an interest in immovable property in accordance with the *lex situs*. In this case, Berchtold died domiciled in Hungary. He left a will in English form, dealing with his real estate in England. By virtue of that will, he put all his freehold estate, which was situated in England, on trust to English trustees. This trust was for sale and conversion with the power to postpone such sale and conversion for as long as they thought fit. The will also provided that the proceeds of sale and the rents and profits of part of the estate which remained unsold were to be held in trust for his son, subject to an annuity to the testator's wife during her life.

The question arose in this case as to whether the proceeds of sale and the rents and profits were interests in movable or immovable property. The court applied English law as the *lex situs* and held that such interests were rights in immovable property. The same line of reasoning was also adopted in *Re Hoyles* (1911); and *Macdonald v Macdonald* (1932).

Hence, as indicated in Chapter 1, the classification of a cause of action for the purposes of conflicts of law is not necessarily identical to the classification made in a purely domestic case. Notwithstanding that the law of the forum plays an important role in respect of classification, whether it be that of a cause of action or a rule of law, English courts are not reluctant to apply a foreign law, for the purposes of classification, in appropriate cases (for full details, see Chapter 1).

8.2 Immovable property

It may be recalled that, in Chapters 2 and 3, it was stated that special jurisdictional rules apply where the subject matter of a dispute before an English court is related to immovable property. These rules vary, depending on whether the immovable property is situated within the EC/EFTA, in which case the Brussels/Lugano rules apply, or whether the immovable property is situated outside the EC/EFTA, in which case the traditional common law rules apply. Once these rules are examined, the issue of choice of law in this context will be considered.

8.2.1 Jurisdiction under the traditional common law rules

Under the traditional rules, where an immovable property is situated outside England, then the court which is said to have competent jurisdiction to determine title to, or the right to possession of, that immovable property is the court of the country where the property is situated. This rule was first established by the House of Lords in *British South Africa Co v Companhia de Moçambique* (1893) in the following terms: English courts have no jurisdiction to entertain an action for the determination of the title to, or the right to possession of, any immovable property situated outside England, or for the recovery of damages for trespass or other torts to such immovable property. Such an action is best tried in the courts of the place where the property is situated.

Until fairly recently, the *Moçambique* rule had limited the jurisdiction of English courts even in cases where the action concerned the question of the recovery of damages for trespass to foreign land, irrespective of whether or not a question of title to the land was in issue, as was held in *St Pierre v South American Stores (Gath and Chaves) Ltd* (1936); and *Hesperides Hotels Ltd v Aegean Turkish Holidays Ltd* (1978). This latter part of the rule, which had been subject to much criticism, was abolished by s 30(1) of the Civil Jurisdiction and Judgments Act 1982 (CJJA). Section 30(1) provides that:

> The jurisdiction of any court in England and Wales or Northern Ireland to entertain proceedings for trespass to, or any other tort affecting, immovable property shall extend to cases in which the property in question is situated outside that part of the UK unless the proceedings are principally concerned with a question of title to, or the right to possession of, that property.

Hence, by virtue of s 30(1) of the CJJA 1982, English courts now have jurisdiction to entertain proceedings for trespass to or any other tort affecting immovable property in a foreign country. This is the case unless the proceedings are principally concerned with the question of title to, or the right to possession of, that property. The application of s 30(1) was examined in the recent case *Re Polly Peck International plc* (1996). The case concerned properties in Northern Cyprus, owned by the plaintiffs, which were appropriated by the Turkish Government. The plaintiffs alleged that Polly Peck, a company in administration, had trespassed on their property by encouraging Polly Peck's subsidiaries to occupy it without authority. The defendants objected to the jurisdiction of the English court and the plaintiffs argued the application of s 30(1) of the CJJA 1982. It was held that, by virtue of this provision, the English court had jurisdiction to hear proceedings for trespass to immovable property, even though the property was situated abroad, provided that the proceedings were not mainly concerned with the question of title or the right to possession of the property. Nevertheless, albeit in an action for trespass it would be necessary to establish ownership, the present claim raised a number of other important questions, for example, whether the defendants themselves had committed trespass, and whether the corporate veil could be pierced to impose liability on Polly Peck for the acts of its subsidiaries. Accordingly, s 30(1) of the CJJA 1982 applied in this case to confer jurisdiction on the English court.

The provisions of s 30, however, are subject to Art 16 of both the Brussels and Lugano Conventions, which allocates exclusive jurisdiction in proceedings which seek to ascertain rights *in rem* in immovable property situated within either the EC or EFTA (see below, 8.2.3).

8.2.2 Exceptions to the *Moçambique* rule

The common law has established three main exceptions to the *Moçambique* rule. They apply where the proceedings are based either on some personal obligations or on the administration of trusts or estates.

The first exception applies in the context where a defendant commits himself by a personal obligation to the plaintiff. In this case, the English court will normally interfere and grant a specific performance ordering him to fulfil his obligation, provided that the court's jurisdiction is *in personam*. This exception can be traced back to *Arglasse v Muschamp* (1862). It was also accepted in the *Moçambique* case, where it was stated that:

> ... courts of equity have, from the time of Lord Hardwicke's decision in *Penn v Baltimore*, exercised jurisdiction *in personam* in relation to foreign land against persons locally within the jurisdiction of the English court in cases of contract, fraud and trust.

The leading case on this exception is *Penn v Baltimore* (1750), where a contract was made in England between the plaintiff and the defendant to settle the boundaries of the then provinces of Pennsylvania and Maryland. In an action for specific performance, Lord Hardwicke granted the decree on the ground that there existed between the parties to the action a personal obligation which, in the view of the court of equity, would be unconscionable not to enforce.

This personal obligation may arise, as Parker J stated in *Deschamps v Miller* (1908), 'out of contract or implied contract, fiduciary relationships or fraud, or other conduct which ... would be unconscionable, and do not depend for their existence on the *locus* of the immovable property'. For example, 'in cases of trusts, specific performance of contracts, foreclosure, or redemption of mortgages, or in the case of land obtained by the defendant by fraud, or other such unconscionable conduct', the English court may assume jurisdiction *in personam*.

However, according to *Re Courtney* (1840), this exception will not apply if the specific performance cannot be effected in the *lex situs*.

The second exception to the *Moçambique* rule applies where the English court has jurisdiction to administer a trust or the estate of a deceased person and some of the assets include foreign land. In such a case, the English court is prepared to determine a dispute over title to the foreign land for the purposes of the administration.

The third exception exists where English courts are asked to entertain an action *in rem* against a ship to enforce a maritime lien on the ship for damage caused to foreign immovable property.

8.2.3 Jurisdiction under the Brussels and Lugano Conventions

Where the immovable property is situated within the EC/EFTA, the same basic principle as that in the *Moçambique* rule is incorporated in Art 16(1) of the Brussels Convention 1968 (as amended by both the San Sebastian and Lugano Conventions). The original text of Art 16(1) provided:

> The following courts shall have jurisdiction, regardless of domicile:
>
> (1)　in proceedings which have as their object rights *in rem* in, or tenancies of, immovable property, the courts of the Contracting State in which the property is situated.

This provision was interpreted by the ECJ in *Rösler v Rottwinkel* (1985) to the effect that Art 16 covered all the obligations of the parties under short term holiday leases, including any action for the recovery of the cost of necessary repairs. This decision was, however, found unsatisfactory and the Brussels Convention was amended on this point both by the San Sebastian Convention and the Lugano Convention, but in slightly different terms. The effect and intent of both amendments was to reverse the ECJ's judgment in the above case. The original Art 16(1) became Art 16(1)(a) in both Conventions, and a new Art 16(1)(b) was added. Art 16(1)(b) of the Lugano Convention provides:

> ... however, in proceedings which have as their object tenancies of immovable property concluded for temporary use for a maximum period of six consecutive months, the courts of the Contracting State in which the defendant is domiciled shall also have jurisdiction, provided that the *tenant* is a *natural person* and neither party is domiciled in the Contracting State in which the property is situated.

An additional requirement was inserted in the equivalent provision of the San Sebastian Convention, that is, the landlord must also be a natural person and must be domiciled in the same Contracting State as the tenant.

It follows from the above provisions that, where an immovable property is situated in England, the English court will have exclusive jurisdiction unless the dispute is concerned with tenancies for temporary use, for a maximum period of six consecutive months and is within the scope of Art 16(1)(b).

Therefore, in addition to rights *in rem*, Art 16(1) covers disputes concerning the respective obligations of the landlord and or tenant under a tenancy agreement. In particular, it covers those rights concerning such issues as the existence or interpretation of the tenancy, its duration, recovery of rent, and so forth. However, according to the ECJ in *Sanders v Van der Putte* (1978), Art 16(1) does not cover an agreement to rent property under a usufructuary lease. In this case, this question was raised within the context of a dispute between two parties domiciled in The Netherlands, in relation to an agreement made under which they arranged that one would take over from the other the running of a business in a shop which the latter had leased in Germany. The defendant refused to perform his part of the agreement and was then sued in the Dutch court as the court of his domicile. He contested the jurisdiction of the Dutch court on the basis of Art 16(1). The ECJ held that the concept of matters relating to tenancies of immovable property within the context of Art 16 must not be interpreted as including an agreement to rent, under a usufructuary lease, a retail business carried on in immovable property rented from a third person by the lessor. Accordingly, Art 16 did not apply to this situation. Similarly, the ECJ held in *Hacker v Euro-Relais GmbH* (1992) that an agreement for a holiday package, including accommodation, for a few weeks was not covered by Art 16(1) so as to confer exclusive jurisdiction on the courts of the Contracting State in which the property was situated. Here, the plaintiff, domiciled in Germany, entered into a contract with the defendant, a German travel agent, for the provision by the latter of a holiday home in The Netherlands. It was also agreed that the defendant would make the necessary ferry reservations for sea crossing for the plaintiff. The holiday fell short of the description given by the defendant and the plaintiff brought an action in the German court, claiming damages. On the question of whether such a contract was within the meaning of tenancy under Art 16(1), the ECJ held that a complex contract of the type which concerned a range of services in return for the payment of a lump sum was outside the scope of Art 16(1), the reason being that the accommodation was not owned by the travel agent, and the latter had also made the travel arrangements for the plaintiff.

However, an annual timeshare agreement appears to fall within the provisions of Art 16 of the Brussels Convention. This was recently held by the Court of Appeal in *Jarrett and Others v Barclays Bank plc* (1997). This case concerned an appeal on three separate actions. The plaintiffs were three couples who had entered into three separate annual timeshare agreements in respect of properties situated in Portugal and Spain. In all three contracts, the plaintiffs had paid an initial sum, part of which was raised from banks under a consumer credit agreement which was expressly regulated by the Consumer Credit Act 1974. In all three cases, the property subject to the contracts was either misrepresented or was never built. The plaintiffs brought proceedings in the English courts against the banks, claiming damages under ss 56 and 75 of the Consumer Credit Act 1974. The defendants contested the jurisdiction of the English courts on the grounds that the claims came within the scope of Art 16(1) of the Convention, for they had as their object tenancy of immovable property. The Court of Appeal held that a timeshare agreement, entitling one part to occupy immovable property owned by another party for a specific period of time in return for payment, was classed as an agreement for tenancy within the meaning of Art 16(1), and therefore conferred exclusive jurisdiction on the courts of the State where the property was situated. Nonetheless, in the present proceedings, the claims were in respect of debtor-creditor-supplier agreements which accorded statutory rights to the debtors by virtue of the Consumer Credit Act 1974, and not the timeshare agreement itself. Accordingly, Art 16(1) did not apply.

8.3 Choice of law

The general rule is that the *lex situs* determines questions of both formal and essential validity of transactions relating to immovable property. Although this rule has been subject to criticisms, on the ground that it is too broad and may lead to harsh results, the rationale behind it is that uniformity with the *lex situs* is crucial, for an immovable property can only be dealt with in a manner permitted by that law. Referral to the *lex situs*, however, is not only restricted to the application of the domestic law of that *situs*, but it means the whole law of the foreign *situs*, including its conflict of laws rules. This is so because there are strong policy considerations in favour of deciding whatever the *lex situs* would have decided. Hence, the doctrine of *renvoi* has been applied in this context. For example, in *Re Ross* (1930), the testatrix, a British subject, died domiciled in Italy. Her wills in respect of her English and Italian estates excluded her son from the list of beneficiaries. This exclusion was allowed by English domestic law, but was contrary to Italian domestic law, which required that one half of her property should go to her son.

The son brought an action in the English court contesting the validity of the wills. The English court referred the essential validity of these wills to Italian law in relation to both the immovable property as the *lex situs*, and the movables as the law of her domicile. Expert evidence showed, however, that an Italian court would apply the law of the testatrix's nationality, and accordingly, the wills were held to be valid (see, also, *Re Duke of Wellington* (1947), where the same principle applied).

With the above principles in mind, the following discussion will illustrate how these principles have been applied to the various issues which may arise in the context of immovables.

8.3.1 Capacity to transfer immovables

Unless a person has capacity to transfer immovables under the *lex situs*, a transfer will be held invalid. This rule was established by the Court of Appeal in *Bank of Africa v Cohen* (1909). A married woman, domiciled in England, made a contract with an English bank whereby she agreed to mortgage her land in South Africa as security for loans made and to be made to her husband. Subsequently, she refused to effect the contract and the bank sued for specific performance. The defendant raised the defence that, by South African law, married women had no capacity to give security for their husband's debts. Both the court of first instance and the Court of Appeal upheld the defence, on the basis that her capacity was governed by the *lex situs*, and accordingly the contract was void.

Similarly, where a person lacks capacity to take (as opposed to transfer) immovables by the *lex situs*, he or she will be denied ownership (see *AG v Parsons* (1956)).

8.3.2 Formal validity of the transfer

The formal validity of a transfer of immovable property is also governed by the *lex situs*. This has been interpreted to mean that, for such a transfer to be valid, it must comply with the formalities required by the domestic law of the *situs*, as if the transfer does not contain foreign elements. For instance, in apparently the only reported English case of *Adams v Clutterbuck* (1883), a conveyance for the right of shooting over land in Scotland was made in England between two domiciled Englishmen. English law, unlike Scots law, required such instruments to be under seal. It was, nevertheless, held that the instrument was valid because it was so by the *lex situs*.

However, if the instrument is to have the effect of a contract, then its formal validity is governed by the Rome Convention 1980 as implemented by the Contracts (Applicable Law) Act 1990, which will be the subject of discussion below, 8.3.4.

8.3.3 Essential validity of the transfer

The essential validity of a transfer of immovable property is also governed by the *lex situs*. For instance, the *lex situs* determines whether gifts to charities are valid (see *Duncan v Lawson* (1889)), whether an estate can be legally created (see *Nelson v Bridport* (1846)), whether a transfer complies with the restraints on alienation (see *Re Ross* (1930)), and whether a transfer infringes the rules as to perpetuities and accumulations (see *Freke v Carbery* (1873)).

8.3.4 Validity of the contract to transfer immovables

A distinction should be made between the validity of a transfer of immovable property and the validity of a contract to transfer immovable property. In the former case, both formal and essential validity of a transaction, which purports to change ownership of the immovable property there and then, must be subject to the law of the *situs*. In the latter case, however, the position is different. Here the question relates, not to the actual transfer, but to the obligations of the party under a contract, the object of which is to transfer some interest in immovable property. Suppose that A entered into a contract with B, whereby he agreed to sell to B a plot of land situated in a foreign country for a certain price. Subsequently, A declined to honour his promise. This brings into play the choice of law rules governing the validity of the contract. Such rules are now contained in the Rome Convention 1980 as implemented by the Contract (Applicable Law) Act 1990. These rules will now be examined.

8.3.5 Formal validity

Article 9(1) of the Rome Convention provides that a contract is formally valid if it satisfies the requirements of the law of the place of contracting or the requirements of the applicable law as determined by virtue of the Convention. So if, in the above example, A and B made the contract in England, then English law would govern its formal validity. Alternatively, if the contract was, by its terms or by implication (as per the Rome Convention) governed by English law, then this contract would be formally valid if it satisfied the requirements of the law of England, irrespective of whether or not it was formally valid by the *lex situs*. At common law, the same principle applied, as may be illustrated in *Re Smith* (1916). In this case, a deed, by which land in the West Indies was charged as security for the repayment of a debt, was executed in England. The parties had also agreed to execute a legal mortgage on this land whenever required. Notwithstanding that the deed was not valid under the *lex situs*, the English court held that, as it satisfied the requirements of the law of England, the deed was valid.

However, a further special requirement is contained in Art 9(6) of the Rome Convention, which deals specifically with the formal validity of a contract, the subject matter of which is a right in immovable property or a right to use immovable property. Such a contract is subject to the mandatory requirements of form of the *lex situs*, provided that, by that law, those 'requirements are imposed irrespective of the country where the contract is concluded and irrespective of the law governing the contract'.

8.3.6 Essential validity

So far as the essential validity of such contracts is concerned, the governing law is the law chosen by the parties (Art 3 of the Rome Convention). In the absence of such a choice, whether it be express or implied, the essential validity of the contract is, by reason of Art 4, governed by the law of the country with which the contract is most closely connected. A presumption is contained in Art 4(3), which provides that such a contract 'is most closely connected with the country where the immovable property is situated'. This presumption may, however, be rebutted where the contract is most closely connected with the law of another country.

At common law, the essential validity of such contracts is determined by the proper law of the contract. For instance, in *British South Africa Co v De Beers Consolidated Mines Ltd* (1910), the essential validity of a contract, which related to land in Rhodesia, was held to be governed by English law as the proper law of the contract.

8.3.7 Capacity

At common law, capacity to make a contract to transfer immovables is governed by the proper law of the contract. In relation to the Rome Convention, as discussed in Chapter 5, questions of capacity of corporations are excluded from the scope of its application. However, when it comes to natural persons, though excluded in general, Art 11 provides that a person may invoke his incapacity resulting from another law only if 'the other party to the contract was aware of this incapacity at the time of the conclusion of the contract or was not aware thereof as a result of negligence', provided that the contract was concluded between persons who are in the same country.

Bearing the above in mind, it is important to note that if a contracting party was subject to some incapacity by the *lex situs*, but not by the proper law of the contract, it would be useless to subject him or her to a decree of specific performance in which the *lex situs* would forbid its implementation. In such a situation, it would be best to subject the party to liability in damages.

8.4 Choice of law and tangible movables

This paragraph is concerned with the determination of the legal system which governs the transfer of proprietary interests in tangible movables (chattels or physical objects). Frequently, such transfers are effected in consequence of a contract, but the law which determines the aspects of the contractual relationship of the parties is not necessarily the same as the one which determines whether the transfer is effected. However, since we are only concerned with proprietary rights and not with contract, it suffices to indicate that the rights and liabilities of the parties under the contract are determined by the proper law of that contract (see Chapter 5).

8.4.1 The applicable law to the transfer

As with immovable property, the basic rule is that the *lex situs*, at the time of the disposition of the property, determines the validity of the transfer of a particular movable. Thus, if a movable property was validly transferred according to its *lex situs* at the time of the disposition, then that transfer would be recognised in England. The leading case is *Cammell v Sewell* (1860), where a cargo of timber was shipped from Russia to Hull, England, on board a Prussian ship. The vessel was seriously damaged off the Norwegian coast. Consequently, the master of the ship sold the damaged timber without obtaining the owners' consent. The goods were subsequently brought to England and sold to the defendants. On an action by the original owners challenging the defendants' title, the English court held that, as the transfer of title was valid in Norway, that is, the *lex situs* at the time of the disposition, that transfer would be recognised in England. Accordingly, the plaintiffs' claim failed.

A more recent illustration of the application of this rule can be found in the case of *Winkworth v Christie Manson and Woods* (1980). Here, works of art were stolen from the plaintiff's house in England and taken to Italy where they were sold to the second defendant. Subsequently, the works were sent back to England to be auctioned by the first defendant. By Italian law, the second defendant had obtained good title when he bought the paintings in Italy. The English court held that, as the *lex situs* at the time of the disposition, that is, Italian law, recognised the transfer as valid, the second defendant had obtained good title. The application of Italian law was justified on the grounds that the transaction in question had taken place in Italy, and that nothing had occurred in England afterwards to deprive the holder of the title under Italian law from his title. Accordingly, the plaintiff's claim failed.

8.4.2 The applicable law to a series of transfers

Where there is a series of transactions affecting goods, the title acquired in the first State continues until divested by a transaction in a second State which validly transfers the title under the law of that State. In other words, where there have been two consecutive transactions in relation to the same movable, the first takes place in one State and the second takes place in another State, it is the law of the second State which determines the validity of the title. For instance, in the Canadian case of *Century Credit Corpn v Richard* (1962), the plaintiff sold and delivered a car to the buyer in Quebec. The contract of sale reserved the title in the car to the seller until full payment of the purchase price was made. The buyer, however, took the car to Ontario, where he sold it to a party who was unaware of the reservation of title. Under Quebec law, the *lex situs* of the first transaction, the reservation of title did not have to be registered in order to be effective. Under Ontario law, however, the reservation of title had to be registered. Moreover, under Ontario law, the first buyer could pass a good title to the second buyer although the former's title was defective under Quebec law. The Ontario court held that the reservation of title made in Quebec did not affect the sale of the car in Ontario, for Ontario law should apply to the second transfer. Accordingly, the second buyer had obtained a good title.

Nonetheless, for the above rule to apply, the second disposition must have the effect of transferring title under the law of the second State, otherwise it will not override the title obtained by virtue of the first transaction. For instance, in the US case of *Goetschius v Brightman* (1927), a car was sold to the buyer in California with a reservation of title clause contained in the contract of sale. The contract also expressly provided that the car was not to be removed from California until it was fully paid for. The buyer, however, took the car to New York without the seller's knowledge and sold it to a *bona fide* purchaser. By the law of California, the *lex situs* of the first transaction, the original seller's title would prevail over that of the second purchaser. However, by the law of New York, a *bona fide* purchaser would acquire good title, but only if the reservation of title clause was not registered in New York, and this was the case. The New York court applied New York law, as the *lex situs*, but held that the original seller's title would be recognised in New York. The reason for this decision was not because of any displacement of the *lex situs*, but because the New York registration requirement did not apply to a Californian reservation of title. In other words, nothing had occurred in New York to render the original seller's title defective under New York law.

The above two cases dealt with the situation where the original seller's title was recognised by the law of the place where the first transaction took place. Where, however, the reverse situation occurs, that is, where the *lex situs* of the first transaction does not recognise the original seller's title but the *lex situs* of the second transaction does, then it appears that his or her title would be governed by the *lex situs* of the second transaction. This may be illustrated by the US case of *Marvin Safe Co v Norton* (1886), where the law of Pennsylvania, the *lex situs* of the first transaction, provided that the original seller's reservation of title, though valid against the first buyer, was not valid against a purchaser from that first buyer. By New Jersey law, however, the title of the original seller would not be overridden. So, when the first buyer took the movable to New Jersey where he sold it to the defendant, the court of New Jersey applied New Jersey law as the *lex situs* of the second transaction, and upheld the original seller's title. This was basically due to the fact that the law of Pennsylvania ceased to operate once the goods were removed to New Jersey.

This principle seems reasonable and appears to meet the requirements of the rule laid down in both *Century Credit* and *Goetschius*. Nevertheless, the New Jersey court in *Dougherty v Krimke* (1929) reached a different conclusion in an identical set of facts. The only difference, however, was that the *lex situs* of the first transaction was that of New York rather than Pennsylvania. Here, the court held that the original seller's title was overridden by the subsequent transaction in New Jersey. Notwithstanding the difficulty of reconciling these two judgments, Dr Morris appears to suggest that *Dougherty* could be distinguished from *Marvin Safe*. Whereas, in the latter case, Pennsylvania law applied to sales taking place in that State, New York law had an extra-territorial effect, in the sense that it applied to all sales taking place anywhere.

8.5 Choice of law and intangible movables

An intangible movable may be described as an interest which is not directly related to a physical object or land, for example, shares, patents, copyrights, debts and negotiable instruments. They may also be referred to as 'choses in action'.

Before examining the rules on choice of law, a distinction has to be drawn between issues of validity of the transaction by which the debt was assigned, and the issue of assignability of the debt, that is, whether or not the debt can be assigned to another person. Accordingly, the choice of the applicable law may vary, depending on which category the issues relate to. In the former case, for example, the issue may relate to capacity, formal or essential validity of the contract of assignment itself, whereas in the latter case, the issue is whether the debt in question is capable of assignment, or to which one of two or more competing assignees the debt is payable, that is the issue of priorities.

8.5.1 Validity of the contract of assignment

For cases falling within the scope of the Rome Convention 1980, questions of formal and essential validity of an assignment are governed by Art 12(1), which provides:

> The mutual obligation of assignor and assignee under a voluntary assignment of a right against another person ('the debtor') shall be governed by the law which under this Convention applies to the contract between the assignor and assignee.

In other words, in the case of essential validity, the applicable law would be the law chosen by the parties (Art 3). In the absence of such a choice, the applicable law is determined by reference to the presumptions in Art 4 of the Convention. Formal validity, however, is determined by the provisions of Art 9 which indicate that an assignment will be formally valid if it satisfies the formal requirements of the applicable law. If both parties were in the same country, the assignment must satisfy the formal requirements of the law of that country and, if they were in different countries, it must satisfy the formal requirements of the law of one of those countries. Moreover, in relation to the issue of capacity, this is excluded from the scope of the Convention save in one limited situation under Art 11, that is, issue of incapacity. As such, issues of capacity must continue to be referred to the common law rules.

Under the traditional rules, the general approach in relation to essential validity, adopted by the English court in *Trendtex Trading Corpn v Crédit Suisse* (1980), was along the same lines as the general approach adopted by the Convention. Issues of formal validity were said to be governed by the law of the place where the transaction was made (see *Republica of Guatemala v Nunez* (1927)).

In relation to capacity, English courts, in the few cases where this issue has been raised, seem to have adopted the law of the place of acting; for instance, in *Lee v Abdy* (1886) where a husband, domiciled in Cape Colony, assigned a policy of life insurance issued by an English company to his wife who was also domiciled in Cape Colony. This assignment, though valid in English law, was void by the law of Cape Colony because the assignee was the wife of the assignor, that is, the wife lacked capacity to accept the assignment. It was held that the assignment was governed by the law of Cape Colony.

Similarly, in *Republica of Guatemala v Nunez* (1927), the President of Guatemala assigned to his son, a minor domiciled in Guatemala, the sum of £20,000, which he had deposited in a London bank. This assignment, though valid by English law, was invalid by Guatemalan law because, *inter alia*, a minor could not accept it unless a judicial trustee had been appointed, and this was not done. Scrutton LJ and Lawrence LJ, the only two judges who dealt with the issue of capacity, stated that such an issue was governed either by the law of domicile or by the law of the place of the transaction.

It has been argued, however, that perhaps what the courts intended to do in the above case was to apply the proper law of the assignment, for the domicile of the parties and the place of acting concurred (see Cheshire and North, *Private International Law*, 12th edn, pp 814–15).

8.5.2 Issues on the nature of the right assigned

A question may arise as to whether the right in question is assignable, or it may arise in relation to priorities as between successive assignments.

8.5.3 Assignability

This is now governed by Art 12(2) of the Rome Convention, which states:

> The law governing the right to which the assignment relates shall determine its assignability, the relationship between the assignee and the debt, or the

conditions under which the assignment can be invoked against the debtor and any question whether the debtor's obligations have been discharged.

Hence, if a question arises as to whether a particular right is assignable, then the law governing the transaction to which the right owes its origin will apply, that is, the law governing the debt or the right.

At common law, the position is very much the same. The proper law of the debt determines whether or not a debt is assignable, as was held in *Campbell Connolly and Co Ltd v Noble* (1963); and *Trendtex Trading Corpn v Crédit Suisse* (1980).

8.5.4 Priorities

This is also governed by Art 12(2) of the Rome Convention, which indicates that the law governing the debt determines the question of priorities. This law has been interpreted to mean the *lex situs* of the debt. For example, in *Macmillan v Bishopsgate Investment Trust plc (No 3)* (1996), the Court of Appeal unanimously decided that issues of priority of title to shares should be determined by their *lex situs*. This was justified on the ground that it was logical to place questions of title to shares on the same footing as other property, notably land and tangible movables.

At common law, the same principle appears to be applicable. This may be illustrated in *Kelly v Selwyn* (1905), where there were two assignments of the same interest in certain English trust funds. The first one was made in 1891 in New York, where the assignor was then domiciled. Notice, however, was not given to the trustees until 12 years later. The second assignment was made in 1894 by a deed executed in England, and immediate notice of which was given to the trustees. Warrington J held that, since the fund was an English trust fund and the English court was the court of jurisdiction, and the testator may have contemplated to administer this fund, then accordingly, the ranking of the assignments must be regulated by the law of England.

Although the court did not make it clear on what basis English law was applied, that is, as the law of the forum, or the law governing the debt, it is, however, suggested that English law was applied as the law governing the debt. Such a suggestion found support in the Jersey case of *Le Feuvre v Sullivan* (1855).

8.6 Foreign expropriation decrees

In this section, the law regarding the effect of decrees or other legislation adopted by foreign governments with the objective of expropriating property will be examined. It happens sometimes that a particular State, by virtue of a decree or other legislation, expropriates certain property belonging to an individual or a corporation. It also happens that, in some instances, the property which is subject to the compulsory acquisition is not within the expropriating State, but is in another State. Suppose, for example, that State A issued a decree expropriating X's property, which consisted of immovables in that State and movables in England. The question which arises here is whether the English court would give effect to that decree.

The answer to this question depends mainly on the *situs* of the property at the time when the foreign law was enacted.

8.6.1 Where the property is in the foreign country

As a general rule, if the property is situated in the expropriating country at the time when the foreign State enacts the law which purported to deprive the owner of his or her title, then English courts will give effect to that law, even if it was of a confiscatory nature. According to *Luther v Sagor* (1921) this is, however, subject to that foreign State or government being recognised by the Crown.

This rule was consolidated by the House of Lords in *Williams and Humbert Ltd v WH Trademarks Ltd* (1986), where it was held that, as a general rule, a foreign confiscatory law will be recognised and given effect by the English courts provided it does not require enforcement in England. In this case, the Spanish Government had compulsorily acquired all the shares in Rumasa, a company incorporated in Spain, as well as the shares in its subsidiaries. Rumasa also owned the full share capital in an English company, Williams and Humbert, which therefore became controlled indirectly by the Spanish Government. Prior to the compulsory acquisition, the English company had assigned one of its trade marks and goodwill to a Jersey company set up for this purpose. Under the agreement, the Jersey company would grant Williams and Humbert licences to use the trade mark on the condition that the Jersey company could terminate the licences if part of the issued share capital or assets of the Spanish company were expropriated. Hence, as a result of the Spanish expropriation, the Jersey company terminated the licences.

In an action in the English court, Williams and Humbert argued, *inter alia*, that the Spanish expropriation should not be recognised, for it seeks to enforce Spanish penal or other public laws in England. The House of Lords held that foreign expropriatory legislation would be recognised as having transferred title/ownership in the property if, at the time, that property was situated within the expropriating State. If, however, the property was situated outside that State, then the foreign State's title/ownership would not be enforced in England. Here, the Spanish legislation had the effect of acquiring the ownership of the shares in the companies in Spain. Accordingly, the Spanish legislation did not amount to indirect enforcement of Spanish penal or other public laws in England.

However, if the expropriation involves discrimination, for example, on racial grounds, it appears that the English court would refuse to recognise it on the grounds of public policy. This can be inferred in the House of Lords' decision in *Oppenheimer v Cattermole* (1976), where the court addressed, *inter alia*, the question of whether a German decree which deprived the plaintiff, an anti-Nazi Jew, of his German nationality would be recognised in England. Indeed, Cross LJ (*obiter*) seems to take this view. He stated that (p 278):

> legislation which takes away without compensation from a section of the citizen body singled out on racial grounds all their property on which the State passing the legislation can lay its hand on and, in addition, deprives them of their citizenship ... constitutes so grave an infringement of human rights that the courts of this country ought to refuse to recognise it as a law at all.

In accordance with *Adams v National Bank of Greece and Athens SA* (1961); and *AG for New Zealand v Ortiz* (1984), this same principle applies where the expropriation attempts to enforce foreign penal or other public laws.

8.6.2 Where the property is in England

Where the property is situated in England at the relevant time, then English courts will not enforce the foreign expropriation law. This may be justified on the ground that, otherwise, the foreign law would be given an extra-territorial effect (see *Lecouturier v Rey* (1910)).

The question which arises at this stage is whether, if the expropriating legislation was recognised in principle, but before the foreign authorities reduced the property into possession it was removed from that country and brought to England, the English court would recognise that law as having divested the owner of his title. Guidance on this matter may be derived from the House of Lords' decision in *AG for New Zealand v Ortiz* (1984). Here, a tribesman found an ancient carving in a swamp in New Zealand. He sold it to the third defendant, a dealer in primitive works of art. That defendant exported it to England in contravention of a New Zealand statute which provided that:

> An historic article knowingly exported or attempted to be exported in breach of this Act shall be forfeited ...

The carving was sold to the first defendant, who then offered it for sale by auction by the second defendant in London. The Attorney General of New Zealand brought an action in the English court alleging that the carving was removed from New Zealand without certificate of permission as required by statute and, accordingly, the Government of New Zealand was entitled to possession of the carving.

The House of Lords held that, on the true construction of the statute, forfeiture took effect only when the historic article was seized by the New Zealand customs or police, and not automatically, immediately the article was exported. The relevant statute was interpreted to mean that the carving was liable to forfeiture, and since no seizure had taken place, the Crown was neither the owner, nor entitled to possession of the carving.

As to whether the New Zealand statute was a 'foreign penal, revenue or public laws', and, therefore, would be unenforceable in England, the House of Lords did not deal with this question. But, equally, their Lordships did not express a conclusion as to the correctness or otherwise of the Court of Appeal's affirmative views which were expressed *obiter*. Whilst Lord Denning MR stated that the New Zealand legislation fell into the category of 'public laws' which would not be enforced in England, Lord Ackner, with whom Lord O'Connor concurred, took the view that it fell into the category of 'penal law', which also was unenforceable in England.

8.7   Succession

Here, the discussion will be confined to the law governing the distribution of the estate of a deceased person, whether movables or immovables, between the beneficiaries. This law may vary, depending on whether the estate consists of movables or immovables, and whether the deceased left a will or died intestate. The discussion will not extend to the question of the administration of the estate. It suffices to say, however, that this is generally governed by English law if the estate is being administered in England.

8.7.1   Intestate succession

If a person dies without leaving a will, then the law governing the distribution of his estate depends on whether it is movables or immovables.

8.7.2   Movables

So far as movable property is concerned, the property is distributed in accordance with the law of the domicile of the deceased at the time of his or her death, as was held in *Re Collens* (1986). This law will determine such questions as the rights of a surviving spouse, the proportions to be given to other relatives, and so forth. If, however, no relatives or next of kin existed, then movables situated in England would pass to the Crown. This is so, unless they are claimed by somebody in the State of domicile as *ultimus heres,* that is a claim of succession. The operation of this latter rule may be illustrated by looking at two English decisions. In *Re Barnett's Trusts* (1902), the deceased died domiciled in Austria, but left property in England. He was heirless, and the Austrian State claimed the property in England. The English court rejected the claim on the ground that it was classified as an issue of administration rather than succession, and accordingly, the property went to the Crown as *bona vacantia*. On the other hand, in *Re Maldonado* (1954), similar facts were involved, but the foreign State claimed the property in England as *ultimus heres.* Here, the English court held that the claim was one of succession and, accordingly, the foreign State was entitled to the property.

8.7.3   Immovables

Intestate succession to immovable property, whether situated in England or in a foreign country, is governed by the *lex situs*, irrespective of the domicile of the deceased. This rule has been criticised as being unsatisfactory, on the ground that it would lead to different kinds of property of a deceased being distributed according to different regimes. The operation of the rule may be illustrated by the case of *Re Collens* (1986). Here, the deceased died intestate and domiciled in Trinidad and Tobago. He left property in Trinidad and Tobago, Barbados and England. Some of the property in England included immovable property. After litigation in Trinidad between his widow and his ex-wife, the widow agreed to receive $1 m in full settlement of any claim against the estate in Trinidad and Tobago. Subsequently, the widow made a claim in relation to the property in England. The English court, although reluctant to see the widow's claim succeed in relation to the English statutory legacy, was unable to divert from the interpretation of English law and, accordingly, allowed the widow's claim.

8.7.4   Testate succession

Where a person dies leaving a will which expresses his or her intentions as to the future of the estate, the governing law is as follows.

8.7.5   Movables

As a general rule, testamentary succession to movable property is governed by the law of the domicile of the deceased at the time of his death for some issues, or at the time of making the will for others. In order to examine how the rules apply, it is necessary to deal with the various issues that may arise.

Capacity

Here, the question may arise as to whether the testator was either old enough to make the will or in a fit mental state to do so. According to the case of *In the Estate of Fuld (No 3)* (1968), the capacity of a testator to make a will is determined by the law of his or her domicile. The controversy, however, arises as to whether the relevant domicile is the domicile at the date of making the will or at the date of the testator's death. The decisive time becomes crucial where the testator has changed his or her domicile after making the will. The view preferred seems to be the time of making the will rather than the time of death, for this would avoid declaring a will invalid according to the law of the domicile at the time of death, when it would be valid by the law of the domicile at the time of making the will.

The question of capacity may also arise in relation to a legatee's capacity to take a bequest under the will. This is determined by either the law of the legatee's domicile or the law of the testator's domicile. Where these laws are conflicting, however, then the English court, according to *Re Hellmann's Will* (1866), would adopt the law which is most favourable to the legatee.

Essential validity

The essential or material validity of a will is determined by the law of the domicile of the testator at the time of his or her death. This rule is not affected by the Wills Act 1963 as this only applies to formal validity. The operation of this rule may be illustrated by the case of *Re Groos* (1915), where a Dutch woman made a will in The Netherlands to the effect that her husband would inherit her movable property, except for the legitimate portion to which her children were entitled. By English law, the law of her domicile at the time of her death, this portion amounted to nothing. By Dutch law, however, the legitimate portion was three quarters of the property. The English court applied English law as the law of the testatrix's domicile at the time of her death.

Where, however, a testator bequeaths a movable property to a legatee domiciled in a foreign country and the legacy, though valid by the law of the domicile of the legatee, is invalid by the law of the testator's domicile because it infringes a rule against perpetuities or accumulations, then according to *Fordyce v Bridges* (1848), the legacy will be held valid.

Construction and effect

Here, the issues concerned are issues of interpretation and issues as to the effect of the will when, for example, a legatee dies and there is no provision in the will to indicate what should happen in such a case. In this context, the applicable law is normally the law of the domicile of the testator at the time the will was made. This is justified on the ground that it is reasonable to assume that, when the testator made his or her will, he or she had the law of his or her own domicile in contemplation. This approach is supported by the English decision of *Re Cunnington* (1924). It is also supported by s 4 of the Wills Act 1963, which provides that the construction of a will shall not be altered by reason of any change in domicile of the testator after the execution of the will.

Nevertheless, this rule on interpretation and effect operates as a presumption and may be rebutted if the testator has manifestly contemplated a different law to apply (see *Re Price* (1900), where it was held that, since the testatrix had stipulated that her will was to be 'considered in England the same as in France', she had contemplated that English law would apply albeit she was domiciled in France).

Formal validity

The choice of law rules in this context are contained in the Wills Act 1963, which implements the International Convention on the Formal Validity of Wills 1961. Section 1 of the Act provides that:

> [A] will shall be treated as properly executed if its execution conformed to the internal law in force in the territory where it was executed, or in the territory where, at the time of its execution or of the testator's death, he was domiciled or had his habitual residence, or in a State of which, at either of those times, he was a national.

It can be seen that the purpose of this section is to avoid the invalidation of wills on formal grounds by allowing compliance with the requirements of the law of one of several countries.

Revocation

In English law, a will may be voluntarily revoked either by a fresh will or by its destruction with the intention of revoking it. On the other hand, it may be automatically revoked by the subsequent marriage of the testator. If a will has been revoked by a subsequent will, s 2(1)(c) of the Wills Act 1963 provides that the subsequent will shall be formally valid if it satisfies the formal requirements of any one of the laws qualified to govern the formal validity of the previous will or any law with which the subsequent will may comply. As to capacity and essential validity of the subsequent will, these are determined by the relevant rules discussed above.

As to the question of whether a will has been revoked by destruction or obliteration, it is suggested that this issue should be determined by the law of the testator's domicile at the time of the purported revocation (see McClean, *Morris – The Conflict of Laws*, 4th edn, pp 359–60; and Cheshire and North, *Private International Law*, 12th edn, p 349).

The issue of whether a will has been revoked by the subsequent marriage of the testator was held by the Court of Appeal, in *Re Martin* (1900), to be determined by the law of the testator's domicile at the time of the marriage.

8.7.6 Immovables

In relation to the capacity of the testator, this is determined by the *lex situs* (see Cheshire and North, *Private International Law*, 12th edn, p 852). In relation to the formal validity of the will, this is determined by s 1 of the Wills Act 1963, the same as wills of movables.

In relation to the question of essential validity, this is determined by the *lex situs* including its choice of law rules, that is, the doctrine of *renvoi* is applicable (see *Re Ross* (1930)). As for construction and effect, there is authority to suggest that the governing law is the law intended by the testator. This is normally presumed to be the law of his or her domicile at the time of making the will. However, if by the *lex situs* it is illegal or impossible to give effect to the terms of the will as construed by the law of the testator's domicile, then the *lex situs* will prevail (see *Re Miller* (1914); and *Philipson-Stow v IRC* (1916)).

Finally, as regards revocation of a will of immovables, the domestic law which would be applied by the *lex situs* will determine the validity of the subsequent will, except in relation to its formal validity, which is governed by s 2(1)(c) of the Wills Act 1963.

LAW OF PROPERTY

Immovable property jurisdiction under the old rules

Where the immovable property is situated outside the EC/EFTA States, the traditional common law rules apply to the effect that English courts have no jurisdiction to try an action for the determination of title to, or the right to possession of, any immovable property situated outside England, irrespective of the parties, domicile and residence. Such an action must be tried in the courts of the *lex situs*.

This rule is subject to s 30 of the CJJA 1982 whereby English courts have jurisdiction to entertain proceedings for trespass to, or any other tort affecting, immovable property situated outside England.

A number of exceptions to this rule are applicable in relation to the enforcement of a personal obligation to the plaintiff and in relation to the administration of trusts or estates in England. In such cases, English courts have the power to try the action even though the property is situated outside England.

Jurisdiction under the Brussels and Lugano Conventions

Where the immovable property is situated within the EC/EFTA States, Art 16(1) of the Conventions ascribes exclusive jurisdiction to the courts of the place where the property is situated.

This exclusive jurisdiction does not, however, cover disputes which have as their object tenancies of immovable property concluded for temporary use for a maximum period of six consecutive months. In such instances, and subject to some qualifications, the courts of the Contracting State in which the defendant is domiciled shall also have jurisdiction.

Choice of law

As a general rule, the law of the place where the property is situated determines questions of both formal and essential validity of transactions relating to immovable property.

The *lex situs* means the whole of that law, including its conflict of laws. Therefore, the doctrine of *renvoi* operates in this context.

Unless a person has capacity to transfer or to take immovable property by the law of the place where the property is situated, the transfer will not be valid.

Validity of the contract to transfer immovable property

Here, the question relates to the obligations of the parties under a contract, the object of which is to transfer immovable property.

The formal validity of such a contract is determined by the law of the place of contracting, or the applicable law allocated by the Rome Convention, subject to the qualification that the contract must comply with the mandatory requirements of the *lex situs* where those requirements are imposed, irrespective of the country where the contract is concluded or irrespective of the governing law.

In relation to essential validity, the applicable law is the law of the country with which the contract is most closely connected.

Choice of law and tangible movables

The *lex situs* determines the validity of the transfer of movable property at the time of the disposition.

Choice of law and intangible movables

Questions of formal and essential validity of an assignment of intangible property are governed by the applicable law of their contract, as determined by the Rome Convention.

Capacity appears to be determined by the law of the place of acting.

The question of whether a particular right can be assigned and the question of priorities seem to be determined by the law governing the assignment.

Foreign expropriation decrees/legislation

If the property is situated within the boundaries of the foreign State at the time when the property was expropriated, then, as a general rule, such an expropriation would be recognised in England.

If, however, the property was outside that State, then English courts would not, as a general rule, recognise the expropriation.

Intestate succession

Movable property will be distributed according to the law of the deceased's domicile at the time of death.

Immovable property will be distributed in accordance with the *lex situs*.

Testate succession

The general rule is that testate succession to movable property is governed by the law of the domicile of the deceased at the time of death for some issues, and at the time of making the will for some others.

In relation to immovable property, the capacity of the testator and the essential validity of the will are determined by the *lex situs*, and the formal validity of the will is determined by the Wills Act 1963.

CHAPTER 9

DOMICILE AT COMMON LAW

9.1 Introduction

For the purposes of jurisdiction in civil and commercial matters, as already seen, English law applies a concept of domicile as defined in ss 41–46 of the Civil Jurisdiction and Judgment Act 1982 (CJJA) (see details below, 9.7). However, a different concept of domicile is adopted in England to determine an individual's personal law. Personal law may be defined as the law of the country to which a person primarily belongs, especially for the purposes of various matters of family law and succession. In other words, the personal law of an individual determines such matters as:

(a) the essential validity of a marriage;

(b) the effect of marriage on the proprietary rights of husband and wife;

(c) wills of movables and succession to movables;

(d) jurisdiction in divorce and nullity of marriage, and to a certain extent, legitimacy of children and adoption; and

(e) certain matters of revenue law.

For the purposes of the above matters, England regards the concept of domicile as the decisive factor. In contrast, civil law jurisdictions regard *nationality* as the decisive factor to determine an individual's personal law. This will clearly create problems of *renvoi*. For instance, in *Re Ross* (1930), Mrs Ross, a British subject domiciled in Italy, died in 1927 leaving movable property in England and Italy, and immovable property in Italy. She left two wills, one in English, leaving her property in England to her niece, and a second one in Italian, leaving her movable and immovable property in Italy to her grandnephew and his mother. Neither will left anything to her only son, who contested the wills on the ground that, under Italian law, he was entitled to a proportion of her property.

With regard to her movable property, it was held that this had to be determined by Italian law as the law of the domicile of the testatrix. However, looking at Italian law, namely, Art 8 of the Italian Code, which provided that succession was regulated by the national law of the deceased, whatever the nature of the property, and Art 9, which stated that the substance and effect of wills were governed by the national law of the testator, the court was of the view that an Italian judge would have referred the subject matter of the dispute to the law of her nationality, that is, British. Hence, by virtue of this *renvoi*, English law was applied and the son's claim failed.

Similarly, in respect of her immovable property, Italian law was applied as the *lex situs*, and by virtue of the same provisions of the Italian Code, it was equally held that the issue would have been referred to English internal law. Again, the son's claim failed.

Another example of *renvoi* can be found in *Re O'Keefe* (1940), where Miss O'Keefe, a British subject of Irish origin, died intestate and domiciled in Italy. By English law, the distribution of her estate, which consisted of movable property, was subject to the law of her domicile, that is Italy. By Italian law, however, this was subject to the law of her nationality, which was British. Accordingly, it was held that the only part of the British empire to which she could be said to have belonged, was the part from which she had originated, namely Ireland (Eire). Therefore, *renvoi* applied, and her estate was distributed according to the law of Ireland.

In order to circumvent this problem of conflict between nationality and domicile, the concept of habitual residence has been selected as the decisive factor to determine an individual's personal law in a number of international conventions seeking to regulate issues of family law; in particular, recognition of divorces. Such an example is the Hague Conference on Private International Law, which refers to habitual residence rather than domicile or nationality. Habitual residence has also been used by the British Parliament in various Acts, such as s 46(1)(b) of the Family Law Act 1986, which provides that a foreign divorce is recognised in England if it is effective under the law of the country where it was obtained, and if, at the date of the commencement of the proceedings, either party to the marriage was habitually resident or domiciled in, or was a national of that country.

As to the meaning of habitual residence, it was examined by the English court in *Cruse v Chittum* (1974). Here, it was held that habitual residence, for the purposes of s 3 of the Recognition of Divorces and Legal Separations Act 1971 (now, s 46 of the Family Law Act 1986), meant 'a regular physical presence which must endure for some time'. It meant 'something more than ordinary residence and something less than domicile'.

9.2   Meaning and definition of domicile

The meaning and definition of domicile were elucidated by the Private International Law Committee in its First Report in 1954 (Cmd 9068) as follows:

> A person's domicile may be defined as meaning the country (in the sense of a territorial unit possessing its own system of law) in which he has his home and intends to live permanently. The law regards every person as having a domicile, whether it be the *domicile of origin* which the law confers on him at birth, or the *domicile of choice* which he may subsequently acquire. The two requisites for the acquisition of a fresh domicile are: (1) residence; and (2) intention to remain permanently, and both these elements must be present before a new domicile

can be acquired. If a person, having acquired a domicile of choice, abandons it without acquiring a fresh one, the law regards his domicile of origin as having revived until a fresh domicile of choice is acquired, even though he may never in fact have returned to his domicile of origin.

Hence, according to this statement, domicile may be defined as the legal system within whose jurisdiction an individual makes his or her home, intending to remain there permanently. It can be seen that the cornerstone underlying the English concept of domicile is *permanent home*. What this in fact means is not clear. Lord Cranworth, in the case of *Whicker v Hume* (1858), declined to clarify this notion and said '... if you do not understand your permanent home, I'm afraid that no illustration drawn from foreign writers or foreign languages will very much help you to it'. What is clear, however, is that no person can lack a domicile, and, in order to meet this end, this concept has been overloaded by complicated rules which resulted in stretching the notion of permanent home beyond the limits of credibility.

There are three types of domicile, the domicile of origin, that is, the domicile which a person acquires at birth; the domicile of choice, which a person of full age acquires by residing in a country other than that of his or her origin, with the intention of settling there permanently; and the domicile of dependency, which a person has by virtue of being dependent. Generally, a child under the age of 16 has a domicile dependent on that of the father if legitimate, and on that of the mother if illegitimate. Each of these types will be considered in turn, but, prior to that, it is important to note that according to *Re Martin* (1900), an individual's domicile must be determined by English law 'according to those principles applicable to domicile which are recognised in this country and are part of its law'. An exception to this rule, however, may be found in s 46(5) of the Family Law Act 1986, which refers to domicile in a country in the context of that country's law.

9.3   Domicile of origin

The domicile of origin is the domicile a person acquires at birth, and remains with that person thereafter until it is replaced by a domicile of dependency or domicile of choice (see *Bell v Kennedy* (1868)). The domicile of origin revives in the absence of any other domicile on the relevant day.

Hence, according to the House of Lords in *Udny v Udny* (1869):

> ... no person shall be without a domicile, and to secure this result the law attributes to every individual as soon as they are born the domicile of his or her father, if the child is legitimate, and the domicile of the mother if illegitimate.

A posthumous child, that is, a child born after his or her father's death, derives his or her domicile of origin from that of the mother. As for the domicile of origin of a foundling, this is derived from the country where he or she is found.

Furthermore, and according to *Henderson v Henderson* (1967), a domicile of origin is the domicile acquired at birth and not the domicile of dependency as at the date of reaching the age of majority.

9.4   Domicile of dependency

It is a well settled rule that no dependent person can acquire a domicile of choice. The domicile of such persons depends on, and changes with, the domicile of the person on whom they are legally dependent. Two classes of persons must be examined, namely, children under the age of 16 and married women. As for mentally disordered persons, it suffices to note that, in general, the domicile of such a person depends on the person to whose care a mentally disordered person has been entrusted.

9.4.1   Children under 16

A child under the age of 16 will be subject to a domicile of dependency if one or both of his parents abandon their domicile of origin to acquire a domicile of choice in a new land.

The rules are partly common law and partly contained in ss 3 and 4 of the Domicile and Matrimonial Proceedings Act 1973 (DMPA). At common law and as a general rule, the domicile of a legitimate child depends on that of the father, provided that the latter is alive and the parents are living together. Once the child reaches the age of 16 or marries under that age, then, according to s 3(1) of the 1973 Act, he or she becomes capable of acquiring an independent domicile. Section 3(1) reads as follows:

> The time at which a person first becomes capable of having an independent domicile shall be when he attains the age of 16 or marries under that age; and in the case of a person who immediately before 1 January 1974 was incapable of having an independent domicile, but had then attained the age of 16 or been married, it shall be that date.

A few points should be made in relation to this provision. First, since the coming into force of the DMPA 1973 on 1 January 1974, the age at which an independent domicile can be acquired has been reduced from 18 to 16. Secondly, a child under the latter age cannot acquire an independent domicile unless he or she marries under that age. Nevertheless, since under English domestic law such a marriage is void, the provision has the effect of only allowing English courts to regard a child, marrying under the age of 16 under a foreign law, as validly married.

Further modifications were brought about by virtue of s 4 of the DMPA 1973, the provisions of which apply only to children whose father and mother are alive but living apart (see s 4(1)). In such circumstances, s 4(2) provides that:

The child's domicile as at the time shall be that of his mother if:

(a) he then has his home with her and has no home with his father; or

(b) he has at any time had her domicile by virtue of para (a) above and has not since had a home with his father.

Hence, where both parents are alive, but living apart, a child's domicile of dependency will be that of the mother, provided that he or she has a home with the mother and no home with the father or, alternatively, provided that he or she has had the mother's domicile by virtue of the above criteria and has not since had a home with the father. This latter provision clearly means that a child who has his or her home with the mother keeps her domicile as his or her domicile of dependency so long as he or she does not later have a home with the father, even though he or she may have ceased to live with the mother. Furthermore, by virtue of s 4(3), a child who has his or her mother's domicile by reason of s 4(2), continues to retain that domicile after the mother's death, provided that the child has not since had a home with the father.

It should be noted at this stage that neither the word home nor the phrase living apart are defined under the Act. It is believed, however, that the latter phrase 'does not imply any breakdown in the relationship between the parents, who may be living apart because of the demands of one parent's work' (McClean, *Morris – The Conflict of Laws*, 4th edn, p 28).

Due to the fact that the main purpose of the DMPA 1973 is to increase the number of instances where the domicile of a child will be dependent on that of the mother, s 4(4) preserves the pre-existing common law rules in which a child's domicile was regarded as being, by dependence, that of the mother; that is to say, the pre-existing rules relating to illegitimate children and those rules relating to legitimate children whose fathers are dead survive the DMPA 1973.

A further improvement is made by virtue of s 4(5), which treats an adopted child as if he or she had been born to the adopted parents.

Nonetheless, the provisions of ss 3 and 4 only apply to ascertain a child's domicile of dependency and do not affect his or her domicile of origin. Moreover, they do not apply to illegitimate children or to children whose parents are both dead. Therefore, for cases falling outside their scope, the common law rules still apply.

Where the domicile of a dependent child changes by reason of the parent's change of domicile or by reason of his or her legitimation, then, according to *Henderson v Henderson* (1967), the new domicile which the child acquires in this way is a domicile of dependency and not a domicile of origin.

Where the child is legitimate and his or her parents are alive and living together, the child's domicile is dependent on that of his or her father. If, however, the father dies, as in *Potinger v Wightman* (1817), thereafter the child takes his or her mother's domicile. This remains the case even if the mother acquires a new domicile, unless the mother's change of domicile was done fraudulently and in order, for example, to obtain some advantage of a law of succession more beneficial to herself. In the *Potinger* case, an Englishman died domiciled in Guernsey leaving seven children, four by a former wife and three by his widow, who was then pregnant with a fourth child. On his death and being intestate, his estate was distributed according to the law of Guernsey as the law of his domicile. A year later, his widow moved back to England with her four children, and from that time she established her domicile there. Three years later, one of her sons died at the age of six, and three years after that another son died at the age of 10. The main issue before the court was whether the estate of the deceased children should be distributed according to the law of England or the law of Guernsey. It was held that, as both the father and mother were natives of England, the return of the mother to England after the father's death was a matter of course and, therefore, did not cast suspicion of an improper motive.

Where a mother changes her domicile after the father's death, but leaves a child permanently resident in the country of her previous domicile, then that child's domicile does not change with that of the mother. Such was the case in *Re Beaumont* (1893), where a widow with four children, all of whom had a Scottish domicile, re-married in Scotland. Shortly thereafter, she and three of her children joined her second husband, who had gone to reside in England permanently. Her fourth child remained in Scotland with her aunt, with whom she had lived since her father's death and where she remained until her death. Stirling J held that the daughter died domiciled in Scotland and stated the rule that:

> ... the change in the domicile of a fatherless infant, which may follow a change of domicile on the part of the mother, is not to be regarded as the necessary consequence of a change of the mother's domicile, but as the result of the exercise by her of a power vested in her for the welfare of the infants, which in their interest she may abstain from exercising even when she changes her own domicile.

Accordingly, as the mother in this case had abstained from exercising her power to change her daughter's domicile by leaving the latter with her aunt, the daughter's domicile remained Scottish.

9.4.2 Married women

Prior to 1 January 1974, the domicile of a married woman was the same as, and changed with, the domicile of her husband. In other words, a married woman's domicile was dependent on that of her husband and, if the husband died or divorced her, then her domicile of dependency continued as her domicile of choice unless and until she acquired a new domicile. This rule was greatly criticised as being 'barbarous' and, consequently, was abolished by s 1 of the DMPA 1973, which provides that:

(1) Subject to sub-s (2) below, the domicile of a married woman as at any time after the coming into force of this section shall, instead of being the same as her husband's by virtue only of marriage, be ascertained by reference to the same factors as in the case of any other individual capable of having an independent domicile.

(2) When immediately before this section came into force a woman was married and then had her husband's domicile by dependence, she is to be treated as retaining that domicile (as a domicile of choice, if it is not also her domicile of origin) unless and until it is changed by acquisition or revival of another domicile either on or after the coming into force of this section.

Section 1(1) means that, since 1 January 1974, a married woman is to be treated as being capable of acquiring an independent domicile from that of her husband. Moreover, s 1(2) deals with transitional cases where a married woman had acquired a domicile of dependency before 1974. A woman who was already married before that date is to be treated as retaining her husband's domicile as a domicile of choice if it was not her domicile of origin, unless and until she abandons it on or after 1 January 1974. The operation of s 1(2) was considered in *IRC v Duchess of Portland* (1982). Here, the Duchess of Portland, who had a Canadian domicile of origin, married her husband, an English domiciliary, in 1948, thus acquiring an English domicile of dependency. The couple set up a house in England, where she intended to stay so long as her husband worked there. Nevertheless, she intended to return to Canada should her husband pre-decease her. Throughout her married life, she maintained close links with Canada, where she returned to visit for 10–12 weeks every summer. She contended that, by virtue of s 1(2) of the DMPA 1973, her English domicile of dependency was changed by the revival of her Canadian domicile of origin.

Nourse J held that the effect of the provisions of s 1 of the DMPA 1973 was to treat women who were married before 1 January 1974 somewhat less favourably than those who marry on or after that date. Immediately before that date, the Duchess had her husband's English domicile by dependency. She was, therefore, to be treated as retaining that domicile as a domicile of choice unless and until it was changed by acquisition or revival of another domicile. In other words, the effect of s 1(2) was to re-impose the domicile of dependency as a domicile of choice. Accordingly, the Duchess had acquired an English domicile of choice, and this was not abandoned since she continued residing in England.

9.5 Domicile of choice

Every independent person is capable of acquiring a domicile of choice by residing in a country, other than the country of origin, with the intention of remaining there permanently. Both the elements of residence and intention must be satisfied before English law can recognise a change of domicile. Although these elements are considered distinct, they are, as the remainder of this section will show, interrelated.

9.5.1 Proof of domicile of choice

It is a well established rule that the onus of proving a change of domicile lies on the party alleging it. How difficult is it to discharge this burden?

Conflicting views have been expressed in relation to the standard of proof required. On the one hand, according to Sir Jocelyn Simon P in *Henderson v Henderson* (1967), clear evidence is required to establish a change of domicile. In particular, to displace the domicile of origin in favour of a domicile of choice, the standard of proof goes beyond a mere balance of probabilities. On the other hand, Scarman J examined the issue in the case of *In the Estate of Fuld (No 3)* (1968). He stated that what has to be proved 'is no mere inclination arising from a passing fancy or thrust upon a man by an external or temporary pressure, but an intention freely formed to reside in a certain territory indefinitely. All the elements of the intention must be shown to exist if the change is to be established'. He, nevertheless, rejected the view that the standard of proof must be beyond reasonable doubt, and he concluded that two things are clear. First, 'unless the judicial conscience is satisfied by evidence of change, the domicile of origin persists'. Secondly, 'the acquisition of a domicile of choice is a serious matter not to be lightly inferred from slight indications or casual words'. Scarman J's approach seems to be the preferred one, for it was endorsed by the Court of Appeal in *Brown v Brown* (1982), and it is also the approach recommended by the Law Commission Report No 168 on the reform of the law of domicile.

9.5.2 Residence

Residence, also referred to as *factum*, in the new homeland is a question of fact. It was defined in *IRC v Duchess of Portland* (1982) as 'physical presence in that country as an inhabitant of it'. So, residence is more than mere physical presence and, therefore, does not cover the situation where, for example, presence in a particular country is for the purpose of holidaymaking. The length of residence in itself is not crucial, provided that the necessary intention exists. For instance, in *Re Flynn* (1968), where the *propositus* (that is, the person whose domicile is in question) had only spent limited periods of time in Jamaica, where he was in the process of building a house, Megarry J held that, whilst his 'work might continue to take him to many parts of the world for long periods ... Jamaica had become his centre of gravity' (p 119). Accordingly, he had acquired a Jamaican domicile of choice.

Notwithstanding that actual residence need not be prolonged, it must be proved to exist at the relevant time, as may be illustrated in *Harrison v Harrison*

(1953). Here, a husband with an English domicile of origin married his wife in 1950 in New Zealand when he was 20 years of age. Prior to their marriage, the parties had decided to live permanently in New Zealand. The husband planned to set up a business there, whereby he would train his own horses, so he decided to come to England, where there were better facilities, for a period of training. The couple arrived in England on 27 March 1951 and, while still in England, he became *sui juris* (that is, reached the age of majority) on 18 June 1951.

On the issue of whether he had acquired a domicile of choice in New Zealand, it was held that both residence and intention are necessary for the acquisition of a domicile of choice. He undoubtedly had the intention, but he did not meet the requirement of residence, for he had not lived in New Zealand since he had become *sui juris*.

Moreover, residence must be intended to create a real link between the individual and his or her alleged new homeland. This was established in *Qureshi v Qureshi* (1971), where a husband of Pakistani nationality came to England to qualify as a Fellow of the Royal College of Surgeons, a qualification which would have greatly enhanced his prospects in Pakistan. On the issue of whether the husband acquired an English domicile of choice, it was held that as his residence in England was only aimed at obtaining the specific qualification of Fellowship, he did not acquire such a domicile.

Finally, as it is possible for an individual to be resident in several countries at the same time, it was established in *Plummer v IRC* (1988) that a domicile of choice can only be acquired in the country of the chief residence.

9.5.3 Intention

The second element which must be satisfied is that the *propositus* must have the intention, also referred to as *animus*, to reside in the new homeland permanently or indefinitely. According to *Udny v Udny* (1869), residence for a limited period of time or for a particular purpose does not satisfy the necessary intention to acquire a domicile of choice. Similarly, an intention conditional upon the occurrence of an act that may or may not take place will not suffice, as may be illustrated in *Cramer v Cramer* (1987). In this case, a married woman with a French domicile of origin had a relationship with a married Englishman. They decided to marry as soon as they were able to obtain a divorce from their respective spouses. In 1985, she was sent by her French employers on a one year's paid detachment with a company in England. Soon after arriving in England with her two younger children, she petitioned for divorce. Her husband argued, however, that the English court lacked jurisdiction, on the ground that she had not acquired an English domicile of choice since she had not yet disposed of her ties in France; that is, she had not terminated her contract of employment, not resolved certain property matters, nor had she resolved the matter of the children's schooling. The Court of Appeal held that the correct approach to determine whether a domicile of choice had been acquired was whether the court was satisfied that there was a clear and settled intention to reside in England indefinitely, and not whether there was a reciprocated desire to marry a British national as soon as possible and live in England. On the facts, the wife's intention to change her domicile had not yet crystallised into a certainty, since it was conditional upon her being able to marry her friend and also upon their relationship continuing on a permanent basis. Had she intended to live in England come what may, she would have satisfied the requirement of intention.

What may be deduced from these principles is that the burden of proving a change of domicile is an extremely heavy one. Indeed, this is so, if one examines two leading House of Lords' decisions, namely *Winans v AG* (1904) and *Ramsay v Liverpool Royal Infirmary* (1930), where it appears that there is almost an irrebuttable presumption against a change of domicile. In *Winans v AG* (1904), Winans was born in the USA in 1823, where he worked in his father's business until 1850. He then resided in Russia until 1859, when his health deteriorated and, on the advice of his doctor, he spent the next winter at a Brighton hotel in England, and in 1860 he rented a house there. From 1860–93, he spent time each year in England, but also time in Scotland, Germany and Russia. From 1893 until he died in 1897, he resided in England. He never bought an estate in England, although he died a millionaire.

Notwithstanding that Winans had resided principally in England for the last 37 years of his life, the House of Lords, by a majority of two to one, held that he did not acquire an English domicile of choice.

Lord Macnaghten stated that the burden of proving that the domicile of origin has been superseded by a domicile of choice was a heavy one. The question to be considered was whether it could be proved with perfect clarity and satisfaction that Winans had, at the time of his death, formed a fixed and settled purpose, a determination, a final and deliberate intention, to abandon his American domicile and settle in England. His Lordship examined Winan's hopes, projects and daily habits, and found that Winans was a person of 'singular tenacity of purpose, self-centred and strangely uncommunicative'. He rarely went into society, and had no intimate friends in England. He had three objects in life. The first was his health, which he nursed with devotion. The remaining two objects which engrossed his thoughts were: first, the construction in the USA of a large fleet of spindle-shaped vessels which would give the USA superiority at sea over Britain; and, secondly, to develop a large property in the USA for the purpose of building docks for the vessels and a house from which he could take personal command of the entire project. Lord Macnaghten concluded that Winans was a sojourner and a stranger when he came to England and remained so until he died. Up to the very last minute, 'he had an expectation or hope of returning to America and seeing his grand scheme inaugurated'. Therefore, he did not acquire a domicile of choice in England.

Lord Halsbury reached a similar conclusion, but only because he found it impossible to infer from the evidence what Winans' intention was.

Lord Lindley, who took a dissenting view, stated that Winans had one, and only one, home and that was England. Moreover, he was satisfied that Winans had given up all serious ideas of returning to his native country.

In *Ramsay v Liverpool Royal Infirmary* (1930), George Bowie, who was born in Glasgow in 1845 with a Scottish domicile of origin, moved to Liverpool in 1892 in order to live on the bounty of his brother. When he first came to Liverpool, he lived in lodgings, but when his brother died 21 years later, he moved into his house, where he lived with his sole surviving sister until she died in 1920. He remained there until he died unmarried in 1927. During his residence in England for the last 36 years of his life, he travelled out on two occasions, once on a short visit to the USA, and once to the Isle of Man on holiday. Despite the fact that he often said that he was proud to be a Glasgow man, he expressed a determination never to return there. In fact, he did not even attend his mother's funeral, and he arranged for his own burial in Liverpool.

The House of Lords unanimously held that he died domiciled in Scotland. Their Lordships declined to uphold the presumption stemming from his prolonged residence in England. In fact, it was deduced that, had his English source of finance stopped, he would have returned to Glasgow. Lord Thankerton stated that mere length of residence by itself was insufficient evidence from which to infer the intention, but the quality of the residence was the decisive factor. For instance, the purchase of a house or estate coupled with long residence therein and non-retention of any home in the domicile of origin, might be sufficient to prove the intention. The long residence of George Bowie in Liverpool was, however, remarkably colourless and suggested little more than inanition.

The above two House of Lords' decisions have been subject to much criticism. They seem to establish a trend, that is, the requirement of intention will not be satisfied if there is a very vague hope of returning to the country of origin. More recent authorities, however, appear to have taken a less rigorous view. They tend to make a distinction between likely and unlikely contingencies. For example, Scarman J, in the case of *In the Estate of Fuld (No 3)* (1968) (p 684), observed that:

> If a man intends to return to the land of his birth upon a clearly foreseen and reasonably anticipated contingency, for example, the end of a job, the intention required by law is lacking; but if he has in mind only a vague possibility, such as making a fortune ... such a state of mind is consistent with the intention required by law.

Hence, if the contingency is not sufficiently clear, it will not prevent the acquisition of a domicile of choice. For example, in *Re Furse* (1980), the *propositus* had an American domicile of origin. In 1923, he came to England with his wife and children. A year later, his wife bought a farm, where he lived for the rest of his life. There was evidence that he would leave England if he was no longer capable of leading an active life on the farm. He died in England at the age of 80. In view of the fact that the *propositus'* intention was to continue living in England and only to leave when he was no longer able to lead an active physical life on the farm, Fox J held that, save on a vague and indefinite contingency, it was clear that he had no intention of leaving England. Accordingly, he had acquired a domicile of choice in England.

If, however, the contingency is clear, then the court asks whether there is a substantial possibility of it occurring. If so, this will prevent the acquisition of a domicile of choice. For example, in *IRC v Bullock* (1976), Mr Bullock, whose domicile of origin was Canadian, came to England in order to join the Royal Air Force. While still in service, he married an English woman. He wished to return to Canada after leaving the RAF, but did not do so, because his wife disliked the idea. Nevertheless, if his wife were to predecease him, it was his intention to return to Canada. The Court of Appeal held that although the establishment of a matrimonial home in a new country was an important factor in deciding whether that new country became the permanent home, it was not conclusive. As Mr Bullock had maintained a firm intention to return to Canada should he survive his wife, which was likely to occur considering the difference in their respective ages, this was not merely a vague aspiration, but amounted to a real determination. Therefore, he could not have had the intention of establishing a permanent home in England, and as such, he had not acquired a domicile of choice there.

On the other hand, if a person changes his or her residence because he or she believes that they will enjoy a better state of health there, this cannot, by itself, be regarded as excluding the necessary intention. This issue arose in *Hoskins v Matthews* (1856), where the testator, whose domicile of origin was English, went to Florence, Italy at the age of 60. He then bought a villa and lived in it except for three or four months each year and until he died 12 years later. There was no doubt that his change of residence was due to a spinal injury, which he thought the warmer climate might cure. His housekeeper stated that, had his state of health allowed him to do so, his wish was to return to England. Turner J held, however, that, in settling in Italy, he was exercising a preference, that is, the desire to enjoy better health, and was not acting upon a necessity in the sense that he was in no immediate danger. Accordingly, he acquired a domicile of choice in Italy. Similarly, where the change in residence of a person is of an involuntary nature, this in itself does not prevent him or her from acquiring a new domicile of choice in that country, if the circumstances indicate a free intention. For instance, in *Donaldson v Donaldson* (1949), wherein an RAF officer was stationed in Florida, where he met and married a woman domiciled there, the fact that he was liable to be posted to another country, and was in fact posted back to England, did not prevent him from acquiring a domicile of choice in Florida, since he had clearly intended to return there to make a permanent home with his wife immediately he was free to do so.

9.6   Abandonment of domicile

With regard to the abandonment of the domicile of dependency, Sir Jocelyn Simon P stated, in *Henderson v Henderson* (1967), that a dependent person will, on independence, retain his or her domicile of dependency as a domicile of choice, albeit it may be abandoned at any time thereafter if the person proves that he or she had no intention of returning to live there permanently.

In relation to the domicile of choice, Megarry J said *obiter*, in *Re Flynn* (1968), that a domicile of choice will be abandoned when, on departing from a country, the intention has merely withered away. There is no need to prove a positive intention not to return, since the death of the old intention suffices without the birth of any new intention.

As for the domicile of origin, this may not be easily abandoned. It cannot be lost by a mere removal of an individual's intention. In fact, according to *Bell v Kennedy* (1868), it endures until a domicile of choice is acquired.

Once a domicile of choice is abandoned, the domicile of origin revives until another domicile of choice is acquired (see *Tee v Tee* (1973)). In *In the Estate of Fuld (No 3)* (1968), Scarman J stated that, if a person has left the territory of his or her domicile of origin with the intention of never returning, although he or she may be resident in a new territory, but his or her mind is not made up yet or evidence is lacking as to what their state of mind is, then the domicile of origin adheres. He further stated that, if he or she has abandoned a domicile of choice which was acquired, then the domicile of origin revives until a new domicile of choice is acquired.

9.7   Domicile for the purposes of jurisdiction in civil and commercial matters

As may be recalled, the CJJA 1982 introduced a new concept of domicile. However, domicile under this Act, unlike the concept of domicile in this chapter, describes a certain type of link between an individual or a company, and a country for the purposes of jurisdiction in civil and commercial matters under RSC Ord 11 r 1 and both the Brussels Convention 1968 and the Lugano Convention 1988. In general terms, under ss 41–46 of the CJJA 1982, domicile is equated with the State where a person or a corporation is resident and the nature and circumstances of their residence indicate a substantial connection with that State (see detailed discussion in Chapter 3).

9.8   Proposals for reform

The foregoing discussion clearly indicates that the concept of domicile has been overloaded by a multitude of cases, which have resulted in making the concept an artificial one. Several attempts have been made to respond to this long standing criticism of the existing law. Two particular defects were identified as long ago as 1954 (First Report of the Private International Law Committee, Cmnd 9068). These are:

(a) the importance attached to the domicile of origin, in particular, that the domicile of origin revives when a domicile of choice is abandoned without another such domicile being acquired, and the heavy burden of proof resting on those who assert that a domicile of origin has been changed; and

(b) the difficulties involved in proving the intention required to acquire a domicile of choice.

The two most recent proposals for reform were made by the Law Commission Working Paper No 88 in 1985, and the Law Commission Report No 168 in 1987. Each of these will be examined separately.

9.8.1   Law Commission Working Paper No 88

In its Working Paper, the Law Commission examined the desirability of substituting domicile with a different connecting factor. It explored the possibility of replacing it by the concept of either habitual residence, or nationality, as a connecting factor. Nevertheless, it was concluded that domicile should continue to be used as a connecting factor.

After considering the present law, the most significant proposal which was made by the Law Commission was the abolition of the domicile of origin. The overall result of this proposal is to make the domicile of origin redundant and, therefore, the peculiar tenacity accorded to the domicile received at birth and the revival of that domicile will not survive.

From this radical proposal stemmed other significant proposed reforms.

Domicile of children

A child under 16 will have the domicile of his or her parents where he or she has a home with them and the parents share a common domicile.

Where the parents do not share a common domicile, then the child's domicile will be that of the mother in all cases. Accordingly, the distinction between a legitimate and an illegitimate child for the purposes of domicile disappears.

Where the child has a home with one parent only, the domicile will be the same as, and changes with, the domicile of that parent.

A child who lives with neither parent is domiciled in the country with which he or she is, for the time being, most closely connected. Thus, orphans and abandoned children can be effectively protected.

Adults

A domicile continues until a new one is acquired.

To acquire a new domicile, it must be shown on the normal civil standard of proof that a person is resident in a country and intends to make a home in that country indefinitely.

No higher or different quality of intention need be required when the alleged change of domicile is from one received at birth than from any other domicile.

Subject to evidence to the contrary, a person should be presumed to intend to make a home indefinitely in a country in which he or she has been habitually resident for a continuous period of seven years since reaching the age of 16.

With regard to mentally incompetent adults, the Law Commission proposed that the domicile of such an adult is the country with which he or she is for the time being most closely connected.

9.8.2 Law Commission Report No 168

In 1987, having received various comments and views on the 1985 proposals, the Law Commission compiled its Report, which differs in certain significant respects from the original proposals in Working Paper No 88. The main differences are as follows.

In relation to children, the test proposed in the draft Bill annexed to the Report is that:

(a) a child is domiciled in the country with which he or she is for the time being most closely connected;

(b) where the child's parents are domiciled in the same country and he or she has his home with either or both of them, then it is to be presumed, unless the contrary is shown, that the child is most closely connected with that country;

(c) where the child's parents are not domiciled in the same country and has a home with one of them but not the other, then it is to be presumed, unless the contrary is shown, that the child is most closely connected with the country in which the parent, with whom he or she has a home, is domiciled.

The earlier proposal for a presumption of domicile after seven years of habitual residence is abandoned.

This proposal is an important step in the process of improving the effectiveness and fairness of the English rules of domicile. If adopted, it will alleviate many of the difficulties facing a *propositus*, especially since it abolishes the tenacity and revival of the domicile of origin and makes it crystal clear that the standard of proving a change of domicile is that of a civil standard.

The Government accepted the proposal in 1991 and it is hoped that legislation will be introduced in the near future.

DOMICILE

The concept of domicile determines an individual's personal law and is defined as the law of the country to which a person primarily belongs.

An individual's domicile must be determined by English law.

Domicile of origin

A domicile of origin is the domicile a person acquires at birth. It remains with him or her until it is replaced by either a domicile of dependency or choice.

A child acquires the domicile of his or her father at birth if legitimate, and that of his or her mother if illegitimate or posthumous. A foundling derives his or her domicile of origin from the country where he or she is found.

Domicile of dependency

A child under the age of 16 is subject to a domicile of dependency if the parents abandon their domicile of origin and acquire a domicile of choice in a new land.

The domicile of dependency of a child is that of his or her father if legitimate, and that of his or her mother if illegitimate.

Since 1974, where the parents are alive but living apart, the child's domicile is that of the mother if he or she then has a home with her and no home with the father, or has a home with the mother and has not since had a home with the father.

An adopted child is treated as if he or she had been born to the adoptive parents.

Where the child is legitimate and the parents are living together, the child's domicile is dependent on that of the father. When the father dies, the child takes the mother's domicile, even if the mother acquires a new domicile, provided that her change of domicile was not done fraudulently.

If the mother changes her domicile but leaves the child behind, then her new domicile will not pass to the child as a domicile of dependency.

Married women

Since 1 January 1974, a married woman is entitled to have a domicile independent from that of her husband.

Domicile of choice

A domicile of choice is acquired by an individual residing in a country, other than the country of his or her origin, with the intention of remaining there permanently.

The onus of proving the acquisition of such a domicile is on the party alleging it, and the burden of proof is a heavy one.

Residence is a question of fact. It has to exist, but need not be prolonged. However, it must indicate a real link between the individual and his or her alleged new homeland.

Intention to reside in the new homeland must be permanent or indefinite. It does not suffice to have the intention conditional upon the occurrence of an act.

Older case law seems to impose an almost irrebuttable presumption against the acquisition of a domicile of choice. More recent cases appear to make a distinction between a likely and unlikely contingency. Where the contingency is not sufficiently clear, it will not prevent the acquisition of a domicile of choice. On the other hand, where it is clear, the court looks at the likely possibility of it happening. If so, this will prevent the acquisition of a domicile of choice.

Abandonment of domicile

A dependent person will, on independence, retain his or her domicile of dependency as a domicile of choice until it is abandoned at any time thereafter.

A domicile of choice will be abandoned when a person departs from a country and the intention to return has withered away.

A domicile of origin endures until a domicile of choice is acquired.

Once a domicile of choice is abandoned, the domicile of origin revives until another domicile of choice is acquired.

CHAPTER 10

MARRIAGE

10.1 Meaning of marriage

In English law, marriage is a contract by which a man and a woman express their consent to create the relationship of husband and wife. This contract, however, differs fundamentally from a commercial contract in the following ways:

(a) as a general rule, it can only be concluded by a formal public act;

(b) it can only be dissolved by a formal public act;

(c) more importantly, it creates a status which is taken into account in relation to, for example, succession, tax, legitimacy of children, and to some extent in relation to immigration laws.

10.1.1 The definition in *Hyde v Hyde*: is it still good law?

In 1866, Lord Penzance, in *Hyde v Hyde* (1866), defined marriage as follows:

> I conceive that marriage, as understood in Christendom, may for this purpose be defined as the *voluntary* union for life of one *man* and one *woman*, to the exclusion of all others.

This common law definition was based on the Christian marriage and, therefore, resulted in the original refusal to recognise marriages celebrated under other rites. For instance, in *Re Bethell* (1888), an Englishman went to South Africa, where he met a woman of the Baralong tribe. They went through a ceremony of marriage in accordance with the customs of that tribe. Stirling J held that such a union, although it might bear the name of marriage in the foreign country where it was formed, was not a valid marriage according to the law of England, for it was not formed on the same basis as marriages throughout Christendom.

It should be noted at this stage, however, that this is no longer the case in relation to most foreign marriages. As shall be seen in due course, in many instances, foreign marriages are recognised in English law. In other words, the above definition, albeit relevant, is no longer comprehensive. Each of the components thereof will be now examined, and an indication as to whether the component in question remains applicable will be stipulated.

10.1.2 Voluntary union

The first component of the above definition is the term 'voluntary union'. It is well established that, if one party to the marriage does not consent to marry the other, the marriage will be regarded as invalid. Lack of consent may emanate from fear for one's life caused by duress as may be illustrated in *Szechter v Szechter* (1971). Here, a husband, his first wife and his secretary were all domiciled in Poland. The secretary, who was imprisoned as a result of being accused of a political crime, suffered from serious ill health. The husband, in order to obtain her release from prison, divorced his wife and married his secretary, who intended to divorce him as soon as they were to leave the country so that he could remarry his wife. All three came to England, and soon after acquiring an English domicile, the secretary petitioned for annulment of her marriage on the ground that the ceremony performed at Warsaw was inoperative due to duress. Sir Jocelyn Simon P upheld her contention and granted the decree of nullity. Similarly, in *Hirani v Hirani* (1982), the Court of Appeal held that duress was capable of vitiating a party's consent to a marriage. In this case, a 19 year old woman, who had been living with her parents in England, was given an ultimatum by them that if she did not consent to an arranged marriage she would be ousted from the family home. The marriage took place, but was not consummated, and after six weeks she deserted her husband. The Court of Appeal held that the crucial question was whether the threats or pressure were such as to overbear the individual's will and destroy the reality of consent. Duress, whatever form it took, was a coercion of the will which had the effect of vitiating consent. Accordingly, the marriage was declared invalid. Note that this component is still good law.

10.1.3 Union for life

As the definition states, the union is required to be for life. This remains part of English law. This requirement, however, does not mean that the marriage must be indissoluble. Indeed, that was the view taken in *Nachimson v Nachimson* (1930), where a marriage between parties domiciled in Russia had been celebrated in Moscow in 1924. At that date, the marriage could be unilaterally dissolved by Russian law and without any proof of causes. On the contention that the marriage 'could not be regarded as a union for life', the Court of Appeal dismissed this argument and held that it was immaterial that, under the local law of the foreign country where the marriage was celebrated, dissolution could be obtained. What was important was that the parties, when they were married, had envisaged that the marriage was potentially indefinite in duration and, therefore, the possibility of its termination by the *lex loci celebrationis* was not relevant.

10.1.4 Union of one man and one woman

A further requirement under this definition, which is still applicable, is that the union must be of one man and one woman. This has been interpreted to mean that a marriage between parties of the same sex is not accepted as a valid marriage. Neither is a marriage between one man and one woman who had been born as a male but underwent a sex change operation accepted as a valid marriage. For instance, in *Corbett v Corbett* (1971), a husband and wife went through a ceremony of marriage in 1963. The wife had been registered at birth as a male and had in 1960 undergone a sex change operation. On a petition for annulment, it was held that a marriage was essentially a relationship between a man and a woman. It was further held that, in order to determine the sex of a party for the purposes of marriage, the law should adopt the chromosomal type, ignoring any operative intervention. Therefore, the wife was not a woman for the purposes of marriage, but 'was from birth and had remained at all times a biological male'. Accordingly, the marriage was declared void.

10.1.5 Union to the exclusion of all others

The final component of the definition is that the union must be of one man and one woman to the exclusion of all others. This was clearly directed at monogamous marriages and resulted in the initial refusal to recognise polygamous or even potentially polygamous marriages. However, over the past century and due to the migration of many people from various social, cultural and religious backgrounds to England, polygamy has come to be accepted for certain purposes, and this will be the subject of discussion below, 10.2.

To sum up, it appears that Lord Penzance's definition in 1866, though no longer comprehensive, is still applicable to a limited extent. Indeed, marriage may still be defined as a union for life of one man and one woman. Christian marriages, however, are no longer the only type of marriages recognised in English law. For instance, in *McCabe v McCabe* (1993), a customary marriage celebrated in Ghana was recognised in English law despite the fact that neither the bride nor the groom were present or represented at the ceremony. As for the component 'to the exclusion of all others', this is no longer correct, for polygamous marriages have been recognised, for various purposes, unless celebrated in England.

Before moving on to deal with polygamy, it must be noted that, prior to 1861, all issues relating to the validity of a marriage used to be referred to the *lex loci celebrationis*. However, in *Brook v Brook* (1861), the House of Lords distinguished between the formal validity of a marriage and its essential validity. In the former case, it was held that such issues were to be governed by the *lex loci celebrationis*. Issues of essential validity, however, were to be determined by the law of the domicile of the parties at the time of the marriage. (Full analysis of this rule will be made below, 10.4 and 10.6.)

10.2 Polygamy

In *Hyde v Hyde* (1866), an Englishman, who had converted to the Mormon faith in 1847, married a Mormon woman in Utah, USA, in 1853. They lived together in Utah until 1856, when the husband went on a mission to what is now Hawaii. On arrival there, he renounced his faith and soon after he became the minister of a dissenting chapel in Derby, England. He petitioned for divorce on the ground of his wife's adultery after she had contracted another marriage in Utah in accordance with the Mormon faith. Lord Penzance assumed that a Mormon marriage was potentially polygamous and declined to adjudicate on the petition on the ground that the matrimonial law of England was adapted to the Christian marriage and was, therefore, inapplicable to polygamy.

Hence, the decision in *Hyde v Hyde* (1866) marked an outright refusal to recognise polygamy, even when the marriage was potentially polygamous, albeit in fact monogamous. Over the past 100 years, however, English law (whether in terms of common law or statute) has sought to break down this old hostility to polygamy and has provided, for certain purposes, for its recognition. For example, in relation to matrimonial relief, s 47(1) of the Matrimonial Causes Act 1973 (MCA), as amended to accommodate the provisions of Pt II of the Private International Law (Miscellaneous Provisions) Act 1995 (PILA), provides:

> A court in England and Wales shall not be precluded from granting matrimonial relief or making a declaration concerning the validity of a marriage by reason only that either party to the marriage is, or has during the subsistence of the marriage been, married to more than one person.

Section 47(1) no longer presents a problem in respect of potentially polygamous marriages, the latter being now recognised by virtue of Pt II of the PILA 1995 (see discussion below, 10.4.3).

Essentially, s 47(1) allows the parties to an actually polygamous marriage to make claims for a wide range of matrimonial relief, such as decrees for divorce, nullity, judicial separation, and declarations under Pt III of the Family Law Act 1986 (FLA) which may involve the determination of the validity of a marriage. The provisions of s 47(1) also have the effect of abolishing the rule in *Hyde v Hyde* (1866), so that the matrimonial law of England now applies to cases of actual polygamy.

Similar improvement has been made at common law and by virtue of Pt II of the PILA 1995 (in force on 8 January 1996), to the effect that, in many circumstances, a polygamous marriage may now be recognised. It should be clear from the outset, however, that a marriage celebrated in England in a polygamous form, whether potential or actual, will not be recognised by English law, regardless of the parties' domicile.

10.2.1 Recognition in England of actually polygamous marriages

The laws of many countries permit polygamy, that is, a man is allowed simultaneously to have more than one wife. Such is the case in all Moslem countries and a number of African countries in which polygamy is allowed under their respective customary laws.

Prior to 8 January 1996, English law had developed a number of principles, by virtue of which English courts would recognise a polygamous marriage, whether be it potentially or actually, for certain purposes. However, due to the adoption of Pt II of the PILA 1995, most of these principles no longer affect potentially polygamous marriages. These marriages have now assumed statutory recognition. Nevertheless, since these principles remain applicable to actually polygamous marriages, they will form the starting point of the discussion.

English courts are prepared to recognise polygamous marriages in order to invalidate a subsequent monogamous marriage celebrated in England, as may be illustrated in *Baindail v Baindail* (1946). In this case, a husband, while domiciled in India, married a Hindu woman in accordance with Hindu rites, whereby polygamy was permitted. Whilst the wife was still alive, he went through another ceremony of marriage with an Englishwoman at a registry office in London. Once the second wife became aware of the previous marriage, she petitioned for a decree of nullity of her marriage. The Court of Appeal held that, as a general rule, the status of an individual depends on his personal law, that is, the law of his domicile. By the law of the husband's domicile at the time of his Hindu marriage, he unquestionably acquired the status of a married man, and that was recognised by English law. Accordingly, the first marriage operated such a bar as to render the second marriage void.

Equally, a polygamous marriage is recognised, even though the wife is a minor under English law. A striking example of such recognition can be illustrated in *Mohammed v Knott* (1969), where a Nigerian man, whilst domiciled in Nigeria, entered into a potentially polygamous marriage with a girl of 13 years of age under Moslem rites. Shortly thereafter, the couple came to England, where a complaint was made against the husband to the effect that the girl, due to her age, was in need of care and protection by virtue of s 2 of the Children and Young Persons Act 1963. It was held that, although the marriage was potentially polygamous, it should be recognised by English law as valid and conferring the status of a wife on the girl.

Polygamous marriages are recognised for the purposes of asserting proprietary rights arising out of a contractual claim against the husband. In *Shahnaz v Rizwan* (1965), the parties to the proceedings were married in India in accordance with Moslem rites. The marriage contract provided that the wife was to be deferred 'dower' payable to her in the event of the husband's death or a divorce. Under Islamic law, such right of dower, once due, was enforceable by a civil action and was regarded as a proprietary right. Following her divorce, the wife brought an action claiming the dower due on the ground that the claim was a lawful contractual one for the purpose of enforcing a proprietary right arising out of a lawful contract of marriage. Conversely, the husband contended that, as the marriage was potentially polygamous, English courts had no jurisdiction over, or did not extend jurisdiction to, the wife's claim. Nonetheless, Winn J upheld the wife's claim, but made it clear that the right she was seeking to enforce was a right *in personam*, arising not out of the relationship of husband and wife but from a contract entered into in contemplation and in consideration of the marriage and was not, therefore, a matrimonial right which the court would refuse to enforce. It should be noted, however, that Winn J's refusal to enforce a matrimonial right was in line with the then existing inability of the English courts to grant matrimonial relief in the context of such marriages. This, however, has changed by virtue of s 47(1) of the MCA 1973, as amended by Pt II of the PILA 1995.

Notwithstanding that the issue of legitimacy of children is, at present, of very limited relevance, it is important to note that children of a valid polygamous marriage are regarded as legitimate: see, for example, *Hashmi v Hashmi* (1972). A Pakistani man and woman were married in 1948, in Pakistan, in accordance with Moslem rites. In 1957, whilst his first marriage was still subsisting, the husband went through a ceremony of marriage in England with an Englishwoman at the Bradford Registry Office. Subsequently, three children were born to them. In 1968, the second wife petitioned for divorce on the ground of cruelty and adultery. On the issue of whether the children to the second marriage would be regarded as legitimate, it was held that because the second marriage would be recognised by Pakistani law, the law of the husband's domicile, a valid subsisting marriage, even though void for the purposes of English law, the children of that marriage would be regarded by English law as legitimate.

Special statutory provisions have been made for wives in polygamous marriages in relation to social security. These are now contained in legislation made under s 12(b) of the Social Security Contributions and Benefits Act 1992 (as amended by Pt II of the PILA 1995), which provides in general terms that a polygamous marriage is treated as having the same consequences as a monogamous marriage, if it has either actually always been monogamous or for any day, and only for any day, throughout which it is in fact monogamous. The effect of this provision is that a polygamous marriage is treated as monogamous for the purposes of statutory protection under Pt IV of the Family Law Act 1996, the latter dealing with domestic violence and the family home. For the purposes of income support, however, the recognition of polygamous marriages is no longer an issue, since the criterion employed by the Income Support (General) Regulations 1987 is in terms of the nature of the relationship between a man and a woman as members of the same household. On the other hand, according to *R v Department of Health ex p Misra* (1996), polygamous marriages are not recognised for the purposes of rights to a widow's pension under the State pension scheme.

Polygamous marriages are also recognised for the purposes of succession. In relation to children of an actually polygamous marriage, it was established in *Bamgbose v Daniel* (1955) that these children can succeed to property in England, provided that the marriage is valid by both the *lex loci celebrationis* and the personal law of the parties. A difficulty arises, however, as to whether a child of a polygamous marriage can succeed to a title of honour. The issue was examined in the *Sinha Peerage Claim* (1946), where it was established by the House of Lords that the eldest son of a potentially polygamous Hindu marriage was entitled to succeed to a peerage conferred on his father, the marriage having become monogamous by change of religion before the claimant was born or the peerage was created. Lord Maugham LC, who delivered the Committee of Privilege's judgment, declined to express a view in relation to a child's succession as heir or his succession to entails, when he was discussing problems which could arise in cases of actually polygamous marriages. He stated:

> If there were several wives, the son of a second or third wife might be the claimant to the dignity to the exclusion of a later born son of the first wife. Our law as to heirship has provided no means of settling such questions as these.

Furthermore, according to the Law Commission Report No 146 (1985), it seems that these problems are restricted to a child of an actually polygamous marriage. Whilst such a child cannot succeed as 'heir', a child of a potentially polygamous marriage can. It must be noted that such a distinction survives Pt II of the PILA 1995, as the latter provides statutory recognition only to potentially polygamous marriages.

10.2.2 Recognition of potentially polygamous marriages

Part II of the PILA 1995 was adopted mainly in order to redress the haphazard way in which the common law rules had applied to validate or recognise potentially polygamous marriages and to provide for statutory recognition of all marriages of this kind. As will be seen in due course, not only does this Part apply to validate potentially polygamous marriages entered into after that date, but also to recognise most such marriages entered into before that date.

10.3 Capacity to marry

A major issue relating to choice of law in the context of marriage is the question of which law governs capacity, otherwise known as essential validity. This question covers a wide range of issues, such as: consanguinity (blood relationships); affinity (relationships created by virtue of marriage); re-marriage; lack of age; and parental consent (unless it is classified as an issue of formalities). As a general rule, capacity to marry is governed by the dual-domicile rule, but subject to some exceptions. Each of these will be examined separately.

10.4 The dual-domicile rule

The dual-domicile rule stems from the traditional theory that capacity to marry is governed by the ante-nuptial domicile of each of the parties. Its effect is that a marriage will only be valid if it is so by the law of the domicile of each contracting party immediately before the marriage. Clearly, this theory has its merits, simply because it tends to preserve equality between the parties by looking to the law of the domicile of each of them. It must be noted, however, that a rival theory, which has been canvassed by academic writers, is that which submits the question of capacity to the law of the intended matrimonial home. This latter theory was stated by Cheshire and North (*Private International Law*, 12th edn, p 587), as follows:

> The basic presumption is that capacity to marry is governed by the law of the husband's domicile at the time of the marriage, for normally it is in the country of that domicile that the parties intend to establish their permanent home. This presumption, however, is rebutted if it can be inferred that the parties at the time of the marriage intended to establish their home and did in fact establish it there within a reasonable time.

These two theories were fully examined by the Law Commission Working Paper No 89 (in 1985), where the view taken was in favour of the dual-domicile theory. Subsequently, in the 1987 Report (No 165), a substantial majority was in favour of this view, but it was decided that no legislative action should be taken in this area, as this is best left to be dealt with by case law. Furthermore, upon examination of case law, especially the more recent ones, it can be seen that the dual-domicile theory, subject to some exceptions which will be considered below, is the favoured one. How does it operate?

10.4.1 Consanguinity and affinity

Most legal systems impose restrictions on marriage between parties who are related. The precise prohibited degree of relationship, however, varies from one legal system to another. Moreover, in some systems the prohibitions are not only restricted to consanguinity, but also to affinity. This will, therefore, often result in couples within the prohibited degrees to visit another country temporarily, where they can validly marry without such restrictions. Are such marriages regarded as valid in the eyes of English law? The House of Lords' decision in *Brook v Brook* (1861) provides authority for the view that such marriages are governed by the dual-domicile rule. In this case, Mr Brook, whose first wife died in 1847, married her sister in Denmark in 1850. Both parties were British subjects and domiciled in England. They had merely gone to Denmark on a temporary visit. The marriage was valid by Danish law, but was void by English law for affinity. The House of Lords held that, as the parties were British subjects and domiciled in England at the time of the marriage and as England was to be their matrimonial residence, the marriage was void. Lord Campbell stated that:

> ... the essentials of the marriage depend on the *lex domicilii*, the law of the country in which the parties are domiciled at the time of the marriage and in which the matrimonial residence is contemplated.

Notwithstanding that this decision has the effect of rejecting the application of Danish law as the law of the place of celebration, it is inconclusive in terms of which of the two theories was applied. In other words, it does not solve the issue of when the domicile of one or both of the parties is different from the country of the intended matrimonial home.

Similar inconclusiveness may be found in *Mette v Mette* (1859), where a marriage was celebrated in Germany between a husband domiciled in England and his deceased wife's half-sister, domiciled in Germany. The marriage was void for affinity by English law, but was valid by German law. It was held that the marriage was void, since there could be no valid contract unless each of the parties was competent to contract with the other. The reasoning clearly supports the dual-domicile rule. Nevertheless, since his Lordship felt the need to add a further reason in his judgment in favour of the matrimonial home theory, namely that the husband 'remained domiciled in this country, and the marriage was with a view to subsequent residence in this country', it is doubtful which of the theories was applied. Later cases, however, have explicitly indicated that the dual-domicile rule was the test to be applied, for example, *Re Paine* (1940), where the wife, a British subject and domiciled in England, visited Germany, where she married her deceased sister's husband, a German subject. This marriage was void in England, but valid in Germany. The couple then lived in England until their respective deaths. On the question of whether the surviving daughter was legitimate for the purposes of succession, the court had to decide the validity of the marriage. Bennett J applied the dual-domicile rule and held that the marriage was void, since the ante-nuptial domicile of the wife attached an incapacity on her to contract such a marriage.

A similar case is that of *Sottomayor v De Barros (No 1)* (1877), where both parties to the marriage were Portuguese first cousins. Both their respective parents had come to England in 1858 and occupied a house jointly in London. At the time of the marriage, the husband was aged 16 and the wife 14. Moreover, the marriage was one of convenience, in order to preserve the Portuguese property of the wife's father from bankruptcy. Although the couple had lived in the same house for six years, the marriage was never consummated. By the law of Portugal, first cousins were incapable of contracting a marriage on the ground of consanguinity, and such a marriage was null and void unless solemnised under a 'papal dispensation'. The wife petitioned for a decree of nullity on the ground of this incapacity. The suit was undefended, but the Queen's Proctor intervened and alleged that, at the time of the marriage, the parties were domiciled in England and not in Portugal and, therefore, the validity of the marriage was to be determined by English domestic law. This question of law was ordered to be determined before the question of fact.

The Court of Appeal held that the personal capacity of the parties must depend on their law of domicile, in this case Portugal, and that law prohibited its subjects within a certain degree of consanguinity from contracting a marriage. Therefore, this imposed on them a personal incapacity, which continued to affect them so long as they were domiciled in that country, and that rendered the marriage invalid.

This latter decision provides a clear and express authority in favour of the dual-domicile rule. Further support can also be found in s 1(3) of the Marriage Enabling Act 1960, which applies in the context of affinity and provides that this section 'does not validate a marriage, if either party to it is, at the time of the marriage, domiciled in a country outside Great Britain, and under the law of that country there cannot be a valid marriage between the parties'.

10.4.2 Re-marriage

The dual-domicile rule appears to apply also to capacity to re-marry. This may be illustrated in *Padolecchia v Padolecchia* (1968), where a man who was domiciled in Italy married there in 1953. In 1958, he was granted a divorce by proxy in Mexico. Neither he nor his wife set foot there. The divorce was recognised in Mexico, but not in Italy. In 1963, he was transferred by his employers to Denmark, where he met a Danish woman domiciled there. In 1964, they both came to England on a one day visit where they were married at a London registry office. After three months of cohabitation, the husband left the matrimonial home in Denmark and never returned. In 1966, he petitioned for a decree of nullity in the English court on the ground that his first marriage was still subsisting at the time of contracting the second marriage. Sir Jocelyn Simon P held that the question to be determined was whether the petitioner's first marriage was still subsisting at the time the second marriage was celebrated, or whether it had been dissolved by the Mexican decree. Applying the dual-domicile rule, he concluded that, at the time of the second marriage, the husband had no capacity to enter into a fresh marriage in England, for Italian law did not recognise the Mexican decree. Accordingly, the second marriage was null and void.

10.4.3 Polygamy

Prior to 8 January 1995, s 11(d) of the MCA 1973 governed the question of capacity to enter into a polygamous marriage. This provision applied the so called dual-domicile rule to this question and read as follows:

> A marriage celebrated after 31 July 1971 shall be void on the following grounds only, that is to say ...:
>
> (d)   in the case of a polygamous marriage entered into outside England and Wales, that either party was at the time of the marriage domiciled in England and Wales.

> For the purposes of para (d) of this sub-section, a marriage may be polygamous although at its inception neither party has any spouse additional to the other.

The impact of this provision was examined by the Court of Appeal in *Hussain v Hussain* (1982), where the husband, domiciled in England, married his wife in Pakistan in 1979 in accordance with Moslem rites. Whilst the marriage was potentially polygamous, it was at all times monogamous. On the wife's petition for judicial separation, the husband argued that the marriage was void by virtue of s 11(d) of the MCA 1973, that is, the marriage was polygamous in nature. The Court of Appeal rejected the husband's argument and interpreted s 11(d) in the following terms: s 11(d) prevented an English domiciliary from entering a polygamous marriage, whether actually or potentially, but a marriage could only be potentially polygamous if at least one of the parties had the capacity to marry a second spouse. The husband was domiciled in England and, therefore, had no capacity to enter an actually or potentially polygamous marriage. Equally, the wife was domiciled in Pakistan, under whose law she was incapable of marrying a second husband. Accordingly, the marriage was valid.

It should be noted that, as a result of the above decision and due to the unsatisfactory state of the law regarding polygamy, the Law Commission, in its Report No 146, recommended the repeal of s 11(d) and proposed that men and women domiciled in England should have capacity to enter a *potentially* polygamous marriage outside the UK. As for capacity to enter an *actually* polygamous marriage, it was proposed that the law should remain the same, that is, no such capacity exists under English law.

Following these recommendations, Pt II of the PILA 1995 was adopted (see draft Bill appended to Law Commission and Scottish Law Commission Joint Report on Polygamous Marriages 1985). As a consequence, the second paragraph of s 11(d) was also amended, to the effect that only actually polygamous marriages are now void where either party was at the time of marriage domiciled in England and Wales. This paragraph now reads as follows:

> For the purposes of para (d) of this sub-section a marriage is not polygamous if at its inception neither party has any spouse additional to the other.

Part II of the PILA 1995 amends the law regarding the validity of potentially polygamous marriages. It extends in application to England and Wales and Scotland. By virtue of ss 5(1) and 7, persons of either sex, domiciled in England and Wales or Scotland, now have the legal capacity to enter into a valid marriage outside the UK which, although celebrated in a polygamous form, is not actually polygamous. Hence, these provisions allow English and Scots courts to recognise all potentially polygamous marriages entered into abroad after 8 January 1996, even if either party is domiciled in England and Wales or Scotland, but provided that there is no other legal impediment for any of the parties to enter into a valid marriage.

By virtue of s 5(2), such marriages are recognised only when the internal law of England and Wales applies to determine their validity. However, where, under the English rules of private international law, the relevant law of another country is applied to determine the validity of a marriage, that law will apply.

More importantly, s 6, which is restricted in application to England and Wales only, ensures that the reforms in s 5 should, in general, apply retrospectively. This provision states as follows:

(1) Section 5 above shall be deemed to apply, and always to have applied, to any marriage entered into before commencement which is not excluded by sub-s (2) or (3) below.

(2) That section does not apply to a marriage a party to which has (before commencement) entered into a later marriage which either:

(a) is valid apart from this section but would be void if s 5 above applied to the earlier marriage; or

(b) is valid by virtue of this section.

(3) That section does not apply to a marriage which has been annulled before commencement, whether by a decree granted in England and Wales or by an annulment obtained elsewhere and recognised in England and Wales at commencement.

(4) An annulment of a marriage resulting from legal proceedings begun before commencement shall be treated for the purposes of sub-s (3) above as having taken effect before that time.

Section 6 has the effect of applying s 5 to marriages celebrated before 8 January 1996. This means that such marriages are regarded as always having been valid. However, this validity is qualified by various exceptions and savings with the result that it does not apply where either party to a potentially polygamous marriage celebrated before the above date has re-married or obtained an annulment of the potentially polygamous marriage. Section 6(6) goes further, to preserve certain property or related rights, such as succession to a dignity or title of honour, which have accrued before the commencement of this Part of the Act.

Furthermore, the retrospective effect is restricted to England and Wales and does not affect Scotland. This is because the then current law in Scotland did not have any clearly established rules which required correction with retrospective effect. The defect in Scots law was mainly that the law on that point was undeveloped. Accordingly, all that was required was to settle the law for the future.

Finally, s 8 provides that the reforms in Pt II do not affect any rule or custom in relation to the marriage of the members of the Royal Family.

10.4.4 Lack of age

In English law, a marriage between persons, either of whom is under the age of 16, is void. In other legal systems, however, the minimum age for marriage may be higher or lower than 16. The question arises here as to what law governs such an issue if one of the parties, not necessarily the party domiciled in England, is under the age of 16. This issue was considered in *Pugh v Pugh* (1951), where the wife was born in Hungary with a Hungarian domicile of origin. In 1945, she went with her parents to Australia, where she met her husband, a British officer domiciled in England. They were married in Australia in 1946 when she was still 15, and they returned to England in 1950. Soon after their arrival, she petitioned for a decree of nullity on the ground of her lack of age at the time of the marriage. By Hungarian law, the marriage was voidable until the wife's 17th birthday, by Australian law the marriage was valid, and by English law it was void. Pearce J held that personal status and capacity to marry were the concern of the country of domicile. Since the husband could not lawfully enter such marriage under his English law of domicile, the marriage was void.

The foregoing discussion clearly indicates that there is strong support for the dual-domicile rule. Nonetheless, the consequences of its application have, on occasion, caused judges to look for other alternatives so that a marriage can be held valid, especially in cases where the parties had been married for several years and have had several children. In some of these instances, English courts applied the intended matrimonial home theory. *Radwan v Radwan (No 2)* (1973) was such a case. Here, the husband was a Moslem domiciled in Egypt and the wife was domiciled in England. They were married before the Egyptian Consul General in Paris in 1951 in polygamous form. At that time, the husband had a wife living in Egypt, whom he divorced one year after his second marriage. The couple lived together in Egypt in accordance with their ante-nuptial intentions. Due to political instability, they moved to England, and in 1956 the husband acquired an English domicile of choice. Eight children were born to the marriage. The wife petitioned for divorce on the ground of cruelty.

On the question of the validity of the marriage, Cumming-Bruce J held that, although the marriage was actually polygamous, it was valid on the basis that the parties intended to live together and did live together for some years in Egypt.

This conclusion, thus, is based on the intended matrimonial home theory. It is to be borne in mind, though, that Cumming-Bruce J concluded his judgment by stating that 'nothing in this judgment bears upon the capacity of minors, the law of affinity, or the effect of bigamy upon capacity to enter into a monogamous union'. Notwithstanding that this decision has been heavily criticised, it may be justified on the ground that, given the fact that the couple had lived together for 19 years and had had eight children, it would have resulted in great injustice had the court held the marriage void.

Another approach has been indicated by the English court in the context of recognising a foreign divorce and capacity to re-marry. This is the law of the country with which the marriage has its most real and substantial connection, that is, the proper law of the marriage. The case in question is *Lawrence v Lawrence* (1985), where the wife, a Brazilian subject, married in that country her first husband, whose domicile of choice was Brazil. In 1970, the wife obtained a divorce in Nevada. This divorce was not recognised in Brazil and, therefore, the wife did not have the capacity to re-marry. One day after the divorce, the wife married in Nevada an American who had been living, and acquired a domicile of choice, in England. The parties intended to live in England and did establish their matrimonial home there. In 1970, the wife left the matrimonial home and returned to live permanently in Brazil. On a petition for declarations as to the validity of the marriage celebrated in Nevada, Lincoln J held that, although the divorce would not be recognised by the law of the wife's domicile at the time of her marriage to the petitioner, she had intended to acquire an English domicile and, since the parties had established their matrimonial home in England, the marriage had a real and substantial connection with England. Accordingly, the court would apply English law and declare that the second marriage was a valid and subsisting marriage.

This proper law approach was strongly rejected by the Law Commission in Working Paper No 89 (1985), on the ground that it is inherently vague and unpredictable and it would introduce an unacceptable degree of uncertainty into an already controversial area of law. When the case of *Lawrence* went to the Court of Appeal, the validity of the marriage was upheld, on the ground that the Nevada divorce was recognised in England.

10.5 Exceptions to the dual-domicile rule

Three exceptions to the dual-domicile rule appear to have been formulated. These are as follows.

The first exception may be drawn from the decision in *Sottomayor v De Barros (No 2)* (1879), where the parties were first cousins of Portuguese origin. Their marriage, which was celebrated in England, was prohibited by Portuguese law unless solemnised by papal dispensation. The couple lived together for six years, but the marriage was never consummated. The wife, after returning to Portugal, petitioned the English court for a decree of nullity on the ground of consanguinity. The Queen's Proctor intervened and it was ordered that the question of law should be argued before the question of fact. The Court of Appeal had held, in *Sottomayor v De Barros (No 1)* (1877), that the issue of capacity to marry was to be governed by the dual-domicile rule. The case was then remitted to the Divorce Division so that the question of fact could be determined. James Hannen P held that the husband was domiciled in England, but the wife was domiciled in Portugal, and that the marriage was valid. In other words, he declined to give effect to the prohibition imposed on the wife by Portuguese law and was obviously in favour of the law of the place of celebration.

This decision, which has never been overruled, appears to have established an exception to the dual-domicile rule. This exception has been reformulated by Dicey and Morris (*Conflict of Laws*, 12th edn, r 10, exception 3) as follows:

> The validity of a marriage celebrated in England between persons of whom the one has an English, and the other a foreign, domicile is not affected by any incapacity which, though existing under the law of such foreign domicile, does not exist under the law of England.

This exception was applied to an incapacity due to religion in the case of *Chetti v Chetti* (1909), where an Englishwoman married a Hindu man, then temporarily resident in England, at a London registry office. The parties cohabited in England, and a few months later the husband returned to India. The wife petitioned for judicial separation on the ground of desertion, and the husband argued that, at the time of the marriage and at all material times since then, he was and remained a Hindu domiciled in India. He further argued that the marriage was invalid on the basis that, by Hindu religion and law, he could not marry a woman from outside his own caste or one who was not by religion a Hindu, and that, by Hindu law, polygamy was permissible. Barnes P, after expressing the view that the husband's disability might not invalidate the marriage in India, held that, even if it had been otherwise, the marriage was valid in England. In his reasoning, Barnes P considered the decision of Lord Hannen in *Sottomayor v De Barros (No 2)* to be decisive in the case before him. He indicated, however, that the only substantial distinction between them was that in that case, the husband was domiciled in England, whereas in the case before him, the wife was domiciled in England. Nevertheless, he took the view that such distinction was not intended by Lord Hannen, and as he felt bound by that decision, he could not come to the conclusion that the distinction ought to produce a different result.

This exception has been taken to mean that when one of the parties 'has an English domicile, a foreign incapacity affecting the other and unknown to English law must be utterly disregarded if the marriage takes place in England' (Cheshire and North, *Private International Law*, 12th edn, p 596). The Law Commission, both in its Working Paper No 89 and Report No 165, criticised this exception on the ground that it gives preference to the *lex loci celebrationis* when it is English, but not when it is foreign. Evidently, this will lead to what are called 'limping marriages', that is, marriages valid in England but invalid in the country of domicile of one of the spouses.

The second exception to the dual-domicile rule applies in relation to the effect of the non-recognition of a divorce on the capacity to re-marry. This is to be found in s 50 of the FLA 1986, which states:

Where, in any part of the United Kingdom:

(a) a divorce or annulment has been granted by a court of civil jurisdiction; or

(b) the validity of a divorce or annulment is recognised by virtue of this Part, the fact that the divorce or annulment would not be recognised elsewhere shall not preclude either party to the marriage from re-marrying in that part of the United Kingdom or cause the re-marriage of either party (wherever the re-marriage takes place) to be treated as invalid in that part.

Thus, s 50 of the FLA 1986 embodies the Court of Appeal decision in *Lawrence v Lawrence* (1985). The rule in s 50, however, is restricted to cases where a foreign divorce is recognised in England; but what if the foreign divorce or annulment is recognised by the law of the domicile of the party intending to re-marry, and not in England? This question was considered in the Canadian case of *Schwebel v Ungar* (1964), where the Supreme Court, though not recognising the divorce, recognised the re-marriage as valid because the wife's status by the law of her domicile where the divorce was recognised was that of a single woman.

A third and final exception to the dual-domicile rule covers prohibitions on re-marriage after a divorce. Where the prohibition is penal in nature, it will be discounted, otherwise it will be upheld; for instance, in *Warter v Warter* (1890) where a husband, domiciled in England but resident in India, divorced his wife in the latter country for adultery. Both parties were prohibited by Indian law from re-marrying before the lapse of six months from the decree absolute. The wife, prior to the expiry of six months, married an English domiciliary in England. It was held that the re-marriage was invalid because of the wife's incapacity under Indian law.

On the other hand, in *Scott v AG* (1886), a couple, domiciled in South Africa, were divorced on the ground of the wife's adultery. By the law of South Africa, a person divorced for adultery was prohibited from re-marrying so long as the other party remained unmarried. However, after the divorce, the wife came to England, where she married an English domiciliary whilst her first husband was still unmarried. Sir James Hannen P upheld the re-marriage, on the ground that the prohibition on the re-marriage in South Africa was penal in nature and should, therefore, be discounted.

10.6 Formal validity of marriage

It is a well established principle that the formal validity of a marriage depends entirely on the law of the place where the ceremony is performed (*lex loci celebrationis*) and, therefore, non-compliance with the requirements of that law will invalidate the marriage, as may be illustrated in *Berthiaume v Dastous* (1930). In this case, a French Canadian woman of the Roman Catholic faith met a French Canadian man of the same faith in Paris, where they were married in a Roman Catholic church. Due to the carelessness of the priest, the marriage was not preceded by a civil ceremony as required by French law. This meant that the marriage, though valid by the law of Quebec, was void by French law.

On the wife's petition for divorce, the Privy Council held that the marriage was void, on the ground that it did not meet the requirements of the *lex loci celebrationis*. This was so irrespective of the domicile of the parties, for the requirements as to formal validity were of an overriding nature.

Thus, the basic rule is that if a marriage does not comply with the formalities of the *lex loci celebrationis*, it will not be valid in that country nor anywhere else. So, what is an issue of formalities? Clearly, the term includes such issues as the requirement of a civil ceremony, the number of witnesses necessary, licensing and necessity to publicise banns, and so forth. In addition, it was established by the Court of Appeal, in *Apt v Apt* (1948), that the question of the validity of a marriage by proxy is classified as an issue of formalities. Here, whilst the wife was resident and domiciled in England, a ceremony of marriage was celebrated in Buenos Aires between her and her husband, who was domiciled and resident in Argentina. The wife did not make an appearance at the ceremony, but she was represented by a person whom, by a power of attorney, she named as her representative to contract the marriage. This marriage was valid by Argentine law but invalid by English law. The Court of Appeal drew a distinction between the method of giving consent and the fact of consent, the former being a matter of form. Accordingly, as the marriage was formally valid by the law of the place of celebration, it was recognised as valid in English law. Equally, in *McCabe v McCabe* (1994), a marriage ceremony was celebrated in Ghana under Akan custom. The man was Irish and the woman was Ghanaian. They lived together in London and neither of them attended the ceremony. He sent £100 and a bottle of gin. Relatives of both parties attended the ceremony, during which the £100 was distributed and the gin drunk as a blessing of the marriage by them. On the issue of formal validity, the Court of Appeal applied Ghanaian law as the *lex loci celebrationis* and upheld the marriage.

Suppose that, at the time a marriage was celebrated, it was formally invalid, and suppose that subsequent legislation was introduced to the effect that such a marriage would become valid. Would the new legislation validate the previously celebrated marriage? This question arose in the case of *Starkowski v AG* (1954), where a wife of Polish domicile of origin entered into her first marriage at a church in Austria in May 1945. At that time, by German marriage law, which was then in force in Austria, a religious ceremony did not constitute a valid marriage since a civil ceremony was required. In June 1945, an Austrian decree was passed to the effect that religious marriages celebrated between 1 April 1945 and the date of the decree should become valid as soon as they were registered in the Family Book. The marriage, however, was not registered until July 1949 and after the wife's second marriage. The House of Lords held that, where there had been retrospective legislation which had the effect of validating an earlier marriage, the balance of justice and convenience was clearly in favour of recognising the validity of such retrospective legislation. Accordingly, the first marriage was valid.

Circumstances may arise where it may be impossible to comply with the *lex loci celebrationis*. Such a problem arose in Europe at the end and in the aftermath of the Second World War, where many people were married without complying with the requirements laid down by the authorities, who often were the Germans. The validity of such marriages was examined in *Taczanowska v Taczanowski* (1957), where the Court of Appeal applied English common law and upheld the formal validity of a marriage in Italy between two Polish nationals, one of whom was serving as an officer with the British armed forces. The marriage, which was celebrated by a Roman Catholic priest, did not comply with the local forms and was, therefore, void by Italian domestic law.

Hence, the general rule is that the formal validity of a marriage is governed by the *lex loci celebrationis*. There are, however, two statutory exceptions and one common law exception.

10.6.1 Consular marriages

The first statutory exception applies in relation to consular marriages and is embodied in the Foreign Marriage Act 1892, as amended by the Foreign Marriage Act 1947 and the Foreign Marriage (Amendment) Act 1988. In general terms, a marriage between parties, one of whom at least is a UK national, solemnised before a marriage officer in a foreign country in accordance with the provision of the Act, will be considered formally valid as if it had been solemnised in, and complied with the legal requirements of, the UK. The term 'UK national' is defined in s 1(2) of the 1892 Act, as inserted by s 1(2) of the 1988 Act, to include a Commonwealth citizen. By virtue of s 11 of the 1892 Act, 'marriage officers' include such persons as consular officers, High Commissioners and British Ambassadors, provided they hold a 'marriage warrant' from the Secretary of State.

Therefore, according to this exception, so long as the foreign marriage complies with the requirements laid down by the Act, it will be held formally valid, though it does not comply with the formalities of the law of the place of celebration.

10.6.2 Marriages of members of British forces serving abroad

A second statutory exception to the general rule is embodied in s 22 of the Foreign Marriage Act 1892, as amended by both the 1947 and the 1988 Acts. This exception applies to marriages entered into by members of Her Majesty's British forces whilst serving abroad. It provides that a marriage solemnised in any foreign territory, apart from the Commonwealth, by a chaplain or an authorised commanding officer with any part of the British naval, military, or air forces serving abroad, will be regarded as valid in law as if it had been solemnised in the UK.

10.6.3 Common law marriages

The third and final exception to the general rule has been established by the common law, and it is invoked in the context of 'common law marriages'. This type of marriage is not what most people believe, that is, the cohabitation of a man and a woman without having gone through any sort of ceremony. Indeed, this type of marriage emerged a very long time ago at a time when canon law marriage was in force. Prior to 1843, the only essential requirement to formal validity was that the couple should take each other as man and wife. However, the House of Lords, in *R v Millis* (1844) imposed the further requirement that an episcopally ordained priest should perform the ceremony. In this case, a marriage celebrated in Ireland by a Presbyterian minister according to the rites of the Presbyterian Church was held to be invalid, on the ground that it was contrary to the common law requirement that the marriage should be celebrated in the presence of an episcopally ordained clergyman.

The nature of this latter requirement has been criticised, and it appears that it does not apply to marriages celebrated outside England and Ireland. For instance, in *Wolfenden v Wolfenden* (1946), where the parties, both Canadian, went through a ceremony of marriage at a Church of Scotland Mission church in a remote part of China, the ceremony was performed by the minister of the Mission without banns or licence. Moreover, the minister was not episcopally ordained, nor was he authorised to perform such a marriage in accordance with the Foreign Marriage Act 1892. The court, after examining the decision in *R v Mills* and subsequent decisions, held that the rule in *R v Mills* had been qualified to apply only to marriages performed in England and Ireland. Additionally, under the circumstances, the parties were unable to celebrate their marriage before such an ordained priest. Accordingly, the marriage was formally valid.

Similarly, in *Penhas v Tan Soo Eng* (1953), a common law marriage performed before a layman in Singapore between a Jewish man and a Chinese woman was held to be valid, for the layman had observed both Jewish and Chinese customs.

This common law exception, unlike the above statutory exceptions, is not confined to marriages of British nationals. This may be illustrated in *Kochanski v Kochanska* (1958), where the parties, born and domiciled in Poland until 1939, were married in Germany in 1945. The ceremony of marriage was solemnised by a Roman Catholic priest according to the rites of the Roman Catholic Church. The ceremony did not, however, comply with the formalities required by German law, because the parties were living in a displaced persons camp whose occupants did not fraternise with the Germans and led the lives of a separate community.

On the question of the formal validity of the marriage, Sachs J held that the presumption that the parties had to subject themselves to German law for the purpose of celebrating their marriage was rebutted and, since the ceremony was one which would constitute an English common law marriage, the marriage was valid.

It must be noted that, for this exception to apply, the parties must have found it virtually impossible to comply with the local law. An example is the case of *Preston v Preston* (1963), where the parties went through a ceremony of marriage in Germany in June 1945. At that time, the husband was domiciled in the western province of Poland and the wife in the central province, the marriage law differing between the two provinces. The marriage was performed by an episcopally ordained priest, but it was void by the law of Germany. The reason why the parties did not comply with the formalities required by German law was that the husband was a member of the Polish forces associated with the Allies, the latter being in belligerent occupation of that part of Germany where the marriage was celebrated. Nevertheless, Cairns J applied English common law and upheld the validity of the marriage on the ground that the *lex loci celebrationis* was not complied with because of the existing extenuating circumstances, and as such the only alternative to determine the formal validity of the marriage was the English common law.

10.7 Characterisation

As a general rule, where the relevant issue in question relates to the essential validity of a marriage, then the dual-domicile rule applies and, where the issue relates to its formal validity, the law of the place of celebration applies. According to what criteria is the relevant issue characterised? The foregoing discussion clearly indicates that capacity to marry is characterised as an issue of essential validity, whereas the form of the marriage ceremony is characterised as an issue of formality. A controversial issue, however, is whether lack of parental consent is an issue of form or an issue of capacity. The general view appears to be that it relates to formalities, irrespective of whether the requirement is imposed by English law or a foreign law. In *Simonin v Mallac* (1860), a Frenchman aged 29 married a Frenchwoman aged 22 in England. The marriage was valid by English domestic law, but was voidable by French law, for neither party had obtained the consent of their respective parents as required by what was then Art 151 of the French Civil Code, which provided that the parties to the marriage were under an obligation to request their parents' consent to marry. Although the marriage was annulled in France on the ground of lack of parental consent, the English court considered lack of consent as an issue of formality and, therefore, subject to English law as the law of the place of celebration, and upheld the validity of the marriage.

Article 148 of the French Civil Code provided a more stringent requirement as to consent than Art 151, namely that 'the son who has not attained the full age of 25 cannot contract a marriage without the consent of his parents'. When the English court decided the above case, a distinction was made between both provisions, and it was indicated that Art 148, which imposed an absolute rather than qualified prohibition on marriages without parental consent, might receive a different interpretation. Nevertheless, this suggested distinction was overlooked in *Ogden v Ogden* (1908). In this case, an Englishwoman, domiciled in England, married in England a 19 year old Frenchman domiciled in France. The marriage took place without the knowledge of either of his parents. Soon after, when the husband's father found out about the marriage, he took his son back to France, where he instituted proceedings to have the marriage annulled in accordance with Art 148 of the French Civil Code, and a nullity decree was granted on that basis.

The parties then re-married, and consequently, the wife's second husband petitioned for a decree of nullity, on the ground that at the time of the second marriage, the wife's first marriage was still subsisting. The Court of Appeal held that the first marriage, though it had been annulled in France, was valid in England, because the requirement of parental consent was a mere formality.

This is a most unsatisfactory decision, for both parties to the first marriage had re-married and the effect of the Court of Appeal decision was to leave the wife married to her first husband who was not only her husband by the law of his domicile, but was also the husband of another woman. Despite the heavy criticism it received, this decision was followed in the case of *Lodge v Lodge* (1963). By way of mitigation, however, it should be borne in mind that French nullity decrees will now be recognised in England by virtue of Pt II of the FLA 1986.

10.8 Preliminary issue – the incidental question

Where an English court is asked to decide a main question which contains a foreign element, such as the parties' capacity to marry, sometimes another subsidiary question may incidentally arise in the course of determining the main question, for example, the validity of an earlier divorce. Such a main question is determined by the English conflict of laws rule, that is, the application of the dual-domicile rule. Should the incidental question be determined by the appropriate English conflict of laws rule, or should it be determined by the appropriate conflict rule of the foreign law which is applied to determine the main question?

Notwithstanding that, in the context of family law, there have been very few decisions where an incidental question has had to be determined, as will be seen, a clear general rule cannot be deduced. The first case to examine is *R v Brentwood Marriage Registrar ex p Arias* (1968), where an Italian man domiciled in Switzerland married a Swiss woman in that country. They were later divorced in Switzerland and the wife re-married. The husband desired to marry, in England, a Spanish national also domiciled in Switzerland. Notice of the marriage was given to the Registrar, who refused to marry them on the ground that, in his view, there was an impediment on the part of the husband. By Swiss law, capacity to marry was governed by the law of the nationality, and by Italian law, the law of his nationality, the divorce of Italian nationals was not recognised. The parties came to England on a temporary basis to evade Swiss law.

The main question here was the husband's capacity to re-marry which, by English conflict of laws, was governed by his Swiss law of domicile, and the incidental question was the validity of the earlier divorce, which was recognised as valid by English conflict of laws, but not recognised by Swiss conflict of laws. The Divisional Court upheld the Registrar's objection and held that the husband did not have capacity to re-marry. In other words, the incidental question was determined in accordance with the Swiss, rather than English, conflict rule.

It should be noted at this stage that the decision in this case would be different now, by virtue of s 50 of the FLA 1986, which does not preclude an English court from recognising a foreign divorce on the ground that it is not recognised elsewhere.

The decision in the above case is to be contrasted with the case of *Perrini v Perrini* (1979), where the husband, an Italian national domiciled and resident in Italy, was married in Italy to an American woman resident in New Jersey when on holiday in Italy. The marriage was never consummated, and the wife returned immediately to New Jersey, where she subsequently obtained a decree of nullity. This decree was not recognised in Italy, under whose law the husband was not free to re-marry. A few years later the husband, while still domiciled in Italy, re-married in London an Englishwoman whom he had met in Italy. Later in the same year, the husband acquired a domicile of choice in England. The wife petitioned for a decree of nullity, on the ground that the husband had no capacity to marry. So the main question was the husband's capacity to marry, and the incidental question was the validity of the New Jersey decree.

Sir Georges Baker P applied English conflict of laws to the incidental question and recognised the New Jersey decree. In other words, the conflict rule which determined the incidental question prevailed over the conflict rule on capacity. Accordingly, the husband was free to re-marry (see also *Lawrence v Lawrence* (1985)).

Prima facie, it seems difficult to reconcile this case with the *Brentwood* case. Nevertheless, if one compares the facts of both cases carefully, it may be seen that, unlike the former case, in this case the husband had already re-married and, as already stated, English courts would uphold a marriage unless there were strong reasons to the contrary. Moreover, whereas in the former case the couple came to England on a temporary visit, in the latter case the husband acquired an English domicile of choice shortly after the second marriage.

The Canadian case of *Schwebel v Ungar* (1964) provides a converse example, where the rule on capacity prevailed over that of the incidental question. Here a husband and wife, both Jews and domiciled in Hungary, decided to emigrate to Israel. In the course of their journey, they stopped at a camp in Italy, where they were divorced by a Jewish ghet. This divorce was not recognised as valid, either by the then law of their domicile, Hungary, or the law of Italy. The parties then acquired a domicile in Israel, and the wife, while so domiciled, married her second husband in Ontario.

When the second husband petitioned for a decree of nullity on the ground of bigamy, the Supreme Court of Canada held that the re-marriage was valid, since the wife had the status of a single person by the law of her ante-nuptial domicile. Hence, the incidental question was determined by the conflict rule applicable to the main question, that is, capacity to marry.

Thus, it can be seen that case law illustrates that the issue of the incidental question does not attract a mechanical determination. Each case is decided on its own facts.

10.9 Public policy

It is a well established principle that English courts would neither enforce nor recognise a right or obligation arising under a foreign law if to do so would be contrary to public policy. What is usually in question is not the rule of a foreign law in the abstract, but the impact of its recognition or enforcement in England. It follows that, if the effect of such a rule is acceptable, then it will be recognised and enforced, otherwise it will be rejected on the ground of public policy.

It may be recalled that, according to the decision in *Hyde v Hyde* (1866), English law used to regard polygamous marriage as against public policy. Nonetheless, this attitude has changed over the years and polygamous marriages are now recognised for most purposes. This is so even if one of the parties was under the English age of puberty, so long as they have capacity under the law of their ante-nuptial domicile. For instance, in *Mohammed v Knott* (1969), a Nigerian Moslem man aged 26 entered into a potentially polygamous marriage in Nigeria with a Nigerian girl aged 13, the marriage being valid by Nigerian law. Shortly thereafter, the couple moved to and cohabited in England. One of the questions before the Court of Appeal was whether a marriage of a 13 year old girl was against English public policy. It was held that since the girl had reached the age of puberty in Nigeria, the marriage was not against public policy.

Similarly, in *Cheni v Cheni* (1965), it was held that a marriage celebrated in Egypt between an uncle and his niece was not contrary to public policy since it was valid by the law of their ante-nuptial domicile. Sir Jocelyn Simon P stated that the true test was 'whether the marriage is so offensive to the conscience of the English court that it should refuse to recognise and give effect to the proper foreign law. In deciding that question, the court will seek to exercise common sense, good manners and a reasonable tolerance.'

MARRIAGE

Meaning and definition

A marriage, as understood in Christendom, may be defined 'as the voluntary union for life of one man and one woman, to the exclusion of all others'.

Where one of the parties does not voluntarily consent to the marriage, the marriage will be declared invalid.

The union must be of one biological man and one biological woman, otherwise it will be void.

Polygamy

Polygamous marriages, when celebrated in a country which allows polygamy, have come to be recognised in English law for most purposes, such as matrimonial relief, proprietary rights arising out of a contractual claim, legitimacy of children, social security, and succession.

Potentially polygamous marriages

Part II of the PILA 1995, which came into force on 8 January 1996, allows English courts to recognise all potentially polygamous marriages celebrated outside the UK where either party to the marriage is domiciled in England. This Part of the Act also applies to Scotland, but has retrospective effect only in England. However, this retrospective effect is subject to some qualifications and savings.

Capacity to marry

As a general rule, capacity to marry is governed by the ante-nuptial domicile of each of the parties immediately before the marriage.

Three exceptions have been adopted:

(a) the validity of a marriage celebrated in England between persons of whom the one has an English, and the other a foreign, domicile is not affected by any incapacity which, though existing under the law of such foreign domicile, does not exist under the law of England;

(b) where the validity of a divorce or annulment is recognised in England, the fact that such divorce or annulment is not recognised elsewhere will not preclude either party to the marriage from re-marrying in England or cause the re-marriage of either party to be treated as invalid;

(c) where the prohibition on re-marriage in the country of domicile is penal in nature, then the English court will ignore it.

Formal validity of marriage

As a general rule, this is determined by the law of place of celebration, but subject to three exceptions:

(a) consular marriages;

(b) marriages of members of the British forces serving abroad;

(c) common law marriages.

Characterisation

The general rule is that characterising the relevant issue is subject to English law.

Capacity to marry is characterised as an issue of essential validity, and is, therefore, subject to the dual-domicile rule, whereas the form of the marriage ceremony is characterised as an issue of formality, and is, therefore, subject to the law of the place of celebration.

Controversy, however, surrounds the issue of lack of parental consent. Case law seems to classify such an issue as one of form.

The incidental question

The examination of case law illustrates that the incidental question does not attract a mechanical rule. Each case is decided on its own facts.

CHAPTER 11

MATRIMONIAL CAUSES AND FINANCIAL RELIEF

11.1 Introduction

As the title indicates, this chapter will examine two major issues in the context of conflict of laws, namely, matrimonial causes and financial relief. The former issue covers such questions as divorce, judicial separation, nullity of marriage, presumption of death and recognition of foreign decrees. The latter issue covers the question of the power of the English court to grant ancillary relief, relief after a foreign decree and maintenance orders. Each of these will be considered separately, and divorce and judicial separation will form the starting point. It must be noted, first, that a new EC Convention on Jurisdiction and the Recognition and Enforcement of Judgments in Matrimonial Matters was signed in Brussels on 27 May 1998. This Convention, when implemented, will regulate jurisdiction, recognition and enforcement of judgments, between Contracting States, in respect of divorce, legal separation, marriage annulment, parental responsibility and child abduction.

11.2 Divorce and judicial separation

This section will deal, first, with the basis on which English courts assume jurisdiction to entertain a divorce or judicial separation decree; and secondly, it will consider whether a question of choice of law arises in this context.

11.2.1 Jurisdiction in England and Wales

The grounds of jurisdiction in respect of divorce and judicial separation were, until recently, governed by s 5(2) of the Domicile and Matrimonial Proceedings Act 1973 (DMPA). These are now contained in s 19(2) of the Family Law Act 1996 (FLA), which stipulates as follows:

The court's jurisdiction is exercisable only if:

(a) at least one of the parties was domiciled in England and Wales on the statement date;

(b) at least one of the parties was habitually resident in England and Wales throughout the period of one year ending with the statement date; or

(c) nullity proceedings are pending in relation to the marriage when the marital proceedings commence.

According to this provision, an English court may assume jurisdiction to entertain proceedings for divorce or judicial separation where any one of the three bases above is satisfied. The first basis applies the connecting factor of domicile, regardless of which of the parties, whether the petitioner or the respondent, is domiciled in England. The time at which domicile is to be determined is the time when the statement of marital breakdown is received by the court (that is, the date of the commencement of the proceedings, see s 20 of the FLA 1996), and not when the case is tried.

It appears that this jurisdictional rule still applies even if the party domiciled in England and Wales at the time of the statement has since changed his or her domicile. This may be deduced from the wording of s 19(2) which stipulates the statement's date as the relevant time.

The second basis of jurisdiction is habitual residence. As with domicile, the relevant date is one year's habitual residence ending at the date of the statement, and not the date of the trial or judgment. According to this basis a spouse, who has never been to England and has no personal connection with England whatsoever, will be able to petition on the basis of the respondent's habitual residence in England and Wales.

Although domicile and habitual residence are determined at the statement date, s 19(2)(c) of the FLA 1996 makes provision for jurisdiction to be assumed on the following further ground: if proceedings are pending for nullity of marriage, in which the court has jurisdiction to entertain by virtue of s 5(3) of the DMPA 1973, then the court has jurisdiction to entertain other proceedings in respect of the same marriage, such as for divorce, or judicial separation, even though there would be no jurisdiction under the FLA 1996. For instance, suppose that a wife, habitually resident in England for one year, petitions the English court for nullity according to s 5(3) of the DMPA 1973. Suppose that, before the petition is heard, the wife abandons her residence in England. The husband, domiciled and resident abroad, wishes to cross-petition for divorce. Notwithstanding that the wife is no longer resident in England, by virtue of s 19(2)(c) of the FLA 1996 the husband's cross-petition can still be heard in the English court, although neither he nor his wife is resident in England. This is because the wife's petition is still pending.

By virtue of s 19(7) of the FLA 1996, the nullity proceedings, which form the third basis of jurisdiction above, mean proceedings in respect of which the court has jurisdiction under s 5(3) of the DMPA 1973. In other words, whilst the jurisdictional grounds in respect of divorce and judicial separation are now set out in the FLA 1996, those grounds in respect of nullity proceedings remain the subject of the DMPA 1973. The latter will be examined below, 11.3. It suffices to note at this stage that the fact that nullity proceedings are pending in the English court is a ground under which the court has jurisdiction in respect of divorce or judicial separation.

11.2.2 Stay of proceedings

The jurisdiction of the English courts to entertain matrimonial proceedings is quite broad. Consequently, this may create the risk that the courts of more than one country may have jurisdiction in relation to the same proceedings. To this end, s 5(6) of the DMPA 1973, which gives effect to Sched 1 (as amended by Sched 3 of the FLA 1996), allows the English court to stay its proceedings where there are concurrent proceedings elsewhere in respect of the same marriage.

By virtue of Sched 1, para 7 (as amended), there is an obligation on the petitioner or cross-petitioner, when proceedings are pending before the English court, to provide particulars of any proceedings, which are known to be continuing in another jurisdiction and are in respect of the marriage or capable of affecting its validity or subsistence. But, before dealing with the relevant provisions on stays, it is important to note that the DMPA 1973 makes a distinction between mandatory and discretionary stays. The former covers cases where the concurrent proceedings are pending in the British Isles, provided that certain requirements are met. In the absence of such requirements, the granting of the stay becomes discretionary.

11.2.3 Mandatory stays

According to Sched 1, para 8 of the DMPA 1973 (as amended by Sched 3, para 6 of the FLA 1996), where, before the beginning of the trial of proceedings for divorce (and only divorce), it appears to the English court that proceedings for divorce *or* nullity in respect of the marriage are pending elsewhere in the British Isles, then it must order a stay of the English proceedings, provided that the parties to the marriage resided in that jurisdiction when the English proceedings began, or they had their last place of residence before those proceedings began in that other jurisdiction; and either of the parties was habitually resident in that jurisdiction for one year ending with the date on which they last resided there together.

As can be seen, this provision on mandatory or obligatory stay only applies to English divorce proceedings where the parties are closely connected with the other relevant jurisdiction in the British Isles. If any of the above requirements is not met, then the question of stay will be considered by virtue of the court's discretionary power.

11.2.4 Discretionary stays

Schedule 1, para 9 of the DMPA 1973 (as amended by Sched 3, para 7 of the FLA 1996) allows for the English courts, at their discretion, to grant a stay. This arises where it appears to the English court, before the beginning of the trial of any marital or matrimonial proceedings (not only divorce), that proceedings in respect of, or capable of affecting, the validity of the same marriage, are pending in another jurisdiction. The court's discretion is to be exercised where it appears that, on the balance of fairness and convenience as between the parties, it is appropriate to dispose of the foreign proceedings before further steps are taken in England. In considering the balance of fairness, Sched 1, para 9(2) of the DMPA 1973 provides that the court must have regard to all the relevant factors, including the convenience of witnesses and delay or expense likely to result from the English proceedings being or not being stayed.

As to the meaning of 'any matrimonial proceedings', this was considered in *Thyssen v Thyssen* (1985), where the husband commenced divorce proceedings in Switzerland, and the wife petitioned for divorce in England. The husband applied for a stay of the English proceedings, but shortly thereafter the stay was dismissed by consent. He then cross-petitioned in the English proceedings, and subsequently the Swiss proceedings were struck out on his application. The wife later returned to Switzerland and then applied for a stay of her English proceedings and her husband's cross-petition. Before the wife's application was heard, interim orders were made in the English proceedings in relation to the custody of the child and ancillary relief. Her application was then dismissed, and on appeal the husband contended, *inter alia*, that the court had no power to stay his cross-petition, because its discretion to do so was only exercisable before the trial or first trial in any matrimonial proceedings, which were taken to include the interim orders made.

The Court of Appeal held that, on its true construction, the phrase trial or first trial in any matrimonial proceedings related only to trial of issues in the main suit and not a hearing relating to custody or ancillary relief. Accordingly, the court had jurisdiction to exercise its discretion to stay the proceedings. Nevertheless, the appeal was dismissed.

Guidance as to the operation of test on stays can be drawn from the small number of reported cases directly concerned with this issue. For instance, in *Shemshadfard v Shemshadfard* (1981), the husband, an Iranian subject, married his third wife, also an Iranian subject, in Iran in 1974. He decided to move to England with her and their young daughter in order to settle them there, although he himself did not intend to leave Iran permanently. He bought a house and business in London, where he installed his wife as manageress. In 1979, the marriage broke down, and as a result the husband sold the business, but left the house, where his wife and daughter continued to live. In the same year, the wife commenced divorce proceedings in England on the ground of the husband's unreasonable behaviour. In 1980, however, the husband issued a petition in Iran seeking a certificate of non-compatibility with the wife, so that he would be relieved of any obligation to maintain her. He then applied to the English court for a stay of the wife's proceedings. Purchas J held that the relevant factors to be considered by the court when considering the balance of fairness and convenience were to be liberally defined. They covered, where appropriate, the remedies which were available in the foreign court, including the possibility or otherwise of dissolution of the marriage there, provision for custody of children and ancillary matters, and the cultural background of the parties. On the facts, he found that the balance of fairness and convenience between the parties was such that it was inappropriate to stay the English proceedings until disposal of the Iranian proceedings. Accordingly, the husband's application for a stay was dismissed. Similarly, in *Gadd v Gadd* (1985), the fact that the wife would receive no financial support in divorce proceedings in Monaco tipped the scales in favour of refusing a stay.

Nonetheless, the unification of the common law and statutory approaches was made by the House of Lords in *De Dampierre v De Dampierre* (1988), where it was held that the *Spiliada* test on stays and *forum non conveniens* was to be applied (see Chapter 2). In *De Dampierre*, both parties were French nationals who had married in France in 1977. In 1979, they moved to London, where they resided, and where the husband was involved in conducting his family's business. In 1982, the child of the marriage was born in London. In 1984, the wife opened a business in New York, where she subsequently moved with her son and refused the husband's request to return to London. The husband commenced divorce proceedings in France and the wife then petitioned for divorce in the English court. The husband applied for a stay of the English proceedings on the basis of the DMPA 1973. The House of Lords held that the same test as that found in *The Spiliada* (1987) applied to cases of stay under the DMPA 1973. The fact that the wife might receive less favourable financial provision were the proceedings to continue in France did not deter the English court from granting a stay, since it was satisfied that substantial justice would be done in France, which is the natural and appropriate forum for the resolution of the dispute.

Similarly, in *T v T* (1995), Thorpe J granted a stay of the English proceedings on the basis that Kenya was the more appropriate forum for the determination of such questions as those concerning a child resident therein and assets situated in that jurisdiction. More recently, in *S v S* (1997), Wilson J applied the *Spiliada* test, and stayed the English divorce proceedings brought by the wife in favour of the proceedings brought in New York by the husband. The parties had married in London in 1987, but had entered into a prenuptial agreement, which was executed in New York in November 1986. When considering the balance of fairness and convenience to determine whether the English proceedings should be stayed, the prenuptial agreement, with its substantial financial provisions, was a major factor which tipped the balance in favour of a stay. The same line of reasoning was adopted in *Butler v Butler* (1997), wherein the husband and wife married in 1991 and lived in Florida. The wife made financial arrangements, negotiated and executed in Florida, to enable the husband to settle certain debts. The wife was a US citizen with no connection with England. The husband, albeit a British citizen, was regarded as a non-resident for UK tax purposes. The marriage broke down, and the husband filed a petition for divorce in England. The wife contested the jurisdiction of the English court and, thereafter, commenced divorce proceedings in Florida, where she additionally sought financial ancilliary relief. The Court of Appeal held that the balance of fairness and convenience resulted in it being more appropriate for the proceedings to be disposed of in Florida, with which the connection was so overwhelming that it was the most convenient and appropriate court in which the dissolution of the marriage should be considered and determined.

11.2.5 Choice of law

Two main headings will be considered in this section, namely divorce and judicial separation.

Divorce

At common law, the only basis for the jurisdiction of the English court in divorce proceedings used to be domicile. As such, English law, as the law of the domicile or the law of the forum, was applied. However, the statutory bases of jurisdiction, first introduced under the Matrimonial Causes Act 1937, for example, a wife can petition the English court on the ground of her husband's domicile prior to his desertion or deportation from England, have led to the possibility that the parties' domicile might not always be English. Nevertheless, the Court of Appeal, in *Zanelli v Zanelli* (1948), assumed that English law was still the applicable law. In this case, the husband, an Italian national domiciled in England, married his wife, an Englishwoman, in England in 1948. Subsequently, he was deported from England, as a result of which he lost his English domicile and reverted to his Italian domicile. On the wife's petition for divorce, the Court of Appeal applied English domestic law without any consideration of a choice of law question.

In relation to divorce under the subsequent 1973 Act, there is no statutory choice of law rule. Indeed, it was the intention of the Law Commission, in its Report No 48, 1972, when proposing the reform which led to 1973 Act, that English domestic law should apply.

Judicial separation

The principal effect of a decree of judicial separation is to entitle the petitioner to live apart from the respondent. It does not, however, dissolve the marriage, nor enable either party to re-marry. This remedy is sought mainly by persons who have religious scruples about divorce. There has never been any doubt that English courts will apply English domestic law, even if the parties are domiciled outside England and Wales.

11.3 Nullity

As in the context of divorce and judicial separation, two main questions will have to be considered, namely jurisdiction and choice of law.

11.3.1 Jurisdiction in England and Wales

Section 5(3) of the DMPA 1973, which remains unaffected by the FLA 1996, governs the question of jurisdiction with regard to nullity proceedings. It provides as follows:

> The court shall have jurisdiction to entertain proceedings for nullity of marriage if (and only if) either of the parties to the marriage:
>
> (a) is domiciled in England and Wales on the date when the proceedings are begun; or
>
> (b) was habitually resident in England and Wales throughout the period of one year ending with that date; or
>
> (c) died before that date and either:
>
>> (i) was at death domiciled in England and Wales; or
>>
>> (ii) had been habitually resident in England and Wales throughout the period of one year ending with the date of death.

As can be seen, the first two bases for jurisdiction are similar to those applicable in respect of divorce and judicial separation. An additional basis under the present provision, which applies only in relation to nullity petitions, is that where either party to the marriage has died before the date when the proceedings for nullity were begun. In this case, the court has jurisdiction if either the deceased was domiciled at death in England, or had been habitually resident in England throughout the period of one year ending with the date of death.

Again, the relevant date, at which the criteria of the first two bases is to be assessed, is the date of the commencement of the proceedings.

11.3.2 Void and voidable marriages

The difficult issue in nullity suits arises in relation to choice of law. One of the main reasons is that a nullity decree is concerned with the validity of the creation of the marriage in question, unlike divorce, which dissolves a marriage that was validly created. This leads to the assertion that the choice of law rules in nullity should be essentially the same as those already examined in relation to the validity of a marriage.

Another difficulty in the context of choice of law in nullity suits stems from the fact that the effects of nullity vary according to the particular ground in issue. Some grounds render a marriage void and some others render it voidable.

Moreover, the difference between void and voidable marriages is very crucial, for according to the case of *Ross Smith v Ross Smith* (1963):

... a void marriage is no marriage. Considered literally, the expression is self-destructive and contradictory. But, without misleading anyone, it serves to denote the situation where a ceremony of marriage does not bring about a marriage.

A voidable marriage, on the other hand, is one which will be regarded as validly created until a decree annulling it has been pronounced by a court of competent jurisdiction (see *De Reneville v De Reneville* (1948)). Accordingly, the annulment of a void marriage has retrospective effect, it considers the marriage as having never existed. As for the annulment of a voidable marriage, the annulment operates only from the date of the decree absolute and, therefore, until that date, the marriage is considered as subsisting.

The grounds on which a marriage is void or voidable in English law are set out in ss 11 and 12 respectively of the Matrimonial Causes Act 1973 (MCA).

11.3.3 Void marriage

In relation to the grounds on which a marriage is void, s 11 states that a marriage celebrated after 31 July 1971 will be void on the following grounds only, that is to say:

(a) that it is not a valid marriage under the provisions of the Marriages Act 1949 to 1970; that is to say where:

    (i) the parties are within the prohibited degrees of relationship;

    (ii) either party is under the age of 16; or

    (iii) the parties have intermarried in the disregard of certain requirements as to the formation of marriage;

(b) that at the time of the marriage either party was already lawfully married;

(c) that the parties are not respectively male and female;

(d) in the case of polygamous marriage entered into outside England and Wales, that either party was at the time of the marriage domiciled in England and Wales.

For the purposes of para (d) of this sub-section a marriage [may be polygamous although] *is not polygamous if* at its inception neither party has any spouse additional to the other [note that the italicised phrase has replaced the phrase in square brackets].

Before moving on to s 12, it is worth noting that s 11(d) has caused mischief to Moslems domiciled in England who contracted marriages by Moslem rites while on visits to their original countries and then returned with their spouses to England. Prior to *Hussain v Hussain* (1982), all such marriages were considered void by virtue of s 11(d). Nevertheless, in this case, the Court of Appeal held that, where the husband is domiciled in England, the marriage is monogamous. Prior to the adoption of Pt II of the PILA 1995, however, this rule did not generally alter the law where the wife was domiciled in England. Therefore, if she married in a Moslem country under Moslem rites, the marriage was potentially polygamous and therefore void by virtue of s 11(d).

Since 8 January 1996, this is no longer the case, for s 11(d) has been amended and the phrase 'may be polygamous although' has been replaced by 'is not polygamous if'. This has the effect that only actually polygamous marriages will now be declared void. Men and women domiciled in England now have capacity to enter a marriage outside the UK which, though polygamous in form, is monogamous in fact, wherever celebrated. However, this excludes from validation any marriages which had already been declared void by a nullity decree, or in the case where either spouse had entered into a later marriage which would be rendered invalid by the retrospective validation of the earlier one.

11.3.4 Voidable marriage

Section 12 of the MCA 1973 provides that a marriage celebrated after 31 July 1971 will be voidable on the following grounds only, that is to say:

(a) that the marriage has not been consummated owing to the incapacity of either party to consummate it;

(b) that the marriage has not been consummated owing to the wilful refusal of the respondent to consummate it;

(c) that either party to the marriage did not validly consent to it, whether in consequence of duress, mistake, unsoundness of mind or otherwise;

(d) that at the time of the marriage either party, though capable of giving a valid consent, was suffering (whether continuously or intermittently) from mental disorder within the meaning of the Mental Health Act 1959 of such a kind or to such an extent as to be unfit for marriage;

(e) that at the time of the marriage the respondent was suffering from venereal disease in a communicable form;

(f) that at the time of the marriage the respondent was pregnant by some person other than the petitioner.

There are bars, however, to the award of a nullity decree for a voidable marriage in all the above cases. According to s 13(1)(a) and (b), the court will not make such award if the respondent can prove that the petitioner knew of the defect, but acted in such a way as to lead him or her to believe that the petitioner would not act upon it, or that it would be unjust on the respondent that the decree be awarded. Moreover, s 13(2) operates a time bar and provides that in all cases, except failure to consummate the marriage, the proceedings will have to be brought within three years of the marriage. Finally, s 13(3) provides that, in relation to grounds (e) and (f) (that is, venereal disease and pregnancy), the court must be satisfied that, at the time of the marriage, the petitioner was ignorant of such facts.

11.3.5 Choice of law

The determination of the proper law in a nullity suit depends on classifying the nature of the defect which constitutes the cause for annulment. In other words, the court has to characterise the defect to decide whether it is one related to the form or essential validity of the marriage. In order to do so, English courts have applied the English rules of characterisation, as may be illustrated in the Canadian case of *Solomon v Walters* (1956). In this case, lack of parental consent as required by the law of the place of celebration, but not by the law of the domicile of the parties, was characterised as an issue of form to which the *lex loci celebrationis* was applied. Accordingly, the marriage was held to be voidable.

A controversial issue is whether defects affecting consent are to be classified as related to formal or essential validity. Lack of consent may take the form of mistaken identity, fraud, duress, coercion, mental illness, and so forth. English courts for many years failed to realise that a choice of law problem existed in such cases and applied English law as the law of the forum, for instance, in the case of *Buckland v Buckland* (1968), where the petitioner, a Maltese man, was charged in 1953 under Maltese law with corruption of a 15 year old girl. Although he claimed that he was innocent, his solicitor advised him that he would inevitably be found guilty and that his only other alternative was to marry the girl. Because he was terrified, he married the girl at a church in Malta, then, a few days later, he left to go to England, where he lived from then on. In 1964, by which time he had acquired an English domicile, he petitioned for the annulment of this marriage, on the ground that it was void for want of consent.

Scarman J declared the marriage null and void. No reference was made to any law other than English law, despite the fact that the only connection with England was that, by the date of the proceedings, the petitioner had acquired an English domicile.

Notwithstanding the decision in the above case, it seems that the weight of judicial opinion favours reference of the issue of consent to the law of domicile. Indeed, this view was adopted by Hodson J in *Way v Way* (1950), where the husband, a British subject domiciled in England, went through a ceremony of marriage in Russia with his wife, a Russian domiciliary. Although he believed that he was legally married, certain formalities required by Russian law had not been complied with. Furthermore, shortly after the marriage, he and his wife intended to return to England, but his wife was not permitted by the Soviet authorities to leave Russia. Subsequently, he petitioned for the annulment of his marriage on the grounds that it did not comply with certain formalities required by Russia. He further contended that the marriage was void for want of consent, since he believed, at the time of the ceremony that his wife would be allowed to accompany him to England. Hodson J held that, in relation to lack of consent, this was to be referred to the personal law of the parties and not the *lex loci celebrationis*. Accordingly, by English law, the personal law of the petitioner, a mistake of the kind pleaded was not sufficient to nullify consent.

On appeal, the marriage was held to be void on the first ground, that is, non-compliance with the Russian formalities.

Hodson J's decision was adopted in the subsequent case of *Szechter v Szechter* (1971), where a Polish professor divorced his wife and married the petitioner, domiciled in Poland, in order to secure her release from prison, and enable her to escape to the West. On arrival to England, she petitioned for annulment of the marriage on the ground of duress. Sir Jocelyn Simon P held that it was for Polish law, as the law of the domicile of the parties at the time of the marriage, to determine the validity of that marriage.

In relation to physical defects or incapacity, the position is equally unclear. In English domestic law, a marriage is voidable if one of the parties is impotent or wilfully refuses to consummate the marriage. The difficulty stems, however, from the fact that, whereas impotence renders a marriage invalid almost everywhere, wilful refusal varies from being a ground for nullity, to a ground for divorce, or, as in some legal systems, it is not an independent ground for relief. What law does the English court apply in such cases?

It was not until 1947 that the possibility of applying a foreign law to such issues was considered for the first time. The landmark case was *Robert v Robert* (1947), where Barnard J characterised wilful refusal as 'an error in the quality of the respondent' to which the *lex loci celebrationis* was applied. His Lordship further considered that if the defect were to be classified as one affecting the capacity of one of the parties to contract a marriage, then the law of the domicile would apply. (Note that this decision was overruled in *De Reneville v De Reneville* (1948), though the question of choice of law was not expressly dissented from.)

An authority in favour of applying the law of domicile may be found in *Ponticelli v Ponticelli* (1958), where the parties were married in Italy by proxy. The wife was domiciled in Italy and the husband was domiciled in England. On the husband's petition for a nullity decree on the ground of wilful refusal, Sachs J had to determine the choice of law issue, for wilful refusal was not a ground for annulment under Italian law. He rejected the classification of such a defect as being an issue of form and applied English law, as the law of the domicile of the husband at the time of the marriage and at the time of the petition.

A further question closely related to the question of applicable law to such physical defects is whether English courts will annul a marriage on grounds unknown to English law. To this end, s 14(1) of the MCA 1973 provides that:

> Where apart from this Act, any matter affecting the validity of a marriage would fall to be determined (in accordance with the rules of private international law) by reference to the law of a country outside England and Wales, nothing in ss 11, 12 or 13(1) above shall:
>
> (a) preclude the determination of that matter as aforesaid; or
>
> (b) require the application to the marriage of the grounds or bar to relief there mentioned except so far as applicable in accordance with those rules.

Hence, there is little doubt that this provision anticipates that English courts will apply a foreign law to nullity petitions in appropriate circumstances. This provision further indicates that English courts may even annul marriages on grounds which are unknown to English law.

11.4 Recognition of foreign divorces, legal separations and annulments

The FLA 1986 was enacted in order to reform the chaotic state of the law relating to recognition of foreign divorces, legal separations and annulments. Prior to this Act, foreign divorces and legal separations were recognised by virtue of the Recognition of Divorces and Legal Separations Act 1971 as amended by the DMPA 1973, and foreign annulments depended for recognition on the common law rules. However, the uncertainty which clouded these rules led the Law Commission in 1984 to examine the law in this area and to propose that essentially the same rules should govern all three matrimonial causes (see Law Commission Report No 137). These recommendations were substantially adopted in Part II of the FLA 1986, which came into force on 4 April 1988. The FLA 1986, as amended by the FLA 1996, has replaced all the pre-existing common law rules in this context.

11.4.1 Decrees granted within the British Isles

Separate rules apply in relation to recognition of divorces, judicial separations and annulments granted elsewhere within the British Isles. A starting point is s 44 of the 1986 Act, which provides that:

> (1) no divorce or annulment obtained in the British Isles shall be recognised unless granted by a court; and
>
> (2) otherwise divorces granted in any part of the British Isles shall be recognised throughout the British Isles.

The provision of this section makes it clear that, unless the divorce or annulment within the British Isles is granted by a court, it will not be recognised. Hence, a man cannot pronounce a *talaq* within these territories and consider himself as validly divorced.

11.4.2 Decrees granted elsewhere by means of proceedings

Where a decree is granted outside the British Isles, s 46 sets out the grounds for recognition and makes a distinction between decrees granted by means of proceedings (s 46(1)) and decrees granted other than by means of proceedings (s 46(2)). According to s 46(1), a divorce, annulment or separation obtained by means of proceedings is recognised if:

(a) it is effective under the law in which it obtained; and

(b) at the relevant date either party to the marriage was:
    (i) habitually resident in the country where the dissolution was obtained; or
    (ii) was domiciled there; or
    (iii) was a national there.

Hence, where the foreign decree is obtained by means of proceedings, the English court will recognise it so long as the decree was effective in the country where it was obtained and provided that either of the parties to the marriage was habitually resident, domiciled or a national of that country. As for the meaning and definition of the term 'proceedings', this will be explored in the context of extra-judicial divorces.

As a general rule, the relevant date under s 46 is the date of the commencement of the foreign proceedings by virtue of which the decree was obtained. Two exceptions, however, exist. The first applies only in relation to foreign annulments where the decree was, by reason of the death of either or both spouses, obtained by another person. In this case, s 46(4) of the FLA 1986 provides that the relevant time is the time of the death of the spouse in question. The second exception applies in relation to cross-proceedings. According to s 47(1)(a), the relevant time is either the time of original proceedings or the time of the cross-proceedings.

11.4.3 Recognition of extra-judicial divorces

A number of jurisdictions permit divorce without recourse to judicial proceedings. This extra-judicial divorce may take a number of forms: it may be a unilateral divorce by the husband; a consensual divorce; or a family/tribal consultation procedure.

In the ancient Islamic law, which is still in force in the Sudan and some parts of East Africa, the husband can divorce his wife simply by pronouncing the word *talaq* three times. There does not have to be any reason, and sometimes the wife does not have to be present.

Under Jewish law, *ghet*, that is, a consensual divorce, is pronounced before, but not granted by, the Beth Din in a rabbinical court.

The question arises here as to whether English courts will recognise such extra-judicial divorces.

Before considering this question, it should be noted that foreign extra-judicial divorces will not be recognised in England by virtue of the Foreign Judgments (Reciprocal Enforcement) Act 1933, as may be illustrated in the case of *Maples v Maples* (1987). Here, the wife married her first husband in Israel in 1968. Later, the couple settled in England, where the marriage broke down, and they went to Beth Din in London where the husband granted the wife and the wife accepted a *ghet* divorce. Subsequently, a rabbinical court in Israel issued a judgment of confirmation, certifying that the necessary requirements had been complied with. On the issue of whether the judgment of confirmation should be recognised in England by virtue of the Foreign Judgments (Reciprocal Enforcement) Act 1933, it was held that the Act did not apply to judgments of marital status.

By virtue of s 44 of the FLA 1986, no divorce or annulment obtained in any part of the British Isles is effective, unless granted by a court of civil jurisdiction. Therefore, *talaq* pronounced in England is invalid, as is a *ghet* obtained before a Beth Din in England.

In relation to extra-judicial divorces obtained elsewhere, s 46(2) of the Act provides for their recognition, but on more stringent grounds than s 46(1). Section 46(2) provides that:

> The validity of an overseas divorce, annulment or legal separation obtained otherwise than by means of proceedings shall be recognised if:
>
> (a) the divorce, annulment or legal separation is effective under the law of the country in which it was obtained; and
>
> (b) at the relevant date:
>
> > (i) each party to the marriage was domiciled in that country; or
> >
> > (ii) either party to the marriage was domiciled in that country and the other party was domiciled in a country under whose law the divorce, annulment or legal separation is recognised as valid; and
> >
> > (iii) neither party to the marriage was habitually resident in the United Kingdom throughout the period of one year immediately preceding that date.

Thus, for a foreign extra-judicial divorce to be recognised in England, it must be effective in the country where it was obtained, and both parties must be either domiciled in that country or, where they are domiciled in different countries, the divorce must be recognised in both countries. This is so, provided that neither party was habitually resident in the UK throughout the period of one year immediately before the divorce.

It was mentioned earlier that an extra-judicial divorce is a divorce obtained other than by means of proceedings. So what constitutes 'proceedings'?

Section 54 states that 'proceedings' means 'judicial or other proceedings'. This phrase was the crucial test in s 2 of the Recognition of Divorces and Legal Separations Act 1971 and it generated case law which presumably remains relevant. In *Quazi v Quazi* (1980), the House of Lords held that a Pakistani *talaq*, effective under the Pakistan Muslim Family Laws Ordinance 1961, which requires notification to the chairman of an arbitration council and postpones the coming into effect of the *talaq* until the expiry of a 90 day period during which a reconciliation might be brought about, was within the phrase 'other proceedings'. It was not essential that there be some State body having power to prevent the parties from dissolving their marriage as of right. Scarman LJ took a wider view and defined 'proceedings' as 'any act or acts, officially recognised as leading to divorce in the country where the divorce was obtained'.

This latter view was adopted in *Zaal v Zaal* (1983), where Bush J held that 'other proceedings' 'did not have to be judicial or quasi-judicial but could be any act or acts officially recognised as leading to divorce in the relevant country'. This wider view is clearly unsatisfactory, for if applied literally it will make the provisions of s 46(2) redundant. Fortunately, in *Chaudhary v Chaudhary* (1985), the Court of Appeal interpreted the statements in *Quazi v Quazi* as requiring the phrase to indicate a narrower category of divorces than all divorces obtained by any means which are effective by the law of the country in which the divorce is obtained. Hence, a *bare talaq*, which is nothing more than a declaration by the husband, was not within the phrase 'other proceedings'.

Last, but not least, it is necessary to consider the question of where a *talaq* may be said to have been obtained. A *bare talaq* seems to be located where the husband speaks the required formula. A *ghet* is probably located where the document is delivered to and accepted by the wife. A problem, however, arises with regard to transnational *talaqs* or *ghets*. For instance, in *R v Secretary of State for the Home Department ex p Fatima* (1986), the husband was a Pakistani national who married in 1968 and had lived in England ever since. In 1978, he purported to divorce his wife by *talaq*. He pronounced the *talaq* in England and made a statutory declaration to that effect to an English solicitor. Copies of this were sent to Pakistan to both the wife and, as required by the Ordinance, to the chairman of the local council. The House of Lords held that the pronouncement of the *talaq* by the husband was the first step in the proceedings by which the *talaq* had been obtained. Accordingly, the proceedings had taken place partly in England and partly in Pakistan. Similarly, in *Berkovits v Grinberg* (1995), Wall J held that a Jewish *ghet*, instituted in England and delivered to the wife in Israel, was not valid, albeit it was effective under the law of Israel.

11.4.4 Grounds for non-recognition

Despite the fact that a foreign decree, whatever its nature, should be recognised in England by virtue of ss 44 and 46, its recognition may be refused by virtue of the policy grounds provided under s 51 of the FLA 1986. All the grounds under this section are discretionary. Section 51(1) provides that:

> Subject to s 52 of this Act, recognition of the validity of:
>
> (a) a divorce, annulment or judicial separation granted by a court of civil jurisdiction in any part of the British Isles; or
>
> (b) an overseas divorce, annulment or legal separation,
>
> may be refused in any part of the UK if the divorce, annulment or separation was granted or obtained at a time when it was irreconcilable with a decision determining the question of the subsistence or validity of the marriage of the parties previously given (whether before or after the commencement of this part) by a court of civil jurisdiction in that part of the UK or by a court elsewhere and recognised or entitled to be recognised in that part of the UK.

Under this provision, recognition may be denied both to other British and overseas divorces, judicial separations and nullity decrees, on the ground of *res judicuatu*.

Section 51(2) only applies to divorce and legal separation and provides that a divorce or legal separation may be refused recognition in England if it was granted at a time when according to English law (including the English rules of the conflict of laws) there was no subsisting marriage between the parties.

It must be noted at this stage that only the above two provisions apply in relation to decrees granted within the British Isles as well as overseas decrees. As for the remaining provisions below, they only apply to overseas decrees.

Section 51(3)(a)(i), which applies only to overseas decrees, provides that an overseas divorce, annulment or judicial separation obtained by means of judicial or other proceedings may be refused recognition in England on the ground of want of proper notice of the proceedings to a party to the marriage. For instance, in *D v D* (1993), both parties came from Ghana where they were validly married pursuant to Ghanaian custom in 1977. A few years later, they came to reside in England. In 1990, the husband left his wife in England and went to Ghana where, unbeknown to the wife, he obtained an order dissolving the marriage in proceedings held before the Customary Arbitration Tribunal. The husband was the plaintiff in the proceedings, and the wife's mother was the defendant. In the course of the proceedings, the defendant protested that she could not deal with the matter without her daughter being either present or notified. It was held that the fact that the wife had no knowledge of the proceedings and that the mother had objected to taking part therein, the divorce would not be recognised for want of proper notice of the proceedings.

Furthermore, by virtue of s 51(3)(a)(ii), an overseas divorce, annulment or judicial separation may be refused recognition in England if it was obtained without a party to the marriage having been given such opportunity to take part in the proceedings.

Section 51(3)(b), which only applies to extra-judicial divorces, provides that a foreign divorce, etc, which is obtained otherwise than by means of judicial or other proceedings, may be refused recognition in England on the ground of the absence of an official document certifying (a) its effectiveness under the law of the country in which it was obtained; or (b) where relevant, that it is recognised as valid in another country in which either party was domiciled.

According to s 51(3)(c), an overseas divorce, etc, may be refused recognition in England if its recognition would be contrary to public policy.

As s 51 repeals s 8 of the 1971 Act, guidance as to the operation of the various provisions may be sought from pre-1986 case law on s 8, which may still be relevant.

In relation to want of opportunity to take part, in *Newmarch v Newmarch* (1978), the court refused to recognise a foreign decree on the ground that, despite the fact that the wife had received notice of proceedings, she was denied an opportunity to take part because her Australian solicitors failed to file an answer to the husband's petition as instructed, so the suit went undefended. And in *Joyce v Joyce* (1979), the wife was unable to afford to travel to Quebec, and could not obtain legal aid from either the English or the Quebec authorities. Moreover, the husband was in arrears in respect of payments to his wife under a maintenance order. Despite the husband's re-marriage, the English court refused to recognise the divorce.

The operation of public policy was illustrated in *Kendall v Kendall* (1977). The husband and wife had their matrimonial home in England. In 1972, the husband was posted by his employers to Bolivia. In 1973, the wife joined him. In 1974, she returned to England with the children. Before she left Bolivia, she was induced by the husband to sign some papers in Spanish, a language she did not understand. The papers asked for a divorce, which she did not want. The husband told her that her signature was necessary to enable the children to leave the country. In 1975, the Bolivian court granted a divorce. This divorce was, however, refused recognition on the ground of public policy.

11.5 Financial relief after overseas divorce

Prior to the coming into force of Pt III of the Matrimonial and Family Proceedings Act 1984 (MFPA) on 16 September 1985, the general rule was that English courts were unable to grant relief on the basis of a foreign divorce. This problem led to proposals for reform made by the Law Commission in 1982 (Report No 117), which were enacted in Pt III of the MFPA 1984. The provisions contained therein apply whether the foreign divorce was obtained before or after Pt III came into effect as was held in *Chebaro v Chebaro* (1986).

Section 12 of the MFPA 1984 applies to the issue of financial relief requested after an overseas divorce and provides that:

(1)   Where:

    (a) a marriage has been dissolved or annulled, or the parties to a marriage have been legally separated, by means of judicial or other proceedings in an overseas country; and

    (b) the divorce, annulment or legal separation is entitled to be recognised as valid in England and Wales,

    either party to the marriage may apply to the court in the manner prescribed by rules of the court for an order for financial relief under this part of this Act.

Two points must be made in relation to this provision. First, s 12 covers annulments and legal separations as well as divorce. Secondly, either party may apply and, therefore, the provision is not limited to wives only.

If a party re-marries, then he or she loses the right to apply for relief by virtue of s 12(2) and (3). It is important to note, however, that no such application may be made unless the applicant satisfies the requirements set out in s 13. That is to say, no application for an order for financial relief shall be made under this part of the MFPA 1984 unless the leave of the court has been obtained in accordance with the rules of the court (s 13(1)), and the court shall not grant leave unless it considers that there is substantial ground for the making of an application for such an order (s 13(2)).

Clearly, s 13(1) operates as a filter mechanism in order to deter frivolous applications and ensure a qualified judge deals with the case (see *Holmes v Holmes* (1989)). And according to s 13(2), the existence of a foreign financial provision order is no bar to the English application. Nevertheless, according to s 13(3), the leave may be granted subject to conditions as the court thinks fit, such as an undertaking not to enforce a foreign order.

Where it appears to the court that the applicant or any child of the family 'is in immediate need of financial assistance', then by virtue of s 14, the court may grant interim orders for maintenance.

A further qualification to the English court jurisdiction is imposed by this Act, namely, that the parties must have a close connection with England in accordance with s 15(1). This provides that an English court will have jurisdiction to entertain an application for an order for financial relief if any of the following jurisdictional requirements are satisfied. That is to say:

(a) either of the parties to the marriage was domiciled in England and Wales on the date of the application for leave under s 13 above or was so domiciled on the date on which the divorce, annulment or legal separation obtained in the overseas country took effect in that country; or

(b) either of the parties to the marriage was habitually resident in England and Wales throughout the period of one year ending with the date of the application for leave or was so resident throughout the period of one year ending with the date on which the divorce, annulment or legal separation obtained in the overseas country took effect in that country; or

(c) either or both of the parties to the marriage had at the date of the application for leave a beneficial interest in possession in a dwelling-house situated in England or Wales which was at some time during the marriage a matrimonial home of the parties to the marriage.

Moreover, where the jurisdiction of the court to entertain proceedings under Pt III of the MFPA 1984 would fall to be determined by reference to the jurisdictional requirements imposed by virtue of Pt I of the CJJA 1982, the relevant provision is that contained in Art 5(2) of the Brussels Convention. This provides that, in matters relating to maintenance, a person domiciled in a Contracting State may be sued in the court for the place where the maintenance creditor is domiciled. Alternatively, if the matter is ancillary to proceedings concerning the status of a person, then that person may be sued in the court which, according to its own law, has jurisdiction to entertain those proceedings. This is so unless the court's jurisdiction is solely based on nationality. In such a case, s 15(2) of the MFPA 1984 provides that satisfying the requirements of s 15(1) above will not obviate the need to satisfy the requirements imposed by virtue of the CJJA 1982. On the other hand, satisfying the requirements imposed by virtue of the CJJA 1982 will obviate the need to satisfy the requirements of s 15(1) of the MFPA 1984.

Even if the jurisdictional criteria are satisfied, the court will not make an automatic order. Indeed, before making an order for financial relief, the court will consider whether, in all the circumstances of the case, it would be appropriate for such an order to be made by a court in England and Wales and, if the court is not satisfied that it would be appropriate, it will dismiss the application (s 16(1) of the MFPA 1984). In exercising its discretion, and according to s 16(2) of the MFPA 1984, the court will consider the following matters:

(a) the connection which the parties to the marriage have with England and Wales;

(b) the connection which those parties have with the country in which the marriage was dissolved or annulled or in which they were legally separated;

(c) the connection which those parties have with any other country outside England and Wales;

(d) any financial benefit which the applicant or a child of the family has received, or is likely to receive, in consequence of the divorce, annulment or legal separation, by virtue of any agreement or the operation of the law of a country outside England and Wales;

(e) in a case where an order has been made by a court in a country outside England and Wales requiring the other party to the marriage to make any payment or transfer any property for the benefit of the applicant or a child of the family, the financial relief given by the order and the extent to which the order has complied with or is likely to be complied with;

(f) any right which the applicant has, or has had, to apply for financial relief from the other party to the party to the marriage under the law of any country outside England and Wales and if the applicant has omitted to exercise that right the reason for that omission;

(g) the availability in England and Wales of any property in respect of which an order under this part of this Act in favour of the applicant could be made;

(h) the extent to which any order made under this part of this Act is likely to be enforceable;

(i) the length of time which elapsed since the date of the divorce, annulment or legal separation.

As to the forms of orders and relief available, these are contained in ss 17–27 of the MFPA 1984 (as amended by the FLA 1996), which make extremely detailed provisions in respect of such issues.

MATRIMONIAL CAUSES AND FINANCIAL RELIEF

Jurisdiction in divorce and legal separation

The English court will have jurisdiction to entertain proceedings for divorce or judicial separation if either of the parties to the marriage were domiciled or habitually resident in England at the time of the proceedings.

Stay of the proceedings

A mandatory stay has to be granted by the English court if it appears that proceedings for divorce or nullity in respect of the same marriage are pending elsewhere in the British Isles; the parties to the marriage have cohabited after its celebration; the place of residence at the date of those proceedings was that of other jurisdiction than in the British Isles; and either party was habitually resident in that jurisdiction for one year ending with the date on which they last resided there together.

A discretionary stay may be granted by the English court where it appears that any matrimonial proceedings capable of affecting the validity of the marriage in question are pending in another jurisdiction. The applicable test is that of *The Spiliada*.

Choice of law

Neither divorce nor judicial separation proceedings provoke a choice of law question. English courts have always applied English law.

Jurisdiction in nullity

An English court has jurisdiction to entertain proceedings for nullity, if either party was habitually resident for one year or domiciled in England, or if either of the parties died before that date and either was at death domiciled in England or had been habitually resident for one year ending with the date of the death.

A nullity decree may declare a marriage either void or voidable.

Choice of law

The applicable law in nullity suits depends on the classification of the relevant issue, that is, whether it is an issue of formal validity or an issue of essential validity.

Lack of parental consent has been classified as an issue of form.

In relation to defects affecting consent, such as fraud, duress, mental illness, and so forth, the weight of judicial opinion seems to favour reference of the issue of consent as one of essential validity and, therefore, subject to the law of domicile.

In relation to physical defects or incapacity, the position is unclear. Such defects have been classified as issues of form in some instances, and as issues of capacity in others.

Recognition of foreign divorces, legal separations and annulments

Where a decree is granted elsewhere than within the British Isles, it will be recognised, unless not granted by a court.

Where a decree is granted elsewhere by means of proceedings, it shall be recognised in England if it is effective under the law where it was obtained and at the relevant time either of the parties to the marriage was habitually resident, domiciled or a national of that country.

Recognition of extra-judicial divorces

An extra-judicial divorce, if pronounced in England, will not be recognised by English courts.

If, on the other hand, it was granted abroad, then it will be recognised if it is effective under the law of the country where it was obtained and, at that date, each party to the marriage was domiciled in that country, or either party was domiciled in that country and the other was domiciled in a country which recognises such a decree, provided that neither party was habitually resident in the UK for one year immediately preceding that date.

Grounds for non-recognition

A foreign decree may be refused recognition on policy grounds, such as want of proper notice, want of opportunity to take part, the absence of an official document, or contrary to public policy.

Financial relief after overseas decrees

Where the foreign decree is entitled to be recognised in England, either party to the marriage may apply to the court for an order for financial relief under the Matrimonial and Family Proceedings Act 1984, provided that either party to the marriage was habitually resident in England for one year ending with the date of the application; domiciled in England; or had a beneficial interest in property situated in England.

Prior to making the order, the court must consider all the relevant circumstances of the case and be satisfied that it would be appropriate to make such an order.

SECTIONS 691, 695 AND 725
OF THE COMPANIES ACT 1985

COMPANIES ACT 1985

(1985 c 6)

691 Documents to be delivered to registrar

(1) When a company incorporated outside Great Britain establishes a place of business in Great Britain, it shall within one month of doing so deliver to the registrar of companies for registration–

(a) a certified copy of the charter, statutes or memorandum and articles of the company or other instrument constituting or defining the company's constitution, and, if the instrument is not written in the English language, a certified translation of it; and

(b) a return in the prescribed form containing–

(i) a list of the company's directors and secretary, containing the particulars specified in the next sub-section;

(ii) a list of the names and addresses of some one or more persons resident in Great Britain authorised to accept on the company's behalf service of process and any notices required to be served on it;

(iii)a list of the documents delivered in compliance with paragraph (a) of this sub-section; and

(iv)a statutory declaration (made by a director or secretary of the company or by any person whose name and address are given in the list required by sub-paragraph (ii), stating the date on which the company's place of business in Great Britain was established ...

695 Service of documents on oversea company

(1) Any process or notice required to be served on an oversea company to which section 691 applies is sufficiently served if addressed to any person whose name has been delivered to the registrar under preceding sections of this Part and left at or sent by post to the address which has been so delivered.

(2) However–

(a) where such a company makes default in delivering to the registrar the name and address of a person resident in Great Britain who is authorised to accept on behalf of the company service of process or notices; or

(b) if at any time all the persons whose names and addresses have been so delivered are dead or have ceased so to reside, or refuse to accept service on the company's behalf, or for any reason cannot be served,

a document may be served on the company by leaving it at, or sending it by post to, any place of business established by the company in Great Britain.

725   Service of documents

(1) A document may be served on a company by leaving it at, or sending it by post to, the company's registered office.

(2) Where a company registered in Scotland carried on business in England and Wales, the process of any court in England and Wales may be served on the company by leaving it at, or sending it by post to, the company's principal place of business in England and Wales, addressed to the manager or other head officer in England and Wales of the company.

(3) Where process is served on a company under sub-section (2), the person issuing out the process shall send a copy of it by post to the company's registered office.

RSC ORDER 11 RULE 1(1) (EXTRACTS)

ORDER 11

Service of process out of the jurisdiction

General introduction: effect of the Civil Jurisdiction and Judgments Act 1982

In 1968, the members of the European Economic Community (EEC) signed a Convention at Brussels on civil jurisdiction and the enforcement of judgments. The United Kingdom acceded to the Convention in 1978, with modifications embodied in the Accession Convention. These Conventions have become part of the law of the United Kingdom by the Civil Jurisdiction and Judgment Act 1982 ('the Act') with effect from 1st January 1987. For further notes and the text of this Act, see Vol 2, Part 8.

The Civil Jurisdiction and Judgments Act 1991 incorporates the Lugano Convention into the 1982 Act. This will enable the EFTA countries, subject to minor modifications, to join the Brussels Convention regime.

The Act, and the rules which given effect to it in the procedure of the High Court have made important alterations; in particular *there is now power to serve writs and other process outside the jurisdiction without leave in a large number of cases.*

Principal cases in which service of writ out of jurisdiction is permissible (Order 11 rule 1)

1 (1) Provided that the writ does not contain any claim mentioned in Order 75 rule 2(1) and is not a writ to which paragraph (2) of this rule applies, service of a writ out of the jurisdiction is permissible with the leave of the Court if in the action begun by the writ:

(a) relief is sought against a person domiciled within the jurisdiction;

(b) an injunction is sought ordering the defendant to do or refrain from doing anything within the jurisdiction (whether or not damages are also claimed in respect of a failure to do or the doing of that thing);

(c) the claim is brought against a person duly served within or out of the jurisdiction and a person out of the jurisdiction is a necessary or a proper party thereto;

(d) the claim is brought to enforce, rescind, dissolve, annul or otherwise affect a contract or to recover damages or obtain other relief in respect of the breach of a contract, being (in either case) a contract which:

   (i) was made within the jurisdiction; or

   (ii) was made by or through an agent trading or residing within the jurisdiction on behalf of a principal trading or residing out of the jurisdiction; or

   (iii) is by its terms or by implication, governed by English law; or

   (iv) contains a term to the effect that the High Court shall have jurisdiction to hear and determine any action in respect of the contract;

(e) the claim is brought in respect of a breach committed within the jurisdiction of a contract made within or out of the jurisdiction, and irrespective of the fact, if such be the case, that the breach was preceded or accompanied by a breach committed out of the jurisdiction that rendered impossible the performance of so much of the contract as ought to have been performed within the jurisdiction;

(f) the claim is founded on a tort and the damage was sustained, or resulted from an act committed, within the jurisdiction;

(g) the whole subject-matter of the action is land situate within the jurisdiction (with or without rents or profits) or the perpetuation of testimony relating to land so situate;

(h) the claim is brought to construe, rectify, set aside or enforce an act, deed, will, contract, obligation or liability affecting land situate within the jurisdiction;

(i) the claim is made for a debt secured on immovable property or is made to assert, declare or determine proprietary or possessory rights, or rights of security, in or over movable property, or to obtain authority to dispose of movable property, situate within the jurisdiction;

(j) the claim is brought to execute the trusts of a written instrument being trusts that ought to be executed according to English law and of which the person to be served with the writ is a trustee, or for any relief or remedy which might be obtained in any such action;

(k) the claim is made for the administration of the estate of a person who died domiciled within the jurisdiction or for any relief or remedy which might be obtained in any such action;

(l) the claim is brought in a probate action within the meaning of Order 76;

(m) the claim is brought to enforce any judgment or arbitral award;

(n) the claim is brought against a defendant not domiciled in Scotland or Northern Ireland in respect of a claim by the Commissioners of Inland Revenue for or in relation to any of the duties or taxes which have been, or are for the time being, placed under their care and management;

(o) the claim is brought under the Nuclear Installations Act 1965 or in respect of contributions under the Social Security Act 1975;

(p) the claim is made for a sum to which the Directive of the Council of the European Communities dated 25th March 1976 No 76/308/EEC applies, and service is to be effected in a country which is a member State of the European Economic Community;

(q) the claim is made under the Drug Trafficking Offences Act 1986;

(r) the claim is made under the Financial Services Act 1986 or the Banking Act 1987;

(s) the claim is made under Part VI of the Criminal Justice Act 1988;

(t) the claim is brought for money had and received or for an account or other relief against the defendant as constructive trustee, and the defendant's alleged liability arises out of acts committed, whether by him or otherwise, within the jurisdiction.

SECTIONS 41 TO 46 OF THE CIVIL JURISDICTION AND JUDGMENTS ACT 1982

DOMICILE

41 (1) Subject to Article 52 (which contains provisions for determining whether a party is domiciled in a Contracting State), the following provisions of this section determine, for the purposes of the 1968 Convention and this Act, whether an individual is domiciled the United Kingdom or in a particular part of, or place in, the United Kingdom or in a State other than a Contracting State.

(2) An individual is domiciled in the United Kingdom if and only if:

(a) he is resident in the United Kingdom; and

(b) the nature and circumstances of his residence indicate that he has a substantial connection with the United Kingdom.

(3) Subject to sub-section (5), and individual is domiciled in a particular part of the United Kingdom if and only if:

(a) he is resident in that part; and

(b) the nature and circumstances of his residence indicate that he has a substantial connection with that part.

(4) An individual is domiciled in a particular place in the United Kingdom if and only if he:

(a) is domiciled in the part of the United Kingdom in which that place is situated; and

(b) is resident in that place.

(5) An individual who is domiciled in the United Kingdom but in whose case the requirements of sub-section (3)(b) are not satisfied in relation to any particular part of the United Kingdom shall be treated as domiciled in the part of the United Kingdom in which he is resident.

(6) In the case of an individual who:

(a) is resident in the United Kingdom, or in a particular part of the United Kingdom; and

(b) has been so resident for the last three months or more,

the requirements of sub-section (2)(b) or, as the case may be, sub-section (3)(b) shall be presumed to be fulfilled unless the contrary is proved.

(7) An individual is domiciled in a State other than a Contracting State if and only if:

(a) he is resident in that State; and

(b) the nature and circumstances of his residence indicate that he has a substantial connection with that State.

42 (1) For the purposes of this Act the seat of a corporation or association (as determined by this section) shall be treated as its domicile.

(2) The following provisions of this section determine where a corporation or association has its seat:

(a) for the purpose of Article 53 (which for the purpose of the 1968 Convention equates the domicile of such a body with its seat); and

(b) for the purposes of this Act other than the provisions mentioned in section 42(1)(b) and (c).

(3) A corporation or association has its seat in the United Kingdom if and only if:

(a) it was incorporated or formed under the law of a part of the United Kingdom and has its registered office or some other official address in the United Kingdom; or

(b) its central management and control is exercised in the United Kingdom.

(4) A corporation or association has its seat in a particular part of the United Kingdom if and only if it has its seat in the United Kingdom and:

(a) it has its registered office or some other official address in that part; or

(b) its central management and control is exercised in that part; or

(c) it has a place of business in that part.

(5) A corporation or association has its seat in a particular place in the United Kingdom if and only if it has its seat in the part of the United Kingdom in which that place is situated and:

(a) it has its registered office or some other official address in that place; or

(b) its central management and control is exercised in that place; or

(c) it has a place of business in that place.

(6) Subject to sub-section (7), a corporation or association has its seat in a State other than the United Kingdom if and only if:

(a) it was incorporated or formed under the law of that State and has its registered office or some other official address there; or

(b) its central management and control is exercised in that State.

(7) A corporation or other association shall not be regarded as having its seat in a Contracting State other than the United Kingdom if it is shown that the courts of that State would not regard it as having its seat there.

(8) In this section:

'business' includes any activity carried on by a corporation or association, and 'place of business' shall be construed accordingly;

'official address', in relation to a corporation or association, means an address which it is required by law to register, notify or maintain for the purpose of receiving notices or other communications.

43 (1) The following provisions of this section determine where a corporation or association has its seat for the purposes of:

(a) Article 16(2) (which confers exclusive jurisdiction over proceedings relating to the formation or dissolution of such bodies, or to the decisions of their organs);

(b) Articles 5A and 16(2) in Schedule 4; and

(c) rules 2(12) and 4(1)(b) in Schedule 8.

(2) A corporation or association has its seat in the United Kingdom if and only if:

(a) it was incorporated or formed under the law of a part of the United Kingdom; or

(b) its central management and control is exercised in the United Kingdom.

(3) A corporation or association has its seat in a particular part of the United Kingdom if and only if it has its seat in the United Kingdom and:

(a) subject to sub-section (5), it was incorporated or formed under the law of that part; or

(b) being incorporated or formed under the law of a State other than the United Kingdom, its central management and control is exercised in that part.

(4) A corporation or association has its seat in a particular place in Scotland if and only if it has its seat in Scotland and:

(a) it has its registered office or some other official address in that place; or

(b) it has no registered office or other official address in Scotland, but its central management and control is exercised in that place.

(5) A corporation or association incorporated or formed under:

(a) an enactment forming part of the law of more than one part of the United Kingdom; or

(b) an instrument having effect in the domestic law of more than one part of the United Kingdom,

shall, if it has a registered office, be taken to have its seat in the part of the United Kingdom in which that office is situated, and not in any other part of the United Kingdom.

(6) Subject to sub-section (7), a corporation or association has its seat in a Contracting State other than the United Kingdom if and only if:

(a) it was incorporated or formed under the law of that State; or

(b) its central management and control is exercised in that State.

(7) A corporation or association shall not be regarded as having its seat in a Contracting State other than the United Kingdom if:

    (a) it has its seat in the United Kingdom by virtue of sub-section (2)(a); or

    (b) it is shown that the courts of that other State would not regard it for the purposes of Article 16(2) as having its seat there.

    (8) In this section 'official address' has the same meaning as in section 42.

44 (1) This section applies to:

    (a) proceedings within Section 3 of Title II of the 1968 Convention (insurance contracts); and

    (b) proceedings within Section 4 of that Title (consumer contracts).

(2) A person who, for the purposes of proceedings to which this section applies, arising out of the operations of a branch, agency or other establishment in the United Kingdom, is deemed for the purposes of the 1968 Convention to be domiciled in the United Kingdom by virtue of:

    (a) Article 8, second paragraph (insurers); or

    (b) Article 13, second paragraph (suppliers of goods, services or credit to consumers),

shall, for the purposes of those proceedings, be treated for the purposes of this Act as so domiciled and as in the part of the United Kingdom in which the branch, agency or establishment in question is situated.

45 (1) The following provisions of this section determine, for the purposes of the 1968 Convention and this Act, where a trust is domiciled.

(2) A trust is domiciled in the United Kingdom if and only if it is by virtue of sub-section (3) domiciled in a part of the United Kingdom.

(3) A trust is domiciled in a part of the United Kingdom if and only if the system of law of that part is the system of law with which the trust has its closet and most real connection.

46 (1) For the purposes of this Act the seat of the Crown (as determined by this section) shall be treated as its domicile.

(2) The following provisions of this section determine where the Crown has its seat:

    (a) for the purposes of the 1968 Convention (in which Article 53 equates the domicile of a legal person with its seat); and

    (b) for the purposes of this Act.

(3) Subject to the provisions of any Order in Council for the time being in force under sub-section (4):

    (a) the Crown in right of Her Majesty's government in the United Kingdom has its seat in every part of, and every place in, the United Kingdom; and

(b) the Crown in right of Her Majesty's government in Northern Ireland has its seat in, and in every place in, Northern Ireland.

(4) Her Majesty may by Order in Council provide that, in the case of proceedings of any specified description against the Crown in right of Her Majesty's government in the United Kingdom, the Crown shall be treated for the purposes of the 1968 Convention and this Act as having its seat in, and in every place in, a specified part of the United Kingdom and not in any other part of the United Kingdom.

(5) An Order in Council under sub-section (4) may frame a description of proceedings in any way, and in particular may do so by reference to the government department or officer of the Crown against which or against whom they fall to be instituted.

(6) Any Order in Council made under this section shall be subject to annulment in pursuance of a resolution of either House of Parliament.

(7) Nothing in this section applies to the Crown otherwise than in right of Her Majesty's government in the United Kingdom or Her Majesty's government in Northern Ireland.

THE CIVIL JURISDICTION AND JUDGMENTS ACT 1982 (AMENDMENT) ORDER 1990

STATUTORY INSTRUMENTS

(1990 No 2591)

JUDGMENTS

THE CIVIL JURISDICTION AND JUDGMENTS ACT 1982

(AMENDMENT) ORDER 1990

Made .... *19th December 1990*

Coming into force in accordance with Article 1

At the Court at Buckingham Palace, the 19th day of December 1990

Present:

The Queen's Most Excellent Majesty in Council

Whereas a Convention on Jurisdiction and the Enforcement of Judgments in Civil and Commercial Matters[a] was signed on 27th September 1968;

And whereas a Protocol on the Interpretation of the Convention by the Court of Justice of the European Communities[b] was signed on 3rd June 1971;

And whereas a Convention on the accession of the Kingdom of Denmark, Ireland and the United Kingdom of Great Britain and Northern Ireland to the Convention[c] signed by Her Majesty's Government on 9th October 1978, was ratified on 7th October 1986 by Her Majesty's Government and entered into force for the United Kingdom on 1st January 1987;

And whereas the Civil Jurisdiction and Judgments Act 1982[d] gave the force of law to these Conventions and to the Protocol in the United Kingdom;

And whereas by section 14(1) of that Act, if at any time it appears to Her Majesty in Council that Her Majesty's Government in the United Kingdom has

---

(a) OJ L304/36, 1978.
(b) OJ L304/50, 1978.
(c) OJ L304/1, 1978.
(d) 1982 c 27, as amended by SI 1989/1346.

agreed to a revision of either of these Conventions or the Protocol, including in particular any revision connected with the accession to the 1968 Convention of one of more further States, Her Majesty may by Order in Council make such modifications of that Act as Her Majesty considers appropriate in consequence of the revision;

And whereas a Convention on the accession of the Kingdom of Spain and the Portuguese Republic to the 1968 Convention[(e)] was signed on 26 May 1989, and in consequence Her Majesty's Government in the United Kingdom has agreed to a revision of the above mentioned Conventions and Protocol:

And whereas each House of Parliament has by a resolution approved a draft of this Order:

Now, therefore, Her Majesty, in exercise of the powers conferred on Her by section 14 of the Civil Jurisdiction and Judgments Act 1982 and of all other powers enabling Her in that behalf, is pleased, by and with the advice of Her Privy Council, to order, and it is hereby ordered, as follows:

1   This Order may be cited as the Civil Jurisdiction and Judgments Act 1982 (Amendment) Order 1990. It shall come into force on the date on which the Convention or the accession of the Kingdom of Spain and the Portuguese Republic to the 1968 Convention and to the Protocol enters into force in respect of the United Kingdom which date shall be notified in the London, Edinburgh and Belfast Gazettes.

2   In this Order 'the Act' means the Civil Jurisdiction and Judgments Act 1982.

3   The following shall be inserted before the final item in section 1(1) of the Act–

    '"the 1989 Accession Convention" means the Convention on the accession of the Kingdom of Spain and the Portuguese Republic to the 1968 Convention and the 1971 Protocol, with the adjustments made to them by the Accession Convention and the 1982 Accession Convention, signed at Donostia – San Sebastian on 26th May 1989.'

4   The following shall be substituted for the final item in section 1(1) of the Act:

    '"the Conventions" means the 1968 Convention, the 1971 Protocol, the Accession Convention, the 1982 Accession Convention and the 1989 Accession Convention.'

5   The following shall be substituted for section 1(2)(a) of the Act–

    '(a) references to, or to any provision of, the 1968 Convention or the 1971 Protocol are references to that Convention, Protocol or provision as amended by the Accession Convention, the 1982 Accession Convention and the 1989 Accession Convention; and'.

(e) OJ L285/1, 1989.

6   The following shall be substituted for section 1(3) of the Act–

'(3) In this Act "Contracting State" means:

(a) one of the original parties to the 1968 Convention (Belgium, the Federal Republic of Germany, France, Italy, Luxembourg and The Netherlands);

or

(b) one of the parties acceding to that Convention under the Accession Convention (Denmark, the Republic of Ireland and the United Kingdom), or under the 1982 Accession Convention (the Hellenic Republic), or under the 1989 Accession Convention (Spain and Portugal),

being a State in respect of which the Accession Convention has entered into force in accordance with Article 39 of that Convention, or being a state in respect of which the 1982 Accession Convention has entered into force in accordance with Article 15 of that Convention, or being a State in respect of which the 1989 Accession Convention has entered into force in accordance with Article 32 of that Convention, as the case might be.'

7   The following shall be substituted for section 2(2) of the Act–

'(2) For convenience of reference there are set out in Schedules 1, 2, 3, 3A and 3B respectively the English texts of–

(a) the 1968 Convention as amended by Titles II and III of the Accession Convention, by Titles II and III of the 1982 Accession Convention and by Titles II and III of, and Annex I(d) to, the 1989 Accession Convention;

(b) the 1971 Protocol as amended by Title IV of the Accession Convention, by Title IV of the 1982 Accession Convention and by Title IV of the 1989 Accession Convention;

(c) Titles V and VI of the Accession Convention (transitional and final provisions) as amended by Title V of the 1989 Accession Convention;

(d) Titles V and VI of the 1982 Accession Convention (transitional and final provisions); and

(e) Titles VI and VII of the 1989 Accession Convention (transitional and final provisions),

being texts prepared from the authentic English texts referred to in Articles 37 and 41 of the Accession Convention, in Article 17 of the 1982 Accession Convention and in Article 34 of the 1989 Accession Convention.'

8   The following shall be inserted after paragraph (c) of section 3(3) of the Act–

': and

(d) the report by Mr Martinho de Almeida Cruz, Mr Manuel Desantes Real and Mr P Jenard on the 1989 Accession Convention.[a]'

9 The following shall be substituted for the first item in section 50 of the Act–

'...: "the Accession Convention", "the 1982 Accession Convention" and "the 1989 Accession Convention" have the meaning given by section 1(1);'.

10 The following shall be substituted for section 39(2)(c) and (d) of the Act–

'(c) any colony'.

11 The following shall be substituted for section 52(2)(c) and (d) of the Act–

'(c) any colony'.

12 (1) The text set out in Schedule 1 to this Order shall be substituted for the text set out in Schedule 1 to the Act.

(2) The text set out in Schedule 2 to this Order shall be substituted for the text set out in Schedule 2 to the Act.

(3) The text set out in Schedule 3 to this Order shall be substituted for the text set out in Schedule 3 to the Act.

(4) The text set out in Schedule 4 to this Order shall be inserted after Schedule 3A to the Act.

GI de Deney
Clerk to the Privy Council

(a) OJ C189/35, 1990.

SCHEDULES

SCHEDULE 1

TEXT OF 1968 CONVENTION, AS AMENDED

ARRANGEMENT OF PROVISIONS

TITLE I   SCOPE (ARTICLE 1)

TITLE II JURISDICTION

Section 1   General provisions (Articles 2–4)

Section 2   Special jurisdiction (Articles 5–6A)

Section 3   Jurisdiction in matters relating to insurance (Articles 7–12A)

Section 4   Jurisdiction over consumer contracts (Articles 13–15)

Section 5   Exclusive jurisdiction (Article 16)

Section 6   Prorogation of jurisdiction (Articles 17 and 18)

Section 7   Examination as to jurisdiction and admissibility (Articles 19 and 20)

Section 8   *Lis pendens* – related actions (Articles 21–23)

Section 9   Provisional, including protective measures (Article 24)

TITLE III RECOGNITION AND ENFORCEMENT

Definition of judgment (Article 25)

Section 1   Recognition (Articles 26–30)

Section 2   Enforcement (Articles 31–45)

Section 3   Common provisions (Articles 46–49)

TITLE IV AUTHENTIC INSTRUMENTS AND COURT SETTLEMENTS (ARTICLES 50 AND 51)

TITLE V GENERAL PROVISIONS (ARTICLES 52 AND 53)

TITLE VI TRANSITIONAL PROVISIONS (ARTICLES 54 AND 54A)

TITLE VII RELATIONSHIP TO OTHER CONVENTIONS (ARTICLES 55–59)

TITLE VIII FINAL PROVISIONS (ARTICLES 60–68)

CONVENTION

ON JURISDICTION AND THE ENFORCEMENT OF JUDGMENTS
IN CIVIL AND COMMERCIAL MATTERS

PREAMBLE

**THE HIGH CONTRACTING PARTIES TO THE TREATY
ESTABLISHING THE EUROPEAN ECONOMIC COMMUNITY**

Desiring to implement the provisions of Article 220 of that Treaty by virtue of which they undertook to secure the simplification of formalities governing the reciprocal recognition and enforcement of judgments of courts or tribunals;

Anxious to strengthen in the Community the legal protection of persons therein established;

Considering that it is necessary for this purpose to determine the international jurisdiction of their courts, to facilitate recognition and to introduce an expeditious procedure for securing the enforcement of judgments, authentic instruments and court settlements;

Have decided to conclude this Convention and to this end have designated as their Plenipotentiaries;

(Designations of Plenipotentiaries of the original six Contracting States)

WHO, meeting within the Council, having exchanged their Full Powers, found in good and due form.

HAVE AGREED AS FOLLOWS:

TITLE I
SCOPE

Article 1

This Convention shall apply in civil and commercial matters whatever the nature of the court or tribunal. It shall not extend, in particular, to revenue, customs or administrative matters.

The Convention shall not apply to–

1 The status or legal capacity of natural persons, rights in property arising out of a matrimonial relationship, wills and succession.

2 Bankruptcy proceedings relating to the winding up of insolvent companies or other legal persons, judicial arrangements, compositions and analogous proceedings.

3 Social security.

4 Arbitration.

TITLE II
JURISDICTION

Section 1
General provisions

Article 2

Subject to the provisions of this Convention, persons domiciled in a Contracting State shall whatever their nationality, be sued in the courts of that State.

Persons who are not nationals of the State in which they are domiciled shall be governed by the rules of jurisdiction applicable to nationals of that State.

Article 3

Persons domiciled in a Contracting State may be sued in the courts of another Contracting State only by virtue of the rules set out in Sections 2–6 of this Title.

In particular the following provisions shall not be applicable as against them–

- in Belgium: Article 15 of the civil code (Code civil – Burgerlijk Wetboek) and Article 638 of the judicial code (Code judiciaire – Gerechtelijk Wetboek).
- in Denmark: Article 246(2) and (3) of the law on civil procedure (Lov om rettend pleje).
- in the Federal Republic of Germany: Article 23 of the code of civil procedure (Zivilprozeβordnung).
- in Greece: Article 40 of the code of civil procedure (Κ ϖ δικας Πολιτικης Δικουομιας).
- in France: Articles 14 and 15 of the civil code (Code civil).
- in Ireland: the rules which enable jurisdiction to be founded on the document instituting the proceedings having been served on the defendant during his temporary presence in Ireland.
- in Italy: Articles 2 and 4, nos 1 and 2 of the code of civil procedure (Codice di procedura civile).
- in Luxembourg: Articles 14 and 15 of the civil code (Code civil).
- in the Netherlands: Articles 126(3) and 127 of the code of civil procedure (Wetboek van Burgerlijke Rechtsvordering).
- in Portugal: Article 651)(c), Article 65(2) and Article 65A(c) of the code of civil procedure (Código de Processo de Trabalho).
- in the United Kingdom: the rules which enable jurisdiction to be founded on:

(a) the document instituting the proceedings having been served on the defendant during his temporary presence in the United Kingdom; or

(b) the presence within the United Kingdom of property belonging to the defendant; or

(c) the seizure by the plaintiff of property situated in the United Kingdom.

Article 4

If the defendant is not domiciled in a Contracting State, the jurisdiction of the courts of each Contracting State shall, subject to the provisions of Article 16, be determined by the law of that State.

As against such a defendant, any person domiciled in a Contracting State may, whatever his nationality, avail himself in that State of the rules of jurisdiction there in force, and in particular those specified in the second paragraph of Article 3, in the same way as the nationals of that State.

Section 2

Special jurisdiction

Article 5

A person domiciled in a Contracting State may, in another Contracting State be sued–

1   In matters relating to a contract, in the courts for the place of performance of the obligation in question; in matters relating to individual contracts of employment this place is that where the employee habitually carries out his work, or if the employee does not habitually carry out his work in any one country, the employer may also be sued in the courts for the place where the business which engaged the employee was or is now situated.

2   In matters relating to maintenance in the courts for the place where the maintenance creditor is domiciled or habitually resident or if the matter is ancillary to proceedings concerning the status of a person in the court which, according to its own law has jurisdiction to entertain those proceedings unless that jurisdiction is based solely on the nationality of one of the parties.

3   In matters relating to tort, delict or quasi-delict in the courts for the place where the harmful event occurred.

4   As regards a civil claim for damages or restitution which is based on an act giving rise to criminal proceedings in the court seised of those proceedings to the extent that that court has jurisdiction under its own law to entertain civil proceedings.

5   As regards a dispute arising out of the operations of a branch, agency or other establishment in the courts for the place in which the branch, agency or other establishment is situated.

6   As settlor, trustee or beneficiary of a trust created by the operation of a statute or by a written instrument or created orally and evidenced in writing in the courts of the Contracting State in which the trust is domiciled.

7   As regards a dispute concerning the payment of remuneration claimed in respect of the salvage of a cargo or freight in the court under the authority of which the cargo or freight in question–

(a) has been arrested to secure such payment; or

(b) could have been so arrested but bail or other security has been given;

provided that this provision shall apply only if it is claimed that the defendant has an interest in the cargo or freight or had such an interest at the time of salvage.

Article 6

A person domiciled in a Contracting State may also be sued–

1   Where he is one of a number of defendants in the courts for the place where any one of them is domiciled.

2   As a third party in an action on a warranty or guarantee or in any other third party proceedings in the court seised of the original proceedings unless these were instituted solely with the object of removing him from the jurisdiction of the court which would be competent in his case.

3   On a counterclaim arising from the same contract or facts on which the original claim was based, in the court in which the original claim is pending.

4   In matters relating to a contract, if the action may be combined with an action against the same defendant in matters relating to rights *in rem* in immovable property, in the court of the Contracting State in which the property is situated.

Article 6a

Where by virtue of this Convention a court of a Contracting State has jurisdiction in actions relating to liability from the use or operation of a ship, that court or any other court substituted for this purpose by the internal law of that State shall also have jurisdiction over claims for limitation of such liability.

Section 3
Jurisdiction in matters relating to insurance

Article 7

In matters relating to insurance, jurisdiction shall be determined by this Section, without the prejudice to the provisions of Articles 4 and 5 point 5.

Article 8

An insurer domiciled in a Contracting State may be sued–

1   In the courts of the State where he is domiciled, or

2   In another Contracting State in the courts for the place where the policy-holder is domiciled, or

3   If he is a co-insurer in the courts of a Contracting State in which proceedings are brought against the leading insurer.

An insurer who is not domiciled in a Contracting State but has a branch agency or other establishment in one of the Contracting States shall in disputes arising out of the operations of the branch agency or establishment be deemed to be domiciled in that State.

Article 9

In respect of liability insurance or insurance of immovable property the insurer may in addition be sued in the courts for the place where the harmful event occurred. The same applies if movable and immovable property are covered by the same insurance policy and both are adversely affected by the same contingency.

Article 10

In respect of liability insurance, the insurer may also, if the law of the court permits it be joined in proceedings which the injured party had brought against the insured.

The provisions of Articles 7, 8 and 9 shall apply to actions brought by the injured party directly against the insurer, where such direct actions are permitted.

If the law governing such direct actions provides that the policy-holder or the insurance may be joined as a party to the action the same court shall have jurisdiction over them.

Article 11

Without prejudice to the provisions of the third paragraph of Article 10 an insurer may bring proceedings only in the courts of the Contracting State in which the defendant is domiciled irrespective of whether he is the policy-holder, the insured or a beneficiary.

The provision of this Section shall not affect the right to bring a counterclaim in the court in which, in accordance with this Section, the original claim is pending.

Article 12

The provisions of this Section may be departed from only by an agreement on jurisdiction–

1   Which is entered into after the dispute has arisen, or

2   Which allows the policy-holder, the insured or a beneficiary to bring proceedings in courts other than those indicated in this Section, or

3   Which is concluded between a policy-holder and an insurer both of whom are domiciled in the same Contracting State and which has the effect of conferring jurisdiction on the courts of that State even if the harmful event were to occur abroad, provided that such an agreement is not contrary to the law of that State, or

4   Which is concluded with a policy-holder who is not domiciled in a Contracting State except in so far as the insurance is compulsory or relates to immovable property in a Contracting State, or

5   Which relates to a contract of insurance in so far as it covers one or more of the risks set out in Article 12a.

Article 12a

The following are the risks referred to in point 5 of Article 12–

1   Any loss of or damage to–
   (a) sea-going ships, installations situated offshore or on the high seas, or aircraft arising from perils which relate to their use for commercial purposes;
   (b) goods in transit other than passengers' baggage where the transit consists of or includes carriage by such ships or aircraft.

2   Any liability other than for bodily injury to passengers or loss of or damage to their baggage–
   (a) arising out of the use of operation of ships, installations or aircraft as referred to in point 1(a) above in so far as the law of the Contracting State in which such aircraft are registered does not prohibit agreements on jurisdiction regarding insurance of such risks;
   (b) for loss or damage caused by goods in transmit as described in point 1(b) above.

3   Any financial loss connected with the use or operation of ships, installations or aircraft as referred to in point 1(a) above, in particular loss of freight or charter-hire.

4   Any risk or interest connected with any of those referred to in points 1 to 3 above.

Section 4

Jurisdiction over consumer contracts

Article 13

In proceedings concerning a contract concluded by a person for a purpose which can be regarded as being outside his trade or profession, hereinafter called 'the consumer', jurisdiction shall be determined by this Section, without prejudice to the provisions of Article 4 and point 5 of Article 5, if it is:

1   A contract for the sale of goods on instalment credit terms, or

2   A contract for a loan repayable by instalments or for any other form of credit, made to finance the sale of goods, or

3   Any other contract for the supply of goods or a contract for the supply of services and:

   (a) in the State of the consumer's domicile the conclusion of the contract was preceded by a specific invitation addressed to him or by advertising; and

   (b) the consumer took in that State the steps necessary for the conclusion of the contract.

Where a consumer enters into a contract with a party who is not domiciled in a Contracting State but has a branch, agency or other establishment in one of the Contracting States, that party shall, in disputes arising out of the operation of the branch, agency or establishment, be deemed to be domiciled in that State.

   This section shall not apply to contracts of transport.

Article 14

A consumer may bring proceedings against the other party to a contract either in the courts of the Contracting State in which that party is domiciled or in the courts of the Contracting State in which he is himself domiciled.

   Proceedings may be brought against a consumer by the other party to the contract only in the courts of the Contracting State in which the consumer is domiciled.

   These provisions shall not affect the right to bring a counterclaim in the court in which, in accordance with this Section, the original claim is pending.

Article 15

The provisions of this Section may be departed from only by an agreement:

1   Which is entered into after the dispute has arisen, or

2   Which allowed the consumer to bring proceedings in courts other than those indicated in this section, or

3   Which is entered into by the consumer and the other party to the contract, both of whom are at the time of conclusion of the contract domiciled or habitually resident in the same Contracting State and which confers jurisdiction on the courts of that State, provided that such an agreement is not contrary to the law of that State.

Section 5
Exclusive jurisdiction

Article 16

The following courts shall have exclusive jurisdiction regardless of domicile:

1   (a) In proceedings which have as their object rights in rem in immovable property or tenancies of immovable property, the courts of the Contracting State in which the property is situated;

    (b) However, in proceedings which have as their object tenancies of immovable property concluded for temporary private use for a maximum period of six consecutive months, the courts of the Contracting State in which the defendant is domiciled shall also have jurisdiction provided that the landlord and the tenant are natural persons and are domiciled in the same Contracting State.

2   In proceedings which have as their object the validity of the constitution, the nullity or the dissolution of companies or other legal persons or associations of natural or legal persons or the decisions of their organs, the courts of the Contracting State in which the company, legal person or association has its seat.

3   In proceedings which have as their object the validity of entries in public registers, the courts of the Contracting State in which the register is kept.

4   In proceedings concerned with the resignation or validity of patents, trade marks, designs or other similar rights required to be deposited or registered, the courts of the Contracting State in which the deposit or registration has been applied for, has taken place or is under the terms of an international convention deemed to have taken place.

5   In proceedings concerned with the enforcement of judgments, the courts of the Contracting State in which the judgment has been or is to be enforced.

Section 6
Prorogation of jurisdiction

Article 17

If the parties, one or more of whom is domiciled in a Contracting State, have agreed that a court or the courts of a Contracting State are to have jurisdiction to settle any disputes which have arisen or which may arise in connection with a particular legal relationship, that court or those courts shall have exclusive jurisdiction. Such an agreement conferring jurisdiction shall be either–

(a) in writing or evidenced in writing, or

(b) in a form which accords with practices which the parties have established between themselves, or

(c) in international trade or commerce, in a form which accords with a usage of which the parties are or ought to have been aware and which in such trade or commerce is widely known to, and regularly observed by parties to contracts of the type involved in the particular trade or commerce concerned.

Where such an agreement is concluded by parties, none of whom is domiciled in a Contracting State, the courts of other Contracting States shall have no jurisdiction over their disputes unless the court or courts chosen have declined jurisdiction.

The court or courts of a Contracting State on which a trust instrument has conferred jurisdiction shall have exclusive jurisdiction in any proceedings brought against a settlor, trustee or beneficiary, if relations between these persons or their rights or obligations under the trust are involved.

Agreements or provisions of a trust instrument conferring jurisdiction shall have no legal force if they are contrary to the provisions of Articles 12 or 15, or if the courts whose jurisdiction they purport to exclude have exclusive jurisdiction by virtue of Article 16.

If an agreement conferring jurisdiction was concluded for the benefit of only one of the parties that party shall retain the right to bring proceedings in any other court which has jurisdiction by virtue of this Convention.

In matters relating to individual contracts of employment an agreement conferring jurisdiction shall have legal force only if it is entered into after the dispute has arisen or if the employee invokes it to seise courts other than those for the defendant's domicile or those specified in Article 5(1).

Article 18

Apart from jurisdiction derived from other provisions of this Convention a court of a Contracting State before whom a defendant enters an appearance shall have jurisdiction. This rule shall not apply where appearance was entered solely to contest the jurisdiction, or where another court has exclusive jurisdiction by virtue of Article 16.

Section 7

Examination as to jurisdiction and admissibility

Article 19

Where a court of the Contracting State is seised of a claim which is principally concerned with a matter over which the courts of another Contracting State have exclusive jurisdiction by virtue of Article 16, it shall declare of its own motion that it has no jurisdiction.

Article 20

Where a defendant domiciled in one Contracting State is sued in a court of another Contracting State and does not enter an appearance, the court shall declare of its own motion that it has no jurisdiction unless its jurisdiction is derived from the provisions of the Convention.

The court shall stay the proceedings so long as it is not shown that the defendant has been able to receive the document instituting the proceedings or an equivalent document in sufficient time to enable him to arrange for his defence, or that all necessary steps have been taken to this end.

The provisions of the foregoing paragraph shall be replaced by those of Article 15 of the Hague Convention of 15th November 1965 on the service abroad of judicial and extrajudicial documents in civil or commercial matters, if the document instituting the proceedings or notice thereof had to be transmitted abroad in accordance with that Convention.

Section 8

Lis pendens – related actions

Article 21

Where proceedings involving the same cause of action and between the same parties are brought in the courts of different Contracting States, any court other than the court first seised shall of its own motion stay its proceedings until such time as the jurisdiction of the court first seised is established.

Where the jurisdiction of the court first seised is established, any court other than the court first seised shall decline jurisdiction in favour of that court.

Article 22

Where related actions are brought in the courts of different Contracting States, any court other than the court first seised may, while the actions are pending at first instance, stay its proceedings.

A court other than the court first seised may also, on the application of one of the parties, decline jurisdiction if the law of that court permits the consolidation of related actions and the court first seised has jurisdiction over both actions.

For the purposes of this Article, actions are deemed to be related where they are so closely connected that it is expedient to hear and determine them together to avoid the risk of irreconcilable judgments resulting from separate proceedings.

Article 23

Where actions come within the exclusive jurisdiction of several courts, any court other than the court first seised shall decline jurisdiction in favour of that court.

Section 9
Provisional including protective measures

Article 24

Application may be made to the courts of a Contracting State for such provisional, including protective measures as may be available under the law of that State, even if, under this Convention, the courts of another Contracting State have jurisdiction as to the substance of the matter.

TITLE III
RECOGNITION AND ENFORCEMENT

Article 25

For the purposes of this Convention 'judgment' means any judgment given by a court or tribunal of a Contracting State, whatever the judgment may be called, including a decree, order, decision or writ of execution as well as the determination of costs or expenses by an officer of the court.

Section 1
Recognition

Article 26

A judgment given in a Contracting State shall be recognised in the other Contracting States without any special procedure being required.

Any interested party who raises the recognition of a judgment as the principal issue in a dispute may, in accordance with the procedures provided for in Sections 2 and 3 of this Title, apply for a decision that the judgment be recognised.

If the outcome of proceedings in a court of a Contracting State depends on the determination of an incidental question of recognition that court shall have jurisdiction over that question.

Article 27

A judgment shall not be recognised–

1 If such recognition is contrary to public policy in the State in which recognition is sought.

2 Where it was given in default of appearance, if the defendant was not duly served with the document which instituted the proceedings or with an equivalent document in sufficient time to enable him to arrange for his defence.

3 If the judgment is irreconcilable with a judgment given in a dispute between the same parties in the State in which recognition is sought.

4 If the court of the State of origin, in order to arrive at its judgment has decided a preliminary question concerning the status or legal capacity of natural persons, rights in property arising out of a matrimonial relationship, wills or succession in a way that conflicts with a rule of the private international law of the State in which the recognition is sought, unless the same result would have been reached by the application of the rules of private international law of that State.

5 If the judgment is irreconcilable with an earlier judgment given in a non-contracting State involving the same cause of action and between the same parties, provided that this latter judgment fulfils the conditions necessary for its recognition in the state addressed.

Article 28

Moreover, a judgment shall not be recognised if it conflicts with the provisions of Sections 3, 4 or 5 of Title II, or in a case provided for in Article 59.

In its examination of the grounds of jurisdiction referred to in the foregoing paragraph, the court or authority applied to shall be bound by the findings of fact on which the court of the State of origin based its jurisdiction.

Subject to the provisions of the first paragraph, the jurisdiction of the court of the State of origin may not be reviewed; the test of public policy referred to in point 1 of Article 27 may not be applied to the rules relating to jurisdiction.

Article 29

Under no circumstances may a foreign judgment be reviewed as to its substance.

Article 30

A court of a Contracting State in which recognition is sought of a judgment given in another Contracting State may stay the proceedings if an ordinary appeal against the judgment has been lodged.

A court of a Contracting State in which recognition is sought of a judgment given in Ireland or the United Kingdom may stay the proceedings if enforcement is suspended in the State of origin, by reason of appeal.

Section 2
Enforcement

Article 31

A judgment given in a Contracting State and enforceable in that State shall be enforced in another Contracting State when, on the application of any interested party, it has been declared enforceable there.

However, in the United Kingdom, such a judgment shall be enforced in England and Wales, in Scotland, or in Northern Ireland when, on the application of any interested party, it has been registered for enforcement in that part of the United Kingdom.

Article 32

1   The application shall be submitted–
    –   in Belgium, to the tribunal de première instance or rechtbank van eerste aanleg,
    –   in Denmark, to the byret,
    –   in the Federal Republic of Germany, to the presiding judge of a chamber of the Landgericcht,
    –   in Greece, to the Μονομελές Πρωτοδικείο,
    –   in Spain, to the Juzgado de Primera Instancia,
    –   in France, to the presiding judge of the tribunal de grande instance,
    –   in Ireland, to the High Court,
    –   in Italy, to the corte d'appello,
    –   in Luxembourg, to the presiding judge of the tribunal d'arrondissement,
    –   in the Netherlands, to the presiding judge of the arrondissementsrechtbank,
    –   in Portugal, to the Tribunal Judicial de Circulo,

- in the United Kingdom–
    (a) in England and Wales, to the High Court of Justice, or in the case of maintenance judgment to the magistrates' court on transmission by the Secretary of State;
    (b) in Scotland, to the Court of Session, or in the case of a maintenance judgment to the Sheriff Court on transmission by the Secretary of State;
    (c) in Northern Ireland, to the High Court of Justice, or in the case of a maintenance judgment to the magistrates' court on transmission by the Secretary of State.

2   The jurisdiction of local courts shall be determined by reference to the place of domicile of the party against whom enforcement is sought. If he is not domiciled in the State in which enforcement is sought, it shall be determined by reference to the place of enforcement.

Article 33

The procedure for making the application shall be governed by the law of the State in which enforcement is sought.

The applicant must given an address for service of process within the area of jurisdiction of the court applied to. However, if the law of the State in which enforcement is sought does not provide for the furnishing of such an address, the applicant shall appoint a representative *ad litem*.

The documents referred to in Articles 46 and 47 shall be attached to the application.

Article 34

The court applied to shall give its decision without delay; the party against whom enforcement is sought shall not at this stage of the proceedings be entitled to make any submissions on the application.

The application may be refused only for one of the reasons specified in Articles 27 and 28.

Under no circumstances may the foreign judgment be reviewed as to its substance.

Article 35

The appropriate officer of the court shall without delay bring the decision given on the application to the notice of the applicant in accordance with the procedure laid down by the law of the State in which enforcement is sought.

Article 36

If enforcement is authorised, the party against whom enforcement is sought may appeal against the decision within one month of service thereof.

If that party is domiciled in a Contracting State other than that in which the decision authorising enforcement was given, the time for appealing shall be two months and shall run from the date of service, either on him in person or at his residence. No extension of time may be granted on account of distance.

Article 37

1   An appeal against the decision authorising enforcement shall be lodged in accordance with the rules governing procedure in contentious matters–

    –   in Belgium, with the tribunal de première instance or rechtbank van eerste aanleg,
    –   in Denmark, with the landsret,
    –   in the Federal Republic of Germany, with Oberlandesgericht,
    –   in Greece, with the εφετείο,
    –   in Spain, with the Audiencia Provincial,
    –   in France, with the cour d'appel,
    –   in Ireland, with the High Court,
    –   in Italy, with the corte d'appello,
    –   in Luxembourg, with the Cour supérieure de justice sitting as a court of civil appeal,
    –   in the Netherlands, with the arrondissementsrechtbank,
    –   in Portugal, with the Tribunal de Relaçäo,
    –   in the United Kingdom–

        (a) in England and Wales, with the High Court of Justice, or in the case of a maintenance judgment with the magistrates' court;
        (b) in Scotland, with the Court of Session, or in the case of a maintenance judgment with the Sheriff Court;
        (c) in Northern Ireland, with the High Court of Justice, or in the case of a maintenance judgment with the magistrates' court.

2   The judgment given on the appeal may be contested only–

    –   in Belgium, Greece, Spain, France, Italy, Luxembourg and in the Netherlands, by an appeal in cassation,
    –   in Denmark, by an appeal to the højesteret, with the leave of the Minister of Justice,
    –   in the Federal Republic of Germany, by a Rechtsbeschwerde,
    –   in Ireland, by an appeal on a point of law to the Supreme Court,
    –   in Portugal, by an appeal on a point of law,
    –   in the United Kingdom, by a single further appeal on a point of law.

Article 38

The court with which the appeal under Article 37(1) is lodged may, on the application of the appellant, stay the proceedings if an ordinary appeal has been lodged against the judgment in the State of origin or if the time for such an appeal has not yet expired; in the latter case, the court may specify the time within which such an appeal is to be lodged.

Where the judgment was given in Ireland or the United Kingdom, any form of appeal available in the State of origin shall be treated as an ordinary appeal for the purposes of the first paragraph.

The court may also make enforcement conditional on the provision of such security as it shall determine.

Article 39

During the time specified for an appeal pursuant to Article 36 and until any such appeal has been determined, no measures of enforcement may be taken other than protective measures taken against the property of the party against whom enforcement is sought.

The decision authorising enforcement shall carry with it the power to proceed to any such protective measures.

Article 40

1   If the application for enforcement is refused, the applicant may appeal–
    – in Belgium, to the cour d'appel or hof van beroep,
    – in Denmark, to the landsret,
    – in the Federal Republic of Germany, to the Oberlandesgericht,
    – in Greece to the εφετείο,
    – in Spain, to the Audiencia Provincial,
    – in France, to the court d'appel,
    – in Ireland, to the High Court,
    – in Italy, to the corte d'appello,
    – in Luxembourg, to the Cour supérieure de justice sitting as a court of civil appeal,
    – in the Netherlands, to the gerechtshof,
    – in Portugal, to the Tribunal da Relaçäo,
    – in the United Kingdom–
        (a) in England and Wales, to the High Court of Justice, or in the case of a maintenance judgment to the magistrates' court;
        (b) in Scotland, to the Court of Session, or in the case of a maintenance judgment to the Sheriff Court;

(c) in Northern Ireland, to the High Court of Justice, or in the case of a maintenance judgment to the magistrates' court.

2 The party against whom enforcement is sought shall be summoned to appear before the appellate court. If he fails to appear, the provisions of the second and third paragraphs of Article 20 shall apply even where he is not domiciled in any of the Contracting States.

Article 41

A judgment given on appeal provided for in Article 40 may be contested only–

- in Belgium, Greece, Spain, France, Italy, Luxembourg and in the Netherlands, by an appeal in cassation,
- in Denmark, by an appeal to the højesteret, with the leave of the Minister of Justice,
- in the Federal Republic of Germany, by a Rechtsbeschwerde,
- in Ireland, by an appeal on a point of law to the Supreme Court,
- in Portugal, by an appeal on a point of law,
- in the United Kingdom, by a single further appeal on a point of law.

Article 42

Where a foreign judgment has been given in respect of several matters and enforcement cannot be authorised for all of them, the court shall authorise enforcement for one or more of them.

An applicant may request partial enforcement of a judgment.

Article 43

A foreign judgment which orders a periodic payment by way of a penalty shall be enforceable in the State in which enforcement is sought only if the amount of the payment has been finally determined by the courts of the State of origin.

Article 44

An applicant who, in the State of origin has benefited from complete or partial legal aid or exemption from costs or expenses shall be entitled in the procedures provided for in Articles 32 to 35 to benefit from the most favourable legal aid or the most extensive exemption from costs or expenses provided for by the law of the State addressed.

However, an applicant who requests the enforcement of a decision given by an administrative authority in Denmark in respect of a maintenance order may, in the State addressed, claim the benefits referred to in the first paragraph if he presents a statement from the Danish Ministry of Justice to the effect that he fulfils the economic requirements to qualify for the grant of complete or partial legal aid or exemption from the costs or expenses.

Article 45

No security, bond or deposit however described shall be required of a party who in one Contracting State applies for enforcement of a judgment given in another Contracting State on the ground that he is a foreign national or that he is not domiciled or resident in the State in which enforcement is sought.

Section 3

Common provisions

Article 46

A party seeking recognition or applying for enforcement of a judgment shall produce–

1 A copy of the judgment which satisfies the conditions necessary to establish authenticity;

2 In the case of a judgment given in default, the original or a certified true copy of the document which establishes that the party in default was served with the document instituting the proceedings or with an equivalent document.

Article 47

A party applying for enforcement shall also produce–

1 Documents which establish that, according to the law of the State of origin the judgment is enforceable and has been served;

2 Where appropriate, a document showing that the applicant is in receipt of legal aid in the State of origin.

Article 48

If the documents specified in point 2 of Articles 46 and 47 are not produced, the court may specify a time for their production, accept equivalent documents or, if it considers that it has sufficient information before it, dispense with their production.

If the court so requires, a translation of the documents shall be produced; the translation shall be certified by a person qualified to do so in one of the Contracting States.

Article 49

No legalisation or other similar formality shall be required in respect of the documents referred to in Articles 46 or 47 or the second paragraph of Article 48, or in respect of a document appointing a representative *ad litem.*

TITLE IV
AUTHENTIC INSTRUMENTS AND COURT SETTLEMENTS

Article 50

A document which has been formally drawn up or registered as an authentic instrument and is enforceable in one Contracting State shall, in another Contracting State, be declared enforceable there, on application made in accordance with procedures provided for in Article 31 *et seq*. The application may be refused only if enforcement of the instrument is contrary to public policy in the State addressed.

The instrument produced must satisfy the conditions necessary to establish its authenticity in the State of origin.

The provisions of Section 3 of Title III shall apply as appropriate.

Article 51

A settlement which has been approved by a court in the course of proceedings and is enforceable in the State in which it was concluded shall be enforceable in the State addressed under the same conditions as authentic instruments.

TITLE V
GENERAL PROVISIONS

Article 52

In order to determine whether a party is domiciled in the Contracting State whose courts are seised of a matter, the Court shall apply its internal law.

If a party is not domiciled in the State whose courts are seised of the matter, then, in order to determine whether the party is domiciled in another Contracting State, the court shall apply the law of that State.

Article 53

For the purposes of this Convention, the seat of a company or other legal person association of natural or legal persons shall be treated as its domicile. However, in order to determine that seat, the court shall apply its rules of private international law.

In order to determine whether a trust is domiciled in the Contracting State whose courts are seised of the matter, the court shall apply its rules of private international law.

TITLE VI
TRANSITIONAL PROVISIONS

Article 54

The provisions of the Convention shall apply only to legal proceedings instituted and to documents formally drawn up or registered as authentic instruments after its entry into force in the State of origin and, where recognition or enforcement of a judgment or authentic instrument is sought, in the State addressed.

However, judgments given after the date of entry into force of this Convention between the State of origin and the State addressed in proceedings instituted before that date shall be recognised and enforced in accordance with the provisions of Title III if jurisdiction was founded upon rules which accorded with those provided for either in Title II of this Convention or in a convention concluded between the State of origin and the State addressed which was in force when the proceedings were instituted.

If the parties to a dispute concerning a contract had agreed in writing before 1st June 1988 for Ireland or before 1st January 1987 for the United Kingdom that the contract was to be governed by the law of Ireland or of a part of the United Kingdom, the courts of Ireland or of that part of the United Kingdom shall retain the right to exercise jurisdiction in the dispute.

Article 54a

For a period of three years from 1st November 1986 for Denmark and from 1 June 1988 for Ireland, jurisdiction in maritime matters shall be determined in these States not only in accordance with the provisions of Title II, but also in accordance with the provisions of paragraphs 1–6 following. However, upon the entry into force of the International Convention relating to the arrest of sea-going ships, signed at Brussels on 10th May 1952, for one of these States, these provisions shall cease to have effect for that State.

1   A person who is domiciled in a Contracting State may be sued in the Courts of one of the States mentioned above in respect of a maritime claim if the ship to which the claim relates or any other ship owned by him has been arrested by judicial process within the territory of the latter State to secure the claim, or could have been so arrested there but bail or other security has been given, and either–

   (a) the claimant is domiciled in the latter State, or

   (b) the claim arose in the latter State, or

   (c) the claim concerns the voyage during which the arrest was made or could have been made, or

(d) the claim arises out of a collision or out of damage caused by a ship to another ship or to goods or persons on board either ship, either by the execution or non-execution of a manoeuvre or by the non-observance of regulations; or

(e) the claim is for salvage; or

(f) the claim is in respect of a mortgage or hypothecation of the ship arrested.

2   A claimant may arrest either the particular ship to which the maritime claim relates, or any other ship which is owned by the person who was, at the time when the maritime claim arose, the owner of the particular ship. However, only the particular ship to which the maritime claim relates may be arrested in respect of the maritime claims set out in (5)(o), (p) or (q) of this Article.

3   Ships shall be deemed to be in the same ownership when all the shares therein are owned by the same person or persons.

4   When in the case of a charter by demise of a ship the charterer alone is liable in respect of a maritime claim relating to that ship, the claimant may arrest that ship or any other ship owned by the charterer, but no other ship owned by the owner may be arrested in respect of such a claim. The same shall apply to any case in which a person other than the owner of a ship is liable in respect of a maritime claim relating to that ship.

5   The expression 'maritime claim' means a claim arising out of one or more of the following:

(a) damage caused by any ship either in collision or otherwise;

(b) loss of life or personal injury caused by any ship or occurring in connection with the operation of any ship;

(c) salvage;

(d) agreement relating to the use or hire of any ship whether by charterparty or otherwise;

(e) agreement relating to the carriage of goods in any ship whether by charterparty or otherwise;

(f) loss of or damage to goods including baggage carried in any ship;

(g) general average;

(h) bottomry;

(i) towage;

(j) pilotage;

(k) goods or materials wherever supplied to a ship for her operation or maintenance;

(l) construction, repair or equipment of any ship or dock charges and dues;

(m) wages of master, officers or crew;

(n) mater's disbursements, including disbursements made by shippers, charters or agents on behalf of a ship or her owner;

(o) dispute as to the title to or ownership of any ship;

(p) disputes between co-owners of any ship as to the ownership, possession, employment or earnings of that ship;

(q) the mortgage of hypothecation of any ship.

6   In Denmark, the expression 'arrest' shall be deemed as regards the maritime claims referred to in 5(o) and (p) of this Article, to include a 'forbud', where that is the only procedure allowed in respect of such a claim under Articles 646 to 653 of the law on civil procedure (lov om rettens pleje).

TITLE VII
RELATIONSHIP TO OTHER CONVENTIONS

Article 55

Subject to the provisions of the second sub-paragraph of Article 54, and of Article 56, this Convention shall, for the States which are parties to it, supersede the following conventions concluded between two or more of them–

–   the Convention between Belgium and France on jurisdiction and the validity and enforcement of judgments, arbitration awards and authentic instruments signed at Paris on 8th July 1899.

–   the Convention between Belgium and the Netherlands on jurisdiction, bankruptcy, and the validity and enforcement of judgments, arbitration awards and authentic instruments, signed at Brussels on 28th March 1925.

–   the Convention between France and Italy on the enforcement of judgments in civil and commercial matters, signed at Rome on 3rd June 1930.

–   the Convention between the United Kingdom and the French Republic providing for the reciprocal enforcement of judgments in civil and commercial matters, with Protocol signed at Paris on 18th January 1934.

–   the Convention between the United Kingdom and the Kingdom of Belgium providing for the reciprocal enforcement of judgments in civil and commercial matters, with Protocol signed at Brussels on 2nd May 1934.

–   the Convention between Germany and Italy on the recognition and enforcement of judgments in civil and commercial matters signed at Rome on 9th March 1936.

- the Convention between the Federal Republic of Germany and the Kingdom of Belgium on the mutual recognition and enforcement of judgments, arbitration awards and authentic instruments in civil and commercial matters, signed at Bonn on 30th June 1958.

- the Convention between the Kingdom of the Netherlands and the Italian Republic on the recognition and enforcement of judgments in civil and commercial matters, signed at Rome on 17th April 1959.

- the Convention between the United Kingdom and the Federal Republic of Germany for the reciprocal recognition and enforcement of judgments in civil and commercial matters signed at Bonn on 14th July 1960.

- the Convention between the Kingdom of Greece and the Federal Republic of Germany for the reciprocal recognition and enforcement of judgments, settlements and authentic instruments in civil and commercial matters, signed in Athens on 4th November 1961.

- the Convention between the Kingdom of Belgium and the Italian Republic on the recognition and enforcement of judgments and other enforceable instruments in civil and commercial matters, signed at Rome on 6th April 1962.

- the Convention between the Kingdom of the Netherlands and the Federal Republic of Germany on the mutual recognition and enforcement of judgments and other enforceable instruments in civil and commercial matters, signed at The Hague on 30th August 1962.

- The Convention between the United Kingdom and the Republic of Italy for the reciprocal recognition and enforcement of judgments in civil and commercial matters, signed at Rome on 7th February 1964, with amending Protocol signed at Rome on 14th July 1970.

- the Convention between the United Kingdom and the Kingdom of the Netherlands providing for the reciprocal recognition and enforcement of judgments in civil matters, signed at The Hague on 17th November 1967.

- the Convention between Spain and France on the recognition and enforcement of judgment arbitration awards in civil and commercial matters signed at Paris on 28th May 1969.

- the Convention between Spain and Italy regarding legal aid and the recognition and enforcement of judgments in civil and commercial matters signed at Madrid on 22nd May 1973.

- the Convention between Spain and the Federal Republic of Germany on the recognition and enforcement of judgments, settlements and enforceable authentic instruments in civil and commercial matters signed at Bonn on 14th November 1983,

and in so far as it is in force–

– the Treaty between Belgium, the Netherlands and Luxembourg on jurisdiction, bankruptcy, and the validity and enforcement of judgments, arbitration awards and authentic instruments signed at Brussels on 24th November 1961.

Article 56

The Treaty and conventions referred to in Article 55 shall continue to have effect in relation to matters to which this Convention does not apply.

They shall continue to have effect in respect of judgments given and documents formally drawn up or registered as authentic instruments before the entry into force of this Convention.

Article 57

1   This Convention shall not affect any conventions to which the Contracting States are or will be parties and which in relation to particular matters, govern jurisdiction or the recognition or enforcement of judgments.

2   With a view to its uniform interpretation, paragraph 1 shall be applied in the following manner–

(a) this Convention shall not prevent a court of a Contracting State which is a party to a convention on a particular matter from assuming jurisdiction in accordance with that Convention, even where the defendant is domiciled in another Contracting State which is not a party to that Convention. The court hearing the action shall, in any event, apply Article 20 of this Convention;

(b) judgments given in a Contracting State by a court in the exercise of jurisdiction provided for in a convention on a particular matter shall be recognised and enforced in the other Contracting State in accordance with this Convention.

Where a Convention on a particular matter to which both the State of origin and the State addressed are parties lays down conditions for the recognition or enforcement of judgments, those conditions shall apply. In any event, the provisions of this Convention which concern the procedure for recognition and enforcement of judgments may be applied.

3   This Convention shall not affect the application of provisions which, in relation to particular matters govern jurisdiction or the recognition or enforcement of judgments and which are or will be contained in acts of the institutions of the European Communities or in national laws harmonised in implementation of such acts.

Article 58

Until such time as the Convention on jurisdiction and the enforcement of judgments in civil and commercial matters signed at Lugano on 16th September 1988 takes effect with regard to France and the Swiss Confederation, this Convention shall not affect the rights granted to the Swiss nationals by the Convention between France and the Swiss Confederation on jurisdiction and enforcement of judgments in civil matters signed at Paris on 15th June 1869.

Article 59

This Convention shall not prevent a Contracting State from assuming, in a convention on the recognition and enforcement of judgments, an obligation towards a third State not to recognise judgments given in other Contracting States against defendants domiciled or habitually resident in the third State where in cases provided for in Article 4, the judgment could only be founded on a ground of jurisdiction specified in the second paragraph of Article 3.

However, a Contracting State may not assume an obligation towards a third State not to recognise a judgment given in another Contracting State by a court basing its jurisdiction on the presence within that State of property belonging to the defendant, or the seizure by the plaintiff of property situated there–

1   If the action is brought to assert or declare proprietary or possessory rights in that property, seeks to obtain authority to dispose of it, or arises from another issue relating to such property, or

2.   If the property constitutes the security for a debt which is the subject matter of the action.

TITLE VIII
FINAL PROVISIONS

Article 60
[Deleted]

Article 61

This Convention shall be ratified by the signatory States. The instruments of ratification shall be deposited with the Secretary General of the Council of the European Communities.

Article 62

This Convention shall enter into force on the first day of the third month following the deposit of the instrument of ratification by the last signatory State to take this step.

Article 63

The Contracting States recognise that any State which becomes a member of the European Economic Community shall be required to accept this Convention as a basis for the negotiations between the Contracting States and that State necessary to ensure the implementation of the last paragraph of Article 220 of the Treaty establishing the European Economic Community.

The necessary adjustments may be the subject of a special convention between the Contracting States of the one part and the new Member States of the other part.

Article 64

The Secretary General of the Council of European Communities shall notify the signatory States of–

(a) the deposit of each instrument of ratification;

(b) the date of entry into force of this Convention;

(c) [deleted];

(d) any declaration received pursuant to Article IV of the Protocol;

(e) any communication made pursuant to Article VI of the Protocol.

Article 65

The Protocol annexed to this Convention by common accord of the Contracting State shall form an integral part thereof.

Article 66

This Convention is concluded for an unlimited period.

Article 67

Any Contracting State may request the revision of this Convention. In this event, a revision conference shall be convened by the President of the Council of the European Communities.

Article 68

This Convention, drawn up in a single original in the Dutch, French, German and Italian languages, all four texts being equally authentic, shall be deposited in the archives of the Secretartiat of the Council of the European Communities. The Secretary General shall transmit a certified copy to the Government of each signatory State.

(Signatures of Plenipotentiaries of the original six Contracting States)

ANNEXED PROTOCOL

Article I

Any person domiciled in Luxembourg who is sued in a court of another Contracting State pursuant to Article 5(1) may refuse to submit to the jurisdiction of that court. If the defendant does not enter an appearance the court shall declare of its own motion that it has no jurisdiction.

An agreement conferring jurisdiction, within the meaning of Article 17, shall be valid with respect to a person domiciled in Luxembourg only if that person has expressly and specifically agreed.

Article II

Without prejudice to any more favourable provisions of national laws, persons domiciled in a Contracting State who are being prosecuted in the criminal courts of another Contracting State of which they are not nationals for an offence which was not intentionally committed may be defended by persons qualified to do so, even if they do not appear in person.

However, the court seised of the matter may order appearance in person; in the case of failure to appear, a judgment given in the civil action without the person concerned having had the opportunity to arrange for his defence need not be recognised or enforced in the other Contracting States.

Article III

In proceedings for the issue of an order for enforcement, no charge, duty or fee calculated by reference to the value of the matter in issue may be levied in the State in which enforcement is sought.

Article IV

Judicial and extrajudicial documents drawn up in one Contracting State which have to be served on persons in another Contracting State shall be transmitted in accordance with the procedures laid down in the conventions and agreements concluded between the Contracting States.

Unless the State in which service is to take place objects by declaration to the Secretary General of the Council of the European Communities, such documents may also be sent by the appropriate public officers of the State in which the document has been drawn up directly to the appropriate public officers of the State in which the addressee is to be found. In this case the officer of the State addressed who is competent to forward it to the addressee. The document shall be forwarded in the manner specified by the law of the State adressed. The forwarding shall be recorded by a certificate sent directly to the officer of the State of origin.

Article V

The jurisdiction specified in Article 6(2) and Article 10 in actions on a warranty or guarantee or any other third party proceedings may not be resorted to in the Federal Republic of Germany. In that State, any person domiciled in another Contracting State may be sued in the courts in pursuance of Articles 68, 72, 73 and 74 of the code of civil procedure (Zivilprozeßordnung) concerning third-party notices.

Judgments given in the other Contracting States by virtue of Article 6(2) or Article 10 shall be recognised and enforced in the Federal Republic of Germany in accordance with Title III. Any effects which judgments given in that State may have on third parties by application of Articles 68, 72, 73 and 74 of the code of civil procedure (Zivilprozeßordnung) shall also be recognised in the other Contracting States.

Article Va

In matters relating to maintenance, the expression 'court' includes the Danish administrative authorities.

Article Vb

In proceedings involving a dispute between the master and a member of the crew of a sea-going ship registered in Denmark or in Ireland, concerning remuneration or other conditions of service, a court in a Contracting State shall establish whether the diplomatic or consular officer responsible for the ship has been notified of the dispute. It shall of its motion decline jurisdiction if the officer, having been duly notified, has exercised the powers accorded to him in the matter by a consular convention, or in the absence of such a convention, has, within the time allowed, raised any objection to the exercise of such jurisdiction.

Article Vc

Articles 52 and 53 of this Convention shall, when applied by Article 69(5) of the Convention for the European Patent for the Common Market, signed at Luxembourg on 15th December 1975, to the provisions relating to 'residence' in the English test of that Convention, operate as if 'residence' in that text were the same as 'domicile' in Articles 52 and 53.

Article Vd

Without prejudice to the jurisdiction of the European Patent Office under the Convention on the Grant of European Patents, signed at Munich on 5th October 1973, the courts of each Contracting State shall have exclusive jurisdiction, regardless of domicile, in proceedings concerned with the registration or validity of any European patent granted for that State which is not a Community patent by virtue of the provisions of Article 86 of the Convention for the European Patent for the Common Market, signed at Luxembourg on 15th December 1975.

Article VI

The Contracting States shall communicate to the Secretary General of the Council of the European Communities the text of any provisions of their laws which amend either those articles of their laws mentioned in the Convention or the lists of courts specified in Section 2 of Title III of the Convention.

SCHEDULE 2

TEXT OF THE 1971 PROTOCOL, AS AMENDED

Article 1

The Court of Justice of the European Communities shall have jurisdiction to give rulings on the interpretation of the Convention on Jurisdiction and the Enforcement of Judgments in Civil and Commercial Matters and of the Protocol annexed to that Convention, signed at Brussels on 27 September 1968, and also on the interpretation of the present Protocol.

The Court of Justice of the European Communities shall also have jurisdiction to give rulings on the interpretation of the Convention on the Accession of the Kingdom of Denmark, Ireland and the United Kingdom of Great Britain and Northern Ireland to the Convention of 27th September 1968 and to this Protocol.

The Court of Justice of the European Communities shall also have jurisdiction to give rulings on the interpretation of the Convention on the Accession of the Hellenic Republic to the Convention of 27th September 1968 and to this Protocol, as adjusted by the 1978 Convention.

The Court of Justice of the European Communities shall also have jurisdiction to give rulings on the interpretation of the Convention on the Accession of the Kingdom of Spain and the Portuguese Republic to the Convention of 27th September 1968 and to this Protocol, as adjusted by the 1978 Convention and the 1982 Convention.

Article 2

The following courts may request the Court of Justice to give preliminary rulings on questions of interpretation:

(1) – in Belgium: la Cour de Cassation – het Hof van Cassatie and le Conseil d'Etat – de Raad van State,

– in Denmark: højesteret,

– in the Federal Republic of Germany: die obersten Gerichtshöfe des Bundes,

– in Greece: τα ανωτατα δικαοτηρια,

– in Spain: el Tribunal Supremo,

– in France: la Cour de Cassation and le Conseil d'Etat,

- in Ireland: the Supreme Court,
- in Italy: la Corte Suprema di Cassazione,
- in Luxembourg: la Cour supérieure de Justice when sitting as Cour de Cassation,
- in the Netherlands: de Hoge Raad,
- in Portugal: o Supremo Tribunal de Justiça and o Supremo Tribunal Administrativo,
- in the United Kingdom: the House of Lords and courts to which application has been made under the second paragraph of Article 37 or under Article 41 of the Convention;

(2) the courts of the Contracting States when they are sitting in an appellate capacity;

(3) in the cases provided for in Article 37 of the Convention, the courts referred to in that Article.

Article 3

(1) Where a question of interpretation of the Convention or one of the other instruments referred to in Article 1 is raised in a case pending before one of the courts listed in point 1 of Article 2, that court shall, if it considers that a decision on the question is necessary to enable it to give judgment, request the Court of Justice to give a ruling thereon.

(2) Where such a question is raised before any court referred to in Article 2(2) or (3), that court may, under the conditions laid down in paragraph (1), request the Court of Justice to give a ruling thereon.

Article 4

(1) The competent authority of a Contracting State may request the Court of Justice to give a ruling on a question of interpretation of the Convention or one of the other instruments referred to in Article 1 if judgments given by courts of that State conflict with the interpretation given either by the Court of Justice of in a judgment of one of the courts of another Contracting State referred to in Article 2(1) or (2). The provisions of this paragraph shall apply only to judgments which have become *res judicata*.

(2) The interpretation given by the Court of Justice in response to such a request shall not affect the judgments which gave rise to the request for interpretation.

(3) The Procurators General of the Courts of Cassation of the Contracting States, or any other authority designated by a Contracting State, shall be entitled to request the Court of Justice for a ruling on interpretation in accordance with paragraph (1).

(4) The Registrar of the Court of Justice shall give notice of the request to the Contracting States, to the Commission and to the Council of the European Communities; they shall then be entitled within two months of the notification to submit statements of case or written observations to the Court.

(5) No fees shall be levied or any costs or expenses awarded in respect of the proceedings provided for in this Article.

Article 5

(1) Except where this Protocol otherwise provides, the provisions of the Treaty establishing the European Economic Community and those of the Protocol on the Statute of the Court of Justice annexed thereto, which are applicable when the Court is requested to give a preliminary ruling, shall also apply to any proceedings for th interpretation of the Convention and the other instruments referred to in Article 1.

(2) The Rules of Procedure of the Court of Justice shall, if necessary, be adjusted and supplemented in accordance with Article 188 of the Treaty establishing the European Economic Community.

Article 6
[Deleted]

Article 7

This protocol shall be ratified by the signatory States. The instruments of ratification shall be deposited with the Secretary General of the Council of the European Communities.

Article 8

This protocol shall enter into force on the first day of the third month following the deposit of the instrument of ratification by the last signatory State to take this step; provided that it shall at the earliest enter into force at the same time as the Convention of 27th September 1968 on Jurisdiction and the Enforcement of Judgments in Civil and Commercial Matters.

Article 9

The Contracting States recognise that any State which becomes a member of the European Economic Community, and to which Article 63 of the Convention on Jurisdiction and the Enforcement of Judgments in Civil and Commercial Matters applies, must accept the provisions of this Protocol, subject to such adjustments as may be required.

Article 10

The Secretary General of the Council of the European Communities shall notify the signatory States of:

(a) the deposit of each instrument of ratification;

(b) the date of entry into force of this Protocol;

(c) any designation received pursuant to Article 4(3);

(d) [deleted].

Article 11

The Contracting States shall communicate to the Secretary General of the Council of the European Communities the texts of any provisions of their laws which necessitate an amendment to the list of courts in Article 2(1)

Article 12

This protocol is concluded for an unlimited period.

Article 13

Any Contracting State may request the revision of this Protocol. In this event, a revision conference shall be convened by the President of the Council of the European communities.

Article 14

This protocol, drawn up in a single original in the Dutch, French, German and Italian languages, all four texts being equally authentic, shall be deposited in the archives of the Secretariat of the Council of the European communities. The Secretary General shall transmit a certified copy to the Government of each signatory State.

THE CIVIL JURISDICTION AND JUDGMENTS ACT 1991

CIVIL JURISDICTION AND JUDGMENTS ACT 1991

(1991 Chapter 12)

ARRANGEMENT OF SECTIONS

Section

SCHEDULES

CIVIL JURISDICTION AND JUDGMENTS ACT 1991

(1991 Chapter 12)

An Act to give effect to the Convention on jurisdiction and the enforcement of judgments in civil and commercial matters, including the Protocols annexed thereto, opened for signature at Lugano on 16th September 1988; and for purposes connected therewith.

[9th May 1991]

BE IT ENACTED by the Queen's most Excellent Majesty, by and with the advice and consent of the Lords Spiritual and Temporal, and Commons, in this present Parliament assembled, and by the authority of the same, as follows–

1.– (1) The Civil Jurisdiction and Judgments Act 1982 (in this Act referred to as 'the 1982 Act') shall have effect with the insertion of the following after section 3–

'**3A.**– (1) The Lugano Convention shall have the force of law in the United Kingdom, and judicial notice shall be taken of it.

(2) For convenience of reference there is set out in Schedule 3C the English text of the Lugano Convention.

3B.–(1) In determining any question as to the meaning or effect of a provision of the Lugano Convention, a court in the United Kingdom shall, in accordance with Protocol No 2 to that Convention, take account of any principles laid down in any relevant decision delivered by a court of any other Lugano Contracting State concerning provisions of the Convention.

(2) Without prejudice to any practice of the courts as to the matters which may be considered apart from this section, the report on the Lugano Convention by Mr P Jenard and Mr G Möller (which is reproduced in the Official Journal of the Communities of 28th July 1990) may be considered in ascertaining the meaning or effect of any provision of the Convention and shall be given such weight as is appropriate in the circumstances.'

(2) In section 9 of the Act, after sub-section (1) (which, as amended, will govern the relationship between other conventions and the 1968 and Lugano Conventions) there shall be inserted–

'(1A)   Any question arising as to whether it is the Lugano Convention or any of the Brussels Conventions which applies in the circumstances of a particular case falls to be determined in accordance with the provisions of Article 54B of the Lugano Convention.'

(3)   After Schedule 3B to that Act there shall be inserted the Schedule 3C set out in Schedule 1 of this Act.

2.–(1)   Section 1 of the 1982 Act (interpretation of references to the Conventions and Contracting States) shall be amended in accordance with the following provisions of this section.

(2) In sub-section (1) in the definitions of 'the Conventions', for the words 'the Conventions' there shall be substituted the words 'the Brussels Convention'.

(3) At the end of that sub-section there shall be added–

'"the Lugano Convention" means the Convention on jurisdiction and the enforcement of judgments in civil and commercial matters (including the Protocols annexed to that Convention) opened for signature at Lugano on 16th September 1988 and signed by the United Kingdom on 18th September 1989.'

(4) In sub-section (2), for paragraph (b) (citation of Articles) there shall be substituted–

'(b) any reference in any provision to a numbered Article without more is a reference–

(i) to the Article so numbered of the 1968 Convention, in so far as the provision applies in relation to that Convention, and

(ii) to the Article so numbered of the Lugano Convention, in so far as the provision applies in relation to that Convention,

and any reference to a sub-division of a numbered Article shall be construed accordingly.'

(5) In sub-section (3) (definitions of 'Contracting State') for the words 'In this Act "Contracting State" means–' there shall be substituted the words–

'In this Act–

"Contracting State", without more, in any provision means–

(a) in the application of the provision in relation to the Brussels Conventions, a Brussels Contracting State; and

(b) in the application of the provision in relation to the Lugano Convention, a Lugano Contracting State;

"Brussels Contracting State" means–'

(6) At the end of that sub-section there shall be added–

'"Lugano Contracting State" means one of the original parties to the Lugano Convention, that is to say–

Austria, Belgium, Denmark, Finland, France, the Federal Republic of Germany, the Hellenic Republic, Iceland, the Republic of Ireland, Italy, Luxembourg, the Netherlands, Norway, Portugal, Spain, Sweden, Switzerland and the United Kingdom,

being a State in relation to which that Convention has taken effect in accordance with paragraph 3 or 4 of Article 61.'

3. The 1982 Act shall have effect with the amendments specified in Schedule 2 to this Act, which are either consequential on the amendments made by sections 1 and 2 above or otherwise for the purpose of implementing the Lugano Convention.

4. The amendments of the 1982 Act made by this Act bind the Crown in accordance with the provisions of section 51 of that Act.

5.–(1) This Act may be cited as the Civil Jurisdiction and Judgments Act 1991.

(2) In this Act–

'the 1982 Act' means the Civil Jurisdiction and Judgments Act 1982;

'the Lugano Convention' has the same meaning as it has in the 1982 Act by virtue of section 2(3) above.

(3) This Act shall come into force on such day as the Lord Chancellor and the Lord Advocate may appoint in an order made by statutory instrument.

(4) This Act extends to Northern Ireland.

SCHEDULES

SCHEDULE 1

SCHEDULE TO BE INSERTED AS SCHEDULE 3C TO THE 1982 ACT

SCHEDULE 3C

TEXT OF THE LUGANO CONVENTION

ARRANGEMENT OF PROVISIONS

TITLE I   SCOPE (ARTICLE 1)

TITLE II   JURISDICTION

Section 1   General provisions (Articles 2–4)

Section 2   Special jurisdiction (Articles 5–6A)

Section 3   Jurisdiction in matters relating to insurance (Articles 7–12A)

Section 4   Jurisdiction over consumer contracts (Articles 13–15)

Section 5   Exclusive jurisdiction (Articles 17–18)

Section 6   Prorogation of jurisdiction (Articles 17–18)

Section 7   Examination as to jurisdiction and admissibility (Articles 19–20)

Section 8   *Lis pendens* – related actions (Articles 21–23)

Section 9   Provisional, including protective, measures (Article 24)

TITLE III RECOGNITION AND ENFORCEMENT

Definition of 'judgment' (Article 25)

Section 1   Recognition (Articles 26–30)

Section 2   Enforcement (Articles 31–45)

Section 3   Common provisions (Articles 46–49)

TITLE IV AUTHENTIC INSTRUMENTS AND COURT SETTLEMENTS (ARTICLES 50–51)

TITLE V   GENERAL PROVISIONS (ARTICLES 52–53)

TITLE VI TRANSITIONAL PROVISIONS (ARTICLES 54–54A)

TITLE VII   RELATIONSHIP TO THE BRUSSELS CONVENTION AND TO OTHER CONVENTIONS (ARTICLES 54B–59)

TITLE VIII   FINAL PROVISIONS (ARTICLES 60–68)

PROTOCOL NO 1 – ON CERTAIN QUESTIONS OF JURISDICTION, PROCEDURE AND ENFORCEMENT

PROTOCOL NO 2 – ON THE UNIFORM INTERPRETATION OF THE CONVENTION

PROTOCOL NO 3 – ON THE APPLICATION OF ARTICLE 57

CONVENTION

ON JURISDICTION AND THE ENFORCEMENT OF JUDGMENTS IN CIVIL AND COMMERCIAL MATTERS

PREAMBLE

The High Contracting Parties to this Convention,

Anxious to strengthen in their territories the legal protection of persons therein established,

Considering that it is necessary for this purpose to determine the international jurisdiction of their courts, to facilitate recognition and to introduce an expeditious procedure for securing the enforcement of judgments, authentic instruments and court settlements,

Aware of the links between them, which have been sanctioned in the economic field by the free trade agreements concluded between the European Economic Community and the States members of the European Free Trade Association,

Taking into account the Brussels Convention of 27th September 1968 on jurisdiction and the enforcement of judgments in civil and commercial matters, as amended by the Accession Conventions under the successive enlargements of the European Communities,

Persuaded that the extension of the principles of that Convention to the States parties to this instrument will strengthen legal and economic co-operation in Europe,

Desiring to ensure as uniform an interpretation as possible of this instrument,

Have in this spirit decided to conclude this Convention and,

Have agreed as follows:

TITLE I
SCOPE

Article 1

This Convention shall apply in civil and commercial matters whatever the nature of the court or tribunal. It shall not extend, in particular, to revenue, customs or administrative matters.

The Convention shall not apply to:

1. the status or legal capacity of natural persons, rights in property arising out of a matrimonial relationship, wills and succession;
2. bankruptcy, proceedings relating to the winding-up of insolvent companies or other legal persons, judicial arrangements, compositions and analogous proceedings;
3. social security;
4. arbitration.

TITLE II
JURISDICTION

Section 1
General provisions

Article 2

Subject to the provisions of this Convention, persons domiciled in a Contracting State shall, whatever their nationality, be sued in the courts of that State.

Persons who are not nationals of the State in which they are domiciled shall be governed by the rules of jurisdiction applicable to nationals of that State.

Article 3

Persons domiciled in a Contracting State may be sued in the court of another Contracting State only by virtue of the rules set out in Sections 2 to 6 of this Title.

In particular the following provisions shall not be applicable as against them:

- in Belgium: Article 15 of the civil code (Code civil – burgerlijk Wetboek) and Article 638 of the judicial code (Code judiciare – Gerechtelijk Wetboek),

- in Denmark: Article 246(2) and (3) of the law on civil procedure (Lov om rettens pleje),

- in the Federal Republic of Germany: Article 23 of the code of civil procedure (Zivilpropzeβordnung),

- in Greece: Article 40 of the code of civil procedure (Κφδικασ πολιτικης δικοϖομίας),

- in France: Articles 14 and 15 of the civil code (Code civil),

- in Ireland: the rules which enable jurisdiction to be founded on the document instituting the proceedings having been served on the defendant during his temporary presence in Ireland,

- in Iceland: Article 77 of the Civil Proceedings Act (lög um meðferð einkamàla I héraði),

- in Italy: Articles 2 and 4, Nos 1 and 2 of the code of civil procedure (Codice di procedura civile),

- in Luxembourg: Articles 14 and 15 of the civil code (Code civil),

- in the Netherlands: Articles 126(3) and 127 of the code of civil procedure (Wetboek van Burgerlijke Rechtsvordering),

- in Norway: Section 32 of the Civil Proceedings Act (tvistemålsloven),

- in Austria: Article 99 of the Law on Court Jurisdiction (Jurisdiktionsnorm),

- in Portugal: Articles 65(1)(c), 65(2) and 65A(c) of the code of civil procedure (Código de Processo de Trabalho),

- in Switzerland: le for du lieu du séquestre/Gerichsstand des Arrestortes/foro del luogo del sequestro within the meaning of Article 4 of the loi fédérale sur le droit international privé/Bundesgesetz über das internationale Privatrecht/legge federale sul diritto internazionale privato,

- in Finland: the second, third and fourth sentences of Section 1 of Chapter 10 of the Code of Judicial Procedure (oikeudenkäymiskaari/ rättengångsbalken),

- in Sweden: the first sentence of Section 3 of Chapter 10 of the Code of Judicial Procedure (Rättengångsbalken),

- in the United Kingdom: the rules which enable jurisdiction to be founded on:

  (a) the document instituting the proceedings having been served on the defendant during his temporary presence in the United Kingdom; or

(b) the presence within the United Kingdom of property belonging to the defendant; or

(c) the seizure by the plaintiff of property situated in the United Kingdom.

Article 4

If the defendant is not domiciled in a Contracting State, the jurisdiction of the courts of each Contracting State shall, subject to the provisions of Article 16, be determined by the law of that State.

As against such a defendant, any person domiciled in a Contracting State may, whatever his nationality, avail himself in that State of the rules of jurisdiction there in force, and in particular those specified in the second paragraph of Article 3, in the same way as the nationals of that State.

Section 2

Special jurisdiction

Article 5

A person domiciled in a Contracting State may, in another Contracting State, be sued:

1. in matters relating to a contract, in the courts for the place of performance of the obligation in question; in matters relating to individual contracts of employment, this place is that where the employee habitually carried out his work, or if the employee does not habitually carry out his work in any one country, this place shall be the place of business through which he was engaged;

2. in matters relating to maintenance, in the courts for the place where the maintenance creditor is domiciled or habitually resident or, if the matter is ancillary to proceedings concerning the status of a person in the court which, according to its own law, has jurisdiction to entertain those proceedings, unless that jurisdiction is based solely on the nationality of one of the parties;

3. in matters relating to tort, delict or quasi-delict, in the courts for the place where the harmful event occurred;

4. as regards a civil claim for damages or restitution which is based on an act giving rise to criminal proceedings, in the court seised of those proceedings, to the extent that the court had jurisdiction under its own law to entertain civil proceedings;

5. as regards a dispute arising out of the operations of a branch, agency or other establishment, in the courts for the place in which the branch, agency or other establishment is situated;

6. in his capacity as settlor, trustee or beneficiary of a trust created by the operation of a statute, or by a written instrument, or created orally and evidenced in writing in the courts of the Contracting State in which the trust is domiciled;

7. as regards a dispute concerning the payment of remuneration claimed in respect of the salvage of a cargo or freight, in the court under the authority of which the cargo or freight in question:

    (a) has been arrested to secure such payment,

        or

    (b) could have been so arrested, but bail or other security has been given;

    provided that this provision shall apply only if it is claimed that the defendant has an interest in the cargo or freight or had such an interest at the time of salvage.

Article 6

A person domiciled in a Contracting State may also be sued:

1. where his is one of a number of defendants, in the courts for the place where any one of them is domiciled;

2. as a third party in an action on a warranty or guarantee or in any other third party proceedings, in the court seised of the original proceedings, unless these were instituted solely with the object of removing him from the jurisdiction of the court which would be competent in his case;

3. on a counterclaim arising from the same contract or facts on which the original claim was based, in the court in which the original claim is pending;

4. in matters relating to a contract, if the action may be combined with an action against the same defendant in matters relating to rights *in rem* in immovable property, in the court of the Contracting State in which the property is situated.

Article 6A

Where by virtue of this Convention a court of a Contracting State has jurisdiction in actions relating to liability arising from the use or operation of a ship, that court, or any other court substituted for this purpose by the internal law of that State, shall also have jurisdiction over claims for limitation of such liability.

Section 3

Jurisdiction in matters relating to insurance

Article 7

In matters relating to insurance, jurisdiction shall be determined by this Section, without prejudice to the provisions of Articles 4 and 5(5).

Article 8

An insurer domiciled in a Contracting State may be sued:

1. in the courts of the State where he is domiciled; or

2. in another Contracting State, in the courts for the place where the policy-holder is domiciled; or

3. if he is a co-insurer, in the courts of a Contracting State in which proceedings are brought against the leading insurer.

An insurer who is not domiciled in a Contracting State but has a branch, agency or other establishment in one of the Contracting States shall, in disputes arising out of the operations of the branch, agency or establishment, he deemed to be domiciled in that State.

Article 9

In respect of liability insurance or insurance of immovable property, the insurer may in addition be sued in the courts for the place where the harmful event occurred. The same applies if movable and immovable property are covered by the same insurance policy and both are adversely affected by the same contingency.

Article 10

In respect of liability insurance, the insurer may also, if the law of the court permits it, be joined in proceedings which the injured party has brought against the insured.

The provisions of Articles 7, 8 and 9 shall apply to actions brought by the injured party directly against the insurer, where such direct actions are permitted.

If the law governing such direct actions provides that the policy-holder or the insured may be joined as a party to the action, the same court shall have jurisdiction over them.

Article 11

Without prejudice to the provisions of the third paragraph of Article 10, an insurer may bring proceedings only in the courts of the Contracting State in which the defendant is domiciled, irrespective of whether he is the policy-holder, the insured or a beneficiary.

The provisions of this Section shall not affect the right to bring a counterclaim in the court in which, in accordance with this Section, the original claim is pending.

Article 12

The provisions of this Section may be departed from only by an agreement on jurisdiction:

1. which is entered into after the dispute has arisen; or

2. which allows the policy-holder, the insured or a beneficiary to bring proceedings in courts other than those indicated in this Section; or

3. which is concluded between a policy-holder and an insurer, both of whom are at the time of conclusion of the contract domiciled or habitually resident in the same Contracting State and which has the effect of conferring jurisdiction on the courts of that State even if the harmful event were to occur abroad, provided that such an agreement is not contrary to the law of the State; or

4. which is concluded with a policy-holder who is not domiciled in a Contracting State, except in so far as the insurance is compulsory or relates to immovable property in a Contracting State; or

5. which relates to a contract of insurance in so far as it covers one or more of the risks set out in Article 12A.

Article 12A

The following are the risks referred to in Article 12(5):

1. any loss of or damage to:
   (a) sea-going ships, installations situated offshore or on the high seas, or aircraft, arising from perils which relate to their use for commercial purposes;
   (b) goods in transit other than passengers' baggage where the transit consists of or includes carriage by such ships or aircraft;

2. any liability, other than for bodily injury to passengers or loss of or damage to their baggage;

(a) arising out of the use or operation of ships, installations or aircraft as referred to in (1)(a) above in so far as the law of the Contracting State in which such aircraft are registered does not prohibit agreements on jurisdiction regarding insurance of such risks;

(b) for loss or damage caused by goods in transit as described in (1)(b) above;

3. any financial loss connected with the use or operation of ships, installations or aircraft as referred to in (1)(a) above, in particular loss of freight or charter-hire;

4. any risk or interest connected with any of those referred to in (1) to (3) above.

Section 4

Jurisdiction over consumer contracts

Article 13

In proceedings concerning a contract concluded by a person for a purpose which can be regarded as being outside his trade or profession, hereinafter called 'the consumer', jurisdiction shall be determined by this Section, without prejudice to the provisions of Articles 4 and 5(5), if it is:

1. a contract for the sale of goods on instalment credit terms; or

2. a contract for a loan repayable by instalments, or for any other form of credit, made to finance the sale of goods; or

3. any other contract for the supply of goods or a contract for the supply of services; and

(a) in the State of the consumer's domicile the conclusion of the contract was preceded by a specific invitation addressed to him or by advertising; and

(b) the consumer took in that State the steps necessary for the conclusion of the contract.

Where a consumer enters into a contract with a party who is not domiciled in a Contracting State but has a branch, agency or other establishment in one of the Contracting States, that party shall, in disputes arising out of the operations of the branch, agency or establishment, be deemed to be domiciled in the State.

This Section shall not apply to contracts of transport.

Article 14

A consumer may bring proceedings against the other party to a contract either in the courts of the Contracting State in which the party is domiciled or in the courts of the Contracting State in which he is himself domiciled.

Proceedings may be brought against a consumer by the other party to the contract only in the courts of the Contracting State in which the consumer is domiciled.

These provisions shall not affect the right to bring a counterclaim in the court in which, in accordance with this Section, the original claim is pending.

Article 15

The provisions of this Section may be departed from only by an agreement:

1. which is entered into after the dispute has arisen; or

2. which allows the consumer to bring proceedings in courts other than those indicated in this Section; or

3. which is entered into by the consumer and the other party to the contract, both of whom are at the time of conclusion of the contract domiciled or habitually resident in the same Contracting State, and which confers jurisdiction on the courts of that State, provided that such an agreement is not contrary to the law of that State.

Section 5

Exclusive jurisdiction

Article 16

The following courts shall have exclusive jurisdiction, regardless of domicile:

1. (a) in proceedings which have as their object rights *in rem* in immovable property or tenancies or immovable property, the courts of the Contracting State in which the property is situated;

    (b) however, in proceedings which have as their object tenancies of immovable property concluded for temporary private use for a maximum period of six consecutive months, the courts of the Contracting State in which the defendant is domiciled shall also have jurisdiction, provided that the tenant is a natural person and neither party is domiciled in the Contracting State in which the property is situated;

2. in proceedings which have as their object the validity of the constitution, the nullity or the dissolution of companies or other legal persons or associations of natural or legal persons, or the decisions of their organs, the courts of the Contracting States in which the company, legal person or association has its seat;

3. in proceedings which have as their object the validity in entries in public registers, the courts of the Contracting State in which the register is kept;

4. in proceedings concerned with the registration or validity of patents, trade marks, designs, or other similar rights required to be deposited or registered, the courts for the Contracting State in which the deposit or registration has been applied for, has taken place or is under the terms of an international convention deemed to have taken place;

5. in proceedings concerned with the enforcement of judgments, the courts of the Contracting States in which the judgement has been or is to be enforced.

Section 6

Prorogation of jurisdiction

Article 17

1. If the parties, one or more of whom is domiciled in a Contracting State, have agreed that a court or the courts of a Contracting State are to have jurisdiction to settle any disputes which have arisen or which may arise in connection with a particular legal relationship, that court or those courts shall have exclusive jurisdiction. Such an agreement conferring jurisdiction shall be either:

   (a) in writing or evidenced in writing; or

   (b) in a form which accords with practices which the parties have established between themselves; or

   (c) in international trade or commerce, in a form which accords with a usage of which the parties are or ought to have been aware and which in such trade or commerce is widely known to, and regularly observed by, parties to contracts of the type involved in the particular trade or commerce concerned.

   Where such an agreement is concluded by parties, none of whom is domiciled in a Contracting State, the courts of other Contracting States shall have no jurisdiction over their disputes unless the court or courts chosen have declined jurisdiction.

2. The court or courts of a Contracting State on which a trust instrument has conferred jurisdiction shall have exclusive jurisdiction in any proceedings brought against a settlor, trustee or beneficiary, if relations between these persons or their rights or obligations under the trust are involved.

3. Agreements or provisions of a trust instrument conferring jurisdiction shall have no legal force if they are contrary to the provisions of Article 12 or 15, or if the courts whose jurisdiction they purport to exclude have exclusive jurisdiction by virtue of Article 16.

4. If an agreement conferring jurisdiction was concluded for the benefit of only one of the parties, that party shall retain the right to bring proceedings in any other court which has jurisdiction by virtue of this Convention.

5. In matters relating to individual contracts of employment an agreement conferring jurisdiction shall have legal force only if it is entered into after the dispute has arisen.

Article 18

Apart from jurisdiction derived from other provisions of this Convention, a court of a Contracting State before whom a defendant enters an appearance shall have jurisdiction. This rule shall not apply where appearance was entered solely to contest the jurisdiction, or where another court has exclusive jurisdiction by virtue of Article 16.

Section 7

Examination as to jurisdiction and admissibility

Article 19

Where a court of a Contracting State is seised of a claim which is principally concerned with a matter over which the courts of another Contracting State have exclusive jurisdiction by virtue of Article 16, it shall declare of its own motion that it has no jurisdiction.

Article 20

Where a defendant domiciled in one Contracting State is sued in a court of another Contracting State and does not enter an appearance, the court shall declare of its own motion that it has no jurisdiction unless its jurisdiction is derived from the provisions of this Convention.

The court shall stay the proceedings so long as it is not shown that the defendant has been able to receive the document instituting the proceedings or an equivalent document in sufficient time to arrange for his defence, or that all necessary steps have been taken to this end.

The provisions of the foregoing paragraph shall be replaced by those of Article 15 of the Hague Convention of 15th November 1965 on the service abroad of judicial and extrajudicial documents in civil or commercial matters, if the document instituting the proceedings or notice thereof had to be transmitted abroad in accordance with that Convention.

Section 8

Lis pendens – related actions

Article 21

Where proceeding involving the same cause of action and between the same parties are brought in the courts of different Contracting State, any court other than the court first seised shall of its own motion stay its proceedings until such time as the jurisdiction of the court first seised is established.

Where the jurisdiction of the court first seised is established, any court other than the court first seised shall decline jurisdiction in favour of that court.

Article 22

Where related actions are brought in the courts of different Contracting States, any court other than the court first seised may, while the actions are pending at first instance, stay its proceedings.

A court other than the court first seised may also, on the application of one of the parties, decline jurisdiction if the law of that court permits the consolidation of related actions and the court first seised has jurisdiction over both actions.

For the purposes of this Article, actions are deemed to be related where they are so closely connected that it is expedient to hear and determine them together to avoid the risk of irreconcilable judgments resulting from separate proceedings.

Article 23

Where actions come within the exclusive jurisdiction of several courts, any court other than the court first seised shall decline jurisdiction in favour of that court.

Section 9
Provisional, including protective measures

Article 24

Applications may be made to the courts of a Contracting State for such provisional, including protective, measures as may be available under the law of that State, even if, under this Convention, the courts of another Contracting State have jurisdiction as to the substance of the matter.

TITLE III
RECOGNITION AND ENFORCEMENT

Article 25

For the purposes of this Convention 'judgment' means any judgment given by a court or tribunal of a Contracting State, whatever the judgment may be called, including a decree, order, decision or writ of execution, as well as the determination of costs or expenses by an officer of the court.

Section 1
Recognition

Article 26

A judgment given in a Contracting State shall be recognised in the other Contracting States without any special procedure being required.

Any interested party who raises the recognition of a judgment as the principal issue in a dispute may, in accordance with the procedures provided for in Sections 2 and 3 of this Title, apply for a decision that the judgment be recognised.

If the outcome of proceedings in a court of a Contracting State depends on the determination of an incidental question of recognition that court shall have jurisdiction over that question.

Article 27

A judgment shall not be recognised:

1. if such recognition is contrary to public policy in the State in which recognition is sought;

2. where it was given in default of appearance, if the defendant was not duly served with the document which instituted the proceedings or with an equivalent document in sufficient time to enable him to arrange for his defence;

3. if the judgment is irreconcilable with a judgment given in a dispute between the same parties in the State in which recognition is sought;

4. if the court of the State or origin, in order to arrive at its judgment, has decided a preliminary question concerning the status or legal capacity of natural persons, rights in property arising out of a matrimonial relationship, will or succession in a way that conflicts with a rule of the private international law of the State in which the recognition is sought, unless the same result would have been reached by the application of the rules of private international law of that State;

5. if the judgment is irreconcilable with an earlier judgment given in a non-Contracting State involving the same cause of action and between the same parties, provided that this latter judgment fulfils the conditions necessary for its recognition in the State addressed.

Article 28

Moreover, a judgment shall not be recognised if it conflicts with the provisions of Section 3, 4 or 5 of Title II or in a case provided for in Article 59.

A judgment may furthermore be refused recognition in any case provided for in Article 54B(3) or 57(4).

In its examination of the grounds of jurisdiction referred to in the foregoing paragraphs, the court or authority applied to shall be bound by the findings of fact on which the court of the State of origin based its jurisdiction.

Subject to the provisions of the first and second paragraphs, the jurisdiction of the court of the State of origin may not be reviewed; the test of public policy referred to in Article 27(1) may not be applied to the rules relating to jurisdiction.

Article 29

Under no circumstances may a foreign judgment be reviewed as to its substance.

Article 30

A court of a Contracting State in which recognition is sought of a judgment given in another Contracting State may stay the proceedings if an ordinary appeal against the judgment has been lodged.

A court of a Contracting State in which recognition is sought of a judgment given in Ireland or the United Kingdom may stay the proceedings if enforcement is suspended in the State of origin by reason of an appeal.

Section 2
Enforcement

Article 31

A judgment given in a Contracting State and enforceable in the State shall be enforced in another Contracting State when, on the application of any interested party, it has been declared there.

However, in the United Kingdom, such a judgment shall be enforced in England and Wales, in Scotland, or in Northern Ireland when, on the application of any interested party, it has been registered for enforcement in that part of the United Kingdom.

Article 32

1. The application shall be submitted:
   - in Belgium, to the tribunal de première instance or rechtbank van eerste annleg,
   - in Denmark, to the byret,
   - in the Federala Republic of Germany, to the presiding judge of a chamber of the Landgericht,
   - in Greece, to the μονομελες πρωτοδικειο,
   - in Spain, to the Juzgado de Primera Instancia,
   - in France, to the presiding judge of the tribunal de grande instances,
   - in Ireland, to the High Court,
   - in Iceland, to the héraðsdómari,
   - in Italy, to the corte d'appello,
   - in Luxembourg, to the presiding judge of the tribunal d'arrondissement,
   - in the Netherlands, to the presiding judge of the arrondissementsrechtbank,
   - in Norway, to the herredsrett or byrett as namsrett,
   - in Austria, to the Landesgericht or the Kreisgericht,
   - in Portugal, to the Tribunal Judicial de Circulo,
   - in Switzerland:
     (a) in respect of judgments ordering the payment of a sum of money, to the judge de la mainlevée/Rechtsöffnungsrichter/giudice competente a pronunciare sul rigetto dell'opposizione, within the framework of the procedure governed by Articles 80 and 81 of the loi fédérale sur la poursuite pour dettes et la faillite/Bundesgesetz

über Schuldbetreibung und Konkurs/legge federale sulla esecuzione e sul fallimento;

(b) in respect of judgment ordering a performance other than the payment of a sum of money, to the juge cantonal d'exequatur compétent/zustündiger kantonaler Vollstreckungsrichter/giudice cantonale competente a pronunciare l'exequatur,

- in Finland, to the ulosotonhaltija/överexekutor,

- in Sweden, to the Svea hovrätt,

- in the United Kingdom:

(a) in England and Wales to the High Court of Justice, or in the case of maintenance judgment to the magistrates' court on transmission by the Secretary of State;

(b) in Scotland, to the Court of Session, or in the case of a maintenance judgment to the Sheriff Court on transmission by the Secretary of State;

(c) in Northern Ireland, to the High Court of Justice, or in the case of a maintenance judgment to the magistrates' court on transmission by the Secretary of State.

2. The jurisdiction of local courts shall be determined by reference to the place of domicile of the party against whom enforcement is sought. If he is not domiciled in the State in which enforcement is sought, it shall be determined by reference to the place of enforcement.

Article 33

The procedure for making the application shall be governed by the law of the State in which enforcement is sought.

The applicant must give an address for service of process within the area of jurisdiction of the court applied to. However, if the law of the State in which enforcement is sought does not provide for the furnishing of such an address, the applicant shall appoint a representative *ad litem*.

The document referred to in Articles 46 and 47 shall be attached to the application.

Article 34

The court applied to shall give its decision without delay; the party against whom enforcement is sought shall not at this stage of the proceedings be entitled to make any submissions on the application.

The application may be refused only for one of the reasons specified in Articles 27 and 28.

Under no circumstances may the foreign judgment be reviewed as to its substance.

Article 35

The appropriate officer of the courts shall without delay bring the decision given on the application to the notice of the applicant in accordance with the procedure laid down by the law of the State in which enforcement is sought.

Article 36

If enforcement is authorised, the party against whom enforcement is sought may appeal against the decision within one month of service thereof.

If that party is domiciled in a Contracting State other than that in which the decision authorising enforcement was given, the time for appealing shall be two months and shall run from the date of service, either on him in person or at his residence. No extension of time may be granted on account of distance.

Article 37

1. An appeal against the decision authorising enforcement shall be lodged in accordance with the rules governing procedure in contentious matters:
   - in Belgium, with the tribunal de Première instance or rechtbank van eerste aanleg,
   - in Denmark, with the landsret,
   - in the Federal Republic of Germany, with the Oberlandesgericht,
   - in Greece, with the εφετείο,
   - in Spain, with the Audiencia Provincial,
   - in France, with the court d'appel,
   - in Ireland, with the High Court,
   - in Iceland, with the héraðsdómari,
   - in Italy, with the corte d'appello,
   - in Luxembourg, with the Cour supérieure de justice sitting as a court of civil appeal,
   - in the Netherlands, with the arrondissementsrechtsbank,
   - in Norway, with the lagmannsrett,
   - in Austria, with the Landesgericht or the Kreisgericht,
   - in Portugal, with the Tribunal da Relaçao,
   - in Switzerland, with the tribunal cantonal/Kantonsgericht/tribunale cantonale
   - in Finland, with the hovioikeus/hovrätt,
   - in the United Kingdom:
     (a) in England and Wales, with the High Court of Justice, or in the case of maintenance judgment with the magistrates' court;

(b) in Scotland, with the Court of Session, or in the case of a maintenance judgment with the Sheriff Court;

(c) in Northern Ireland, with the High Court of Justice, or in the case of maintenance judgment with the magistrates' court.

2. The judgment given on the appeal may be contested only:

   - in Belgium, Greece, Spain, France, Italy, Luxembourg and in the Netherlands, by an appeal in cassation,

   - in Denmark, by an appeal to the højesteret, with the leave of the Minister of Justice,

   - in the Federal Republic of Germany, by a Rechtsbeschwerde,

   - in Ireland, by an appeal on a point of law to the Supreme Court,

   - in Iceland, by an appeal to the Hæstiréttur,

   - in Norway, by an appeal (Kjæremål or anke) to the Hoyesteretts Kjæremålsutvalg or Hoyesterett,

   - in Austria, in the case of an appeal, by a Revisionsrekurs and, in the case of opposition proceedings, by a Berufung with the possibility of a Revision,

   - In Portugal, by an appeal on a point of law,

   - in Switzerland, by a recours de droit public devant le tribunal féderal/staatsrechtliche Beschwerede beim βundesgericht/ricorso di diritto pubblico davanti al tribunale federale,

   - in Finland, by an appeal to the korkein oikeus/högsta domstolen,

   - in Sweden, by an appeal to the högsta domstolen,

   - in the United Kingdom, by a single further appeal on a point of law.

Article 38

The court with which the appeal under the first paragraph of Article 37 is lodged may, on the application of the appellant, stay the proceedings if an ordinary appeal has been lodged against the judgment in the State of origin or if the time for such an appeal has not yet expired; in the latter case, the court may specify the time within which such an appeal is to be lodged.

Where the judgment was given in Ireland or the United Kingdom, any form of appeal available in the State of origin shall be treated as an ordinary appeal for the purposes of the first paragraph.

The court may also make enforcement conditional on the provision of such security as it shall determine.

Article 39

During the time specified for an appeal pursuant to Article 36 and until any such appeal has been determined, no measures of enforcement may be taken other than protective measures taken against the property of the party against whom enforcement is sought.

The decision authorising enforcement shall carry with it the power to proceed to any such protective measures.

Article 40

1. If the application for enforcement is refused, the applicant may appeal:
   - in Belgium, to the cour d'appel or hof van beroep,
   - in Denmark, to the landsret,
   - in the Federal Republic of Germany, to the Oberlandesgericht,
   - in Greece, to the εφετείο,
   - in Spain, to the Audiencia Provincial,
   - in France, to the cour d'appel,
   - in Ireland, to the High Court,
   - in Iceland, to the héraðsdómari,
   - in Italy, to the corte d'appello,
   - in Luxembourg, to the Court supérieure de justice sitting as a court of civil appeal,
   - in the Netherlands, to the gerechtshof,
   - in Norway, to the lagmannsrett,
   - in Austria, to the Landesgericht or the Kreisgericht,
   - in Portugal, to the Tribunal da Relaçäo,
   - in Switzerland, to the tribunal cantonal/Kantonsgericht/tribunale cantonale,
   - in Finland, to the hovioikeus/hovrätt,
   - in Sweden, to the Svea hovrätt,
   - in the United Kingdom:
     (a) in England and Wales, to the High Court of Justice, or in the case of a maintenance judgment to the magistrates' court;
     (b) in Scotland, to the Court of Session, or in the case of a maintenance judgment ot the Sheriff Court;
     (c) in Northern Ireland, to the High Court of Justice, or in the case of a maintenance judgment to the magistrates' court.

2. The party against whom enforcement is sought shall be summoned to appear before the appellate court. If he fails to appear, the provisions of the second and third paragraphs of Article 20 shall apply even where he is not domiciled in any of the Contracting States.

Article 41

A judgment given on an appeal provided for in Article 40 may be contested only:

- in Belgium, Greece, Spain, France, Italy, Luxembourg and in the Netherlands by an appeal in cassation,
- in Denmark, by an appeal to the højesteret, with the leave of the Minister of Justice,
- in the Federal Republic of Germany, by a Rechtsbeschwerde,
- in Ireland, by an appeal on a point of law to the Supreme Court,
- in Iceland, by an appeal to the Hæstiréttur,
- in Norway, by an appeal (Kjæremål or anke) to the Hoyesteretts kjæremålsutvalg or Hoyesterett,
- in Austria, by a Revisionsrekurs,
- in Portugal, by an appeal on a point of law,
- in Switzerland, by a recours d droit public devant le tribunal fédéral/staatsrechtliche Beschwerde beim bundesgericht/ricorso di diritto pubblico davanti al tribunale federale,
- in Finland, by an appeal to the korkein oikeus/högsta domstolen,
- in Sweden, in an appeal to the högsta domstolen,
- in the United Kingdom, by a single further appeal on a point of law.

Article 42

Where a foreign judgment has been given in respect of several matters and enforcement cannot be authorised for all of them, the court shall authorise enforcement for one or more of them.

An application may request partial enforcement of a judgment.

Article 43

A foreign judgment which orders a periodic payment by way of a penalty shall be enforceable in the State in which enforcement is sought only if the amount of the payment has been finally determined by the courts of the State of origin.

Article 44

An applicant who, in the State of origin, has benefited from complete or partial legal aid or exemption from costs or expenses, shall be entitled, in the procedures provided for in Articles 32 to 35, to benefit from the most favourable legal aid or the most extensive exemption from costs or expenses provided for by the law of the State addressed.

However, an applicant who requests the enforcement of a decision given by an administrative authority in Denmark or in Iceland in respect of a maintenance order may, in the State addressed, claim the benefits referred to in the first paragraph if he presents a statement from, respectively, the Danish Ministry of Justice or the Icelandic Ministry of Justice to the effect that he fulfils the economic requirements to qualify for the grant of complete or partial legal aid or exemption from costs or expenses.

Article 45

No security, bond or deposit, however described, shall be required of a party who in one Contracting State applies for enforcement of a judgment given in another Contracting State on the ground that he is a foreign national or that he is not domiciled or resident in the State in which enforcement is sought.

Section 3

Common provisions

Article 46

A party seeking recognition or applying for enforcement of a judgment shall produce:

1. a copy of the judgment which satisfied the conditions necessary to establish its authenticity;

2. in the case of a judgment given in default, the original or a certified true copy of the document which establishes that the party in default was served with the document instituting the proceedings or with an equivalent document.

Article 47

A party applying for enforcement shall also produce:

1. documents which establish that, according to the law of the State of origin, the judgment is enforceable and has been served;

2. where appropriate, a document showing that the applicant is in receipt of legal aid in the State of origin.

Article 48

If the documents specified in Article 46(2) and Article 47(2) are not produced, the court may specify a time for their production, accept equivalent documents or, if it considers that it has sufficient information before it, dispense with their production.

If the court so requires, a translation of the documents shall be produced; the translation shall be certified by a person qualified to do so in one of the Contracting States.

Article 49

No legislation or other similar formality shall be required in respect of the documents referred to in Article 46 or 47 or the second paragraph of Article 48, or in respect of a document appointing a representative *ad litem*.

TITLE IV

AUTHENTIC INSTRUMENTS AND COURT SETTLEMENTS

Article 50

A document which has been formally drawn up or registered as an authentic instrument and is enforceable in one Contracting State shall, in another Contracting State, be declared enforceable there, on application made in accordance with the procedures provided for in Articles 31 *et seq*. The application may be refused only if enforcement of the instrument is contrary to public policy in the State addressed.

The instrument produced must satisfy the conditions necessary to establish its authenticity in the State of origin.

The provisions of Section 3 of Title III shall apply as appropriate.

Article 51

A settlement which has been approved by a court in the course of proceedings and is enforceable in the State in which it was concluded shall be enforceable in the State addressed under the same conditions as authentic instruments.

TITLE V

GENERAL PROVISIONS

Article 52

In order to determine whether a party is domiciled in the Contracting State whose courts are seised of a matter, the court shall apply its internal law.

If a party is not domiciled in the State whose courts are seised of the mater, then, in order to determine whether the party is domiciled in another Contracting State, the court shall apply the law of that State.

Article 53

For the purposes of this Convention, the seat of a company or other legal person or association of natural or legal persons shall be treated as its domicile. However, in order to determine that seat, the court shall apply its rules of private international law.

In order to determine whether a trust is domiciled in the Contracting State whose courts are seised of the matter, the court shall apply its rules of private international law.

TITLE VI

TRANSITIONAL PROVISIONS

Article 54

The provisions of this Convention shall apply only to legal proceedings instituted and to documents formally drawn up or registered as authentic instruments after its entry into force in the State of origin and, where recognition or enforcement of a judgement or authentic instrument is sought, in the State addressed.

However, judgments given after the date of entry into force of this Convention between the State of origin and the State addressed in proceedings instituted before the date shall be recognised and enforced in accordance with the provisions of Title III if jurisdiction was founded upon rules which accorded with those provided for either in Title II of this Convention or in a convention concluded between the State of origin and the State addressed which was in force when the proceedings were instituted.

If the parties to a dispute concerning a contract had agreed in writing before the entry into force of this Convention that the contract was to be governed by the law of Ireland or of a part of the United Kingdom, the courts of Ireland or of that part of the United Kingdom shall retain the right to exercise jurisdiction in the dispute.

Article 54A

For a period of three years from the entry into force of this Convention for Denmark, Greece, Ireland, Iceland, Norway, Finland and Sweden, respectively, jurisdiction in maritime matters shall be determined in these States not only in accordance with the provisions of Title II, but also in accordance with the provisions of paragraphs 1 to 7 following. However, upon the entry into force of the International Convention relating to the arrest of sea-going ships, signed at Brussels on 10th May 1952, for one of these States, these provisions shall cease to have effect for that State.

1. A person who is domiciled in a Contracting States may be sued in the courts of one of the States mentioned above in respect of a maritime claim if the ship to which the claim relates or any other ship owned by him has been arrested by judicial process within the territory of the latter State to secure the claim, or could have been so arrested there but bail or other security has been given, and either:

    (a) the claimant is domiciled in the latter State; or

    (b) the claim arose in the latter State; or

    (c) the claim concerns the voyage during which the arrest was made or could have been made; or

    (d) the claim arises out of a collision or out of damage caused by a ship to another ship or to goods   or persons on board either ship, either by the execution or non-execution of a manoeuvre or by the non-observance of regulations; or

    (e) the claim is for salvage; or

    (f) the claim is in respect of a mortgage or hypothecation of the ship arrested.

2. A claimant may arrest either the particular ship to which the maritime claims relates, or any other ship which is owned by the person who was, at the time when the maritime claim arose, the owner of the particular ship. However, only the particular ship to which the maritime claim relates may be arrested in respect of the maritime claims set out in 5.(o), (p) or (q) of this Article.

3. Ships shall be deemed to be in the same ownership when all the shares therein are owned by the same person or persons.

4. When in the case of a charter by demise of a ship the charterer alone is liable in respect of a maritime claim relating to that ship, the claimant may arrest that ship or any other ship owned by the charterer, but no other ship owned by the owner may be arrested in respect of such claim. The same shall apply to any case in which a person other than the owner of a ship is liable in respect of a maritime claim relating to that ship.

5. The expression 'maritime claim' means a claim arising out of one or more of the following:

    (a) damage caused by any ship either in collision or otherwise;

(b) loss of life or personal injury caused by any ship or occurring in connection with the operation of any ship;

(c) salvage;

(d) agreement relating to the use or hire of any ship whether by charterparty or otherwise;

(e) agreement relating to the carriage of goods in any ship whether by charterparty or otherwise;

(f) loss of or damage to goods including baggage carried in any ship;

(g) general average;

(h) bottomry;

(i) towage;

(j) pilotage;

(k) goods or materials wherever supplied to a ship for her operation or maintenance;

(l) construction, repair or equipment of any ship or dock charges and dues;

(m) wages of masters, officers or crew;

(n) master's disbursements, including disbursement made by shippers, charterers or agents on behalf of a ship or her owner;

(o) dispute as to the title to or ownership of any ship;

(p) disputes between co-owners of any ship as to the ownership, possession, employment or earnings of that ship;

(q) the mortgage or hypothecation of any ship.

6. In Denmark, the expression 'arrest' shall be deemed, as regards the maritime claims referred to in 5.(o) and (p) of this Article, to include a 'forbud', where that is the only procedure allowed in respect of such a claim under Articles 646 to 653 of the law on civil procedure (lov om rettens pleje).

7. In Iceland, the expression 'arrest' shall be deemed, as regards the maritime claims referred to in 5.(o) and (p) of this Article, to include a 'lögbann', where that is the only procedure allowed in respect of such a claim under Chapter III of the law on arrest and injunction (lög um kyrrsetningu og lögbann).

TITLE VII

RELATIONSHIP TO THE BRUSSELS CONVENTION AND TO OTHER CONVENTIONS

Article 54B

1. This Convention shall not prejudice the application by the Member States of the European Communities of the Convention on Jurisdiction and the Enforcement of Judgments in Civil and Commercial Matters, signed at Brussels on 27th September 1968 and of the Protocol on interpretation of that Convention by the Court of Justice, signed at Luxembourg on 3rd June 1971, as amended by the Conventions of Accession to the said Convention and the said Protocol by the States acceding to the European Communities, all of these Conventions and the Protocol being hereinafter referred to as the 'Brussels Convention'.

2. However, this Convention shall in any event be applied:

    (a) in matters of jurisdiction, where the defendant is domiciled in the territory of a Contracting State which is not a member of the European Communities, or where Article 16 or 17 of this Convention confers a jurisdiction on the courts of such a Contracting State;

    (b) in relation to a *lis pendens* or to related actions as provided for in Articles 21 and 22, when proceedings are instituted in a Contracting State which is not a member of the European Communities and in a Contracting State which is a member of the European Communities;

    (c) in matters of recognition and enforcement, where either the State of origin or the State addressed is not a member of the European Communities.

3. In addition to the grounds provided for in Title III recognition or enforcement may be refused if the ground of jurisdiction on which the judgment has been based differs from that resulting from the Convention and recognition or enforcement is sought against a party who is domiciled in a Contracting State which is not a member of the European Communities, unless the judgment may otherwise be recognised or enforced under any rule of law in the State addressed.

Article 55

Subject to the provisions of the second paragraph of Article 54 and of Article 56, this Convention shall, for the States which are parties to it, supersede the following conventions concluded between two or more of them:

- the Convention between the Swiss Confederation and France on jurisdiction and enforcement of judgments in civil matters, signed at Paris on 15th June 1869,
- the Treaty between the Swiss Confederation and Spain on the mutual enforcement of judgments in civil or commercial matters, signed at Madrid on 19th November 1896,
- the Convention between the Swiss Confederation and the German Reich on the recognition and enforcement of judgments and arbitration awards, signed at Berne on 2nd November 1929,
- the Convention between Denmark, Finland, Iceland, Norway, and Sweden on the recognition and enforcement of judgments, signed at Copenhagen on 16th March 1932,
- the Convention between the Swiss Confederation and Italy on the recognition and enforcement of judgments, signed at Rome on 3rd January 1933,
- the Convention between Sweden and the Swiss Confederation on the recognition and enforcement of judgments and arbitral awards, signed at Stockholm on 15th January 1936,
- the Convention between the Kingdom of Belgium and Austria on the reciprocal recognition and enforcement of judgments and authentic instruments relating to maintenance obligations, signed at Vienna on 25th October 1957,
- the Convention between the Swiss Confederation and Belgium on the recognition and enforcement of judgments and arbitration awards, signed at Berne, on 29th April 1959,
- the Convention between the Federal Republic of Germany and Austria on the reciprocal recognition and enforcement of judgments, settlements and authentic instruments in civil and commercial matters, signed at Vienna on 6th June 1959,
- the Convention between the Kingdom of Belgium and Austria on the reciprocal recognition and enforcement of judgments, arbitral awards and authentic instruments in civil and commercial matters, signed at Vienna on 16th June 1959,
- the Convention between Austria and the Swiss Confederation on the recognition and enforcement of judgments, signed at Berne on 16th December 1960,
- the Convention between Norway and the United Kingdom providing for the reciprocal recognition and enforcement of judgments in civil matters, signed at London on 12th June 1961,
- the Convention between the United Kingdom and Austria providing for the reciprocal recognition and enforcement of judgments in civil

and commercial matters, signed at Vienna on 14th July 1961, with amending Protocol signed at London on 6th March 1970,

- the Convention between the Kingdom of the Netherlands and Austria on the reciprocal recognition and enforcement of judgments and authentic instruments in civil and commercial matters, signed at The Hague on 6th February 1963,

- the Convention between France and Austria on the recognition and enforcement of judgments and authentic instruments in civil and commercial matters, signed at Vienna on 15th July 1966,

- the Convention between Luxembourg and Austria on the recognition and enforcement of judgments and authentic instruments in civil and commercial matters, signed at Luxembourg on 29th July 1971,

- the Convention between Italy and Austria on the recognition and enforcement of judgments in civil and commercial matters, of judicial settlements and of authentic instruments, signed at Rome on 16th November 1971,

- the Convention between Norway and the Federal Republic of Germany on the recognition and enforcement of judgments and enforceable documents, in civil and commercial matters, signed at Oslo on 17th June 1977,

- the Convention between Denmark, Finland, Iceland, Norway and Sweden on the recognition and enforcement of judgments in civil matters, signed at Copenhagen on 11th October 1977,

- the Convention between Austria and Sweden on the recognition and enforcement of judgments in civil matters, signed at Stockholm on 16th September 1982,

- the Convention between Austria and Spain on the recognition and enforcement of judgments, settlements and enforceable authentic instruments in civil and commercial matters, signed at Vienna on 17th February 1984,

- the Convention between Norway and Austria on the recognition and enforcement of judgments in civil matters, signed at Vienna on 21st May 1984, and

- the Convention between Finland and Austria on the recognition and enforcement of judgment in civil matters, signed at Vienna on 17th November 1986.

Article 56

The Treaty and the conventions referred to in Article 55 shall continue to have effect in relation to matters to which this Convention does not apply.

They shall continue to have effect in respect of judgments given and documents formally drawn up or registered as authentic instruments before the entry into force of this Convention.

Article 57

1. This Convention shall not affect any conventions to which the Contracting States are or will be parties and which, in relation to particular matters, govern jurisdiction or the recognition or enforcement of judgments.

2. This Convention shall not prevent a court of a Contracting State which is party to a convention referred to in the first paragraph from assuming jurisdiction in accordance with that convention, even where the defendant is domiciled in a Contracting State which is not a party to that convention. The court hearing the action shall, in any event, apply Article 20 of this Convention.

3. Judgments given in a Contracting State by a court in the exercise of jurisdiction provided for in a convention referred to in the first paragraph shall be recognised and enforced in the other Contracting States in accordance with Title III of this Convention.

4. In addition to the grounds provided for in Title III, recognition or enforcement may be refused if the State addressed is not a contracting party to a convention referred to in the first paragraph and the person against whom recognition or enforcement is sought is domiciled in that State, unless the judgment may otherwise be recognised or enforced under any rule of law in the State addressed.

5. Where a convention referred to in the first paragraph to which both the State of origin and the State addressed are parties lays down conditions for the recognition or enforcement of judgments, those conditions shall apply. In any event, the provisions of this Convention which concern the procedures for recognition and enforcement of judgments may be applied.

Article 58
[None]

Article 59

The Convention shall not prevent a Contracting State from assuming, in a convention on the recognition and enforcement of judgments, an obligation towards a third State not to recognise judgments given in other Contracting States against defendant domiciled or habitually resident in the third State where, in cases provided for in Article 4, the judgment could only be founded on a ground of jurisdiction specified in the second paragraph of Article 3.

However, a Contracting State may not assume an obligation towards a third State not to recognise a judgment given in another Contracting State by a court basing its jurisdiction on the presence within that State of property belonging to the defendant, or the seizure by the plaintiff of property situated there:

1. if the action is brought to assert or declare proprietary or possessory rights in that property, seeks to obtain authority to dispose of it, or arises from another issue relating to such property, or

2. if the property constitutes the security for a debt which is the subject matter of the action.

TITLE VIII

FINAL PROVISIONS

Article 60

The following may be parties to this Convention:

(a) States which, at the time of the opening of this Convention for signature, are members of the European Communities or of the European Free Trade Association;

(b) States which, after the opening of the Convention for signature, become members of the European Communities or the European Free Trade Association;

(c) States invited to accede in accordance with Article 62(1)(b).

Article 61

1. This Convention shall be opened for signature by the States members of the European Communities or of the European Free Trade Association.

2. The Convention shall be submitted for ratification by the signatory States. The instruments of ratification shall be deposited with the Swiss Federal Council.

3. The Convention shall enter into force on the first day of the third month following the date on which two States, of which one is a member of the European Communities and the other a member of the European Free Trade Association, deposit their instruments of ratification.

4. The Convention shall take effect in relation to any other signatory State on the first day of the third month following the deposit of its instrument of ratification.

Article 62

1. After entering into force this Convention shall be open to accession by:

    (a) the States referred to in Article 60(b);

    (b) other States which have been invited to accede upon a request made by one of the Contracting States to the depository State. The depository State shall invite the State concerned to accede only if, after having communicated the contents of the communications that this State intends to make in accordance with Article 63, it has obtained the unanimous agreement of the signatory States and the Contracting States referred to in Article 60(a) and (b).

2. If an acceding State wishes to furnish details for the purposes of Protocol No 1, negotiations shall be entered into to that end. A negotiating conference shall be convened by the Swiss Federal Council.

3. In respect of an acceding State, the Convention shall take effect on the first day of the third month following the deposit of its instrument of accession.

4. However, in respect of an acceding State referred to in paragraph 1(a) or (b), the Convention shall take effect only in relations between the acceding State and the Contracting States which have not made any objections to the accession before the first day of the third month following the deposit of the instrument of accession.

Article 63

Each acceding State shall, when depositing its instrument of accession, communicate the information required for the application of Articles 3, 32, 37, 40, 41 and 55 of this Convention and furnish, if need be, the details prescribed during the negotiations for the purposes of Protocol No 1.

Article 64

1. This Convention is concluded for an initial period of five years from the date of its entry into force in accordance with Article 61(3), even in the case of States which ratify it or accede to it after that date.

2. At the end of the initial five-year period, the Convention shall be automatically renewed from year to year.

3. Upon the expiry of the initial five-year period, any Contracting State may, at any time, denounce the Convention by sending a notification to the Swiss Federal Council.

4. The denunciation shall take effect at the end of the calendar year following the expiry of a period of six months from the date of receipt by the Swiss Federal council of the notification of denunciation.

Article 65

The following are annexed to this Convention:

- a Protocol No 1, on certain questions of jurisdiction, procedure and enforcement,
- a Protocol No 2, on the uniform interpretation of the Convention,
- a Protocol No 3, on the application of Article 57.

These Protocols shall form an integral part of the Convention.

Article 66

Any Contracting State may request the revision of this Convention. To that end, the Swiss Federal Council shall issue invitations to a revision conference within a period of six months from the date of the request for revision.

Article 67

The Swiss Federal Council shall notify the States represented at the Diplomatic Conference of Lugano and the States who have later acceded to the Convention of:

(a) the deposit of each instrument of ratification or accession;

(b) the dates of entry into force of this Convention in respect of the Contracting States;

(c) any denunciation received pursuant to Article 64;

(d) any declaration received pursuant to Article Ia of Protocol No 1;

(e) any declaration received pursuant to Article Ib of Protocol No 1;

(f) any declaration received pursuant to Article IV of Protocol No 1;

(g) any communication made pursuant to Article VI of Protocol No 1.

Article 68

This Convention, drawn up in a single original in the Danish, Dutch, English, Finnish, French, German, Greek, Icelandic, Irish, Italian, Norwegian, Portuguese, Spanish and Swedish language, all fourteen texts being equally authentic, shall be deposited in the archives of the Swiss Federal Council. The Swiss Federal Council shall transmit a certified copy to the Government of each State represented at the Diplomatic Conference of Lugano and to the Government of each acceding State.

PROTOCOL No 1

ON CERTAIN QUESTIONS OF JURISDICTION, PROCEDURE AND ENFORCEMENT

The High Contracting Parties have agreed upon the following provisions, which shall be annexed to the Convention:

Article I

Any person domiciled in Luxembourg who is sued in a court of another Contracting State pursuant to Article 5(1) may refuse to submit to the jurisdiction of that court. If the defendant does not enter an appearance the court shall declare of its own motion that it has no jurisdiction.

An agreement conferring jurisdiction, within the meaning of Article 17, shall be valid with respect to a person domiciled in Luxembourg only if that person has expressly and specifically so agreed.

Article Ia

1. Switzerland reserves the right to declare, at the time of depositing its instrument of ratification, that a judgment given in another Contracting State shall be neither recognised nor enforced in Switzerland if the following conditions are met:

   (a) the jurisdiction of the court which has given the judgment is based only on Article 5(1) of this Convention; and

   (b) the defendant was domiciled in Switzerland at the time of the introduction of the proceedings; for the purposes of this Article, a company or other legal person is considered to be domiciled in Switzerland if it has its registered seat and the effective centre of activities in Switzerland; and

   (c) the defendant raises an objection to the recognition or enforcement of the judgment in Switzerland, provided that he has not waived the benefit of the declaration foreseen under this paragraph.

2. This reservation shall not apply to the extent that at the time recognition or enforcement is sought a derogation has been granted from Article 59 of the Swiss Federal Constitution. The Swiss Government shall communicate such derogations to the signatory States and the acceding States.

3. This reservation shall cease to have effect on 31st December 1999. It may be withdrawn at any time.

Article Ib

Any Contracting State may, by declaration made at the time of signing or of deposit of its instrument or ratification or of accession, reserve the right, notwithstanding the provisions of Article 28, not to recognise and enforce judgments given in the other Contracting States if the jurisdiction of the court of the State of origin is based, pursuant to Article 16(1)(b), exclusively on the domicile of the defendant in the State of origin, and the property is situated in the territory of the State which entered the reservation.

Article II

Without prejudice to any more favourable provisions of national laws, persons domiciled in a Contracting State who are being prosecuted in the criminal courts of another Contracting State of which they are not nationals for an offence which was not intentionally committed may be defended by persons qualified to do so, even if they do not appear in person.

However, the court seised of the matter may order appearance in person; in the case of failure to appear, a judgment given in the civil action without the person concerned having had the opportunity to arrange for his defence need not be recognised in the other Contracting States.

Article III

In proceedings for the issue of an order for enforcement, no charge, duty or fee calculated by reference to the value of the matter in issue may be levied in the State in which enforcement is sought.

Article IV

Judicial and extrajudicial documents drawn up in one Contracting State which have to be served on persons in another Contracting State shall be transmitted in accordance with the procedures laid down in the conventions and agreements concluded between the Contracting States.

Unless the State in which service is to take place objects by declaration to the Swiss Federal Council, such documents may also be sent by the appropriate public officers of the State in which the document has been drawn up directly to the appropriate public officers of the State in which the addressee is to be found. In this case the officer of the State of origin shall send a copy of the document to the officer of the State applied to who is competent to forward it to the addressee. The document shall be forwarded in the manner specified by the law of the State applied to. The forwarding shall be recorded by a certificate sent directly to the officer of the State of origin.

Article V

The jurisdiction specified in Articles 6(2) and 10 in actions on a warranty or guarantee or in any other third party proceedings may not be resorted to in the

Federal Republic of Germany, in Spain, in Austria and in Switzerland. Any person domiciled in another Contracting State may be sued in the courts:

- of the Federal Republic of Germany, pursuant to Articles 68, 72, 73 and 74 of the code of civil procedure (Zivilprozeβordnung) concerning third-party notices,
- of Spain, pursuant to Article 1482 of the civil code,
- of Austria, pursuant to Article 21 of the code of civil procedure (Zivilprozeβordnung) concerning third-party notices,
- of Switzerland, pursuant to the appropriate provisions concerning third-party notices of the cantonal codes of civil procedure.

Judgments given in the other Contracting States by virtue of Article 6(2) or Article 10 shall be recognised and enforced in the Federal Republic of Germany, in Spain, in Austria and in Switzerland in accordance with Title III. Any effects which judgments given in these States may have on third parties by application of the provisions in the preceding paragraph shall also be recognised in the other Contracting States.

Article Va

In matters relating to maintenance, the expression 'court' includes the Danish, Icelandic and Norwegian administrative authorities.

In civil and commercial matters, the expression 'court' includes the Finnish ulosotonhaltja/överexekutor.

Article Vb

In proceedings involving a dispute between the master and a member of the crew of a sea-going ship registered in Denmark, in Greece, in Ireland, in Iceland, in Norway, in Portugal or in Sweden concerning remuneration or other conditions of service, a court in a Contracting State shall establish whether the diplomatic or consular officer responsible for the ship has been notified of the dispute. It shall stay the proceedings so long as he has not been notified. It shall of its own motion decline jurisdiction if the officer, having been duly notified, has exercised the powers accorded to him in the matter by a consular convention, or in the absence of such a convention has, within the time allowed, raised any objection to the exercise of such jurisdiction.

Article Vc
[None]

Article Vd

Without prejudice to the jurisdiction of the European Patent Officer under the Convention on the grant of European patents, signed at Munich on 5th October 1973, the courts of each Contracting State shall have exclusive jurisdiction, regardless of domicile, in proceedings concerned with the registration or validity of any European patent granted for that State which is not a Community patent by virtue of the provision of Article 86 of the Convention for the European patent for the common market, signed at Luxembourg on 15th December 1975.

Article VI

The Contracting States shall communicate to the Swiss Federal Council the text of any provisions of their laws which amend either those provisions of their laws mentioned in the Convention or the lists of courts specified in Section 2 of Title III.

PROTOCOL No 2

ON THE UNIFORM INTERPRETATION OF THE CONVENTION

Preamble

The High Contracting Parties,

Having regard to Article 65 of this Convention,

Considering the substantial link between this Convention and the Brussels Convention,

Considering that the Court of Justice of the European Communities by virtue of the Protocol of 3rd June 1971 has jurisdiction to give rulings on the interpretation of the provisions of the Brussels Convention,

Being aware of the rulings delivered by the Court of Justice of the European Communities on the interpretation of the Brussels Convention up to the time of signature of this Convention,

Considering that the negotiations which led to the conclusion of the Convention were based on the Brussels Convention in the light of these rulings,

Desiring to prevent, in full deference to the independence of the courts, divergent interpretations and to arrive at as uniform an interpretation as possible of the provisions of the Convention which are substantially reproduced in this Convention,

Have agreed as follows:

Article 1

The court of each Contracting State shall, when applying and interpreting the provisions of the Convention, pay due account to the principles laid down by any relevant decision delivered by courts of the other Contracting States concerning provisions of this Convention.

Article 2

1. The Contracting Parties agree to set up a system of exchange of information concerning judgments delivered pursuant to this Convention as well as relevant judgments under the Brussels Convention. This system shall comprise:
    - transmission to a central body by the competent authorities of judgments delivered by the courts of last instance and the Court of Justice of the European Communities as well as judgments of particular importance which have become final and have been delivered pursuant to this Convention or the Brussels Convention,
    - classification of these judgments by the central body including, as far as necessary, the drawing-up and publication of translations and abstracts,
    - communication by the central body of the relevant documents to the competent national authorities of all signatories and acceding States to the Convention and to the Commission of the European Communities.

2. The central body is the Registrar of the Court of Justice of the European Communities.

Article 3

1. A Standing Committee shall be set up for the purposes of this Protocol.

2. The Committee shall be composed of representatives appointed by each signatory and acceding State.

3. The European Communities (Commission, Court of Justice and General Secretariat of the Council) and the European Free Trade Association may attend the meetings as observers.

Article 4

1. At the request of a Contracting Party, the depository of the Convention shall convene meetings of the Committee for the purpose of exchanging views on the functioning of the Convention and in particular on:
    - the development of the case law as communicated under the first indent of Article 2(1),
    - the application of Article 57 of the Convention.

2. The Committee, in the light of these exchanges, may also examine the appropriateness of starting on particular topics a revision of the Convention and make recommendations.

PROTOCOL No 3
ON THE APPLICATION OF ARTICLE 57

The High Contracting Parties have agreed as follows:

1. For the purposes of the Convention, provisions which, in relation to particular matters, govern jurisdiction or the recognition or enforcement of judgments and which are, or will be, contained in acts of the institutions of the European Communities shall be treated in the same way as the conventions referred to in paragraph 1 of Article 57.

2. If one Contracting State is of the opinion that a provision contained in an act of the institutions of the European Communities is incompatible with the Convention, the Contracting States shall promptly consider amending the Convention pursuant to Article 66, without prejudice to the procedure established by Protocol No 2.

SCHEDULE 2
OTHER AMENDMENTS OF THE 1982 ACT

1. The words 'Brussels Conventions' shall be substituted for the word 'Conventions' wherever occurring in section 2 (the Conventions to have the force of law) and section 3 (interpretation of the Conventions).

2. In section 4(1) (enforcement of judgments other than maintenance orders) and section 5(1) (recognition and enforcement of maintenance orders) after the words 'an application under Article 31' there shall be inserted the words 'of the 1968 Convention or of the Lugano Convention'.

3. In section 6 (appeals under Article 37, second paragraph and Article 41)–

   (a) in sub-section (1), after the words 'referred to' there shall be inserted the words 'in the 1968 Convention and the Lugano Convention'; and

   (b) in sub-section (3), after the words 'referred to' there shall be inserted the words 'in each of those Conventions'.

4. In section 9 (provisions supplementary to Title VII of the 1968 Convention) in sub-section (1)–

   (a) after the words 'Title VII of the 1968 Convention' there shall be inserted the words 'and apart from Article 54B, of Title VII of the Lugano Convention'; and

   (b) for the words 'that convention' there shall be substituted the words 'the Convention in question'.

5. In section 10 (allocation within UK of jurisdiction in proceedings with respect to trusts and consumer contracts in respect of which the 1968 Convention confers jurisdiction on UK courts generally) in sub-section (1), after the words 'the 1968 Convention' there shall be inserted the words 'or the Lugano Convention'.

6. In section 11 (proof and admissibility of certain judgments and related documents for the purposes of the 1968 Convention) in sub-section (1), after the words 'For the purposes of the 1968 Convention' there shall be inserted the words 'and the Lugano Convention'.

7. In section 12 (provision for issue of copies of, and certificates in connection with, UK judgments for purposes of the 1968 Convention) after the words 'the 1968 Convention' there shall be inserted the words 'or the Lugano Convention'.

8. In section 13 (modifications to cover authentic instruments and court settlements) in sub-section (1)–

    (a) after the words 'the 1968 Convention' in paragraph (a) there shall be inserted the words 'or the Lugano Convention';

    (b) after the words 'Title IV of the 1968 Convention' there shall be inserted the words 'or, as the case may be, Title IV of the Lugano Convention'; and

    (c) for the words 'that Convention' there shall be substituted the words 'the Convention in question'.

9. In section 14 (modifications consequential on revision of the Conventions)–

    (a) for the words 'any of the Conventions' wherever occurring in sub-sections (1) and (3), there shall be substituted the words 'the Lugano Convention or any of the Brussels Conventions'; and

    (b) in sub-section (1), after the words 'any revision connected with the accession to' there shall be inserted the words 'the Lugano Convention or'.

10. In section 15 (interpretation of Part I)–

    (a) in sub-section (1), in the definition of 'maintenance order', after the words 'maintenance judgment within the meaning of the 1968 Convention' there shall be inserted the words 'or, as the case may be, the Lugano Convention'; and

    (b) in sub-section (3), after the words 'authorised or required by the 1968 Convention' there shall be inserted the words 'the Lugano Convention'.

11. In section 16 (allocation within UK of jurisdiction in certain civil proceedings)–

(a) in paragraph (a) of sub-section (1), for the word 'the Convention' there shall be substituted the words 'that or any other Convention';

(b) in paragraph (b) of that sub-section, after the words 'Article 16' there shall be inserted the words 'of the 1968 Convention'; and

(c) in sub-section (4), after the words 'subject to the 1968 Convention' there shall be inserted the words 'and the Lugano Convention'.

12. The words 'Brussels or Lugano Contracting State' shall be substituted for the words 'Contracting State' wherever occurring in each of the following provisions, that is to say–

(a) in sub-sections (1)(a) and (3)(a) of section 25 (interim relief for England and Wales or Northern Ireland in the absence of substantive proceedings);

(b) in sub-sections (2)(a) and (3)(a) and (d) of section 27 (which makes for Scotland similar provision to that made in section 25 for England and Wales); and

(c) in section 28 (application of section 1 of the Administration of Justice (Scotland) Act 1972);

and, in section 25(1)(b), for the words 'the Convention' there shall be substituted the words 'that or any other Convention'.

13. In section 30 (proceedings in England and Wales or Northern Ireland for torts to immovable property) in sub-section (2), after the words 'subject to the 1968 Convention' there shall be inserted the words 'and the Lugano Convention'.

14. In section 32 (overseas judgments given in proceedings brought in breach of agreement for settlement of disputes) in sub-section (4) (saving for judgments required to be recognised or enforce in UK under the 1968 Convention, etc) in paragraph (a) after the words 'under the 1968 Convention' there shall be inserted the words 'or the Lugano Convention'.

15. In section 33 (certain steps not to amount to submission to the jurisdiction of an overseas court) in sub-section (2) (saving for judgments required to be recognised or enforced in England and Wales or Northern Ireland under the 1968 Convention) after the words 'under the 1968 Convention' there shall be inserted the words 'or the Lugano Convention'.

16. In section 41 (determination of domicile of individuals for the purposes of the 1968 Convention, etc) in sub-section (1), after the words 'for the purposes of the 1968 Convention' there shall be inserted the words 'the Lugano Convention'.

17. In section 42 (domicile and seat of corporation or association) in sub-section (2)(a), after the words 'for the purposes of the 1968 Convention'

there shall be inserted the words 'or, as the case may be, the Lugano Convention.'

18. In section 43 (seat of corporation or association for purposes of Article 16(2) and related provisions) in sub-section (1)(a), after the words 'Article 16(2)' there shall be inserted the words 'of the 1968 Convention or of the Lugano Convention'.

19.– (1) In section 44 (persons deemed to be domiciled in UK for certain purposes) in sub-section (1)–

(a) in paragraph (a) (which provides that the section applies to proceedings within Section 3 of Title II of the 1968 Convention) after the words 'the 1968 Convention' there shall be inserted the words 'or Section 3 of Title II of the Lugano Convention'; and

(b) in paragraph (b) (proceedings within Section 2 of that Title) for the words 'that Title' there shall be substituted the words 'Title II of either of those Conventions'.

(2) In sub-section (2) of that section after the words 'is deemed for the purposes of the 1968 Convention' there shall be inserted the words 'or, as the case may be, of the Lugano Convention'.

20. In section 45 (domicile of trusts) in sub-section (1), after the words 'for the purposes of the 1968 Convention' there shall be inserted the words 'the Lugano Convention'.

21.– (1) In section 46 (domicile and seat of the Crown) in sub-section (2)(a), after the words 'for the purposes of the 1968 Convention' there shall be inserted the words 'and the Lugano Convention' and for the words '– in which, there shall be substituted the words '– in each of which'.

(2) In sub-section (4) of that section (Order in Council with respect to seat of the Crown) after the words 'for the purposes of the 1968 Convention' there shall be inserted the words 'the Lugano Convention'.

22. In section 46 (modifications occasioned by decisions of the European Court as to meaning or effect of the Conventions) for the word 'Conventions', wherever occurring, there shall be substituted the words 'Brussels Conventions'.

23. In section 48 (matters for which rules of court may provide)–

(a) in sub-section (1), for the words 'or the Conventions' there shall be substituted the words 'the Lugano Convention or the Brussels Conventions'; and

(b) in sub-section (3), for the words 'the Conventions' there shall be substituted the words 'the Lugano Convention, the Brussels Conventions'.

24. In section 49 (saving for powers to stay, sist, strike our or dismiss proceedings where to do so is not inconsistent with the 1968 Convention) after the words 'the 1968 Convention' there shall be inserted the words 'or, as the case may be, the Lugano Convention'.

25. In section 50 (general interpretation) the following definitions shall be inserted at the appropriate places–

    "'Brussels Contracting State" has the meaning given by section 1(3)';

    "'The Brussels Conventions" has the meaning given by section 1(1)';

    "'Lugano Contracting State" has the meaning given by section 1(3)';

    "'the Lugano Convention" has the meaning given by section 1(1)',

    and the entry relating to 'the Conventions' is hereby repealed.

SCHEDULES 4 TO 9 OF THE CIVIL JURISDICTION AND JUDGMENTS ACT 1982 – THE MODIFIED CONVENTION

SCHEDULE 4

TITLE II OF 1968 CONVENTION, AS MODIFIED FOR ALLOCATION OF JURISDICTION WITHIN UK

TITLE II

JURISDICTION

Section 1

General provisions

Article 2

Subject to the provisions of this Title, persons domiciled in a part of the United Kingdom shall ... be sued in the courts of that part.

Article 3

Persons domiciled in a part of the United Kingdom may be sued in the courts of another part of the United Kingdom only by virtue of the rules set out in Sections 2, 4, 5 and 6 of this Title.

Section 2

Special jurisdiction

Article 5

A person domiciled in a part of the United Kingdom may, in another part of the United Kingdom, be sued:

(1) in matters relating to a contract, in the courts for the place of performance of the obligations in question; in matters relating to individual contracts of employment, this place is that where the employee habitually carries out his work or if the employee does not habitually carry out his work in any one country, the employer may also be sued in the courts for the place where the business which engaged the employee was or is now situated;

(2) in matters relating to maintenance, in the courts for the place where the maintenance creditor is domiciled or habitually resident or, if the matter is ancillary to proceedings concerning the status of a person, in the court which, according to its own law, has jurisdiction to entertain those proceedings, unless that jurisdiction is based solely on the nationality of one of the parties;

(3) in matters relating to tort, delict or quasi-delict, in the courts for the place where the harmful event occurred or in the case of a threatened wrong is likely to occur;

(4) as regards a civil claim for damages or restitution which is based on an act giving rise to criminal proceedings, in the court seised of those proceedings, to the extent that the court has jurisdiction under its own law to entertain civil proceedings;

(5) as regards a dispute arising out of the operations of a branch, agency or other establishment, in the courts for the place in which the branch agency or other establishment is situated.

(6) in his capacity as a settlor, trustee or beneficiary of a trust created by the operation of a statute, or by a written instrument, or created orally and evidenced in writing, in the courts of the part of the United Kingdom in which the trust is domiciled;

(7) as regards a dispute concerning the payment of remuneration claimed in respect of the salvage of a cargo or freight, in the court under the authority of which the cargo or freight in question–

(a) has been arrested to secure such payment; or

(b) could have been so arrested, but bail or other security has been given;

provided that this provision shall apply only if it is claimed that the defendant has an interest in the cargo or freight or had such an interest at the time of salvage;

(8) in proceedings–

(a) concerning a debt secured on immovable property;

or

(b) which are brought to assert, declare or determine proprietary or possessory rights, or rights of security, in or over movable property, or to obtain authority to dispose of movable property,

in the courts of the part of the United Kingdom in which the property is situated.

Article 5A

Proceedings which have as their object a decision of an organ of a company or other legal person or of an association of natural or legal persons may, without prejudice to the other provisions of this Title, be brought in the courts of the part of the United Kingdom in which that company, legal person or association has its seat.

Article 6

A person domiciled in a part of the United Kingdom may, in another part of the United Kingdom, also be sued:

(1) where he is one of a number of defendants, in the courts for the place where any one of them is domiciled;

(2) as a third party in an action on a warranty of guarantee or in any other third party proceedings, in the court seised of the original proceedings, unless these were instituted solely with the object of removing him from the jurisdiction of the court which would be competent in his case;

(3) on a counterclaim arising from the same contract or facts on which the original claim was based, in the court in which the original claim is pending.

Article 6A

Where by virtue of this Title a court of a part of the United Kingdom has jurisdiction in actions relating to liability arising from the use or operation of a ship, that court, or any other court substituted for this purpose by the internal law of that part, shall also have jurisdiction over claims for limitation of such liability.

Section 4

Jurisdiction over consumer contracts

Article 13

In proceedings concerning a contract concluded by a person for a purpose which can be regarded as being outside his trade or profession, hereinafter called 'the consumer', jurisdiction shall be determined by this Section, without prejudice to the provisions of Articles 5(5) and (8)(b), if it is:

(1) a contract for the sale of goods on instalment credit terms, or

(2) a contract for a loan repayable by instalments, or for any other form of credit, made to finance the sale of goods, or

(3) any other contract for the supply of goods or a contract for the supply of services and the consumer took in the part of the United Kingdom in which he is domiciled the steps necessary for the conclusion of the contract.

This Section shall not apply to contracts of transport or insurance.

Article 14

A consumer may bring proceedings against the other party to a contract either in the courts of the part of the United Kingdom in which that party is domiciled or in the courts of the part of the United Kingdom in which he is himself domiciled.

Proceedings may be brought against a consumer by the other party to the contract only in the courts of the part of the United Kingdom in which the consumer is domiciled.

These provisions shall not affect the right to bring a counterclaim in the court in which, in accordance with this Section, the original claim is pending.

Article 15

The provisions of this Section may be departed from only by an agreement:

(1) which is entered into after the dispute has arisen,

or

(2) which allows the consumer to bring proceedings in courts other than those indicated in this Section,

or

(3) which is entered into by the consumer and other party to the contract, both of whom are at the time of conclusion of the contract domiciled or habitually resident in the same part of the United Kingdom, and which confers jurisdiction on the courts of that part, provided that such an agreement is not contrary to the law of that part.

Section 5

Exclusive jurisdiction

Article 16

The following courts shall have exclusive jurisdiction, regardless of domicile:

(1) (a) in proceedings which have as their object right *in rem* in, or tenancies of, immovable property, the courts of the part of the United Kingdom in which the property is situated;

(b) however, in proceedings which have as their object tenancies of immovable property concluded for temporary use for a maximum period of six consecutive months, the courts of the United Kingdom shall have jurisdicition, provided that the landlord and the tenant are natural persons and are domiciled in the same part of the United Kingdom;

(2) in proceedings which have as their object the validity of the constitution, the nullity or the dissolution of companies or other legal persons or associations of natural or legal persons, the courts of the part of the United Kingdom in which the company, legal person or association has its seat;

(3) in proceedings which have as their object the validity of entries in public registers, the courts of the part of the United Kingdom in which the register is kept ...;

(5) in proceedings concerned with the enforcement of judgments, the courts of the part of the United Kingdom in which the judgment has been or is to be enforced.

Section 6

Prorogation of jurisdiction

Article 17

If the parties have agreed that a court or the courts of a part of the United Kingdom are to have jurisdiction to settle any disputes which have arisen or which may arise in connection with a particular legal relationship, and, apart from this Schedule, the agreement would be effective to confer jurisdiction under the law of that part, that court or those courts shall have jurisdiction.

The court or courts of a part of the United Kingdom on which a trust instrument has conferred jurisdiction shall have jurisdiction in any proceedings brought against a settlor, trustee or beneficiary, if relations between these persons or their rights or obligations under the trust are involved.

Agreements or provisions of a trust instrument conferring jurisdiction shall have no legal force if they are contrary to the provisions of Article 15, or if the courts, whose jurisdiction they purport to exclude have exclusive jurisdiction by virtue of Article 16.

In matters relating to individual contracts of employment an agreement conferring jurisdiction shall have legal force only if it is entered into after the dispute has arisen or if the employee invokes it to seise courts other than those for the defendant's domicile or those specified in Article 5(1).

Article 18

Apart from jurisdiction derived from other provisions of this Title, a court of a part of the United Kingdom before whom a defendant enters an appearance shall have jurisdiction. This rule shall not apply where appearance was entered solely to contest the jurisdiction, or where another court has exclusive jurisdiction by virtue of Article 16.

Section 7

Examination as to jurisdiction and admissibility

Article 19

Where a court of a part of the United Kingdom is seised of a claim which is principally concerned with a matter over which the courts of another part of the United Kingdom have exclusive jurisdiction by virtue of Article 16, it shall declare of its own motion that it has no jurisdiction.

Article 20

Where a defendant domiciled in one part of the United Kingdom is sued in a court of another part of the United Kingdom and does not enter an appearance, the court shall declare of its own motion that it has no jurisdiction unless its jurisdiction is derived from the provisions of this Title.

The court shall stay the proceedings so long as it is not shown that the defendant has been able to receive the document instituting the proceedings or an equivalent document in sufficient time to enable him to arrange for his defence, or that all necessary steps have been taken to this end.

Section 9

Provisions, including protective, measures

Article 24

Application may be made to the courts of a part of the United Kingdom for such provisions, including provisional, including protective, measures as may be available under the law of that part, even if, under this Title, the courts of another part of the United Kingdom have jurisdiction as to the substance of the matter.

SCHEDULE 5
PROCEEDINGS EXCLUDED FROM SCHEDULE 4

PROCEEDINGS UNDER THE COMPANIES ACTS

1. Proceedings for the winding up of a company under the Companies Act 1948 or the Companies Act (Northern Ireland) 1960, or proceedings relating to a company as respects which jurisdiction is conferred on the court having winding up jurisdiction under either of those Acts.

PATENTS, TRADE MARKS, DESIGNS AND SIMILAR RIGHTS

2. Proceedings concerned with the registration of validity of patents, trade marks, designs or other similar rights required to be deposited or registered.

PROTECTION OF TRADING INTERESTS ACT 1980

3. Proceedings under section 6 of the Protection of Trading Interests Act 1980 (recovery of sums paid or obtained pursuant to a judgment for multiple damages).

APPEALS, ETC, FROM TRIBUNALS

4. Proceedings on appeal form, or for review of, decisions of tribunals.

MAINTENANCE AND SIMILAR PAYMENTS TO LOCAL AND OTHER PUBLIC AUTHORITIES

5. Proceedings for, or otherwise relating to, an order under any of the following provisions–
   (a) paragraph 23 of Schedule 2 to the Children Act 1989 (contributions in respect of children in care, etc);
   (b) section 49 or 50 of the Child Care Act 1980, section 81 of the Social Work (Scotland) Act 1968 or section 159 of the Children and Young Persons Act (Northern Ireland) 1968 (applications for, or for variation of, affiliation orders in respect of children in care, etc);
   (c) section 43 of the National Assistance Act 1948, section 18 of the Supplementary Benefits Act 1976, Article 101 of the Health and Personal Social Services (Northern Ireland) Order 1972 or Article 23 of the Supplementary Benefits (Northern Ireland) Order 1977 (recovery of cost of assistance or benefit from person liable to maintain the assisted person);

(d) section 44 of the National Assistance Act 1948, section 19 of the Supplementary Benefits Act 1976, Article 102 of the Health and Personal Social Services (Northern Ireland) Order 1972 or Article 24 of the Supplementary Benefits (Northern Ireland) Order 1977 (applications for, or for variation of, affiliation orders in respect of children for whom assistance or benefit provided).

PROCEEDINGS UNDER CERTAIN CONVENTIONS, ETC

6. Proceedings brought in any court in pursuance of–

(a) any statutory provision which, in the case of any convention to which Article 57 applies (conventions relating to specific matters which override the general rules in the 1968 Convention), implements the convention or makes provision with respect to jurisdiction in any field to which the convention relates; and

(b) any rule of law so far as it has the effect of implementing any such convention.

CERTAIN ADMIRALTY PROCEEDINGS IN SCOTLAND

7. Proceedings in Scotland in an Admiralty cause where the jurisdiction of the Court of Session or, as the case may be, of the sheriff is based on arrestment *in rem* or *ad fundandam jurisdictionem* of a ship, cargo or freight.

REGISTER OF AIRCRAFT MORTGAGES

8. Proceedings for the rectification of the register of aircraft mortgages kept by the Civil Aviation Authority.

CONTINENTAL SHELF ACT 1964

9. Proceedings brought in any court in pursuance of an order under section 3 of the Continental Shelf Act 1964.

SCHEDULE 6

ENFORCEMENT OF UK JUDGMENTS (MONEY PROVISIONS)

PRELIMINARY

1. In this Schedule–

'judgment' means any judgment to which section 18 applies and references to the giving of a judgment shall be construed accordingly;

'money provision' means a provision for the payment of one or more sums of money;

'prescribed' means prescribed by rules of court.

CERTIFICATES IN RESPECT OF JUDGMENTS

2.– (1) Any interested party who wishes to secure that enforcement in another part of the United Kingdom of any money provisions contained in a judgment may apply for a certificate under this Schedule.

(2) The application shall be made in the prescribed manner to the proper officer of the original court, that is to say–

(a) in relation to a judgment within paragraph (a) of the definition of 'judgment' in section 18(2), the court by which the judgment or order was given or made;

(b) in relation to a judgment within paragraph (b) of that definition, the court in which the judgement or order is entered;

(c) in relation to a judgment within paragraph (c) of that definition, the court in whose books the document is registered;

(d) in relation to a judgment within paragraph (d) of that definition, the tribunal by which the award or order was made;

(e) in relation to a judgment within paragraph (e) of that definition, the court which gave the judgment or made the order by virtue of which the award has become enforceable as mentioned in that paragraph.

3. A certificate shall not be issued under this Schedule in respect of a judgment unless under the law of the part of the United Kingdom in which the judgment was given–

(a) either–

(i) the time for bringing an appeal against the judgment has expired, no such appeal having been brought within that time;

or

(ii) such an appeal having been brought within that time, that appeal has been finally disposed of; and

(b) enforcement of the judgment is not for the time being stayed or suspended, and the time available for its enforcement has not expired.

4.– (1) Subject to paragraph 3, on an application under paragraph 2 the proper officer shall issue to the applicant a certificate in the prescribed form–

(a) stating the sum or aggregate of the sums (including any costs or expenses) payable under the money provisions contained in the judgment, the rate of interest, if any, payable thereon and the date or time from which any such interest began to accrue;

(b) stating that the conditions specified in paragraph 3(a) and (b) are satisfied in relation to the judgment; and

(c) containing such other particulars as may be prescribed.

(2) More than one certificate may be issued under this Schedule (simultaneously or at different times) in respect of the same judgment.

REGISTRATION OF CERTIFICATES

5.– (1) Where a certificate has been issued under this Schedule in any part of the United Kingdom, any interested party may, within six months from the date of its issue, apply in the prescribed manner to the proper officer of the superior court in any other part of the United Kingdom for the certificate to be registered in that court.

(2) In this paragraph 'superior court' means, in relation to England and Wales or Northern Ireland, the High Court and, in relation to Scotland, the Court of Session.

(3) Where an application is duly made under this paragraph to the proper officer of a superior court, he shall register the certificate in that court in the prescribed manner.

GENERAL EFFECT OF REGISTRATION

6.– (1) A certificate registered under this Schedule shall, for the purposes of its enforcement, be of the same force and effect, the registering court shall have in relation to its enforcement the same powers, and proceedings for or with respect to its enforcement may be taken, as if the certificate had been a judgment originally given in the registering court and had (where relevant) been entered.

(2) Sub-paragraph (1) is subject to the following provisions of this Schedule and to any provision made by rules of court as to the manner in which and the conditions subject to which a certificate registered under this Schedule may be enforced.

COSTS OR EXPENSES

7. Where a certificate is registered under this Schedule, the reasonable costs or expenses of and incidental to the obtaining of the certificate and its registration shall be recoverable as if they were costs or expenses stated in the certificate to be payable under a money provision contained in the original judgment.

INTEREST

8.– (1) Subject to any provision, made under sub-paragraph (2), the debt resulting, apart from paragraph 7, from the registration of the certificate shall carry interest at the rate, if any, stated in the certificate from the date or time so stated.

(2) Provision may be made by rules of court as to the manner in which and the periods by reference to which any interest payable by virtue of sub-paragraph (1) is to be calculated and paid, including provision for such interest to cease to accrue as from a prescribed date.

(3) All such sums as are recoverable by virtue of paragraph 7 carry interest as if they were the subject of an order for costs or expenses made by the registering court on the date of registration of the certificate.

(4) Except as provided by this paragraph sums payable by virtue of the registration of a certificate under this Schedule shall not carry interest.

STAY OR SISTING OF ENFORCEMENT IN CERTAIN CASES

9. Where a certificate in respect of a judgment has been registered under this Schedule, the registering court may, if it is satisfied that any person against whom it is sought to enforce the certificate is entitled and intends to apply under the law of the part of the United Kingdom in which the judgment was given for any remedy which would result in the setting aside or quashing of the judgment, stay (or, in Scotland, sist) proceedings for the enforcement of the certificate, on such terms as it thinks fit, for such period as appears to the court to be reasonably sufficient to enable the application to be disposed of.

CASES IN WHICH REGISTRATION OF A CERTIFICATE MUST OR MAY BE SET ASIDE

10. Where a certificate has been registered under this Schedule, the registering court–

(a) shall set aside the registration if, on an application made by any interested party, it is satisfied that the registration was contrary to the provisions of this Schedule;

(b) may set aside the registration if, on an application so made, it is satisfied that the matter in dispute in the proceedings in which the judgment in question was given had previously been the subject of a judgment by another court or tribunal having jurisdiction in the matter.

SCHEDULE 7

ENFORCEMENT OF UK JUDGMENTS (NON-MONEY PROVISIONS)

PRELIMINARY

1. In this Schedule–

'judgment' means any judgment to which section 18 applies and references to the giving of a judgment shall be construed accordingly;

'non-money provision' means a provision for any relief or remedy not requiring payment of a sum of money;

'prescribed' means prescribed by rules of court.

CERTIFIED COPIES OF JUDGMENTS

2.– (1) Any interested party who wishes to secure the enforcement in another part of the United Kingdom of any non-money provisions contained in a judgment may apply for a certified copy of the judgment.

(2) The application shall be made in the prescribed manner to the proper officer of the original court, that is to say–

(a) in relation to a judgment within paragraph (a) of the definition of 'judgment' in section 18(2), the court by which the judgment or order was given or made;

(b) in relation to a judgment within paragraph (b) of that definition, the court in which the judgment or order is entered;

(c) in relation to a judgment within paragraph (c) of that definition, the court in whose books the document is registered;

(d) in relation to a judgment within paragraph (d) of that definition, the tribunal by which the award or order was made;

(e) in relation to a judgment within paragraph (e) of that definition, the court which gave the judgment or made the order by virtue of which the award has become enforceable as mentioned in that paragraph.

3. A certified copy of a judgment shall not be issued under this Schedule unless under the law of the part of the United Kingdom in which the judgment was given–

(a) either–

(i) the time for bringing an appeal against the judgment has expired, no such appeal having been brought within that time,

or

(ii) such an appeal having been brought within that time, that appeal has been finally disposed of; and

(b) enforcement of the judgment is not for the time being stayed or suspended, and the time available for its enforcement has not expired.

4.– (1) Subject to paragraph 3, on an application under paragraph 2 the proper officer shall issue to the applicant–

(a) a certified copy of the judgment (including any money provisions or excepted provisions which it may contain); and

(b) a certificate stating that the conditions specified in paragraph 3(a) and (b) are satisfied in relation to the judgment.

(2) In sub-paragraph (1)(a) 'excepted provision' means any provision of a judgment which is excepted from the application of section 18 by sub-section (5) of that section.

(3) There may be issued under this Schedule (simultaneously or at different times)–

(a) more than one certified copy of the same judgment; and

(b) more than one certificate in respect of the same judgment.

REGISTRATION OF JUDGMENTS

5.– (1) Where a certified copy of a judgment has been issued under this Schedule in any part of the United Kingdom, any interested party may apply in the prescribed manner to the superior court in any other part of the United Kingdom for the judgment to be registered in that court.

(2) In this paragraph 'superior court' means, in relation to England Wales or Northern Ireland, the High Court and, in relation to Scotland, the Court of Session.

(3) An application under this paragraph for the registration of a judgment must be accompanied by–

(a) a certified copy of the judgment issued under this Schedule; and

(b) a certificate is issued under paragraph 4(1)(b) in respect of the judgment not more than six months before the date of the application.

(4) Subject to sub-paragraph (5), where an application under this paragraph is duly made to a superior court, the court shall order the whole of the judgment as set out in the certified copy to be registered in that court in the prescribed manner.

(5) A judgment shall not be registered under this Schedule by the superior court in any part of the United Kingdom if compliance with the non-money provisions contained in the judgment would involve a breach of the law of that part of the United Kingdom.

GENERAL EFFECT OF REGISTRATION

6.– (1) The non-money provisions contained in a judgment registered under this Schedule shall, for the purposes of their enforcement, be of the same force and effect, the registering court shall have in relation to their enforcement the same powers, and proceedings for or with respect to their enforcement may be taken, as if the judgment containing them had been originally given in the registering court and had (where relevant) been entered.

(2) Sub-paragraph (1) is subject to the following provisions of this Schedule and to any provision made by rules of the court as to the manner in which and conditions subject to which the non-money provisions contained in a judgment registered under this Schedule may be enforced.

COSTS OR EXPENSES

7.– (1) Where a judgment is registered under this Schedule, the reasonable costs or expenses of and incidental to–

(a) the obtaining of the certified copy of the judgment and of the necessary certificate under paragraph 4(1)(b) in respect of it; and

(b) the registration of the judgment,

shall be recoverable as if on the date of registration there had also been registered in the registering court a certificate under Schedule 6 in respect of the judgment and as if those costs or expenses stated in that certificate to be payable under a money provision contained in the judgment.

(2) All such sums as are recoverable by virtue of sub-paragraph (1) shall carry interest as if they were the subject of an order for costs or expenses made by the registering court on the date of registration of the judgment.

STAY OR SISTING OF ENFORCEMENT IN CERTAIN CASES

8. Where a judgment has been registered under this Schedule, the registering court may, if it is satisfied that any person against whom it is sought to enforce the judgment is entitled and intends to apply under the law of the part of the United Kingdom in which the judgment was given for any remedy which would result in the setting aside or quashing of the judgment, stay (or, in Scotland sist) proceedings for the enforcement of the judgment, on such terms as it thinks fit, for such period as appears to the court to be reasonably sufficient to enable the application to be disposed of.

CASES IN WHICH REGISTERED JUDGMENT MUST OR MAY BE SET ASIDE

9. Where a judgment has been registered under this Schedule, the registering court–

> (a) shall set aside the registration if, on an application made by any interested party, it is satisfied that te registration was contrary to the provisions of this Schedule;
>
> (b) may set aside the registration if, on an application so made, it is satisfied that the matter in dispute in the proceedings in which the judgment was given had previously been the subject of a judgment by another court or tribunal having jurisdiction in the matter.

SCHEDULE 8

RULES AS TO JURISDICTION IN SCOTLAND

GENERAL

1. Subject to the following Rules, persons shall be sued i the courts for the place where they are domiciled.

SPECIAL JURISDICTION

2. Subject to Rules 3 (jurisdiction over consumer contracts), 4 (exclusive jurisdiction) and 5 (prorogation) a person may also be sued–

(1) where he has no fixed residence, in a court within whose jurisdiction he is personally cited;

(2) in matters relating to a contract, in the courts for the place of performance of the obligation in question;

(3) in matters relating to delict or quasi-delict, in the courts for the place where the harmful event occurred;

(4) as regards a civil claim for damages or restitution which is based on an act giving rise to criminal proceedings, in the court seised of those proceedings to the extent that that court has jurisdiction to entertain civil proceedings;

(5) in matters relating to maintenance, in the courts for the place where the maintenance creditor is domiciled or habitually resident or, if the matter is ancillary to proceedings concerning the status of a person, in the court which has jurisdiction to entertain those proceedings, provided that an action for adherence and ailment or of affiliation and ailment shall be treated as a matter relating to maintenance which is not ancillary to proceedings concerning the status of a person, and provided also that–

(a) where a local authority exercises its power to raise an action under section 44(7) of the National Assistance Act 1948 or under section 8(1) of the Social Work (Scotland) Act 1968; and

(b) where the Secretary of State exercises his power to raise an action under section 19(8)(a) of the Supplementary Benefits Act 1976;

this Rule shall apply as if the reference to the maintenance creditor were a reference to the mother of the child;

(6) as regards a dispute arising out of the operations of a branch, agency or other establishment, in the courts for the place in which the branch, agency or other establishment is situated;

(7) in his capacity as settlor, trustee or beneficiary of a trust domiciled in Scotland created by the operation of a statute, or by a written instrument, or created orally and evidenced in writing, in the Court of Session, or the appropriate sheriff court within the meaning of section 24A of the Trusts (Scotland) Act 1921;

(8) where he is not domiciled in the United Kingdom, in the courts for any place where–

(a) any movable property belonging to him has been arrested; or

(b) any immovable property in which he has any beneficial interest is situated;

(9) in proceedings which are brought to asset, declare or determine proprietary or possessory rights, or rights of security, in or over movable property, or to obtain authority to dispose of movable property, in the courts for the place where the property is situated;

(10) in proceedings for interdict, in the courts for the place where it is alleged that the wrong is likely to be committed;

(11) in proceedings concerning a debt secured over immovable property, in the courts for the place where the property is situated;

(12) in proceedings which have as their object a decision of an organ of a company or other legal person or of an association of natural or legal persons, in the courts for the place where that company, legal person or association has its seat;

(13) in proceedings concerning an arbitration which is conducted in Scotland or in which the procedure is governed by Scots law, in the Court of Session;

(14) in proceedings principally concerned with the registration in the United Kingdom or the validity in the United Kingdom of patents, trade marks, designs or other similar rights required to be deposited or registered, in the Court of Session;

(15)(a) where he is one of a number of defenders, in the courts for the place where any one of them is domiciled

(b) as a third party in an action on a warranty or guarantee or in any other third party proceedings, in the court seised of the original proceedings, unless these were instituted solely with the object of removing him from the jurisdiction of the court which would be competent in his case;

(c) on a counterclaim arising from the same contract or facts on which the original claim was based, i the court in which the original claim is pending.

JURISDICTION OVER CONSUMER CONTRACTS

3.– (1) In proceedings concerning a contract concluded by a person for a purpose which can be regarded as being outside his trade or profession hereinafter called the 'consumer', subject to Rule 4 (exclusive jurisdiction), jurisdiction shall be determined by this Rule if it is–

(a) a contract for the sale of goods on instalment credit terms; or

(b) a contract for a loan repayable by instalments, or for any other form of credit, made to finance the sale of goods; or

(c) any other contract for the supply of goods or a contract for the supply of services, if–

(i) the consumer took in Scotland the steps necessary for the conclusion of the contract; or

(ii) proceedings are brought in Scotland by virtue of section 10(3).

(2) This Rule shall not apply to contracts of transport or contracts of insurance.

(3) A consumer may bring proceedings against the other party to a contract only in–

(a) the courts for the place in which that party is domiciled;

(b) the courts for the place in which he is himself domiciled;

or

(c) any court having jurisdiction by virtue of Rule 2(6) or (9).

(4) Proceedings may be brought against a consumer by the other party to the contract only in the courts for the place where the consumer is domiciled or any court having jurisdiction under Rule 2(9).

(5) Nothing in this Rule shall affect the right to bring a counterclaim in the court in which, in accordance with this Rule, the original claim is pending.

(6) The provisions of this Rule may be departed from only by an agreement–

(a) which is entered into after the dispute has arisen; or

(b) which allows the consumer to bring proceedings in a court other than a court indicated in this Rule.

EXCLUSIVE JURISDICTION

4.– (1) Notwithstanding anything contained in any of Rules 1 to above or 5 to 8 below, the following courts shall have exclusive jurisdiction–

(a) in proceedings which have as their object rights in rem in, or tenancies of, immovable property, the courts for the place where the property is situated;

(b) in proceedings which have as their object the validity of the constitution, the nullity or the dissolution of companies or other legal persons or associations of natural or legal persons, the courts for the place where the company, legal person or association has its seat;

(c) in proceedings which have as their object the validity of entries in public registers, the courts for the place where the register is kept;

(d) in proceedings concerned with the enforcement of judgments, the courts for the place where the judgment has been or is to be enforced.

(2) Nothing in paragraph (1)(c) above affects jurisdiction in any proceedings concerning the validity of entries in registers of patents, trade marks, designs, or other similar rights required to be deposited or registered.

(3) No court shall exercise jurisdiction in a case where immovable property, the seat of a body mentioned in paragraph (1)(b) above, a public register or the place where a judgment has been or is to be enforced is situated outside Scotland and where paragraph (1) above would apply if the property, seat, register or, as the case may be, place of enforcement were situated in Scotland.

PROROGATION OF JURISDICTION

5.– (1) If the parties have agreed that a court is to have jurisdiction to settle any disputes which have arisen or which may arise in connection with a particular legal relationship, that court shall have exclusive jurisdiction.

(2) Such an agreement conferring jurisdiction shall be either in writing or evidenced in writing or, in trade or commerce, in a form which accords with practices in that trade or commerce of which the parties are or ought to have been aware.

(3) The court on which a trust instrument has conferred jurisdiction shall have exclusive jurisdiction in any proceedings brought against a settlor, trustee or beneficiary, if relations between these persons or their rights or obligations under the trust are involved.

(4) Where an agreement or a trust instrument confers jurisdiction on the courts of the United Kingdom or of Scotland, proceedings to which paragraph (1) or, as the case may be, (3) above applies may be brought in any court in Scotland.

(5) Agreements or provisions of a trust instrument conferring jurisdiction shall have no legal force if the courts whose jurisdiction they purport to exclude have exclusive jurisdiction by virtue of Rule 4 or where Rule 4(3) applies.

6.– (1) Apart from jurisdiction derived from other provisions of this Schedule, a court before whom a defender enters an appearance shall have jurisdiction.

(2) This Rule shall not apply where appearance was entered solely to contest jurisdiction, or where another court has exclusive jurisdiction by virtue of Rule 4 or where Rule 4(3) applies.

EXAMINATION AS TO JURISDICTION AND ADMISSIBILITY

7. Where a court is seised of a claim which is principally concerned with a matter over which another court has exclusive jurisdiction by virtue of Rule 4, or where it is precluded from exercising, jurisdiction by Rule 4(3), it shall declare of its own motion that it has no jurisdiction.

8. Where in any case a court has no jurisdiction which is compatible with this Act, and the defender does not enter an appearance, the court shall declare of its own motion that it has no jurisdiction.

SCHEDULE 9

PROCEEDINGS EXCLUDED FROM SCHEDULE 8

1. Proceedings concerning the status or legal capacity of natural persons (including proceedings for separation) other than proceedings which consist solely of proceedings for adherence and aliment or of affiliation and aliment.

2. Proceedings for regulating the custody of children.

3. Proceedings relating to tutory and curatory and all proceedings relating to the management of the affairs of persons who are incapable of managing their own affairs.

4. Proceedings in respect of sequestration in bankruptcy; or the winding up of a company or other legal person; or proceedings in respect of a judicial arrangement or judicial composition with creditors.

5. Proceedings relating to a company where, by any enactment, jurisdiction in respect of those proceedings is conferred on the court having jurisdiction to wind it up.

6. Admiralty causes in sor far as the jurisdiction is based on arrestment *in rem* or *ad fundandam jurisdictionem* of a ship, cargo or freight.

7. Commissary proceedings.

8. Proceedings for the rectification of the register of aircraft mortgages kept by the Civil Aviation Authority.

9. Proceedings under section 7(3) of the Civil Aviation (Eurocontrol) Act 1962 (recovery of charges for air navigation services and proceedings for damages against Eurocontrol).

10. Proceedings brought in pursuance of an order under section 3 of the Continental Shelf Act 1964.

11. Proceedings under section 6 of the Protection of Trading Interests Act 1980 (recovery of sums paid or obtained pursuant to a judgment for multiple damages).

12. Appeals from or review of decisions of tribunals.

13. Proceedings which are not in substance proceedings in which a decree against any person is sought.

14. Proceedings brought in any court in pursuance of–

(a) any statutory provision which, in the case of any convention to which Article 57 applies (conventions relating to specific matters which override the general rules in the 1968 Convention), implements the convention; and

(b) any rule of law so far as it has the effect of implementing any such convention.

SECTIONS 9 TO 12 AND 14 OF THE ADMINISTRATION OF JUSTICE ACT 1920

ADMINISTRATION OF JUSTICE ACT 1920

(10 and 11 Geo 5 c 81)

9   Enforcement in the United Kingdom of judgments obtained in superior courts in other British dominions

(1) Where a judgment has been obtained in a superior court in any part of His Majesty's dominions outside the United Kingdom to which this Part of this Act extends, the judgment creditor may apply to the High Court in England or [Northern] Ireland, or to the Court of Session in Scotland, at any time within twelve months after the date of the judgment, or such longer period as may be allowed by the court, to have the judgment registered in the court, and on any such application the court may, if in all the circumstances of the case they think it just and convenient that the judgment should be enforced in the United Kingdom, and subject to the provisions of this section, order the judgment to be registered accordingly.

(2) No judgment shall be ordered to be registered under this section if–

(a) the original court acted without jurisdiction; or

(b) the judgment debtor, being a person who was neither carrying on business nor ordinarily resident within the jurisdiction of the original court, did not voluntarily appear or otherwise submit or agree to submit to the jurisdiction of that court; or

(c) the judgment debtor, being the defendant in the proceedings, was not duly served with the process of the original court and did not appear, notwithstanding that he was ordinarily resident or was carrying on business within the jurisdiction of that court or agreed to submit to the jurisdiction of that court; or

(d) the judgment was obtained by fraud; or

(e) the judgment debtor satisfies the registering court either that an appeal is pending, or that he is entitled and intends to appeal, against the judgment; or

(f) the judgment was in respect of a cause of action which for reasons of public policy or for some other similar reason could not have been entertained by the registering court.

(3) Where a judgment is registered under this section–

(a) the judgment shall, as from the date of registration, be of the same force and effect, and proceedings may be taken thereon, as if it had been a judgment originally obtained or entered up on the date of registration in the registering court;

(b) the registering court shall have the same control and jurisdiction over the judgment as it has over similar judgments given by itself, but in so far only as relates to execution under this section;

(c) the reasonable costs of and incidental to the registration of the judgment (including the cost of obtaining a certified copy thereof from the original court and of the application for registration) shall be recoverable in like manner as if they were sums payable under the judgment ...

(5) In any action brought in any court in the United Kingdom on any judgment which might be ordered to be registered under this section, the plaintiff shall not be entitled to recover any costs of the action unless an application to register the judgment under this section has previously been refused or unless the court otherwise orders.

10 Issue of certificates of judgment obtained in the United Kingdom

(1) Where–

(a) a judgment has been obtained in the High Court in England or Northern Ireland, or in the Court of Session in Scotland, against any person; and

(b) the judgment creditor wishes to secure the enforcement of the judgment in a part of Her Majesty's dominions outside the United Kingdom to which this Part of this Act extends,

the court shall, on an application made by the judgment creditor, issue to him a certified copy of the judgment.

(2) The reference in the preceding subsection to Her Majesty's dominions shall be construed as if that subsection had come into force in its present form at the commencement of this Act ...

12 Interpretation

(1) In this Part of this Act, unless the context otherwise requires–

The expression 'judgment' means any judgment or order given or made by a court in any civil proceedings, whether before or after the passing of this Act, whereby any sum of money is made payable, and includes an award in proceedings on an arbitration if the award has, in pursuance of the law in force in the place where it was made, become enforceable in the same manner as a judgment given by a court in that place;

The expression 'original court' in relation to any judgment means the court by which the judgment was given;

The expression 'registering court' in relation to any judgment means the court by which the judgment was registered;

The expression 'judgment creditor' means the person by whom the judgment was obtained, and includes the successors and assigns of that person;

The expression 'judgment debtor' means the person against whom the judgment was given, and includes any person against whom the judgment is enforceable in the place where it was given.

(2) Subject to rules of court, any of the powers conferred by this Part of this Act on any court may be exercised by a judge of the court.

14 Extent of Part II of the Act

(1) Where His Majesty is satisfied that reciprocal provisions have been made by the legislature of any part of His Majesty's dominions outside the United Kingdom for the enforcement within that part of His dominions of judgment obtained in the High Court in England, the Court of Session in Scotland, and the High Court in Ireland, His Majesty may by Order in Council declare that this Part of this Act shall extend to that part of His dominions, and on any such Order being made this Part of this Act shall extend accordingly.

(2) An Order in Council under this section may be varied or revoked by a subsequent Order.

(3) Her Majesty may by Order in Council under this section consolidate any Orders in Council under this section which are in force when the consolidating Order is made.

SECTIONS 1, 2 AND 4 TO 6 OF THE FOREIGN JUDGMENTS (RECIPROCAL ENFORCEMENT) ACT 1933

FOREIGN JUDGMENTS (RECIPROCAL ENFORCEMENT) ACT 1933

(23 and 24 Geo 5 c 13)

PART 1

REGISTRATION OF FOREIGN JUDGMENTS

1 Power to extend Part I of Act to foreign countries giving reciprocal treatment

(1) If, in the case of a foreign country, His Majesty is satisfied that, in the event of the benefits conferred by this Part of the Act being extended to, or to any particular class of, judgments given in the courts of that country or in any particular class of those courts, substantial reciprocity of treatment will be assured as regards the enforcement in that country of similar judgments given in similar courts of the United Kingdom, He may by Order in Council direct–

  (a) that this part of this Act shall extend to that country;

  (b) that such courts of that country as are specified in the Order shall be recognised courts in that country for the purposes of this Part of this Act; and

  (c) that judgments of any such recognised court, or such judgments of any class so specified shall, if within sub-section (2) of this section, be judgments to which this Part of this Act applies.

(2) Subject to sub-section (2A) of this section, a judgment of a recognised court is within this sub-section if it satisfies the following conditions, namely–

  (a) it is either final and conclusive as between the judgment debtor and the judgment creditor or requires the former to make interim payment to the latter; and

  (b) there is payable under it a sum of money, not being a sum payable in respect of taxes or other charges of a like nature or in respect of a fine or other penalty; and

  (c) it is given after the coming into force of the Order in Council which made that court a recognised court.

(2A) The following judgments of a recognised court are not within sub-section (2) of this section–

(a) a judgment given by that court on appeal from a court which is not a recognised court;

(b) a judgment or other instrument which is regarded for the purposes of its enforcement as a judgment of that court but which was given or made in another country;

(c) a judgment given by that court in proceedings founded on a judgment of court of another country and having as their object the enforcement of that judgment.

(3) For the purposes of this section, a judgment shall be deemed to be final and conclusive notwithstanding that an appeal may be pending against it, or that it may still be subject to appeal, in the courts of the country of the original court.

(4) His Majesty may be subsequent Order in Council vary or revoke any Order previously made under this section.

(5) Any Order in Council made under this section before its amendment by the Civil Jurisdiction and Judgments Act 1982 which deems any court of a foreign country to be a superior court of that country for the purposes of this part of this Act shall (without prejudice to sub-section (4) of this section) have effect from the time of that amendment as if it is provided for that court to be a recognised court of that country for those purposes, and for any final and conclusive judgment of that court, if within sub-section (2) of this section, to be a judgment to which this Part of the Act applies.

2 Application for, and effect of, registration of foreign judgment

(1) A person, being a judgment creditor under a judgment to which this Part of this Act applies, may apply to the High Court at any time within six years after the date of the judgment, or, where there have been proceedings by way of appeal against the judgment, after the date of the last judgment given in those proceedings, to have the judgment registered in the High Court, and on any such application the court shall, subject to proof of the prescribed matters and to the other provisions of this Act, order the judgment to be registered: provided that a judgment shall not be registered if at the date of the application—

(a) it has been wholly satisfied; or

(b) it could not be enforced by execution in the country of the original court.

(2) Subject to the provisions of this Act with respect to the setting aside of registration—

(a) a registered judgment shall, for the purposes of execution, be of the same force and effect; and

(b) proceedings may be taken on a registered judgment; and

(c) the sum for which a judgment is registered shall carry interest; and

(d) the registering court shall have the same control over the execution of a registered judgment,

as if the judgment had been a judgment originally given in the registering court and entered on the date of registration: provided that execution shall not issue on the judgment so long as, under this Part of the Act and the Rules of Court made thereunder, it is competent for any party to make an application to have the registration of the judgment set aside, or, where such an application is made, until after the application has been finally determined.

(4) If, at the date of the application for registration the judgment of the original court has been partly satisfied, the judgment shall not be registered in respect of the whole sum payable under the judgment of the original court, but only in respect of the balance remaining payable at that date.

(5) If, on an application for the registration of a judgment, it appears to the registering court that the judgment is in respect of different matters and that some, but not all, of the provisions of the judgment are such that if those provisions had been contained in separate judgments those judgments could properly have been registered, the judgment may be registered in respect of the provisions aforesaid but not in respect of any other provisions contained therein.

(6) In addition to the sum of money payable under the judgment of the original court, including any interest which by the law of the country of the original court becomes due under the judgment up to the time of registration, the judgment shall be registered for the reasonable costs of and incidental to registration, including the costs of obtaining a certified copy of the judgment from the original court ...

4 Cases in which registered judgments must, or may, be set aside

(1) On an application in that behalf duly made by any party against whom a registered judgment may be enforced, the registration of the judgment–

(a) shall be set aside if the registering court is satisfied–

(i) that the judgment is not a judgment to which this Part of this Act applies or was registered in contravention of the foregoing provisions of this Act; or

(ii) that the courts of the country of the original court had no jurisdiction in the circumstances of the case; or

(iii) that the judgment debtor, being the defendant in the proceedings in the original court, did not (notwithstanding that process may have been duly served on him in accordance with the law of the country of the original court) receive notice of those proceedings in sufficient time to enable him to defend the proceedings and did not appear; or

(iv) that the judgment was obtained by fraud; or

(v) that the enforcement of the judgment would be contrary to public policy in the country of the registering court; or

(vi) that the rights under the judgment are not vested in the person by whom the application for registration was made;

(b) may be set aside if the registering court is satisfied that the matter in dispute in the proceedings in the original court had previously to the date of the judgment in the original court been the subject of a final and conclusive judgment by a court having jurisdiction in the matter.

(2) For the purposes of this section the courts of the country of the original court shall, subject to the provisions of sub-section (3) of this section, be deemed to have had jurisdiction–

(a) in the case of a judgment given in an action *in personam*–

(i) if the judgment debtor, being a defendant in the original court, submitted to the jurisdiction of that court by voluntarily appearing in the proceedings; or

(ii) if the judgment debtor was plaintiff in, or counterclaimed in, the proceedings in the original court; or

(iii) if the judgment debtor, being a defendant in the original court, had before the commencement of the proceedings, agreed in respect of the subject matter of the proceedings, to submit to the jurisdiction of that court or of the courts of the country of that court; or

(iv) if the judgment debtor, being a defendant in the original court, was at the time when the proceedings were instituted resident in, or being a body corporate had its principal place of business in, the country of that court; or

(v) if the judgment debtor, being a defendant in the original court, had an office or place of business in the country of that court and the proceedings in that court were in respect of a transaction effected through or at the office or place;

(b) in the case of a judgment given in an action of which the subject matter was immovable property or in an action in rem of which the subject matter was movable property, if the property in question was at the time of the proceedings in the original court situate in the country of that court;

(c) in the case of a judgment given in an action other than any such action as is mentioned in paragraph (a) or paragraph (b) of this sub-section, if the jurisdiction of the original court is recognised by the law of the registering court.

(3) Notwithstanding anything in sub-section (2) of this section, the courts of the country of the original court shall not be deemed to have had jurisdiction–

(a) if the subject matter of the proceedings was immovable property outside the country of the original court; or

(b) if the judgment debtor, being a defendant in the original proceedings, was a person who under the rules of public international law was entitled to immunity from the jurisdiction of the courts of the country of the original court and did not submit to the jurisdiction of that court.

5 Powers of registering court on application to set aside registration

(1) If, on an application to set aside the registration of a judgment, the applicant satisfies the registering court either that an appeal is pending, or that he is entitled and intends to appeal, against the judgment, the court, if it thinks fit, may, on such terms as it may think just, either set aside the registration or adjourn the application to set aside the registration until after the expiration of such period as appears to the court to be reasonably sufficient to enable the applicant to take the necessary steps to have the appeal disposed of by competent tribunal.

(2) Where the registration of a judgment is set aside under the last foregoing sub-section, or solely for the reason that the judgment was not at the date of the application for registration enforceable by execution in the country of the original court, the setting aside of the registration shall not prejudice a further application to register the judgment when the appeal has been disposed of or if and when the judgment becomes enforceable by execution in that country, as the case may be.

(3) Where the registration of a judgment is set aside solely for the reason that the judgment, notwithstanding that it had at the date of the application for registration been partly satisfied, was registered for the whole sum payable thereunder, the registering court shall, on the application of the judgment creditor, order judgment to be registered for the balance remaining payable at that date.

6 Foreign judgments which can be registered not to be enforceable otherwise

No proceedings for the recovery of a sum payable under a foreign judgment, being a judgment to which this Part of this Act applies, other than proceedings by way of registration of the judgment, shall be entertained by any court in the United Kingdom.

SECTIONS 32 TO 34 OF THE CIVIL JURISDICTION AND JUDGMENTS ACT 1982

32–(1) Subject to the following provisions of this section a judgment given by a court of an overseas country in any proceedings shall not be recognised or enforced in the United Kingdom if–

 (a) the bringing of those proceedings in that court was contrary to an agreement under which the dispute in question was to be settled otherwise than by proceedings in the courts of that country; and

 (b) those proceedings were not brought in that court by, or with the agreement of, the person against whom the judgment was given; and

 (c) that person did not counterclaim in the proceedings or otherwise submit to the jurisdiction of that court.

 (2) Sub-section (1) does not apply where the agreement referred to in paragraph (a) of that sub-section was illegal, void or unenforceable or was incapable of being performed for reasons not attributable to the fault of the party bringing the proceedings in which the judgment was given.

 (3) In determining whether a judgment given by a court of an overseas country should be recognised or enforced in the United Kingdom, a court in the United Kingdom shall not be bound by any decision of the overseas court relating to any of the matters mentioned in sub-section (1) or (2).

 (4) Nothing in sub-section (1) shall affect the recognition or enforcement in the United Kingdom of–

 (a) a judgment which is required to be recognised or enforced there under the 1968 Convention;

 (b) a judgment to which Part I of the Foreign Judgments (Reciprocal Enforcement) Act 1933 applies by virtue of section 4 of the Carriage of Goods by Road Act 1965, section 17(4) of the Nuclear Installations Act 1965, section 13(3) of the Merchant Shipping (Oil Pollution) Act 1971, section 5 of the Carriage by Railway Act 1972, section 6 of the International Transport Conventions Act 1983, section 5 of the Carriage of Passengers by Road Act 1974 or section 6(4) of the Merchant Shipping Act 1974.

33–(1) For the purposes of determining whether a judgment given by a court of an overseas country should be recognised or enforced in England and Wales or Northern Ireland, the person against whom the judgment was given shall not be regarded as having submitted to the jurisdiction of the court by reason only of the fact that he appeared (conditionally or otherwise) in the proceedings for all or any one or more of the following purposes, namely–

(a) to contest the jurisdiction of the court;

(b) to ask the court to dismiss or stay the proceedings on the ground that the dispute in question should be submitted to arbitration or to the determination of the courts of another country;

(c) to protect, or obtain the release of, property seized or threatened with seizure in the proceedings.

(2) Nothing in this section shall affect the recognition or enforcement in England and Wales or Northern Ireland of a judgment which is required to be recognised or enforced there under the 1968 Convention.

34 No proceedings may be brought by a person in England and Wales or Northern Ireland on a cause of action in respect of which a judgment has been given in his favour in proceedings between the same parties, or their privies, in a court in another part of the United Kingdom or in a court of an overseas country, unless that judgment is not enforceable or entitled to recognition in England and Wales or, as the case may be, in Northern Ireland.

THE CONTRACTS (APPLICABLE LAW) ACT 1990

CONTRACTS (APPLICABLE LAW) ACT 1990

(1990 Chapter 36)

An Act to make provision as to the law applicable to contractual obligations in the case of conflict of laws.

[26th July 1990]

BE IT ENACTED by the Queen's most Excellent Majesty, by and with the advice and consent of the Lords Spiritual and Temporal, and Commons, in this present Parliament assembled, and by the authority of the same, as follows–

1. In this Act–

   (a) 'the Rome Convention' means the Convention on the law applicable to contractual obligations opened for signature in Rome on 19th June 1980 and signed by the United Kingdom on 7th December 1981;

   (b) 'the Luxembourg Convention' means the Convention on the accession of the Hellenic Republic to the Rome Convention signed by the United Kingdom in Luxembourg on 10th April 1984; and

   (c) 'the Brussels Protocol' means the first Protocol on the interpretation of the Rome Convention by the European Court signed by the United Kingdom in Brussels on 19th December 1988;

   (d) the 'Funchal Convention' means the Convention on the accession of the Kingdom of Spain and the Portuguese Republic to the Rome Convention and the Brussels Protocol, with adjustments made to the Rome Convention by the Luxembourg Convention, signed by the United Kingdom in Funchal on 18th May 1992,

and the Rome Convention, the Luxembourg Convention and the Brussels Protocol are together referred to as 'the Conventions'.

2.– (1) Subject to sub-sections (2) and (3) below, the Conventions shall have the force of law in the United Kingdom.

(2) Articles 7(1) and 10(1)(e) of the Rome Convention shall not have the force of law in the United Kingdom.

(3) Notwithstanding Article 19(2) of the Rome Convention, the Conventions shall apply in the case of conflicts between the laws of different parts of the United Kingdom.

(4) For ease of reference there are set out in Schedules 1, 2 and 3 to this Act respectively the English texts of–

(a) the Rome Convention;

(b) the Luxembourg Convention;

(c) the Brussels Protocol; and

(c) the Funchal Convention.

3.– (1) Any question as to the meaning or effect of any provision of the Conventions shall, if not referred to the European Court in accordance with the Brussels Protocol, be determined in accordance with the principles laid down by, and any relevant decision of, the European Court.

(2) Judicial notice shall be taken of any decision of, or expression of opinion by, the European Court on any such question.

(3) Without prejudice to any practice of the courts as to the matters which may be considered apart from this sub-section–

(a) the report on the Rome Convention by Professor Mario Giuliano and Professor Paul Lagarde which is reproduced in the Official Journal of the Communities of 31st October 1980 may be considered in ascertaining the meaning or effect of any provision of that Convention; and

(b) any report on the Brussels Protocol which is reproduced in the Official Journal of the Communities may be considered in ascertaining the meaning or effect of any provision of that Protocol.

4.– (1) If at any time it appears to Her Majesty in Council that Her Majesty's Government in the United Kingdom–

(a) have agreed to a revision of any of the Conventions (including, in particular, any revision connected with the accession to the Rome Convention of any state); or

(b) have given notification in accordance with Article 22(3) of the Rome Convention that either or both of the provisions mentioned in section 2(2) above shall have the force of law in the United Kingdom.

Her Majesty may by Order in Council make such consequential modifications of this Act or any other statutory provision, whenever passed or made, as Her Majesty considers appropriate.

(2) An Order in Council under sub-section (1) above shall not be made unless a draft of the Order has been laid before Parliament and approved by a resolution of each House.

(3) In sub-section (1) above–

'modifications' includes additions, omissions and alterations;

'revision' means an omission from, addition to or alteration of any of the Conventions and includes replacement of any of the Conventions to any extent by another convention, protocol or other description of international agreement; and 'statutory provision' means any provision contained in an Act, or in any Northern Ireland legislation, or in–

(a) subordinate legislation (as defined in section 21(1) of the Interpretation Act 1978); or

(b) any instrument of a legislative character made under any Northern Ireland legislation.

5. The enactments specified in Schedule 4 to this Act shall have effect subject to the amendments specified in that Schedule.

6. This Act binds the Crown.

7. This Act shall come into force on such day as the Lord Chancellor and the Lord Advocate may by order made by statutory instrument appoint; and different days may be appointed for different provisions or different purposes.

8.– (1) This Act extends to Northern Ireland.

(2) Her Majesty may by Order in Council direct that all or any of the provisions of this Act shall extend to any of the following territories, namely–

(a) the Isle of Man;

(b) any of the Channel Islands;

(c) Gibraltar;

(d) the Sovereign Base Areas of Akrotiri and Dhekelia (that is to say, the areas mentioned in section 2(1) of the Cyprus Act 1960).

(3) An Order in Council under sub-section (2) above may modify this Act in its application to any of the territories mentioned in that sub-section and may contain such supplementary provisions as Her Majesty considers appropriate; and in this sub-section 'modify' shall be construed in accordance with section 4 above.

9. This Act may be cited as the Contracts (Applicable Law) Act 1990.

SCHEDULES

SCHEDULE 1

THE ROME CONVENTION

The High Contracting Parties to the Treaty establishing the European Economic Community,

Anxious to continue in the field of private international law the work of unification of law which has already been done within the Community, in particular in the field of jurisdiction and enforcement of judgments,

Wishing to establish uniform rules concerning the law applicable to contractual obligations,

Have agreed as follows:

TITLE I

SCOPE OF THE CONVENTION

Article 1

Scope of the Convention

1. The rules of this Convention shall apply to contractual obligations in any situation involving a choice between the laws of different countries.

2. They shall not apply to:

   (a) questions involving the status or legal capacity of natural persons, without prejudice to Article 11;

   (b) contractual obligations relating to:
   - wills and succession,
   - rights in property arising out of a matrimonial relationship,
   - rights and duties arising out of a family relationship, parentage, marriage or affinity, including maintenance obligations in respect of children who are not legitimate;

   (c) obligations arising under bills of exchange, cheques and promissory notes and other negotiable instruments to the extent that the obligations under such other negotiable instruments arise out of their negotiable character;

   (d) arbitration agreements and agreements on the choice of court;

   (e) questions governed by the law of companies and other bodies corporate or unincorporate such as the creation, by registration or otherwise, legal capacity, internal organisation or winding up of companies and other bodies corporate or unincorporate and the personal liability of officers and members as such for the obligations of the company or body;

   (f) the question whether an agent is able to bind a principal, or an organ to bind a company or body corporate or unincorporate, to a third party;

   (g) the constitution of trusts and the relationship between settlors, trustees and beneficiaries;

   (h) evidence and procedure, without prejudice to Article 14.

3. The rules of this Convention do not apply to contracts of insurance which cover risks situated in the territories of the Member States of the European Economic Community. In order to determine whether a risk is situated in these territories the court shall apply its internal law.

4. The preceding paragraph does not apply to contracts of re-insurance.

Article 2

Application of law non-Contracting States

Any law specified by this Convention shall be applied whether or not it is the law of a Contracting State.

TITLE II

UNIFORM RULES

Article 3

Freedom of choice

1. A contract shall be governed by the law chosen by the parties. The choice must express or demonstrated with reasonably certainty by the terms of the contract or the circumstances of the case. By their choice the parties can select the law applicable to the whole or a part only of the contract.

2. The parties may at any time agree to subject the contract to a law other than which previously governed it, whether as a result of an earlier choice under this Article or of other provisions of this Convention. Any variation by the parties of the law to be applied made after the conclusion of the contract shall not prejudice its formal validity under Article 9 or adversely affect the rights of third parties.

3. The fact that the parties have chosen a foreign law, whether or not accompanied by the choice of a foreign tribunal, shall not, where all the other elements relevant to the situation at the time of the choice are connected with one country only, prejudice the application of rules of the law of that country which cannot be derogated from by contract, hereinafter called 'mandatory rules'.

4. The existence and validity of the consent of the parties as to the choice of the applicable law shall be determined in accordance with the provisions of Articles 8, 9 and 11.

Article 4

Applicable law in the absence of choice

1. To the extent that the law applicable to the contract has not been chosen in accordance with Article 3, the contract shall be governed by the law of the country with which it is most closely connected. Nevertheless, a severable part of the contract which has a closer connection with another country may by way of exception by governed by the law of that other country.

2. Subject to the provisions of paragraph 5 of this Article, it shall be presumed that the contract is most closely connected with the country where the party who is to effect the performance which is characteristic of the contract has, at the time of conclusion of the contract, his habitual residence, or, in the case of a body corporate or unincorporate, its central administration. However, if the contract is entered into in the course of that party's trade or profession, that country shall be the country in which the principal place of business is situated or, where under the terms of the contract the performance is to be effected through a place of business other than the principal place of business, the country in which that other place of business is situated.

3. Notwithstanding the provisions of paragraph 2 of this Article, to the extent that the subject matter of the contract is a right in immovable property or a right to use immovable property it shall be presumed that the contract is most closely connected with the country where the immovable property is situated.

4. A contract for the carriage of goods shall not be subject to the presumption in paragraph 2. In such a contract if the country in which, at the time the contract is concluded, the carrier has his principal place of business is also the country in which the place of loading or the place of discharge of the principal place of business of the consignor is situated, it shall be presumed that the contract is most closely connected with that country. In applying this paragraph single voyage charterparties and other contracts the main purpose of which is the carriage of goods shall be treated as contracts for the carriage of goods.

5. Paragraph 2 shall not apply if the characteristic performance cannot be determined, and the presumptions in paragraphs 2, 3 and 4 shall be disregarded if it appears from the circumstances as a whole that the contract is more closely connected with another country.

Article 5

Certain consumer contracts

1. This Article applies to a contract the object of which is the supply of goods or services to a person ('the consumer') for a purpose which can be regarded as being outside his trade or profession, or a contract for the provision of credit for that object.

2. Notwithstanding the provisions of Article 3, a choice of law made by the parties shall not have the result of depriving the consumer of the protection afforded to him by the mandatory rules of the law of the country in which he has his habitual residence:

– if in that country the conclusion of the contract was preceded by a specific invitation addressed to him or by advertising, and he had taken in that country all the steps necessary on his part for the conclusion of the contract, or

— if the other party or his agent received the consumer's order in that country,

or

— if the contract is for the sale of goods and the consumer travelled from that country to another country and there gave his order, provided that the consumer's journey was arranged by the seller for the purpose of inducing the consumer to buy.

3. Notwithstanding the provisions of Article 4, a contract to which this Article applies shall, in the absence of choice in accordance with Article 3, be governed by the law of the country in which the consumer has his habitual residence if it is entered into in the circumstances described in paragraph 2 of this Article.

4. This Article shall not apply to:

(a) a contract of carriage;

(b) a contract for the supply of services where the services are to be supplied to the consumer exclusively in a country other than that in which he has his habitual residence.

5. Notwithstanding the provisions of paragraph 4, this Article shall apply to a contract which, for an inclusive price, provides for a combination of travel and accommodation.

Article 6

Individual employment contracts

Notwithstanding the provisions of Article 3, in a contract of employment a choice of law made by the parties shall not have the result of depriving the employee of the protection afforded to him by the mandatory rules of the law which would be applicable under paragraph 2 in the absence of choice.

Notwithstanding the provisions of Article 4, a contract of employment shall, in the absence of choice in accordance with Article 3, be governed:

(a) by the law of the country in which the employee habitually carries out his work in performance of the contract, even if he is temporarily employed in another country; or

(b) if the employee does not habitually carry out his work in any one country, by the law of the country in which the place of business through which he was engaged is situated,

unless it appears from the circumstances as a whole that the contract is more closely connected with another country, in which case the contract shall be governed by the law of the country.

Article 7

Mandatory rules

1. When applying under this Convention the law of a country, effect may be given to the mandatory rules of the law of another country with which the situation has a close connection, if and in so far as, under the law of the latter country, those rules must be applied whatever the law applicable to the contract. In considering whether to give effect to these mandatory rules, regard shall be had to their nature and purpose and to the consequences of their application or non-application.

2. Nothing in this Convention shall restrict the application of the rules of the law of the forum in a situation where they are mandatory irrespective of the law otherwise applicable to the contract.

Article 8

Material validity

1. The existence and validity of a contract, or of any term of a contract, shall be determined by the law which would govern it under this Convention if the contract or term were valid.

2. Nevertheless a party may rely upon the law of the country in which he has his habitual residence to establish that he did not consent if it appears from the circumstances that it would not be reasonable to determine the effect of his conduct in accordance with the law specified in the preceding paragraph.

Article 9

Formal validity

1. A contract concluded between persons who are in the same country is formally valid if it satisfies the formal requirement of the law which governs it under this Convention or of the law of the country where it is concluded.

2. A contract concluded between persons who are in different countries is formally valid if it satisfies the formal requirements of the law which governs it under this Convention or of the law of one of those countries.

3. Where a contract is concluded by an agent, the country in which the agent acts is the relevant country for the purposes of paragraphs 1 and 2.

4. An act intended to have legal effect relating to an existing or contemplated contract is formally valid if it satisfies the formal requirements of the law which under this Convention governs or would govern the contract or of the law of the country where the act was done.

5. The provisions of the preceding paragraphs shall not apply to a contract to which Article 5 applies, concluded in the circumstances described in paragraph 2 of Article 5. The formal validity of such a contract is governed by the law of the country in which the consumer has his habitual residence.

6. Notwithstanding paragraphs 1 to 4 of this Article, a contract the subject matter of which is a right in immovable property or a right to use immovable property shall be subject to the mandatory requirements of form of the law of the country where the property is situated if by that law those requirements are imposed irrespective of the country where the contract is concluded and irrespective of the law governing the contract.

Article 10

Scope of the applicable law

1. The law applicable to a contract by virtue of Articles 3 to 6 and 12 of this Convention shall govern in particular:

- (a) interpretation;
- (b) performance;
- (c) within the limits of the powers conferred on the court by its procedural law, the consequences of breach, including the assessment of damages in so far as it is governed by rules of law;
- (d) the various ways of extinguishing obligations, and prescription and limitation of actions;
- (e) the consequences of nullity of the contract.

2. In relation to the manner of performance and the steps to be taken in the event of defective performance regard shall be had to the law of the country in which performance takes place.

Article 11

Incapacity

In a contract concluded between persons who are in the same country, a natural person who would have capacity under the law of that country may invoke his incapacity resulting from another law only if the other party to the contract was aware of this incapacity at the time of the conclusion of the contract or was not aware thereof as a result of negligence.

Article 12

Voluntary assignment

1. The mutual obligations of assignor and assignee under a voluntary assignment of a right against another person ('the debtor') shall be governed by the law which under this Convention applies to the contract between the assignor and assignee.

2. The law governing the right to which the assignment relates shall determine its assignability, the relationship between the assignee and the debtor, the conditions under which the assignment can be invoked against the debtor and any question whether the debtor's obligations have been discharged.

Article 13

Subrogation

1. Where a person ('the creditor') has a contractual claim upon another ('the debtor'), and a third person has a duty to satisfy the creditor, or has in fact satisfied the creditor in discharge of that duty, the law which governs the third person's duty to satisfy the creditor shall determine whether the third person is entitled to exercise against the debtor the rights which the creditor had against the debtor under the law governing their relationship and, if so, whether he may do so in full or only to a limited extent.

2. The same rule applies where several persons are subject to the same contractual claim and one of them has satisfied the creditor.

Article 14

Burden of proof, etc

1. The law governing the contract under this Convention applies to the extent that it contains, in the law of contract, rules which raise presumptions of law or determine the burden of proof.

2. A contract or an act intended to have legal effect may be proved by any mode of proof recognised by the law of the forum or by any of the laws referred to in Article 9 under which that contract or act is formally valid, provided that such mode of proof can be administered by the forum.

Article 15

Exclusion of renvoi

The application of the law of any country specified by this Convention means the application of the rules of law in force in that country other than its rules of private international law.

Article 16

'Ordre public'

The application of a rule of the law of any country specified by this Convention may be refused only if such application is manifestly incompatible with the public policy ('*ordre public*') of the forum.

Article 17

No retrospective effect

This Convention shall apply in a Contracting State to contracts made after the date on which this Convention has entered into force with respect to that State.

Article 18

Uniform interpretation

In the interpretation and application of the preceding uniform rules, regard shall be had to their international character and to the desirability of achieving uniformity in their interpretation and application.

Article 19

States with more than one legal system

1. Where a State comprises several territorial units each of which has its own rules of law in respect of contractual obligations, each territorial unit shall be considered as a country for the purposes of identifying the law applicable under this Convention.

2. A State within which different territorial units have their own rules of law in respect of contractual obligations shall not be bound to apply this Convention to conflicts solely between the laws of such units.

Article 20

Precedence of Community law

This Convention shall not affect the application of provisions which, in relation to particular matters, lay down choice of law rules relating to contractual obligations and which are or will be contained in acts of the institutions of the European Communities or in national laws harmonised in implementation of such acts.

Article 21

Relationship with other conventions

This Convention shall not prejudice the application of international conventions to which a Contracting State is, or becomes, a party.

Article 22

Reservations

1. Any Contracting State may, at the time of signature, ratification, acceptance, or approval, reserve the right not to apply:

(a) the provisions of Article 7(1);

(b) the provisions of Article 10 (1)(e) ...

3. Any Contracting State may at any time withdraw a reservation which it has made; the reservation shall cease to have effect on the first day of the third calendar month after notification of the withdrawal.

TITLE III

FINAL PROVISIONS

Article 23

1. If, after the date on which this Convention has entered into force for a Contracting State, that State wishes to adopt any new choice of law rule in regard to any particular category of contract within the scope of this Convention, it shall communicate its intention to the other signatory States through the Secretary General of the Council of the European Communities.

2. Any signatory State may, within six months from the date of the communication made to the Secretary General, request him to arrange consultations between signatory States in order to reach agreement.

3. If no signatory State has requested consultations within this period or if within two years following the communication made to the Secretary General no agreement is reached in the course of consultations, the Contracting State concerned may amend its law in the manner indicated. The measures taken by that State shall be brought to the knowledge of the other signatory States through the Secretary General of the Council of the European Communities.

Article 24

1. If, after the date on which this Convention has entered into force with respect to a Contracting State, that State wishes to become a party to a multilateral convention whose principal aim or one of whose principal aims is to lay down rules of private international law concerning any of the matters governed by this Convention, the procedure set out in Article 23 shall apply.

However, the period of two years, referred to in paragraph 3 of that Article, shall be reduced to one year.

2. The procedure referred to in the preceding paragraph need not be followed if a Contracting State or one of the European Communities is already a party to the multilateral convention, or if its object is to revise a convention concluded within the framework of the Treaties establishing the European Communities.

Article 25

If a Contracting State considers that the unification achieved by this Convention is prejudiced by the conclusion of agreements not covered by Article 24(1), that State may request the Secretary General of the Council of the European Communities to arrange consultations between the signatory States of this Convention.

Article 26

Any Contracting State may request the revision of this Convention. In this event a revision conference shall be convened by the President of the Council of the European Communities.

Article 27

1. This Convention shall apply to the European territories of the Contracting States, including Greenland, and to the entire territory of the French Republic.

2. Notwithstanding paragraph 1:

(a) this Convention shall not apply to the Faroe Islands, unless the Kingdom of Denmark makes a declaration to the contrary;

(b) this Convention shall not apply to any European territory situated outside the United Kingdom for the international relations of which the United Kingdom is responsible, unless the United Kingdom makes a declaration to the contrary in respect of any such territory;

(c) this Convention shall apply to the Netherlands Antilles, if the Kingdom of the Netherlands makes a declaration to that effect.

3. Such declarations may be made at any time by notifying the Secretary General of the Council of the European Communities.

4. Proceedings brought to the United Kingdom on appeal from courts in one of the territories referred to in paragraph 2(b) shall be deemed to be proceedings taking place in those courts.

Article 28

1. This Convention shall be open from 19 June 1980 for signature by the States party to the Treaty establishing the European Economic Community.

2. This Convention shall be subject to ratification, acceptance or approval by the signatory States. The instruments of ratification, acceptance or approval shall be deposited with the Secretary General of the Council of the European Communities.

Article 29

1. This Convention shall enter into force on the first day of the third month following the deposit of the seventh instrument of ratification, acceptance or approval.

2. This Convention shall enter into force for each signatory State ratifying, accepting or approving at a later date on the first day of the third month following the deposit of its instrument of ratification, acceptance or approval.

Article 30

1. This Convention shall remain in force for 10 years from the date of its entry into force in accordance with Article 29(1) , even for States for which it enters into force at a later date.

2. If there has been no denunciation it shall be renewed tacitly every five years.

3. A Contracting State which wishes to denounce shall, not less than six months before the expiration of the period of 10 or five years, as the case may be, give notice to the Secretary General of the Council of the European Communities. Denunciation may be limited to any territory to which the Convention has been extended by a declaration under Article 27(2).

4. The denunciation shall have effect only in relation to the State which has notified it. The Convention will remain in force as between all other Contracting States.

Article 31

The Secretary General of the Council of the European Communities shall notify the States party to the Treaty establishing the European Economic Community of:

(a) the signatures;

(b) the deposit of each instrument of ratification, acceptance or approval;

(c) the date of entry into force of this Convention;

(d) communications made in pursuance of Articles 23, 24, 25, 26 27 and 30;

(e) the reservations and withdrawals of reservations referred to in Article 22.

Article 32

The Protocol annexed to this Convention shall form an integral part thereof.

Article 33

This Convention, drawn up in a single original in the Danish, Dutch, English, French, German, Irish and Italian languages, these texts being equally authentic shall be deposited in the archives of the Secretariat of the Council of the European Communities. The Secretary General shall transmit a certified copy thereof to the Government of each signatory State.

PROTOCOL

The High Contracting Parties have agreed upon the following provision which shall be annexed to the Convention.

Notwithstanding the provisions of the Convention, Denmark may retain the rules contained in Soloven (Statute on Maritime Law) paragraph 169 concerning the applicable law in matters relating to carriage of goods by sea and may revise these rules without following the procedure prescribed in Article 23 of the Convention.

SCHEDULE 2

THE LUXEMBOURG CONVENTION

The High Contracting Parties to the Treaty establishing the European Economic Community,

Considering that the Hellenic Republic, in becoming a Member of the Community, undertook to accede to the Convention on the law applicable to contractual obligations, opened for signature in Rome on 19th June 1980,

Have decided to conclude this Convention, and to this end have designated as their plenipotentiaries:

(Designation of plenipotentiaries)

Who, meeting within the Council, having exchanged their full powers, found in good and due form,

Have agreed as follows:

Article 1

The Hellenic Republic hereby accedes to the Convention on the law applicable to contractual obligations, opened for signature in Rome on 19th June 1990.

Article 2

The Secretary General of the Council of the European Communities shall transmit a certified copy of the Convention on the law applicable to contractual obligations in the Danish, Dutch, English, French, German, Irish and Italian languages to the Government of the Hellenic Republic.

The text of the Convention on the law applicable to contractual obligations in the Green language is annexed hereto. The text in the Greek language shall be authentic under the same conditions as the other texts of the Convention on the law applicable to contractual obligations.

Article 3

This Convention shall be ratified by the Signatory States. The instruments of ratification shall be deposited with the Secretary General of the Council of the European Communities.

Article 4

This Convention shall enter into force, as between the States which have ratified it, on the first day of the third month following the deposit of the last instrument of ratification by the Hellenic Republic and seven States which have ratified the Convention on the law applicable to contractual obligations.

This Convention shall enter into force for each Contracting State which subsequently ratifies it on the first day of the third month following the deposit of its instrument of ratification.

Article 5

The Secretary General of the Council of the European Communities shall notify the signatory States of:

(a) the deposit of each instrument of ratification;

(b) the dates of entry into force of this Convention for Contracting States.

Article 6

This Convention, drawn up in a single original in the Danish, Dutch, English, French, German, Greek, Irish and Italian languages, all eight texts being equally authentic, shall be deposited in the archives of the General Secretariat of the Council of the European Communities. The Secretary General shall transmit a certified copy to the Government of each Signatory State.

SCHEDULE 3

THE BRUSSELS PROTOCOL

The High Contracting Parties to the Treaty establishing the European Economic Community,

Having regard to the Joint Declaration annexed to the Convention on the law applicable to contractual obligations, opened for signature in Rome on 19 June 1980,

Have decided to conclude a Protocol conferring jurisdiction on the Court of Justice of the European Communities to interpret that Convention, and to this end have designated as their Plenipotentiaries:

(Designation of plenipotentiaries)

Who, meeting within the Council of the European Communities, having exchanged their full powers, found in good and due form,

Have agreed as follows:

Article 1

The Court of Justice of the European Communities shall have jurisdiction to give rulings on the interpretation of–

(a) the Convention on the law applicable to contractual obligations, opened, opened for signature in Rome on 19 June 1980, hereinafter referred to as 'the Rome Convention';

(b) the Convention on accession to the Rome Convention by the States which have become Members of the European Communities since the date on which it was opened for signature;

(c) this Protocol.

Article 2

Any of the courts referred to below may request the Court of Justice to give a preliminary ruling on a question raised in a case pending before it and concerning interpretation of the provisions contained in the instruments referred to in Article 1 if that court considers that a decision on the question is necessary to enable it to give judgment:

(a) – in Belgium:

la Cour de cassation (het Hof Van Cassatie) and le Conseil d'Etat (de Raad Van State),

– in Denmark:

Højesteret,

– in the Federal Republic of Germany:

die obersten Gerichtschöfe des Bundes,
- in Greece:
τα ανωτατα Αικαστηφια,
- in Spain:
el Tribunal Supremo,
- in France
la Cour de cassation and le Conseil d'Etat,
- in Ireland:
the Supreme Court,
- in Italy:
la Corte suprema di cassazione and il Consiglio di Stato,
- in Luxembourg:
la Court Superieure de Justice, when sitting as Cour de cassation,
- in the Netherlands:
de Hoge Raad,
- in Portugal:
o Supremo Tribunal de Justiça and o Supremo Tribunal Administrativo,
- in the United Kingdom
the House of Lords and other courts from which no further appeal is possible;

(b) the courts of the Contracting States when acting as appeal courts.

Article 3

1. The competent authority of a Contracting State may request the Court of Justice to give a ruling on a question of interpretation of the provisions contained in the instruments referred to in Article 1 if judgments given by courts of that State conflict with the interpretation given either by the Court of Justice or in a judgment of one of the courts of another Contracting State referred to in Article 2. The provisions of this paragraph shall apply only to judgments which have become *res judicata*.

2. The interpretation given by the Court of Justice in response to such a request shall not affect the judgments which gave rise to the request for interpretation.

3. The Procurators General of the Supreme Courts of Appeal of the Contracting States, or any other authority designated by a Contracting State, shall be entitled to request the Court of Justice for a ruling on interpretation in accordance with paragraph 1.

4. The Registrar of the Court of Justice shall give notice of the request to the Contracting States, to the Commission and to the Council of the European Communities; they shall then be entitled within two months of the notification to submit statements of case or written observations to the Court.

5. No fees shall be levied or any costs or expenses awarded in respect of the proceedings provided for in this Article.

Article 4

1. Except where this Protocol provides, the provisions of the Treaty establishing the European Economic Community and those of the Protocol on the Statute of the Court of Justice annexed thereto, which are applicable when the Court is requested to give a preliminary ruling, shall also apply to any proceedings for the interpretation of the instruments referred to in Article 1.

2. The Rules of Procedure of the Court of Justice shall, if necessary, be adjusted and supplemental in accordance with Article 188 of the Treaty establishing the European Economic Community.

Article 5

This Protocol shall be subject to ratification by the Signatory States. The instruments of ratification shall be deposited with the Secretary General of the Council of the European Communities.

Article 6

1. To enter into force, this Protocol must be ratified by seven States in respect of which the Rome Convention is in force. This Protocol shall enter into force on the first day of the third month following the deposit of the instrument of ratification by the last such State to take this step. If, however, the Second Protocol conferring on the Court of Justice of the European Communities certain powers to interpret the Convention on the law applicable to contractual obligations, opened for signature in Rome on 19th June 1980, concluded in Brussels on 19th December 1988, enters into force on a later date, this Protocol shall enter into force on the date of entry into force of the Second Protocol.

2. Any ratification subsequent to the entry into force of this Protocol shall take effect on the first day of the third month following the deposit of the instrument of ratification provided that the ratification, acceptance or approval of the Rome Convention by the State in question has become effective.

Article 7

The Secretary General of the Council of the European Communities shall notify the Signatory States of:

(a) the deposit of each instrument of ratification;

(b) the date of entry into force of this Protocol;

(c) any designation communicated pursuant to Article 3(3);

(d) any communication made pursuant to Article 8.

Article 8

The Contracting States shall communicate to the Secretary General of the Council of the European Communities the texts of any provisions of their laws which necessitate an amendment to the list of courts in Article 2(a).

Article 9

This Protocol shall have effect for as long as the Rome Convention remains in force under the conditions laid down in Article 30 of that Convention.

Article 10

Any Contracting State may request the revision of this Protocol. In this event, a revision conference shall be convened by the President of the Council of the European Communities.

Article 11

This Protocol, drawn up in a single original in the Danish, Dutch, English, French, German, Greek, Irish, Italian, Portuguese and Spanish languages, all 10 texts being equally authentic, shall be deposited in the archives of the General Secretariat of the Council of the European Communities. The Secretary General shall transmit a certified copy to the Government of each Signatory State.

SCHEDULE 4

CONSEQUENTIAL AMENDMENTS

THE EQUAL PAY ACT 1970 (c 41)

THE EQUAL PAY ACT (NORTHERN IRELAND) 1970 (c 32 (NI))

1. In section 1(11) of the Equal Pay Act 1970 and section 1(12) of the Equal Pay Act (Northern Ireland) 1970 for the words 'proper law of' there shall be substituted the words 'law applicable to'.

THE CONSUMER CREDIT ACT 1974 (c 39)

2. In sections 43(2)(c) and 145(3)(c) and (4)(b) of the Consumer Credit Act 1974, for the words 'proper law of', in each place where they occur, there shall be substituted the words 'law applicable to'.

THE PATENTS ACT 1977 (C 37)

3. In section 82(5) and (6) of the Patents Act 1977, for the words 'proper law of' there shall be substituted the words 'law applicable to'.

THE UNFAIR CONTRACT TERMS ACT 1977 (C 50)

4. In section 27(1) of the Unfair Contract Terms Act 1977, for the words 'proper law of' there shall be substituted the words 'law applicable to' and for the words 'of the proper law' there shall be substituted the words 'of the law applicable to the contract'.

THE AVIATION SECURITY ACT 1982 (C 36)

5. In section 19(5) of the Aviation Security Act 1982, for the words 'of which the proper law' there shall be substituted the words 'the law applicable to which'.

THE INCOME AND CORPORATION TAXES ACT 1988 (C 1)

6. In section 347B(1)(a) of the Income and Corporation Taxes Act 1988, for the words 'proper law of' there shall be substituted the words 'law applicable to'.

PRIVATE INTERNATIONAL LAW (MISCELLANEOUS PROVISIONS) ACT 1995

PRIVATE INTERNATIONAL LAW (MISCELLANEOUS PROVISIONS) ACT 1995

(1995 Chapter 42)

ARRANGEMENT OF SECTIONS

PART I

INTEREST ON JUDGMENT DEBTS AND ARBITRAL AWARDS

PART II

VALIDITY OF MARRIAGES UNDER A LAW WHICH PERMITS POLYGAMY

PART III

CHOICE OF LAW IN TORT AND DELICT

PART IV

SUPPLEMENTAL

16 Commencement

17 Modification of Northern Ireland Act 1974

18 Extent

19 Short title

SCHEDULE

– Consequential and minor amendments relating to Part II.

PRIVATE INTERNATIONAL LAW (MISCELLANEOUS PROVISIONS) ACT 1995

(1995 Chapter 42)

An Act to make provision about interest on judgment debts and arbitral awards expressed in a currency other than sterling; to make further provision as to marriages entered into by unmarried persons under a law which permits polygamy; to make provision for choice of law rules in tort and delict; and for connected purposes. [8th November 1995]

BE IT ENACTED by the Queen's most Excellent Majesty, by and with the advice and consent of the Lords Spiritual and Temporal, and Commons, in this present Parliament assembled, and by the authority of the same as follows–

PART I

INTEREST ON JUDGMENT DEBTS AND ARBITRAL AWARDS

1.– (1) In the Administration of justice Act 1970, after section 44 (interest on judgment debts) there shall be inserted the following section–

'44A.– (1)Where a judgment is given for a sum expressed in a currency other than sterling and the judgment debt is one to which section 17 of the Judgments Act 1838 applies, the court may order that the interest rate applicable to the debt shall be such rate as the court thinks fit.

(2) Where the court makes such an order, section 17 of the Judgments Act 1838 shall have effect in relation to the judgment debt as if the rate specified in the order were substituted for the rate specified in that section.'

(2) Sub-section (1) above does not apply in relation to a judgment given before the commencement of this section.

2. In section 74 of the County Courts Act 1984 (interest on judgment debts, etc), after sub-section (5) there shall be inserted the following sub-section–

'(5A) The power conferred by sub-section (1) includes power to make provision enabling a county court to order that the rate of interest applicable to a sum expressed in a currency other than sterling shall be such rate as the court thinks fit (instead of the rate otherwise applicable).'

3.– (1) In the Arbitration Act 1950, for section 20 (interest on awards) there shall be substituted the following section–

'20.–(1)A sum directed to be paid by an award shall, unless the award otherwise directs, carry interest as from the date of the award.

(2) The rate of interest shall be–

(a) the rate for judgment debts specified in section 17 of the judgments Act 1838 at the date of the award; or

(b) if the power under sub-section (3) below is exercised, the rate specified in the award.

(3) Where the sum is expressed in a currency other than sterling, the award may specify such rate as the arbitrator or umpire thinks fit instead of the rate mentioned in sub-section (2)(a) above.'

(2) Sub-section (1) above does not apply in relation to an award made before the commencement of this section.

4.– (1) In section 24(1) of the Crown Proceedings Act 1947 (interest on debts, etc), after the word 'interest' there shall be inserted the words 'and section 44A of the Administration of Justice Act 1970 (which enables the court to order an appropriate rate for a judgment debt expressed in a currency other than sterling)'.

(2) In Schedule 11 to the Agricultural Holdings Act 1986, in paragraph 22 (interest on awards), for the words 'same rate as a judgment debt' there shall be substituted the words 'the same rate as that specified in section 17 of the judgments Act 1838 at the date of the award'.

A corresponding amendment shall be deemed to have been made in paragraph 20B of Schedule 6 to the Agricultural Holdings Act 1948 in relation to any case to which it continues to apply.

(3) In section 10(3) of the Drug Trafficking Act 1994 (interest on sums unpaid under confiscation orders), for the words from 'that' to the end there shall be substituted the words 'the same rate as that specified in section 17 of the Judgments Act 1838 (interest on civil judgment debts)'.

PART II

VALIDITY OF MARRIAGES UNDER A LAW WHICH PERMITS POLYGAMY

5.– (1) A marriage entered into outside England and Wales between parties neither of whom is already married is not void under the law of England and Wales on the ground that it is entered into under a law which permits polygamy and that either party is domiciled in England and Wales.

(2) This section does not affect the determination of the validity of a marriage by reference to the law of another country to the extent that it falls to be so determined in accordance with the rules of private international law.

6.– (1) Section 5 above shall be deemed to apply, and always to have applied, to any marriage entered into before commencement which is not excluded by sub-section (2) or (3) below.

(2) That section does not apply to a marriage a party to which has (before commencement) entered into a later marriage which either–

(a) is valid from this section but would be void if section 5 above applied to the earlier marriage; or

(b) is valid by virtue of this section.

(3) That section does not apply to a marriage which has been annulled before commencement, whether by a decree granted in England and Wales or by annulment obtained elsewhere and recognised in England and Wales at commencement.

(4) An annulment of a marriage resulting from legal proceedings begun before commencement shall be treated for the purposes of sub-section (3) above as having taken effect before that time.

(5) For the purposes of sub-sections (3) and (4) above a marriage which has been declared to be invalid by a court of competent jurisdiction in any proceedings concerning either the validity of the marriage or any right dependent on its validity shall be treated as having been annulled.

(6) Nothing in section 5 above, in its application to marriages entered into before commencement–

(a) gives or affects any entitlement to an interest–

(i) under the will or codicil of, or on the intestacy of, a person who died before commencement; or

(ii) under a settlement or other disposition of property made before that time (otherwise than by will or codicil);

(b) gives or affect any entitlement to a benefit, allowance, pension or other payment–

(i) payable before, or in respect of a period before, commencement; or

(ii) payable in respect of the death of a person before that time;

(c) affects tax in respect of a period or event before commencement; or

(d) affects the succession to any dignity or title of honour.

(7) In this section 'commencement' means the commencement of this Part.

7.– (1) A person domiciled in Scotland does not lack capacity to enter into a marriage by reason only that the marriage is entered into under a law which permits polygamy.

(2) For the avoidance of doubt, a marriage valid by the law of Scotland and entered into–

(a) under a law which permits polygamy; and

(b) at a time when neither party is already married,

has, so long as neither party marries a second spouse during the subsistence of the marriage, the same effects for all purposes of the law of Scotland as a marriage entered into under a law which does not permit polygamy.

8.– (1) Nothing in this Part affects any law or custom relating to the marriage of members of the Royal Family.

(2) The enactments specified in the Schedule to this Act (which contains consequential amendments and amendments removing unnecessary references to potentially polygamous marriages) are amended in accordance with that Schedule.

(3) Nothing in that Schedule affects either the generality of any enactment empowering the making of subordinate legislation or any such legislation made before the commencement of this Part.

PART III

CHOICE OF LAW IN TORT AND DELICT

9.– (1) The rules in this Part apply for choosing the law (in this Part referred to as 'the applicable law') to be used for determining issues relating to tort or (for the purposes of the law of Scotland) delict.

(2) The characterisation for the purposes of private international law of issues arising in a claim as issues relating to tort or delict is a matter for the courts of the forum.

(3) The rules in this Part do not apply in relation to issues arising in any claim excluded from the operation of this Part by section 13 below.

(4) The applicable law shall be used for determining the issues arising in a claim, including in particular the question whether an actionable tort or delict has occurred.

(5) The applicable law to be used for determining the issues arising in a claim shall exclude any choice of law rules forming part of the law of the country or countries concerned.

(6) For the avoidance of doubt (and without prejudice to the operation of section 14 below) this Part applies in relation to events occurring in the forum as it applies in relation to events occurring in any other country.

(7) In this Part as it extends to any country within the United Kingdom, 'the forum' means England and Wales, Scotland or Northern Ireland, as the case may be.

(8) In this Part 'delict' includes quasi-delict.

10. The rules of the common law, in so far as they–

(a) require actionability under both the law of the forum and the law of another country for the purpose of determining whether a tort or delict is actionable; or

(b) allow (as an exception from the rules falling within paragraph (a) above) for the law of a single country to be applied for the purpose of determining the issues, or any of the issues, arising in the case in question,

are hereby abolished so far as they apply to any claim in tort or delict which is not excluded from the operation of this Part by section 13 below.

11.– (1) The general rule is that the applicable law is the law of the country in which the events constituting the tort or delict in question occur.

(2) Where elements of those events occur in different countries, the applicable law under the general rule is to be taken as being–

(a) for a cause of action in respect of personal injury caused to an individual or death resulting from personal injury the law of the country where the individual was when he sustained the injury;

(b) for a cause of action in respect of damage to property, the law of the country where the property was when it was damaged; and

(c) in any other case, the law of the country in which the most significant element or elements of those events occurred.

(3) In this section 'personal injury' includes disease or any impairment of physical or mental condition.

12.– (1) If it appears, in all the circumstances, from a comparison of–

(a) the significance of the factors which connect a tort or delict with the country whose law would be the applicable law under the general rule; and

(b) the significance of any factors connecting the tort or delict with another country,

that it is substantially more appropriate for the applicable law for determining the issues arising in the case, or any of those issues, to be the law of the other country, the general rule is displaced and the applicable law for determining those issues or that issue (as the case may be) is the law of that other country.

(2) The factors that may be taken into account as connecting a tort or delict with a country for the purposes of this section include, in particular, factors relating to the parties, to any of the events which constitute the tort or delict in question or to any of the circumstances or consequences of those events.

13.– (1) Nothing in this Part applies to the affect the determination of issues arising in any defamation claim.

(2) For the purposes of this section 'defamation claim' means–

(a) any claim under the law of any part of the United Kingdom for libel or slander or for slander of title, slander of goods or other malicious falsehood and any claim under the law of Scotland for verbal injury; and

(b) any claim under the law of any other country corresponding to or otherwise in the nature of a claim mentioned in paragraph (a) above.

14.– (1) Nothing in this Part applies to acts or omissions giving rise to a claim which occur before the commencement of this Part.

(2) Nothing in this Part affects any rules of law (including rules of private international law) except those abolished by section 10 above.

(3) Without prejudice to the generality of sub-section (2) above, nothing in this Part–

(a) authorises the application of the law of a country outside the forum as the applicable law for determining issues arising in any claim in so far as to do so–

(i) would conflict with principles of public policy; or

(ii) would give effect to such penal, revenue or other public law as would not otherwise be enforceable under the law of the forum; or

(b) affects any rules of evidence, pleading or practice or authorises questions of procedure in any proceedings to be determined otherwise than in accordance with the law of the forum.

(4) This Part has effect without prejudice to the operation of any rule of law which either has effect notwithstanding the rules of private international law applicable in the particular circumstances or modifies the rules of private international law that would otherwise be so applicable.

15.– (1) This Part applies in relation to claims by or against the Crown as it applies in relation to claims to which the Crown is not a party.

(2) In sub-section (1) above a reference to the Crown does not include a reference to Her Majesty in Her private capacity or to Her Majesty in right of Her Duchy of Lancaster or to the Duke of Cornwall.

(3) Without prejudice to the generality of section 14(2) above, nothing in this section affects any rule of law as to whether proceedings of any description may be brought against the Crown.

PART IV

SUPPLEMENTAL

16.– (1) Part I shall come into force on such day as the Lord Chancellor may be order made by statutory instrument appoint; and different days may be appointed for different provisions.

(2) Part II shall come into force at the end of the period of two months beginning with the day on which this Act is passed.

(3) Part III shall come into force on such day as the Lord Chancellor and the Lord Advocate may by order made by statutory instrument appoint; and different days may be appointed for the commencement of Part III as it extends to England and Wales, Scotland or Northern Ireland.

17. An Order in Council under paragraph 1(1)(b) of Schedule 1 to the Northern Ireland Act 1974 (legislation for Northern Ireland in the interim period) which contains a statement that it is only made for purposes corresponding to the purposes of any provision of Part II shall not be subject to paragraph 1(4) and (5) of that Schedule (requirement for affirmative resolution procedure) but shall be subject to annulment in pursuance of a resolution of either House of Parliament.

18.– (1) Any amendment made by this Act has the same extent as the enactment being amended.

(2) In Part II, sections 5 and 6 extend to England and Wales only, section 7 extends to Scotland only and section 8 extends to England and Wales and Scotland.

(3) Part III extends to England and Wales, Scotland and Northern Ireland.

19.– This Act may be cited as the Private International Law (Miscellaneous Provisions) Act 1995.

SCHEDULE

CONSEQUENTIAL AND MINOR AMENDMENTS RELATING TO PART II

MATRIMONIAL PROCEEDINGS (POLYGAMOUS MARRIAGES) ACT 1972 (C 38)

1.– (1) Section 2 of the Matrimonial Proceedings (Polygamous Marriages) Act 1972 (matrimonial relief, etc, in relation to polygamous marriages: Scotland) shall be amended as follows.

(2) In sub-section (1) for the words 'the marriage' onwards there shall be substituted the words 'either party to the marriage is, or has during the subsistence of the marriage been, married to more than one person'.

(3) For sub-section (3) there shall be substituted–

'(3) Provision may be made by rules of court–

(a) for requiring notice of proceedings brought by virtue of this section to be served on any additional spouse of a party to the marriage in question; and

(b for conferring on any such additional spouse the right to be heard in the proceedings,

in such cases as may be specified in the rules.'

MATRIMONIAL CAUSES ACT 1973 (C 18)

2.– (1) The Matrimonial Causes Act 1973 shall be amended as follows.

(2) In section 11 (grounds on which a marriage is void), for the words 'may be polygamous although' there shall be substituted the words 'is not polygamous if'.

(3) In section 47 (matrimonial relief and declarations in respect of polygamous marriage)–

(a) in sub-section (1), for the words 'the marriage' onwards there shall be substituted the words 'either party to the marriage is, or has during the subsistence of the marriage been, married to more than one person'; and

(b) for sub-section (4) there shall be substituted–

'(4) Provision may be made by rules of court–

(a) for requiring notice of proceedings brought by virtue of this section to be served on any additional spouse of a party to the marriage in question; and

(b) for conferring on any such additional spouse the right to be heard in the proceedings;

in such cases as may be specified in the rules.'

MATRIMONIAL HOMES ACT 1983 (C 19)

3. In section 10 of the Matrimonial Homes Act 1983 (interpretation), for sub-section (2) there shall be substituted–

'(2) It is hereby declared that this Act applies as between the parties to a marriage notwithstanding that either of them is, or has at any time during the marriage's subsistence been, married to more than one person.'

SOCIAL SECURITY CONTRIBUTIONS AND BENEFITS ACT 1992 (C 4)

4.– (1) The Social Security Contributions and Benefits Act 1992 shall be amended as follows.

(2) In section 121(1)(b) (regulations as to application of provisions of Parts I to IV to polygamous marriages), for the words following 'section' there shall be substituted the words 'applies, a marriage during the subsistence of which a party to it is at any time married to more than one person is to be treated as having, or as not having, the same consequences as any other marriage.'

(3) In section 147(5) (regulations as to application of provisions of Part IX to polygamous marriages), for the words following 'in which' there shall be substituted the words 'a marriage during the subsistence of which a party to it is at any time married to more than one person is to be treated for the purposes of this Part of this Act as having, or not having, the same consequences as any other marriage.'

SECTIONS 1 TO 4 OF
THE WILLS ACT 1963

WILLS ACT 1963

(1963 c 44)

1 General rule as to formal validity

A will shall be treated as properly executed if its execution conformed to the internal law in force in the territory where it was executed, or in the territory where, at the time of its execution or of the testator's death, he was domiciled or had his habitual residence, or in a state of which, at either of those times, he was a national.

2 Additional rules

(1) Without prejudice to the preceding section, the following shall be treated as properly executed–

  (a) a will executed on board a vessel or aircraft of any description, if the execution of the will conformed to the internal law in force in the territory with which, having regard to its registration (if any) and other relevant circumstances, the vessel or aircraft may be taken to have been most closely connected;

  (b) a will so far as it disposes of immovable property, if its execution conformed to the internal law in force in the territory where the property was situated;

  (c) a will so far as it revokes a will which under this Act would be treated as properly executed or revokes a provision which under this Act would be treated as comprised in a properly executed will, if the execution of the later will conformed to any law by reference to which the revoked will or provision would be so treated;

  (d) a will so far as it exercises a power of appointment, if the execution of the will conformed to the law governing the essential validity of the power.

(2) A will so far as it exercises a power of appointment shall not be treated as improperly executed by reason only that its execution was not in accordance with any formal requirements contained in the instrument creating the power.

3 Certain requirements to be treated as formal

Where (whether in pursuance of this Act or not) a law in force outside the United Kingdom falls to be applied in relation to a will, any requirement of that law whereby special formalities are to be observed by testators answering a particular description, or witnesses to the execution of a will are to possess certain qualifications, shall be treated, notwithstanding any rule of that law to the contrary, as a formal requirement only.

4 Construction of wills

The construction of a will shall not be altered by reason of any change in the testator's domicile after the execution of the will.

SECTIONS 1, 3 TO 5 AND SCHEDULE 1, PARAGRAPHS 1 TO 10 OF THE DOMICILE AND MATRIMONIAL PROCEEDINGS ACT 1973

DOMICILE AND MATRIMONIAL PROCEEDINGS ACT 1973

(1973 c 45)

1 Abolition of wife's dependent domicile

(1) Subject to sub-section (2) below, the domicile of a married woman as at any time after the coming into force of this section shall, instead of being the same as her husband's by virtue only of marriage, be ascertained by reference to the same factors as in the case of any other individual capable of having an independent domicile.

(2) Where immediately before this section came into force a woman was married and then had her husband's domicile by dependence, she is to be treated as retaining that domicile (as a domicile of choice, if it is not also her domicile of origin) unless and until it is changed by acquisition or revival of another domicile either on or after the coming into force of this section.

(3) This section extends to England and Wales, Scotland and Northern Ireland.

3 Age at which independent domicile can be acquired

(1) The time at which a person first becomes capable of having an independent domicile shall be when he attains the age of sixteen or marries under that age; and in the case of a person who immediately before 1 January 1974 was incapable or having an independent domicile, but has attained the age of sixteen of been married, it shall be that date.

(2) This section extends to England and Wales, Scotland and Northern Ireland.

4 Dependent domicile of child not living with his father

(1) Sub-section (2) of this section shall have effect with respect to the dependent domicile of a child as at any time after the coming into force of this section when his father and mother are alive but living apart.

(2) The child's domicile as at that time shall be that of his mother if–

(a) he then has his home with her and has no home with his father;

(b) he has at any time had her domicile by virtue of paragraph (a) above and has not since had a home with his father.

(3) As at any time after the coming into force of this section, the domicile of a child whose mother is dead shall be that which she last had before she died if at her death he had her domicile by virtue of sub-section (2) above and he has not since had a home with his father.

(4) Nothing in this section prejudices any existing rule of law as to the cases in which a child's domicile is regarded as being, by dependence, that of his mother.

(5) In this section, 'child' means a person incapable of having an independent domicile; and in its application to a child who has been adopted, references to his father and his mother shall be construed as references to his adoptive father and mother.

(6) This section extends to England and Wales, Scotland and Northern Ireland.

5 Jurisdiction in matrimonial proceedings (England and Wales)

(1) Sub-sections (2) to (5) below shall have effect, subject to section 6(3) and (4) of this Act, with respect to the jurisdiction of the court to entertain–

- (a) proceedings for divorce, judicial separation or nullity of marriage; and

- (b) proceedings for death to be presumed and a marriage to be dissolved in pursuance to section 19 of the Matrimonial Causes Act 1973,

and in this Part of this Act 'the court' means the High Court and a divorce county court within the meaning of the Matrimonial Causes Act 1967.

(2) The court shall have jurisdiction to entertain proceedings for divorce or judicial separation if (and only if) either of the parties to the marriage–

- (a) is domiciled in England and Wales on the date when the proceedings are begun; or

- (b) was habitually resident in England and Wales throughout the period of one year ending with that date.

(3) The court shall have jurisdiction to entertain proceedings for nullity of marriage if (and only if) either of the parties to the marriage–

- (a) is domiciled in England and Wales on the date when the proceedings are begun; or

- (b) was habitually resident in England and Wales throughout the period of one year ending with that date; or

- (c) died before that date and either–

  - (i) was at death domiciled in England and Wales, or

  - (ii) had been habitually resident in England and Wales throughout the period of one year ending with the date of death.

(4) The court shall have jurisdiction to entertain proceedings for death to be presumed and a marriage to be dissolved if (and only if) the petitioner–

(a) is domiciled in England and Wales on the date when the proceedings are begun; or

(b) was habitually resident in England and Wales throughout the period of one year ending with that date.

(5) The court shall, at any time when proceedings are pending in respect of which it has jurisdiction by virtue of sub-section (2) or (3) above (or of this sub-section), also have jurisdiction to entertain other proceedings, in respect of the same marriage, for divorce, judicial separation or nullity of marriage, notwithstanding that jurisdiction would not be exercisable under sub-section (2) or (3).

(6) Schedule 1 to this Act shall have effect as to the cases in which matrimonial proceedings in England and Wales are to be, or may be, stayed by the court where there are concurrent proceedings in respect of the same marriage, and as to the other matters dealt with in that Schedule; but nothing in the Schedule–

(a) requires or authorises a stay of proceedings which are pending when this section comes into force; or

(b) prejudices any power to stay proceedings which is exercisable by the court apart from the Schedule.

SCHEDULE 1

STAYING OF MATRIMONIAL PROCEEDINGS (ENGLAND AND WALES)

INTERPRETATION

1. The following five paragraphs have effect for the interpretation of this Schedule.

2. 'Matrimonial proceedings' means any proceedings so far as they are one or more of the five following kinds, namely, proceedings for–

divorce,

judicial separation,

nullity of marriage,

a declaration as to the validity of a marriage of the petitioner, and

a declaration as to the subsistence of such a marriage.

3.– (1) 'Another jurisdiction' means any country outside England and Wales.

(2) 'Related jurisdiction' means any of the following countries, namely, Scotland, Northern Ireland, Jersey, Guernsey, and the Isle of Man (the reference to Guernsey being treated as including Alderney and Sark).

4.– (1) References to the trial or first trial in any proceedings do not include references to the separate trial of an issue as to jurisdiction only.

(2) For the purposes of this Schedule, proceedings in the court are continuing if they are pending and not stayed.

5. Any reference in this Schedule to proceedings in another jurisdiction is to proceedings in a court of that jurisdiction, and to any proceedings in that jurisdiction, which are of a description prescribed for the purposes of this paragraph; and provision may be made by rules of court as to when proceedings of any description in another jurisdiction are continuing for the purposes of this Schedule.

6. 'Prescribed' means prescribed by rules of court

DUTY TO FURNISH PARTICULARS OF CONCURRENT PROCEEDINGS IN ANOTHER JURISDICTION

7. While matrimonial proceedings are pending in the court in respect of a marriage and the trial or first trial in those proceedings has not begun, it shall be the duty of any person who is a petitioner in the proceedings, or is a respondent and has in his answer included a prayer for relief, to furnish, in such manner and to such persons and on such occasions as may be prescribed, such particulars as may be prescribed of any proceedings which–

(a) he knows to be continuing in another jurisdiction; and

(b) are in respect of that marriage or capable of affecting its validity or subsistence.

OBLIGATORY STAYS

8.– (1) Where before the beginning of the trial or first trial in any proceedings for divorce which are continuing in the court it appears to the court on the application of a party to the marriage–

(a) that in respect of the same marriage proceedings for divorce or nullity of marriage are continuing in a related jurisdiction; and

(b) that the parties to the marriage have resided together after its celebration; and

(c) that the place where they resided together when the proceedings in the court were begun or, if they did not then reside together, where they last resided together before those proceedings were begun, is in that jurisdiction; and

(d) that either of the said parties was habitually resident in that jurisdiction throughout the year ending with the date on which they last resided together before the date on which the proceedings in the court were begun, it shall be the duty of the court, subject to paragraph 10 (2) below, to order that the proceedings in the court be stayed.

(2) References in sub-paragraph (1) above to the proceedings in the court are, in the case of proceedings which are not only proceedings for divorce, to the proceedings so far as they are proceedings for divorce.

DISCRETIONARY STAYS

9.– (1) Where before the beginning of the trial or first trial in any matrimonial proceedings which are continuing in the court it appears to the court–

- (a) that any proceedings in respect of the marriage in question, or capable of affecting its validity or subsistence, are continuing in another jurisdiction; and
- (b) that the balance of fairness (including convenience) as between parties to the marriage is such that it is appropriate for the proceedings in that jurisdiction to be disposed of before further steps are taken in the proceedings in the court or in those proceedings so far as they consist of a particular kind of matrimonial proceedings,

the court may then, if it thinks fit, order that the proceedings in the court be stayed or, as the case may be, that those proceedings be stayed so far as they consist of proceedings of that kind.

(2) In considering the balance of fairness and convenience for the purposes of sub-paragraph (1)(b) above, the court shall have regard to all factors appearing to be relevant, including the convenience of witnesses and any delay or expense which may result from those proceedings being stayed, or not being stayed.

(3) In the case of any proceedings so far as they are proceedings for divorce, the court shall not exercise the power conferred on it by sub-paragraph (1) above while an application under paragraph 8 above in respect of the proceedings is pending.

(4) If, at any time after the beginning of the trial or first trial in any matrimonial proceedings which are pending in the court, the court declares by order that it is satisfied that a person has failed to perform the duty imposed on him in respect of the proceedings by paragraph 7 above, sub-paragraph (1) above shall have effect in relation to those proceedings and, to the other proceedings by reference to which the declaration is made, as if the words 'before the beginning of the trial or first trial' were omitted; but no action shall lie in respect of the failure of a person to perform such a duty.

SUPPLEMENTARY

10.– (1) Where an order staying proceedings is in force in pursuance of paragraph 8 or 9 above, the court may, if it thinks fit, on the application of a party to the proceedings, discharge the order if it appears to the court that the other proceedings by reference to which the order was made are stayed or concluded, or that a party to those other proceedings has delayed unreasonably in prosecuting them.

(2) If the court discharges an order staying any proceedings and made in pursuance of paragraph 8 above, the court shall not again stay those proceedings in pursuance of that paragraph.

SECTIONS 12 TO 16 OF THE MATRIMONIAL AND FAMILY PROCEEDINGS ACT 1984

MATRIMONIAL AND FAMILY PROCEEDINGS ACT 1984

(1984 c 42)

12 Application for financial relief after overseas divorce

(1) Where–

    (a) a marriage has been dissolved or annulled, or the parties to a marriage have been legally separated, by means of judicial or other proceedings in an overseas country; and

    (b) the divorce, annulment or legal separation is entitled to be recognised as valid in England and Wales,

either party to the marriage may apply to the court in the manner prescribed by rules of court for an order for financial relief under this Part of this Act.

(2) If after a marriage has been dissolved or annulled in an overseas country one of the parties to the marriage remarries that party shall not be entitled to make an application in relation to that marriage.

(3) For the avoidance of doubt it is hereby declared that the reference in sub-section (2) above to the remarriage includes a reference to a marriage which is by law void or voidable ...

13 Leave of the court required for applications for financial relief

(1) No application for an order for financial relief shall be made under this Part of this Act unless the leave of the court has been obtained in accordance with the rules of court; and the court shall not grant leave unless it considers that there is substantial ground for the making of an application for such an order.

(2) The court may grant leave under this section notwithstanding that an order has been made by a court in a country outside England and Wales requiring the other party to the marriage to make any payment or transfer any property to the applicant or a child of the family.

(3) Leave under this section may be granted subject to such conditions as the court thinks fit.

14 Interim orders for maintenance

(1) Where leave is granted under section 13 above for the making of an application for an order for financial relief and it appears to the court that the applicant or any child of the family is in immediate need of financial assistance, the court may make an interim order for maintenance, that is to say, an order requiring the other party to the marriage, to make to the applicant or to the child such periodical payments, and for such term, being a term beginning not earlier than the date of the grant of leave and ending with the date of the determination of the application for an order for financial relief, as the court thinks reasonable.

(2) If it appears to the court that the court has jurisdiction to entertain the application for an order for financial relief by reason only of paragraph (c) of section 15(1) below the court shall not make an interim order under this section.

(3) An interim order under sub-section (1) above may be made subject to such conditions as the court thinks fit.

15 Jurisdiction of the court

(1) Subject to sub-section (2) below, the court shall have jurisdiction to entertain an application for an order for financial relief if any of the following jurisdictional requirements are satisfied, that is to say–

(a) either of the parties to the marriage was domiciled in England and Wales on the date of the application for leave under section 13 above or was so domiciled on the date on which the divorce annulment or legal separation obtained in the overseas country took effect in that country; or

(b) either of the parties to the marriage was habitually resident in England and Wales throughout the period of one year ending with the date of the application for leave or was so resident throughout the period of one year ending with the date on which the divorce, annulment or legal separation obtained in the overseas country took effect in that country; or

(c) either or both of the parties to the marriage had at the date of the application for leave a beneficial interest in possession in a dwelling-house situated in England or Wales which was at some time during the marriage a matrimonial home of the parties to the marriage.

(2) Where the jurisdiction of the court to entertain proceedings under this Part of this Act would fall to be determined by reference to the jurisdictional requirements imposed by virtue of Part I of the Civil Jurisdiction and Judgments Act 1982 (implementation of certain European conventions) then–

(a) satisfaction of the requirements of sub-section (1) above shall not obviate the need to satisfy the requirements imposed by virtue of Part I of that Act; and

(b) satisfaction of the requirements imposed by virtue of Part I of that Act shall obviate the need to satisfy the requirements of sub-section (1) above,

and the court shall entertain or not entertain the proceedings accordingly.

16 Duty of the court to consider whether England and Wales is appropriate venue for application

(1) Before making an order for financial relief the court shall consider whether in all the circumstances of the case it would be appropriate for such an order to be made by a court in England and Wales and if the court is not satisfied that it would be appropriate, the court shall dismiss the application.

(2) The court shall in particular have regard to the following matters–

(a) the connection which the parties to the marriage have with England and Wales;

(b) the connection which those parties have with the country in which the marriage was dissolved or annulled or in which they were legally separated;

(c) the connection which those parties have with any other country outside England and Wales;

(d) any financial benefit which the applicant or a child of the family received, or is likely to receive, in consequence of the divorce, annulment or legal separation, by virtue of any agreement or the operation of the law of a country outside England and Wales;

(e) in a case where an order has been made by a court in a country outside England and Wales requiring the other party to the marriage to make any payment or transfer any property for the benefit of the applicant or a child of the family, the financial relief given by the order and the extent to which the order has been complied with or is likely to be complied with;

(f) any right which the applicant has, or has had, to apply for financial relief from the other party to the marriage under the law of any country outside England and Wales and if the applicant has omitted to exercise that right the reason for that omission;

(g) the availability in England and Wales of any property in respect of which an order under this Part of this Act in favour of the applicant could be made;

(h) the extent to which any order made under this Part of this Act is likely to be enforceable;

(i) the length of time which has elapsed since the date of the divorce, annulment or legal separation.

SECTIONS 44 TO 52 OF THE
FAMILY LAW ACT 1986

FAMILY LAW ACT 1986

(1986 c 55)

PART II

RECOGNITION OF DIVORCES, ANNULMENTS
AND LEGAL SEPARATIONS

44 Recognition in United Kingdom of divorces, annulments and judicial separations granted in the British Islands

(1) Subject to section 52(4) and (5)(a) of this Act, no divorce or annulment obtained in any part of the British Islands shall be regarded as effective in any part of the United Kingdom unless granted by a court of civil jurisdiction.

(2) Subject to section 51 of this Act, the validity of any divorce, annulment or judicial separation granted by a court of civil jurisdiction in any part of the British Islands shall be recognised throughout the United Kingdom.

45 Recognition in the United Kingdom of overseas divorces, annulments and legal separations

Subject to sections 51 and 52 of this Act, the validity of a divorce, annulment or legal separation obtained in a country outside the British Islands (in this Part referred to as an overseas divorce, annulment or legal separation) shall be recognised in the United Kingdom if, and only if, it is entitled to recognition–

(a) by virtue of sections 46 to 49 of this Act; or

(b) by virtue of any enactment other than this Part.

46 Grounds for recognition

(1) The validity of an overseas divorce, annulment or legal separation obtained by means of proceedings shall be recognised if–

(a) the divorce, annulment or legal separation is effective under the law of the country in which it was obtained; and

(b) at the relevant date either party to the marriage–

(i) was habitually resident in the country in which the divorce, annulment or legal separation was obtained; or

431

    (ii) was domiciled in that country; or

    (iii) was a national of that country.

(2) The validity of an overseas divorce, annulment or legal separation obtained otherwise than by means of proceedings shall be recognised if–

    (a) the divorce, annulment or legal separation is effective under the law of the country in which it was obtained;

    (b) at the relevant date–

        (i) each party to the marriage was domiciled in that country; or

        (ii) either party to the marriage was domiciled in that country and the other party was domiciled in a country under whose law the divorce, annulment or legal separation is recognised as valid; and

    (c) neither party to the marriage was habitually resident in the United Kingdom throughout the period of one year immediately preceding that date.

(3) In this section 'the relevant date' means–

    (a) in the case of an overseas divorce, annulment or legal separation obtained by means of proceedings, the date of the commencement of the proceedings;

    (b) in the case of an overseas divorce, annulment or legal separation obtained by means of proceedings, the date on which it was obtained.

(4) Where in the case of an overseas annulment, the relevant date fell after the death of either party to the marriage, any reference in sub-section (1) or (2) above to that date shall be construed in relation to that party as a reference to the date of death.

(5) For the purposes of this section, a party to a marriage shall be treated as domiciled in a country if he was domiciled in that country either according to the law of that country in family matters or according to the law of the part of the United Kingdom in which the question of recognition arises.

47 Cross-proceedings and divorces following legal separations

(1) Where there have been cross-proceedings, the validity of an overseas divorce, annulment or legal separation obtained either in the original proceedings or in the cross-proceedings shall be recognised if–

    (a) the requirements of section 46(1)(b)(i), (ii) or (iii) of this Act are satisfied in relation to the date of the commencement either of the original proceedings or of the cross-proceedings, and

    (b) the validity of the divorce, annulment or legal separation is otherwise entitled to recognition by virtue of the provisions of this Part.

(2) Where a legal separation, the validity of which is entitled to recognition by virtue of the provisions of section 46 of this Act or of sub-section (1) above, is converted, in the country in which it was obtained, into a divorce which is effective under the law of that country, the validity of the divorce shall be recognised whether or not it would itself be entitled to recognition by virtue of those provisions.

48 Proof of facts relevant to recognition

(1) For the purpose of deciding whether an overseas divorce, annulment or legal separation obtained by means of proceedings is entitled to recognition by virtue of section 46 and 47 of this Act, any findings of fact made (whether expressly or by implication) in the proceedings and on the basis of which jurisdiction was assumed in the proceedings shall–

    (a) if both parties to the marriage took part in the proceedings, be conclusive evidence of the fact found; and

    (b) in any other case, be sufficient proof of that fact unless the contrary be shown.

(2) In this section 'finding of fact' includes a finding that either party to the marriage–

    (a) was habitually resident in the country in which the divorce, annulment or legal separation was obtained; or

    (b) was under the law of that country domiciled there; or

    (c) was a national of that country.

(3) For the purposes of sub-section (1)(a) above, a party to the marriage who has appeared in judicial proceedings shall be treated as having taken part in them.

49 Modifications of Part II in relation to countries comprising territories having different systems of law

(1) In relation to a country comprising territories in which different systems of law are in force in matters of divorce, annulment or legal separation, the provisions of this Part mentioned in sub-sections (2) to (5) below shall have effect subject to the modifications there specified.

(2) In the case of a divorce, annulment or legal separation the recognition of the validity of which depends on whether the requirements of sub-section (1)(b)(i) or (ii) of section 46 of this Act are satisfied, that section and, in the case of a legal separation, section 47(2) of this Act shall have effect as if each territory were a separate country.

(3) In the case of a divorce, annulment or legal separation the recognition of the validity of which depends on whether the requirements of sub-section (1)(b)(iii) of section 46 of this Act are satisfied–

(a) that section shall have effect as if for paragraph (a) of sub-section (1) there were substituted the following paragraph–

'(a) the divorce, annulment or legal separation is effective throughout the country in which it was obtained'; and

(b) in the case of a legal separation, section 47(2) of this Act shall have effect as if for the words 'is effective under the law of that country' there were substituted the words 'is effective throughout that country'.

(4) In the case of a divorce, annulment or legal separation the recognition of the validity of which depends on whether the requirements of sub-section (2)(b) of section 46 of this Act are satisfied, that section and section 52(3) and (4) of this Act and, in the case of a legal separation, section 47(2) of this Act shall have effect as if each territory were a separate country.

(5) Paragraphs (a) and (b) of section 48(2) of this Act shall each have effect as if each territory were a separate country.

50 Non-recognition of divorce or annulment in another jurisdiction no bar to remarriage

Where in any part of the United Kingdom–

(a) a divorce or annulment has been granted by a court of civil jurisdiction, or

(b) the validity of a divorce or annulment is recognised by virtue of this Part,

the fact that the divorce or annulment would not be recognised elsewhere shall not preclude either party to the marriage from remarrying in that part of the United Kingdom or cause the remarriage of either party (wherever the marriage takes place) to be treated as invalid in that part.

51 Refusal of recognition

(1) Subject to section 52 of this Act, recognition of the validity of–

(a) a divorce, annulment or judicial separation granted by a court of civil jurisdiction in any part of the British Islands, or

(b) an overseas divorce, annulment or legal separation,

may be refused in any part of the United Kingdom if the divorce, annulment or separation was granted or obtained at a time when it was irreconcilable with a decision determining the question of the subsistence or validity of the marriage of the parties previously given (whether before of after the commencement of this Part) by a court of civil jurisdiction in that part of the United Kingdom or by a court elsewhere and recognised or entitled to be recognised in that part of the United Kingdom.

(2) Subject to section 52 of this Act, recognition of the validity of–

(a) a divorce or judicial separation granted by a court of civil jurisdiction in any part of the British Islands, or

(b) an overseas divorce or legal separation,

may be refused in any part of the United Kingdom if the divorce or separation was granted or obtained at a time when, according to the law of that part of the United Kingdom (including its rules of private international law and the provisions of this Part), there was no subsisting marriage between the parties.

(3) Subject to section 52 of this Act, recognition by virtue of section 45 of the Act of the validity of the overseas divorce, annulment or legal separation may be refused if–

(a) in the case of a divorce, annulment or legal separation obtained by means of proceedings, it was obtained–

(i) without such steps having been taken for giving notice of the proceedings to a party to the marriage as, having regards to the nature of the proceedings and all the circumstances, should reasonably have been take; or

(ii) without a party to the marriage having been given (for any reason other that lack of notice) such opportunity to take part in the proceedings as, having regard to those matters, he should reasonably have been given; or

(b) in the case of a divorce, annulment or legal separation obtained otherwise than by means of proceedings–

(i) there is no official document certifying that the divorce, annulment or legal separation is effective under the law of the country in which it was obtained; or

(ii) where either party to the marriage was domiciled in another country at the relevant date, there is no official document certifying that the divorce, annulment or legal separation is recognised as valid under the law of that other country; or

(c) in either case, recognition of the divorce, annulment or legal separation would be manifestly contrary to public policy.

(4) In this section–

'official', in relation to a document certifying that a divorce, annulment or legal separation is effective, or is recognised as valid under the law of any country, means issued by a person or body appointed or recognised for the purpose under that law;

'the relevant date' had the same meaning as in section 46 of this Act;

and sub-section (5) of that section shall apply for the purposes of this section as it applies for the purposes of that section.

(5) Nothing in this Part shall be construed as requiring the recognition of any finding of fault made in any proceedings for divorce, annulment or separation or of any maintenance, custody or other ancillary order made in any such proceedings.

52 Provisions as to divorces, annulments, etc, obtained before commencement of Part II

(1) The provisions of this Part shall apply–

   (a) to a divorce, annulment or judicial separation granted by a court of civil jurisdiction in the British Islands before the date of the commencement of this Part, and

   (b) to an overseas divorce, annulment or legal separation obtained before that date,

as well as to one granted on or after that date.

(2) In the case of such a divorce, annulment or separation as is mentioned in sub-section (1)(a) or (b) above, the provisions of this Part shall require or, as the case may be, preclude the recognition of its validity in relation to any time before that date as well as in relation to any subsequent time, but those provisions shall not–

   (a) affect any property to which any person became entitled before that date, or

   (b) affect the recognition of the validity of the divorce, annulment or separation if that matter has been decided by any competent court in the British Islands before that date.

(3) Sub-sections (1) and (2) above shall apply in relation to any divorce or judicial separation granted by a court of civil jurisdiction in the British Islands before the date of the commencement of this Part whether granted before or after the commencement of section 1 of the Recognition of Divorces and Legal Separations Act 1971.

(4) The validity of any divorce, annulment or legal separation mentioned in sub-section (5) below shall be recognised in the United Kingdom whether or not it is entitled to recognition by virtue of any of the foregoing provisions of this Part.

(5) The divorces, annulments and legal separations referred to in sub-section (4) above are–

   (a) a divorce which was obtained in the British Islands before 1 January 1974 and was recognised as valid under rules of law applicable before that date;

(b) an overseas divorce which was recognised as valid under the Recognition of Divorces and Legal Separations Act 1971 and was not affected by section 16(2) of the Domicile and Matrimonial Proceedings Act 1973 (proceedings otherwise than in a court of law where both parties resident in the United Kingdom);

(c) a divorce of which the decree was registered under section 1 of the Indian and Colonial Divorce Jurisdiction Act 1926;

(d) a divorce or annulment which was recognised as valid under section 4 of the Matrimonial Causes (War Marriages) Act 1944; and

(e) an overseas legal separation which was recognised as valid under the Recognition of Divorces and Legal Separations Act 1971.

SECTIONS 19 TO 20 OF THE FAMILY LAW ACT 1996

FAMILY LAW ACT 1996

(1996 c 27)

Jurisdiction and commencement of proceedings

19.– (1) In this section 'the court's jurisdiction' means–

(a) the jurisdiction of the court under this Part to entertain marital proceedings; and

(b) any other jurisdiction conferred on the court under this Part, or any other enactment, in consequence of the making of a statement.

(2) The court's jurisdiction is exercisable only if–

(a) at least one of the parties was domiciled in England and Wales on the statement date;

(b) at least one of the parties was habitually resident in England and Wales throughout the period of one year ending with the statement date; or

(c) nullity proceedings are pending in relation to the marriage when the marital proceedings commence.

(3) Sub-section (4) applies if–

(a) a separation order is in force; or

(b) an order preventing divorce has been cancelled.

(4) The court–

(a) continue to have jurisdiction to entertain an application made by reference to the order referred to in sub-section (3); and

(b) may exercise any other jurisdiction which is conferred on it in consequence of such an application.

(5) Schedule 3 amends Schedule 1 to the Domicile and Matrimonial Proceedings Act 1973 (orders to stay proceedings where there are proceedings in other jurisdictions).

(6) The court's jurisdiction is exercisable subject to any order for a stay under Schedule 1 to that Act.

(7) In this section–

'nullity proceedings' means proceedings in respect of which the court has jurisdiction under section 5(3) of the Domicile and Matrimonial Proceedings Act 1973; and

'statement date' means the date on which the relevant statement was received by the court.

20.– (1) The receipt by the court of a statement is to be treated as the commencement of proceedings.

(2) The proceedings are to be known as marital proceedings.

(3) Marital proceedings are also–

(a) separation proceedings, if an application for a separation order has been made under section 3 by reference to the statement and not withdrawn;

(b) divorce proceedings, if an application for a divorce order has been made under section 3 by reference to the statement and not withdrawn.

(4) Marital proceedings are to be treated as being both divorce proceedings and separation proceedings at any time when no application by reference to the statement, either for a divorce order or for a separation order, is outstanding.

(5) Proceedings which are commenced by the making of an application under section 4(3) are also marital proceedings and divorce proceedings.

(6) Marital proceedings come to an end–

(a) on the making of a separation order;

(b) on the making of a divorce order;

(c) on the withdrawal of the statement by a notice in accordance with section 5(3)(a);

(d) at the end of the specified period mentioned in section 5(3)(b), if no application under section 3 by reference to the statement is outstanding;

(e) on the withdrawal of all such applications which are outstanding at the end of that period;

(f) on the withdrawal of an application under section 4(3).

SECTIONS 11 TO 14 AND 47 OF THE MATRIMONIAL CAUSES ACT 1973

MATRIMONIAL CAUSES ACT 1973

(1973 c 18)

11 Grounds on which a marriage is void

A marriage celebrated after 31st July 1971 shall be void on the following grounds, that is to say–

  (a) that it is not a valid marriage under the provisions of the Marriage Act 1949 to 1986 (that is to say where–

   (i) the parties are within the prohibited degrees of relationship;

   (ii) either party is under the age of sixteen; or

   (iii)the parties have intermarried in disregard of certain requirements as to the formation of marriage);

  (b) that at the time of the marriage either party was already lawfully married;

  (c) that the parties are not respectively male and female;

  (d) in the case of a polygamous marriage entered into outside England and Wales, that either party was at the time of the marriage domiciled in England and Wales.

For the purposes of paragraph (d) of this sub-section a marriage is not polygamous if at its inception neither party has any spouse additional to the other.

12 Grounds on which a marriage is voidable

A marriage celebrated after 31st July 1971 shall be voidable on the following grounds only, that is to say–

  (a) that the marriage has not been consummated owing to the incapacity of either party to consummate it;

  (b) that the marriage has not been consummated owing to the wilful refusal of the respondent to consummate it;

  (c) that either party to the marriage did not validly consent to it, whether in consequence of duress, mistake, unsoundness of mind or otherwise;

  (d) that at the time of the marriage either party, though capable of giving a valid consent, was suffering (whether continuously or intermittently) from mental disorder within the meaning of the Mental Health Act 1983 of such kind to such an extent as to be unfitted for marriage;

(e) that at the time of the marriage the respondent was suffering from venereal disease in a communicable form;

(f) that at the time of the marriage the respondent was pregnant by some person other than the petitioner.

13 Bars to relief where marriage is voidable

(1) The court shall not, in proceedings instituted after 31st July 1971, grant a decree of nullity on the ground that a marriage is voidable if the respondent satisfies the court–

(a) that the petitioner, with the knowledge that it was open to him to have the marriage avoided, so conducted himself in relation to the respondent as to lead the respondent reasonably to believe that he would not seek to do so; and

(b) that it would be unjust to the respondent to grant the decree.

(2) Without prejudice to sub-section (1) above, the court shall not grant a decree of nullity by virtue of section 12 above on the grounds mentioned in paragraph (c), (d), (e) or (f) of that section unless–

(a) it is satisfied that proceedings were instituted within the period of three years from the date of the marriage, or

(b) leave for the institution of proceedings after the expiration of that period has been granted under sub-section (4) below.

(3) Without prejudice to sub-sections (1) and (2) above, the court shall not grant a decree of nullity by virtue of section 12 above on the grounds mentioned in paragraph (e) or (f) of that section unless it is satisfied that the petitioner was at the time of the marriage ignorant of the facts alleged.

(4) In the case of proceedings for the grant of a decree of nullity by virtue of section 12 above on the grounds mentioned in paragraph (c), (d), (e) or (f) of that section, a judge of the court may, on an application made to him, grant leave for the institution of proceedings after the expiration of the period of three years from the date of the marriage if–

(a) he is satisfied that the petitioner has at some time during that period suffered from mental disorder within the meaning of the Mental Health Act 1983, and

(b) he considers that in all the circumstances of the case it would be just to grant leave for the institution of proceedings.

(5) An application for leave under sub-section (4) above may be made after the expiration of the period of three years from the date of the marriage.

14 Marriages governed by foreign law or celebrated abroad under English law

(1) Where, apart from this Act, any matters affecting the validity of a marriage would fall to be determined (in accordance with the rules of private international law) by reference to the law of a country outside England and Wales, nothing in section 11, 12 or 13(1) above shall–

(a) preclude the determination of that matter as aforesaid; or

(b) require the application to the marriage of the grounds or bar there mentioned except so far as applicable in accordance with those rules.

(2) In the case of a marriage which purports to have been celebrated under the Foreign Marriage Acts 1892 to 1947 or has taken place outside England and Wales and purports to be a marriage under common law, section 11 above is without prejudice to any ground on which the marriage may be void under those Acts or, as the case may be, by virtue of the rules governing the celebration of marriages outside England and Wales under common law.

47 Matrimonial relief and declarations of validity in respect of polygamous marriages

(1) A court in England and Wales shall not be precluded from granting matrimonial relief or making a declaration concerning the validity of a marriage by reason only that either party to the marriage is, or has during the subsistence of the marriage been, married to more than one person.

(2) In this section 'matrimonial relief' means–

(a) any decree under Part I of this Act;

(b) a financial provision order under section 27 above;

(c) an order under section 35 above altering a maintenance agreement;

(d) an order under any provision of this Act which confers a power exercisable in connection with, or in connection with proceedings for, any such decree or order as is mentioned in paragraphs (a) to (c) above;

(dd) an order under Part III of the Matrimonial and Family Proceedings Act 1984;

(e) an order under Part I of the Domestic Proceedings and Magistrates' Courts Act 1978.

(3) In this section 'a declaration concerning the validity of a marriage' means any declaration under Part III of the Family Law Act 1986 involving a determination as to the validity of a marriage.

(4) Provision may be made by rules of court–

(a) for requiring notice of proceedings brought by virtue of this section to be served on any additional spouse of a party to the marriage in question; and

(b) for conferring on any such additional spouse the right to be heard in the proceedings,

in such cases as may be specified in the rules.

FURTHER READING

In general, readers may refer to the following textbooks which provide an excellent coverage of this area of law.

Clarkson, C and Hill, J, *Jaffey on the Conflict of Laws*, 1997, London: Butterworths

Collins, L, *Dicey and Morris on the Conflict of Laws*, 12th edn, 1993 and supplements, London: Sweet & Maxwell

Mayss, A and Reed, A, *European Business Litigation*, 1998, London: Ashgate

McClean, J, *Morris: The Conflict of Laws*, 4th edn, 1993, London: Sweet & Maxwell

North, P and Fawcett, J, *Cheshire and North's Private International Law*, 12th edn, 1992, London: Butterworths

Chapter 1, Nature and Scope of Conflict of Laws

Briggs, A, 'Conflict of laws: postponing the future?' (1989) 9 OJLS 251

Fawcett, J, 'The interrelationships of jurisdiction and choice of law in private international law' [1991] Current Legal Problems 39

Fentiman, R, 'Foreign law in English courts' (1992) 108 LQR 142

Morris, J, 'The renvoi in New York' (1951) 4 ILQ 268

Chapter 2, Jurisdiction of the English Court in Commercial Disputes: the Common Law Rules

Collins, L, '*The Siskina* again: an opportunity missed' (1996) 112 LQR 8

Fawcett, J, 'Trial in England and abroad: the underlying policy considerations' (1989) 9 OJLS 205

Peel, E, 'Exclusive jurisdiction agreements: purity and pragmatism in the conflict of laws' [1998] LMCLQ 182

Chapter 3, Jurisdiction of the English Court in Commercial Disputes: the Brussels and Lugano Conventions

'Almeida Cruz-Desantes Real-Jenard Report', OJ C189/35, 1990

Bell, A, 'Negative declarations in transnational litigation' (1995) 111 LQR 674

Collins, L, 'Negative declarations and the Brussels Convention' (1992) 109 LQR 545

Hartley, T, 'Unnecessary Europeanisation under the Brussels Jurisdiction and Judgments Convention: the case of the dissatisfied sub-purchaser' (1993) 18 EL Rev 506

Hill, J, 'Jurisdiction in matters relating to a contract under the Brussels Convention' (1995) 44 ICLQ 591

'Jenard Report', OJ C59/1, 1979

'Jenard-Möller Report', OJ C189/57, 1990

Minor, J, 'The Lugano Convention: some problems of interpretation' (1990) 27 CML Rev 507

'Schlosser Report', OJ C59/71, 1979

Chapter 4, Recognition and Enforcement of Foreign Judgments

'Almeida Cruz-Desantes Real-Jenard Report', OJ C189/35, 1990

Briggs, A, 'Which foreign judgments should we recognise today?' (1987) 36 ICLQ 240

'Jenard Report', OJ C59/1, 1979

'Jenard-Möller Report', OJ C189/57, 1990

'Schlosser Report', OJ C59/71, 1979

Von Mehren, A, 'Recognition and enforcement of sister-State judgments: reflections on general theory and current practice in the European Economic Community and the United States' (1981) 81 Col LR 1044

Chapter 5, Choice of Law in Contract

'Giuliano-Lagarde Report', OJ C282/1, 1980

Lando, O, 'The EEC Convention on the law applicable to contractual obligations' (1987) 24 CML Rev 159

Mann, F, 'The proper law of the contract – an obituary' (1991) 107 LQR 553

Morse, CG, 'Letters of credit and the Rome Convention' [1994] LMCLQ 560

Morse, CG, 'Consumer contracts, employment contracts and the Rome Convention' (1992) 41 ICLQ 1

Reynolds, F, 'Illegality by *lex loci solutionis*' (1992) 108 LQR 553

Chapter 6, Choice of Law in Tort

Briggs, A, 'A choice of law in tort and delict' [1995] LMCLQ 519

Carter, P, 'The Private International Law (Miscellaneous Provisions) Act 1995' (1996) 112 LQR 190

Law Commission, *Choice of Law in Tort and Delict*, Report No 193, 1990, London: HMSO

Morse, CG, 'Torts in private international law: a new statutory framework' (1996) 45 ICLQ 888

North, P, 'Contract as a tort defence in the conflict of laws' (1977) 26 ICLQ 914

Chapter 7, Judgments in Foreign Currency

Bowles, R and Whelan, C, 'Law Commission Working Paper No 80 – Private International Law: Foreign Money Liabilities' (1982) 45 MLR 434

Knott, JA, 'Foreign currency judgments in tort: an illustration of the wealth-time continuum' (1980) 43 MLR 18

Law Commission, *Private International Law: Foreign Money Liabilities*, Working Paper No 80, 1981, London: HMSO

Law Commission, *Private International Law: Foreign Money Liabilities*, Report No 124, 1983, London: HMSO

Chapter 8, Law of Property

Mann, F, 'Rumasa in America' (1988) 104 LQR 346

Nott, S, 'Title to illegally exported items of historic or artistic worth' (1984) 33 ICLQ 203

Rogerson, P, 'The situs of debts in the conflict of laws – illogical, artificial and misleading' [1990] CLJ 441

Moshinsky, M, 'The assignment of debts in the conflict of laws' (1992) 108 LQR 591

Chapter 9, Domicile at Common Law

Carter, P, 'Domicil: the case for radical reform in the United Kingdom' (1987) 36 ICLQ 713

Fawcett, J, 'Result selection in domicile cases' (1985) 5 OJLS 378

Fentiman, R, 'Domicile revisited' [1991] CLJ 445

Law Commission, *Private International Law: the Law of Domicile*, Report No 168, 1987, London: HMSO

Pilkington, M, 'Illegal residence and the acquisition of a domicile of choice' (1984) 33 ICLQ 885

Wade, J, 'Domicile: a re-examination of certain rules' (1983) 32 ICLQ 1

Chapter 10, Marriage

Clarkson, C, 'Marriage in England: favouring the *lex fori*' (1990) 10 OJLS 80

Davie, M, 'The break-up of essential validity of marriage choice of law rules in English conflict of laws' (1994) 23 Anglo-Am L Rev 32

Fentiman, R, 'Activity in the law of status: domicile, marriage and the Law Commission' (1986) 6 OJLS 353

Gotlieb, A, 'The incidental question revisited – theory and practice in the conflict of laws' (1977) 26 ICLQ 734

Hartley, T, 'The policy bases of the English conflict of laws of marriage' (1972) 35 MLR 571

Karsten, IG, 'Capacity to contract a polygamous marriage' (1973) 36 MLR 291

Chapter 11, Matrimonial Causes and Financial Relief

Beaumont, P and Moir, G, 'Brussels Convention II: a new private international instrument in family matters for the European Union of the European Community?' (1995) 20 EL Rev 268

Law Commission, *Private International Law: Recognition of Foreign Nullity Decrees and Related Matters*, Report No 137, 1984, London: HMSO

Pilkington, M, 'Transnational divorces under the Family Law Act 1986' (1988) 37 ICLQ 131

Smart, P, 'The recognition of extra-judicial divorces' (1985) 34 ICLQ 392

Young, J, 'The recognition of extra-judicial divorces in the UK' (1987) 7 LS 78

INDEX